TO THE GREATER GLORY

A HISTORY OF THE IRISH JESUITS

LOUIS McREDMOND

GILL AND MACMILLAN

Published in Ireland by
Gill and Macmillan Ltd
Goldenbridge
Dublin 8
with associated companies in
Auckland, Delhi, Gaborone, Hamburg, Harare,
Hong Kong, Johannesburg, Kuala Lumpur, Lagos, London,
Manzini, Melbourne, Mexico City, Nairobi,
New York, Singapore, Tokyo
© Louis McRedmond 1991
Index compiled by Helen Litton
Print origination by Seton Music Graphics Ltd, Bantry, Co. Cork
Printed by Colour Books Ltd, Dublin

British Library Cataloguing in Publication Data

McRedmond, Louis
To the greater glory: A history of the Irish Jesuits.
I. Title
271.009417

ISBN 0–7171–1833–9

A.M.D.G.

Ignatii Sancti filiis
nationis Hibernicae,
quibus multa
non verbis
explicanda
auctor debet,
hoc opusculum
humiliter
ac grato animo
dedicatum est

L.D.S.

CONTENTS

FOREWORD

JESUITS first began to work in Ireland nearly 450 years ago and we have been part of the apostolate of the Catholic Church in Ireland almost continuously since 1598. Our work has always been dedicated to carrying forward the inspiration of our founder, St Ignatius Loyola, despite difficulties, despite our own mistakes and those of others, in times of persecution and in times of peace. The story of the Irish Jesuits is fascinating, but it is not well known.

Now, when we are celebrating the 500th anniversary of the birth of St Ignatius and the 450th anniversary of the Order which he founded, it seems appropriate to publish a history of the Jesuits in Ireland and to remember Irish Jesuits who worked abroad. We want to do this in a spirit of gratitude, discovering more about our past and sharing it with others, so that it may encourage us as we face today's challenges and give us confidence as we approach a new millennium.

Louis McRedmond is an experienced journalist and historian, with a great interest in Church matters, both past and present. He was asked to write this book because we were well aware of his talents and because we wanted an objective writer, able to apportion praise or blame. The text which he has produced has more than justified the confidence we placed in him, but we do not want it to be regarded as an 'official' history. *To the Greater Glory* is an account of the Irish Jesuit story from the pen of a talented writer, who felt free to make his own judgments throughout the book.

I am grateful to Louis McRedmond for giving so much of his time to the project. I hope that this book will encourage other scholars to begin detailed studies of particular aspects of our history. I am sure that my fellow Jesuits, our colleagues, our friends and many people interested in Ireland's history, will find this book both enlightening and entertaining.

Philip Harnett, S.J.
Provincial
July 1991

INTRODUCTION

INSTEAD of 'A History of the Irish Jesuits', I should have subtitled it 'Towards a History...'. I have painted a landscape with figures. Scientific exploration still needs to be put in hand since only part of the story is visible, easily depicted with the aid of the books and printed documents to which, for the most part, I have confined my researches. A landscape, however, reveals hills and valleys, flora and fauna, which may lure a professional explorer to investigate further. It is my hope that the present modest history will prove a spur to production of the authoritative study-in-depth of the Irish Jesuits crying out to be written.

I said a landscape with figures. The figures, the individual Jesuits, tell us much. No two of these warm-blooded, warm-hearted men are the same, although they mostly fall into a few recognisable categories: Holywood and Kenney building to blueprints; Nugent and Delany hyper-active in giving substance to ideas sprung from fertile minds; Knoles and O'Callaghan surviving on what to earthbound observers must have seemed irrational hope; Finlay and McGarry envisaging the needs to be met, in times of radical change, of a State about to be born or a Church in the trauma of renewal. The backdrop of the country's history reveals their endeavours in high relief. The Irish Jesuits were at Kinsale and in Cromwellian Drogheda, the Confederation of Kilkenny knew them well and they were found with the dispossessed after Limerick; they provided a home-from-home for O'Connell, schooling for James Joyce, an intellectual stiffening for the emergent sociology of the New Ireland upon which so many aspects of our modern economics, industrial relations, educational theory and political priorities have been constructed. They trained priests for penal Ireland in their continental colleges. They rescued a university at home. They gave a status to Catholicism in Australia which it lacked until they came.

These are highlights to outsiders. From within the Society of Jesus, to the Jesuits themselves, such activities may be only the discharging of some tasks among many, and other work may well be judged of equal or greater importance towards the service and salvation of mankind which Saint Ignatius urged them to pursue. Who can measure the achievement of the preachers, an O'Kearney in the country places recovering from the devastation of the Elizabethan wars, a Cullen ameliorating with his *Irish Messenger* the stresses of a popular religion too dominated by the God of stern judgment rather than the God of mercy? Who can quantify the good done in a lifetime of teaching in Ireland, or running a mission station in Zambia, or writing books of mystical theology, or battling against a bureaucratic system on behalf of homeless children? Who can estimate the effects of martyrdom, of dying for faith like Dominic Collins on the scaffold at Youghal or out of the selfless doing of duty, like Willie Doyle in Flanders? The Jesuit agenda is wider than the sophisticated may appreciate.

My first reason for hoping that a more expansive history of the Irish Jesuits will one day be put in hand is that I am conscious of my own limitations, not merely those of time and space, which could be overcome with more of each commodity, but also those which restrict the extent to which an outsider can enter the Jesuit mind. The profundity of the *Spiritual Exercises*, the broad sweep of the Constitutions, the stimulus of the *Ratio Studiorum* — the very idea that the educative process can be comprehended as a unity, however little attainable in practice — and the four centuries of experience that lie behind the lengthy formation of a Jesuit, all these inevitably mean that even those of us who have been pupils in their schools and have remained in constant contact with them cannot presume to have the same reaction to events, contemporary or past, as they do — and especially not the identical feeling for what matters in their story. I hope I do not depart too far from their self-perception, but Jesuits must not expect to find in this book the Society precisely as they know it. They may find an image of the Society as it appears to sympathetic and not uninformed non-Jesuits. They will, I am sure, accept this as a service to their understanding of themselves and a yardstick of some use to the Irish Jesuit historian who must be commissioned to produce in time the definitive history. Here I should add that, for the sake of simplifying the point I want to make, I put to one side the variety of opinion among Jesuits themselves!

My second reason for wanting a major history of the Irish Jesuits to be undertaken is that it seems to me to be a chapter of both Irish and Jesuit history which has been extra-ordinarily downplayed. The antiquity of the Irish Mission, going back to the lifetime of Saint Ignatius; its untypical character, being for much of its existence carried out in a country violently disrupted by political as well as religious tensions; its intimate association with the generalate in Rome; its European and foreign missionary dimensions dating from the sixteenth century — all these give it an importance beyond its physical scale. Its survival despite successive bouts of intense persecution and more prolonged anti-Catholic discrimination, despite suppression too, was not unique but, combined with the Mission's other features, make it a very special case in which the qualities and the policies of the Society can be seen enduring under pressure incredibly severe. If ever the Ignatian norm of adaptability to place and circumstance needed to be invoked it was in Ireland long ago, and invoked it was. Very little of this is known, known even to Irish Jesuits. Yet Irish Jesuit historians of high calibre have done splendid work on aspects of the story through research in the Irish, Roman and other archives. Much of what they have written remains unpublished. It should be brought together and made the core of the Jesuit *magnum opus* which I believe to be called for.

Meanwhile, there is my modest offering. I make one plea in terms I have already used elsewhere. Those who know me will not doubt my ecumenical credentials or my respect for

Christian traditions other than that to which I belong. But my subject is history, and the times of which I have to write include centuries marked by deep division and discord between Christians, mutual suspicion and hatred, often leading to most unChristian — even savage — persecution, especially when religion was recruited to advance the priorities of state. Because in Ireland the victims of this phenomenon were for the most part Catholics, and it is on them I must concentrate, please do not imagine I have forgotten the fires of Smithfield or the St Bartholomew's Day Massacre, the Spanish Inquisition or the Revocation of the Edict of Nantes. Nothing done in Ireland to Catholics lacks its counterpart for Protestants elsewhere — or at home, for that matter, for we had the barbarous drownings at Portadown, the barn-burning at Scullabogue, the piking of Protestants on Wexford bridge. All that I condemn. But it is with the general, and generally dismal, experience of Irish Catholics that the earlier part of my story has to do. I trust I can tell it with blame to none for belonging to the age in which fate cast them to live their lives.

Considerations not altogether different arise in the later part of the narrative. In the nineteenth century and into the twentieth, the denominational character of schools and universities formed the subject of much public debate. Each Church endeavoured to strengthen its own institutions and keep its adherents out of those with a different allegiance or with no allegiance at all. Because the ecumenical and liberal temper of the present time admits of arguments in favour of inter-denominational or non-denominational schooling some readers may be tempted to judge the past by current standards. On the contemporary argument, happily, I have no occasion to pronounce. But I would stress the intellectual impropriety of denigrating anybody because he or she, in an altogether different historical context, did not adopt attitudes in fashion today. It is salutary to remember that the man who first called the university institutions in Belfast, Cork and Galway 'godless colleges' was an evangelical Protestant remote from any sympathy with the Roman ecclesiastics who would soon be thundering their denunciations in the phrase he invented. Standards were shared across the denominational divide. It will also be noticed how much effort went into ensuring that Catholics were educationally enabled to enter, and advance in, the professions, aspire to public office and become effective leaders at national as well as community level. This should not be seen, in its nineteenth century context, as an attempt to secure denominational advantage. Its purpose was rather to rectify denominational disadvantage, to liberalise, not to discriminate.

I have many people to thank. Father Fergus O'Donoghue, S.J., and Father Thomas Morrissey, S.J., put at my disposal their impressively comprehensive theses, without which my coverage of the first hundred years would have been little more than a chronology stiffened with legend: my debt to these historians, and to Father Morrissey in addition for his work on William Delany and on the evolution of Mungret, will be evident from many references in the Notes. Pádraig Folan generously made me photocopies of the archival material which he had assembled for his history of the Galway Jesuits from a manuscript compilation put together by Father James Rabbitte in the 1930s; this enabled me to write not only an account of the early decades of St Ignatius' College and Church but also to give some insights to Jesuit community life in the Victorian age. Michael Gill was my principal collaborator in the production of the book; his never failing support involved professional efficiency in having the text processed by his highly competent staff at Gill and Macmillan, maintaining liaison with the Jesuits and administering psychological therapy to calm my panic in the face of relentlessly receding deadlines. For the Society of Jesus, Father Frank Sammon, S.J., co-ordinated the exercise with benevolent diplomacy.

A number of friends, unsolicited, kindly sent me useful books, quotations or information when they heard I had undertaken the project. These included Father Jack Leonard, S.J., Father Austin Flannery, O.P., Betty O'Connell, John More O'Ferrall, Seán Mac Réamoinn and the late Mary Purcell. I must single out Father Henry Peel, O.P., who took the trouble to transcribe extended extracts from the correspondence of Archbishop Troy. These threw new light on the attempts to seize the Irish Mission Funds during the

Suppression. I have presented Father Peel's information as
Note 11 to Chapter 4. Others who assisted me in various ways
were Dermot Roantree, Carmel Doolan, Margaret More
O'Ferrall, Pat Stephenson, Neil Porter and Patrick Power,
Ambassador of Ireland to the Holy See; among the Jesuits
who come to my aid were Father Philip Fogarty, S.J., Father
Stephen Redmond, S.J., and Father Thomas O'Brien, S.J.
Thomas Kinsella's very fine translations of Irish poetry
published by the Dolmen Press in the collection *An Duanaire*
were of special help in dealing with the earlier centuries
since they made it possible to illuminate the authentic Gaelic
thought-process for readers of an English-language text. I
am, of course, indebted to all the authors listed in the Biblio-
graphy. I gained access to a number of their writings only
through the courtesy and scholarly guidance of Father
Brendan Woods, S.J., in the Milltown Library, who also very
tolerantly allowed me to take away a dozen volumes or more
and retain them for over a year. Peter Costello, Father
Redmond and Jesuits in a number of houses around the
country provided me with photographs, the original sources
of which were so varied (and often unknown) that I am
unable to acknowledge them individually but I record my
gratitude for them all. Father Joseph Veale, S.J., Father Brian
Lennon, S.J., and Father O'Donoghue read the text in typescript with great diligence; they made many wise comments
and many suggestions, most of which I was able to adopt.

I have to stress that the opinions I voice in the book are
solely my own. This is no ritual exculpation of authors,
advisors or others on whose knowledge I have drawn. I am
very well aware that no reader, and certainly no Jesuit, is
likely to agree with everything I have to say, or the way I say
it, or the emphasis I give to particular episodes or persons. I
therefore repeat that nobody other than I should be held
responsible for any attitude I take it on myself to express. I
offer only one man's perspective on a long and complex
story, which can be validly seen from other angles and be
fairly interpreted by other norms. If what I have written
encourages such further reflection I shall be content.

Lastly and above all, I have to record my deep gratitude to
Father Philip Harnett, S.J., Provincial of Ireland, for trusting

me with the task of making known what the Society of Jesus did in and for our country, and for the Irish Church, through four and a half centuries of apostolic endeavour. He subjected me to no constraint, accepting that I would judge the Jesuits as I saw fit, warts and all. The shortcomings did not, in the end, seem of great significance but they will be found here in due proportion to the virtues. The virtues predominate, for the Irish Jesuits strove by every means they knew to discharge the mandate given the Society by Pope Julius III, in wording substantially composed by Saint Ignatius himself and his original companions:

> To strive especially for the defence and propagation of the faith and for the progress of souls in Christian life and doctrine, by means of public preaching, lectures and any other ministration whatsoever of the word of God, and further by means of the Spiritual Exercises, the education of children and unlettered persons in Christianity, and the spiritual consolation of Christ's faithful through hearing confessions and administering the other sacraments . . . show(ing) itself no less useful in reconciling the estranged, in holily assisting and serving those who are found in prisons or hospitals, and indeed in performing any other works of charity, according to what will seem expedient for the glory of God and the common good.*

All this the Irish Jesuits did among their own compatriots. They carried out the selfsame mission in Asia, Africa and the Antipodes. Their service has been unremitting. It continues still. They merit profound and grateful admiration.

---

* From the bull *Exposcit debitum*. Translation in Ganss, par.3 'The Formula of the Institute' (preceding the Constitutions).

1

LIGHT HORSEMEN

SOFT rain immersing an Irish woodland, water lapping idly upon a pebbled lakeshore, a brown immensity of bog spreading off to distant pale blue hills: poets can fashion fancy from such scenes, and painters too, and emigrants dreaming of home. A foreigner accustomed to the shimmer and heat of a southern sun, another familiar with the cosily furnished houses of bourgeois towns nestling below lofty bell-towers, would be less inclined to wax lyrical in the chill, dank damp of February in Donegal or Mayo. Paschase Broet and Alfonso Salmeron, priests in the newly-founded Society of Jesus and members of the small band of companions who had earlier grouped themselves around Ignatius Loyola, shuddered at the sight of this 'wild region' where they often found themselves 'hungry and thirsty' and without shelter for the night.[1] Broet came from Picardy in Northern France on the border of Flanders, Salmeron from proud Toledo in the heart of Spain. They were the first Jesuits to set foot in Ireland and were sent by Ignatius himself at the request of Pope Paul III, who appointed them papal nuncios. Their visit occupied most of Lent in the year 1542 and proved to be appropriately penitential.

Mere physical hardship, although they could not but be aware of it, was the least of the features of Gaelic Ireland to trouble men who had been instructed to live frugally and poorly.[2] Just as they failed to remark on the beauty of the landscape, when they met the people they failed to recognise the echo of the troubadours in their poetry and the intricate web of relationships making up their legal system and governing their daily lives. But they may have spotted more obvious, if trivial, phenomena — like the way a handsome young man at a fair was sure to attract attention:

> Wives, pretending not to look,
> Plait their hair in front of you.
> With fingers through her lovely hair
> One of them is studying you.[3]

Whether it was the same youth or not who boasted,

> I got a kiss more sweet than honey
>   from a man's wife, for love,
> and I'll get no taste from any kiss
>   till doomsday, after that,[4]

the foreigners could not have understood him, for they lacked any knowledge of the Irish language. For the same reason they would have been unaware of a clandestine lover's fear of discovery:

> In the chapel, in the abbey,
>   the churchyard or the open air,
> if we two should chance to meet don't look,
>   and I won't look at you.[5]

While the nuances may have escaped them, however, the Frenchman and Spaniard could not avoid observing the number of illegitimate relationships, among churchmen as well as laity, and involving incestuous unions as well as adultery.[6] So they generalised. They saw a morass of immorality as they saw the soggy marshlands and brambly forests that covered the country. They did not suspect that the loose living harboured a degree of hedonism which made it in no way more moral but much less barbaric than they supposed. Petrarch, had he access to the contemporary Irish literature, would have recognised the phenomenon as would other poetasters from medieval Provence or Renaissance Italy.

Passing visitors could hardly have been expected, on the other hand, to appreciate how the laws relating to inheritance were a major part of the reason why most people's homes were simple wattle-and-daub 'beehive' shelters rather than solid houses of timber or stone. It was not, after all, as if the Irish were unable to build permanent structures. Not only did the clandestine lover fear to be identified in various ecclesiastical buildings but he also worried about gossip 'in the cottages or the big house'[7] and in fact the countryside was dotted with fortified enclosures, stone tower-houses and small castles. If the majority of the Gaelic population, including some of the chieftains, used humbler dwellings, it was because land was frequently redistributed on the death of its occupier. To retain what were considered the benefits of this system meant accepting a degree of mobility which dissuaded investment in costly building enterprises.[8] Another practice making for mobility, at least among the poorer countryfolk, was transhumance or booleying by which herds were moved to upland pastures in summertime while the lowlying meadowland renewed itself:[9] a method of farming employed to this day in Alpine and other continental districts but for some reason thought primitive by the Elizabethan English.[10]

For want of knowing *why* people lived as they did, travellers from Europe, England and even the Irish seaports and towns of the English-dominated 'pale' around Dublin assumed that the deficiencies of Gaelic society sprang from the ignorance of the uncivilised. It occurred to very few that they might be looking at an *alternative* civilisation, or at any rate an alternative way of organising society and defining its priorities. In saying this, no exaggerated case need be made for the alleged virtues of a Gaelic Ireland marked by incessant violence, much crude behaviour and little appreciation of artistic endeavour other than wordcraft. This was, to tell the truth, the once hugely promising 'abortive civilisation' of Celtic Christianity[11] in advanced decay. But by the same token, it was *not* a state of aboriginal primitiveness where everything had yet to be learned, where knowledge had yet to be inculcated of values loftier than bare survival and the satisfaction of greed. 'Sweet is the scholar's life,' wrote a poet, '. . . the sweetest lot in Ireland'[12] and another advised, Polonius-like,

> On ample learning's mighty ocean be,
> my boy, a good sailor . . .

> Take a copious draught each day
> from wisdom's noble spring.
> It won't taste sour in your mouth.
> Knowledge is a hold on bliss.[13]

The shock of immersion in an alien culture and the barrier of language left the first Jesuit emissaries unimpressed by Ireland and convinced that the people were barbarous.[14] British travellers, from Giraldus Cambrensis[15] in the twelfth century to Fynes Moryson[16] at the end of the Elizabethan period, came away with the same impression.

The misjudgment ran deep. The Gaelic Irish possessed an already ancient literature, acknowledged an elaborate code of rights and duties, had been Christian for a millennium and showed no desire to exchange their manner of living — however much it had degenerated — for an alternative system; indeed to some extent, possibly exaggerated, they had absorbed into their culture the descendants of Norman invaders (who had crossed over from Britain four centuries earlier) rather than adapt to Norman feudalism. Communication with a people so conscious of, and wedded to, their own identity could not be conducted with any hope of success in the terms addressed to savages whose race-memory was nothing but myth and whose lifestyle was no more than an inherited technique for tribal survival. The distinction between barbarity and decadence had important implications for those outside the country planning policies, whether political or pastoral, for dealing with the Irish.

Broadly speaking, the political approach of English administrations, based on the assumption that the Irish were uncivilised, required the *imposition* of an alternative structure of society with different allegiances, a different legal system, different agricultural methods, different property rights . . . and eventually a different religion. Colonists were settled throughout wide tracts of the country to demonstrate the better way and, of course, to ensure a loyalist presence among the untrustworthy natives. By contrast, the pastoral approach of the Catholic Church, when faced with the challenge of the new religion, was to *accept* the traditions, the folk-memory, the popular faith, and seek to strengthen the moral fibre of the people by wooing them out of their laxity. The bulk of the nation, not surprisingly, responded to acceptance and resisted imposition. Thus was drawn up a blueprint for the subsequent history of Ireland.

It was probably inevitable. The first Jesuits with their foreigners' reaction to sixteenth-century Gaelic Ireland would scarcely have favoured the acceptance of much that struck them as typical of the country and its people. But how could reform be imposed? The civil power, with whom the Church used to seek collaboration in the past (as when it conferred the lordship of Ireland on King Henry II so that he might remove alleged abuses), had broken with Rome and was no longer a potential ally. The centralised papacy which could decree detailed change lay far in the future. Indeed, in the 1540s the Church as a whole was still awaiting its own reform and Father Salmeron would play a part in it as a theologian at the Council of Trent.[17] Meanwhile, if religion in Ireland were to be strengthened and the moral fibre of the people to be tightened, the people's collaboration would be needed.

It can be argued that the Broet-Salmeron mission was inadequately prepared. Allowing for the inordinate time which it took for news to come from Ireland to Rome (about five months for a letter), not to mention the paucity of news sent in the first place, the Pope decided almost hastily on the dispatch of nuncios. It was only in the mid-1530s that Henry VIII began to flex his muscles in Ireland; not until 1536 did he proclaim himself Supreme Head of the Church there; by the time the Irish parliament declared him King (rather than Lord) of Ireland the nuncios were already named and girding themselves for the long journey via Scotland. Because the appeals for help against Tudor aggression which moved the Pope to act came mainly from the Irish chieftains, he sent his delegates to the Gaelic province of Ulster instead of the 'English Ireland' of the towns, where they might have learned more about the political situation and the effect of the royal schism on popular religion.

None of this is to say that preliminary discussions on the purpose of the mission were neglected,[18] but rather that the difficulties to be overcome were insufficiently assessed. It can be questioned whether the members of a year-old ten-man-strong order[19] were as clear about the means they should employ to carry out the tasks they were given as they would be a few years later when their numbers had dramatically increased and the manner in which they were expected to discharge any duties laid upon them had been clarified. Certainly, these nuncios to Ireland seem to have taken literally Ignatius's metaphor, that Jesuits were to be 'light horsemen . . . ready . . . to go everywhere and skirmish on all sides'.[20] It was not the happiest turn of phrase, for it implied a superficial attitude contradicting the thoroughness which Ignatius demanded of himself and his brethren. Be that as it may, Broet and Salmeron contented themselves with a quick reconnaissance which met the Pope's need for information up to a point but omitted the immersion in local conditions — staying long enough, for example, to learn something of the language and customs — which would become instinctive everywhere among their confrères in the future. One Jesuit, indeed, already prefigured that Jesuit sympathy with foreign cultures which in time would have such an impact in countries as far apart as China and Paraguay. Francis Xavier received his commission to go to the Indies in the same month as his two colleagues were chosen for Ireland. It is thought that Ignatius may have originally intended him for the Irish mission.[21] It stuns the mind to contemplate what might have happened had his dynamism and capacity for responding to others been brought to bear on the Irish situation.

As it happened, nearly twenty years were to pass before the Jesuits renewed their interest in Ireland: Ignatius, no doubt influenced by the pessimistic reports of Broet and Salmeron, felt that nothing useful could be achieved in so troubled a country.[22] The reputation of the order was growing rapidly, however, and the Counter-Reformation was gathering steam on the continent under the stimulus of Trent. Catholic leaders in Ireland, especially among the clergy, saw the need for the kind of moral uplift and strengthening of commitment which the Jesuits could be counted on to provide. They kept up an insistent battery of appeals to Rome, and Diego Laynez, who succeeded Ignatius as General, finally yielded. This time the Jesuits' approach was altogether more professional. They identified the twin threat to the Catholic religion among the people: an inadequate popular understanding of the faith and the resumed promotion (after the brief reign of the Catholic Mary Tudor) of a schismatic Church which by this stage could be termed Protestant. They concluded that the best means of tackling both these hazards lay in education and they looked to the towns as the places in Ireland most likely to react favourably to what the Jesuits had to offer.

The towns were largely peopled by the *Sean-Gaill*, the 'Old Foreigners' known in Irish history as the 'Old English'. They were descended from the Norman invaders of earlier centuries, or more commonly from the Anglo-Saxon retainers and tradesmen who accompanied the Normans. These townsfolk spoke the English language, while being fluent in Irish as well, and had adopted fewer Gaelic customs than their counterparts in the country districts. They felt an affinity with the English Crown that was lacking among the Gaels but they clung as tenaciously as their Gaelic compatriots to their Catholic heritage despite the pressures brought to bear on them at the time of the English Reformation.

The source of the new approach towards the problems of Ireland can be easily surmised. Father David Wolfe, a native of Limerick, had joined the Society in Italy, become rector of a college in Modena and founder of another in the Alpine district of the Valtelline. He had therefore become imbued with the educational standards of the Society at the same time as the reforms of the Council of Trent were taking hold. He represented the refurbished and revitalised Catholicism of the day. He also knew his own country from the standpoint of a town-dweller of Old English stock. This disposed him to distinguish between English political and religious objectives: he had no fundamental objection to the first[23] but was naturally determined to resist the latter. In this bifurcation of government policy in Ireland, Wolfe's Achilles' heel can perhaps be detected, for the Elizabethan officials and garrison made no such clearcut subdivision of their objectives. They were guided by the single-minded purpose of imposing the royal will on Church and State alike and were prepared to do no more towards keeping them separate than to suspend from time to time the campaign against the Roman

Church when they judged it more important to woo the loyalty of urban Catholics.

Interestingly, the reigning Pope — the dour, determined and reformist Paul IV — shared the English view of the intertwined concerns of the sacred and the secular. When it was decided in 1560 to send Wolfe to Ireland the Pope appointed him a nuncio apostolic, like his Jesuit predecessors, and charged him[24] not only with various duties regarding religion but also with finding out the state of 'fortresses and munitions'. An instruction to make contact with the Catholic leaders and encourage them to continue steadfast in defending the faith could be read in the circumstances of the time as a political as well as a religious commission. Paul IV was not a Pope with whose directives men readily quibbled and it may be assumed that Wolfe uncomplainingly agreed, like a good Jesuit, to carry out the wishes of the Holy Father even when these threatened to distract him from the pastoral and educational roles which were his special competence. In these activities, too, the Pope had specific instructions for him. He was to report on the quality of the Irish clergy and their preaching, which would probably be easy enough, and reprimand bishops if he found them failing in their duty, which would call for all the tact he could summon up.

Wolfe's own inclination and experience, as well as a growing awareness in the Society of Jesus that education was a most important buttress of faith in any community,[25] found reflection in the further command to set up grammar schools if he could, and persuade parents to send their children to them. Neither for these nor any other work 'undertaken for the salvation of souls' was he to accept reward: an interesting and perceptive recognition of the case for free 'secondary education'. What Wolfe made of the authority given him after he had been in Ireland some years to found a university modelled on Paris or Louvain is unclear. Oddly enough, the same encouragement to open a university like Louvain would be addressed by Pope Pius IX to the Irish bishops nearly three centuries later. On each occasion it exposed abysmal ignorance of the social conditions and political circumstances of Ireland and serves still as a healthy caution against unthinking admiration for the supposed wisdom of the Vatican and its access to reliable information. Papal policy, then as now, was normally elaborated not by the Pope himself but by his bureaucracy, the Roman curia. A surviving letter of Broet's refers to 'the very reverend cardinals, who planned and directed our mission. . . .'[26] They were not always the most sagacious planners!

Three significant features stand out in the instructions given to Wolfe, however, which were no doubt in part at least drawn up on his advice. The first was a determination to bring Ireland into the mainstream of reformed Catholicism at an early point, when the thrust of the Council of Trent had become evident but its deliberations were not yet over. Secondly, attention was to be paid to political and even military factors which in the era of wars of religion were seen to bear directly on the concerns of the Church. Finally, a Jesuit was considered the best qualified person to assume the difficult and dangerous obligations of such a mission.

David Wolfe landed at Cork on 20 January 1561, and it is said that 'vast crowds flocked from places as much as sixty miles distant to receive his ministrations'.[27] This would seem to imply a shortage of priests or a grave sense of sin which could be relieved by confessing to the Pope's representative. The latter possibility may be borne out by Wolfe's observation that although the Irish 'are much given to vice, they are free from heresy'.[28] Not that 'heresy' in the form of the state Church was much of a problem just then: many were waiting to see whether Elizabeth, on the throne for merely two years, might not eventually decide that she was a Catholic after all like her half-sister, Queen Mary, under whom the old religion had been officially restored for a short time in the 1550s. Rome, to be sure, was out of favour again but the Irish had coped with that before. Their tactics were crude but effective. Gaelic chieftains, the heads of Old English families, city corporations and even some bishops swore allegiance to the monarch and a number of them took the oath acknowledging the King or the Queen as supreme head or governor (Elizabeth's title) of the Church. They then went home, ignored the clergy and the rites of the new religion and resumed their worship of God in the traditional manner, especially by attending Mass. The Crown forces were too thin

on the ground in Gaelic areas and in the old Anglo-Irish
lordships to do much about this during the opening years of
Elizabeth's reign, while in the towns they were anxious to
avoid rebellion and so did little to promote religious change
beyond handing the churches over once more to the priests
and bishops of the state Church.

Wolfe had therefore a relatively free hand during the early
years of his mission, especially in the towns of the southern
province of Munster. To cope with the shortage of priests
and to overcome the disedifying lives of some of them, he
quickly sought out candidates for the priesthood and sent
them to the continent to be properly educated. One consequence was what a modern writer has called 'a mild vocation-
explosion to the Jesuit order from Ireland',[29] for a number
of these young men were attracted by the nuncio's style and
zeal. Another result was the increasing vigilance of the
English authorities when they came to realise how government objectives were being undermined by the strengthening of the papist clergy. They took to keeping a close
watch on ships leaving or entering Irish ports, since they
shared the view of Catholic churchmen like David Wolfe that
the introduction of worthy and able priests would guarantee
the survival of the old faith. What one tried to achieve, the
other worked hard to prevent.

The nuncio had less success in setting up schools, not so
much initially because of government obstruction as because
of resistance by the Catholic bishops: what objection they
had is unclear, other than possible resentment at the wide
powers conferred by the Pope on a mere priest. The urgency
could scarcely be questioned as the government was already
planning the establishment of schools under state control[30]
and the paucity of competent teachers available to Wolfe also
underlined the imperative need for an educated laity. Wolfe
managed to have schools opened in several Munster towns,[31]
including his native Limerick where he founded a grammar
school which he consigned to the care of a relative, Edmund
Daniel, who was a scholastic (a Jesuit who has completed his
noviceship but not the years of study prior to ordination)
and Father William Good, an English member of the Society.[32]
The refusal of the bishops to co-operate in educational

projects can only have confirmed Wolfe in his belief that the choice of suitable clerics to be made bishops in Ireland was of vital importance. The lack of discipline, the neglect of preaching and the sheer immorality common among the priests — concubinage was widespread — would have been a further stimulus to reform the episcopate whose neglect had allowed the situation to develop which the poet pithily summed up:

> Gold priests, wooden chalices
> in Ireland in Patrick's time.
>> Golden chalices, wooden priests,
>> as the wretched world stands now.[33]

Whether it was in general a happy precedent to have bishops chosen by a nuncio, even a nuncio native to the country, must remain an open question. Given the degenerate condition of the Irish Church and the conniving for place in Gaelic and urban Ireland alike, it met immediate needs satisfactorily. Wolfe's recommendations were accepted by the papacy and three of his nominees — Bishops O'Herlihy of Ross, Mac Congail of Raphoe and O'Hart of Achonry — not only went to Rome to be consecrated but then made their way to Trent where they joined the Council in its closing stages.[34] Wolfe's protégés also included Limerick-born Richard Creagh, the saintly Archbishop of Armagh who was to be Primate for a full twenty years, many of which he spent imprisoned in Dublin Castle and the Tower of London.[35] Through such leaders, as through the Jesuits and other priests returning from the continental colleges to which the nuncio had sent them, the Catholic Church in Ireland became consciously part of the international communion centred on Rome at the very time when burgeoning Calvinism in France and the Netherlands, and Anglicanism in England, were about to challenge its claim on the soul of Europe with more determination than had been seen since Luther led half of Germany away from Roman allegiance a generation before. This intimate identification of Irish Catholicism with the embattled Church on the European mainland was David Wolfe's lasting contribution to his country's history.

As the 1560s progressed, Queen Elizabeth's religio-political attitude became both less enigmatic and indisputably Protestant. Public acknowledgment of Catholic belief, and especially of the spiritual authority of the Pope, invited arrest, fines and imprisonment. Wolfe was jailed in 1567, his Limerick school closed down the following year, and other clergy, including Primate Creagh, were arrested. Rebellion flared up in west Munster, close to Limerick, led by James Fitzmaurice Fitzgerald, cousin to the Earl of Desmond, who denounced the Queen for bringing pressure on the Irish 'to forsake the catholic faith by God unto his church given'.[36] Retrospective blessing for the revolt could be read into the excommunication of Elizabeth by Pope Pius V in 1570, which *inter alia* absolved her subjects from any oath of loyalty to her and extended the excommunication to those who continued to yield her obedience.[37]

The Pope, of course, had wider considerations in mind than events in Ireland but it is difficult with hindsight to see the excommunication, which in fact purported to depose the Queen in the now anachronistic manner of the high medieval papacy, as anything but disastrous. It gave the government in England, and by extension in Ireland, valid reason to represent the adherents of Rome as traitors. It demolished the credibility of those Catholics who, like Wolfe, had proclaimed them-selves loyal subjects in all secular matters. And it laid the foundation for the long-popular Protestant belief that Jesuits were spies, *agents provocateurs*, sinister and unscrupulous manipulators dedicated to the destruction of rulers and regimes which refused to bend the knee to Rome.

The Jesuits contributed to the growth of this caricature of themselves in two ways. In the first place, out of loyalty to the Pope and virtually immediately, some Jesuits began actively to collaborate with rebellion and to seek foreign aid against the Queen. Wolfe was among them and when he escaped from prison in 1572 he went to Spain to lobby for an expedition in support of Fitzmaurice and for the replacement of Elizabeth by a Catholic king of Ireland: his choice was Don John of Austria,[38] recently the victor in the sea-battle of Lepanto against the Turks. The English, who had an extensive network of spies on the continent, were well aware of what was going on and also knew that theological justifications for rebellion against a heretic ruler were attracting much interest in the University of Louvain, where there were many English and several Irish exiles and where there were Jesuits both on the staff and among the students.[39] This provided the second cause for suspicion and indeed represented the embryonic stirring of a theme which would in time provoke much hostility against the Society in Catholic as well as Protestant kingdoms, and especially in France. It would be the source, too, of serious dissension between Jesuits themselves.

Meanwhile the English authorities in Ireland responded with vigour to the threat of political subversion following the excommunication of the Queen. They seized Wolfe's cousin, Edmund Daniel, the Jesuit scholastic who had been teaching in the Limerick school, demanded that he take the Oath of Supremacy renouncing the Pope and, when he refused, condemned him to death. After the brutal manner of the day, he was hanged, drawn and quartered (that is, disembowelled while still alive and then dismembered) in Cork on 25 October 1572. The date should loom more prominently than it does in the annals of the Society, for Edmund Daniel was 'the first Jesuit to shed his blood for the faith on European soil'.[40] In Cork also 'on the eve of St Patrick's Day' in 1575 the Jesuit priest Edmund O'Donnell of Limerick suffered the same penalty for the same refusal to acknowledge the Queen's supremacy in the Church. Perhaps significantly, O'Donnell seems to have been found guilty of the further offences of 'obstinate adherence to Popery' and 'propagating Popish doctrines'.[41]

If a distinction can be made between these two inadequately reported martyrdoms, it lies in the stress placed in the later case on matters of religious belief as well as on civil disobedience. Of course, the civil disobedience amounting to treason, which would have been the judge's understanding of refusal to swear the Oath of Supremacy, was an assertion of religious belief by the Jesuits concerned. Arraignment on the more general charge of propagating Popish doctrine suggests a hardening of lines — the invocation of creed as a measure of loyalty, which had long been possible under statute but was sparingly invoked in Ireland until the Queen had been excommunicated. Other clergy, and laity too, were to suffer

death now, from Archbishop Dermot O'Hurley of Cashel to
the Wexford baker, Matthew Lambert, whose offence was to
have given shelter to fugitives who included Father Robert
Rochford.[42] Rochford, himself from Wexford, was a well-
known Jesuit, 'a proper divine, an exact philosopher and very
good antiquary' according to Richard Stanyhurst. As late as
1577, Rochford had been conducting a school at Youghal
together with his Jesuit colleague, Charles Lea, a native of
nearby Cloyne, but by 1581 he had to leave Ireland because
of the hazard he represented for all who associated with him:
five sailors had been executed with Lambert for trying to get
the fugitives a passage out of the country. Rochford's departure
marked the end of the mission begun by David Wolfe twenty
years before.

Wolfe's success could be measured ironically by the alarm
of government agents at the mere mention of a Jesuit in the
vicinity. Regardless of rank, whoever was thought to have harboured one was interrogated, as were the Earl and Countess
of Kildare when suspected of helping Rochford.[43] Maurice
Eustace, a young man who wanted to join the Society in
Belgium, was arrested when he went home to Ireland to
obtain his parents' consent. He denied any involvement in
rebellion, but the judge told him: 'Out of your own mouth I
judge you; for as you affirm you are a Jesuit, every prudent
man will say you are guilty of the crime of which you are
charged.'[44] And on that basis they hanged him in 1588.

More positive evidence of the mission's effectiveness was
the failure of the Anglican Church to win allegiance from
the Irish, whether of Gaelic or Old English stock, whether in
town or countryside. Of course, this cannot be attributed solely
to the handful of Jesuits at work in Ireland, but it seems fair
to claim that their influence exceeded their numbers: Wolfe,
as nuncio, brought a degree of discipline to the disorganised
hierarchy and gave a powerful impulse to the training of
priests abroad so that the Irish clergy, both secular and regular,
came rapidly to represent the fresh spirit engendered in
Catholicism by the Council of Trent. These priests were
theologically well-formed, disposed to see their vocation as a
crusade, determined to inculcate moral behaviour and the
ordered practice of religion among their compatriots as well

as resistance to Protestantism. The Jesuits also appreciated the key role of education in producing a self-confident laity; the establishment of schools, some in fixed locations, others itinerant, was a distinctive feature of their mission. It would be wrong to suggest that Irish religion by the 1580s had developed an altogether new character. Overhaul was required on far too great a scale to be brought about in so short a time by a small cadre of churchmen, no matter how dedicated. But defects had been diagnosed and remedial action set in motion. It was the beginning of the modernisation and revivification which would give the Catholic Church in Ireland precisely the stiffening it needed to withstand the strain of political oppression and religious persecution.

So much on the credit side. There was a darker aspect too. It was a time of chaotic upheaval in Ireland. The Northern chieftains blew hot and cool in their relations with England, now supporting, now opposing, the officialdom in Dublin Castle, consistent only in their refusal to abandon a jot of their traditional status in Gaelic society, and for the most part avoiding any truck with the Anglican Church. Some of the lords of Norman ancestry — Fitzmaurice in Munster, Baltinglass on the borders of the Pale — rose in revolt specifically to defend the Roman Catholic faith. The motives of those who supported them could not always be identified with such clarity: both there and in Connacht the control of hereditary fiefdoms often seemed a more important consideration than matters of religion.

Sometimes the Irish compromised with English governors; time and again they repudiated compromises arrived at. As a survival tactic it could be understood and was perhaps not reprehensible in people who felt no loyalty towards the overbearing Tudor bureaucrats manifestly bent on exterminating the lifestyle of generations, not to mention extirpating the Church against which the Irish bore no grudges of the kind so long endemic in England. To the English administrators, however, Irish undependability looked like treachery and adhesion to Rome like treason. They responded accordingly. Their armies marched to and fro across the provinces, trampling, ravaging, burning, levying contributions by way of supplies and taxes. We should not, in hindsight, wax unduly indignant. In those days, it was the way of armies everywhere, of Catholic armies in France and Lutheran armies in Germany, of Spaniards in the Netherlands and Swedes from the Baltic to Bohemia. Everywhere as well it brought misery and resentment. It was so in Ireland.

The Jesuits, sadly, proved less perceptive in this situation than might have been expected. The most influential among them took up a political stance, committing themselves to those Irish leaders in revolt against English domination. That could scarcely be criticised, given the ferocious implementation of anti-Catholic and even anti-Jesuit governmental measures. It was another matter when Jesuits sought to define and promote the steps to be taken towards a political resolution of the conflict in Ireland . . . becoming, as it were, politicians themselves. Wolfe in particular asked the King of Spain to send soldiers and the Pope to send money. This in effect meant obtaining valuable aid for military incompetents like Fitzmaurice or unpredictable O'Neills, O'Donnells and other chieftains who would do a deal with the Lord Deputy if it seemed to be in their interest, notwithstanding the pleas they sent to continental potentates for assistance 'in consideration of [their] defence of the Romish faith'.[45] Some of them, indeed, were capable also of burning churches and harassing clergy when denied the tribute they claimed as their due.[46] Wolfe, in his zeal, saw only the advantage to Catholicism in defeating the Protestant forces of the English Crown. Foreign monarchs were more calculating. Philip II of Spain long held back rather than provoke Elizabeth into allying herself with the French against him, while the French, when approached in their turn, could detect no advantage in encouraging English-Spanish collaboration.[47] The Papacy, having excommunicated the Queen and absolved her subjects from their allegiance, had to provide some help but the only result was the devastation of West Munster by the soldiery sent to quench the papal-sparked last flicker of Fitzmaurice's revolt in 1579.

The only military result, that is to say. Consequences followed for religion which were disastrous and would continue for many years. The lobbying abroad by Irish clerics, their use of the excommunication of Elizabeth to justify their cause and the influx of aid from the continent convinced the royal authorities that nothing would be gained by turning a blind eye to the persistent Catholicism of the people. Oppression became active persecution. Torture and the gallows claimed numerous victims, charged indiscriminately with common crimes and offences related to religion: all ranked as disturbance of the Queen's peace. To be sure, such awfulness was increasingly the norm in Europe wherever the Catholic and Reformed Churches were in collision and it would go far towards drowning out the few voices that spoke the language of Christian tolerance: Peter Canisius, for example, who had already pleaded, 'Let us confine ourselves to expounding Catholic doctrine; we shall obtain far greater and better results than by force and polemics',[48] or Martin Becanus who would soon argue in favour of 'keeping faith with heretics'.[49] These were Jesuit voices, incidentally, but their message never penetrated to Ireland where the division was not only between Catholic and Protestant but between native and stranger, between familiar ways and alien, between what was seen to belong and what was being imposed. In the tension-laden air such contrasts simply could not admit of the charitable concept underlying Canisius's description of those who differed from him in religion as his 'separated brethren'.[50]

Wolfe did his best by his lights. If his activities at the Spanish court added to the tensions at home, they left intact his major achievement of demonstrating what the Irish Church had to do to by way of internal discipline, education and spiritual renewal in order to survive the tribulations which had begun to gather round it. He resumed his work in Ireland in 1575. 'Under circumstances not clarified by known documents, his connections with the Society were severed in 1576–1577.'[51] He died about the end of 1578. That year brought a horrifying event which was fortuitously to link Wolfe's mission with the next Jesuit enterprise in Ireland, destined to begin two decades later. In August 1578, Bishop Patrick O'Hely of Mayo — a diocese now absorbed into Tuam — and his chaplain, Conor O'Rourke, were arrested in County Limerick on their way home from the continent. On the night before they were to be hanged in the market-town of Kilmallock a young priest contrived to visit O'Rourke and minister to him: a particularly brave undertaking in the circumstances. The priest was James Archer from Kilkenny. He would be heard of again.[52]

Like all the Irish towns, Kilkenny had remained Catholic despite the royal administration based there. Archer probably attended the highly regarded grammar school favoured by Catholic families and run by Dr Peter White, a layman and former fellow of Oriel College, Oxford. When young Archer showed an inclination towards the priesthood, he was sent for higher studies to the university of Louvain; it can scarcely be doubted that this reflected the influence of Wolfe's policy which was most effectively felt among the Old English population of the urban centres. Louvain at the time must have been abuzz with news and opinions. English Catholic exiles thronged there, for it was convenient to the Flemish ports. The Calvinist Dutch, a mere fifty miles away, were locked in warfare, part-nationalist and part-religious, with the Spaniards. Commercial contact continued meanwhile between Belgium and the German states, some of them Catholic, some Protestant. Adding spice to the debates engendered by all this was the recent excommunication of Queen Elizabeth by Pope Pius V. Robert Bellarmine, an Italian Jesuit scholastic not yet ordained, was preaching and elaborating his theories on the residual rights of the papacy to intervene in secular affairs when the good of religion required it, a position approved by the English cleric, William Allen. Another Englishman in Louvain, Nicholas Sanders, was arguing less subtly that the good of religion demanded an invasion of England by Catholic forces — most likely from Spain — to put down the heretic Queen. The sad impracticality, so common in exile communities, rings hauntingly through such English asseverations.

To an Irish boy, of course, they were not at all impractical. He came from a country where the old religion survived intact, the Church structures still functioned — if somewhat erratically — and the Queen had lost whatever loyalty she once commanded, not least in towns like Kilkenny. He must have been saying as much in Louvain because the spies reported him and when he came home as an ordained priest in 1577 the Lord President (the English governor) of Munster noted the return of 'James Archer of Kilkenny, a detestable enemy of the Word of God [who] did swear against Her Majesty's jurisdiction in Louvain. . .'. Dr Sanders turned up a little later to support Fitzmaurice and died a lonely death as a fugitive in the Irish woods. Archer can only have been confirmed in the belief that it was a pious objective to seek to overthrow the Queen's authority. It would be rash to assume that this impelled him towards the Jesuits, but for reasons unknown he sought entry to the Society and began his novitiate in Rome in 1581. From here he moved on to the Jesuit Collegio Romano, where he was exposed not only to the jurist Francisco Suarez, who favoured papal authority above regal, but also to Bellarmine again who had been brought back from Louvain and installed in the aptly named chair of Controversial Theology.

These eminent thinkers were elaborating theory at an elevated and abstract level. Nobody ever accused Archer of intellectual brilliance — his superiors in fact considered him somewhat mediocre — and it may be that he took the theory more literally than his mentors intended. At any rate, the ambition to promote insurrection in Ireland never left him despite the years he was to spend as a chaplain to the Spanish armies in the Netherlands and later in Spain itself as Vice-Rector of the Irish College at Salamanca, founded by Thomas White, a fellow Jesuit from Clonmel. (This was the first of many colleges established specifically for Irish clerical students on the continent during the penal era: the second, at Lisbon, would be set up shortly afterwards by yet another Jesuit, John Howling of Wexford). Archer must have been less than reticent in expressing his opinions, for he caught the attention of the spies once more and during his service on the continent was listed in reports to the English government among a group of alleged plotters said to be planning to assassinate the Queen. With modern espionage in its infancy and the spies anxious to show results, such reports have to be discounted, although it is less easy to argue that Archer gave no grounds for misrepresentation to eavesdroppers.

Through the English Jesuit, Robert Persons, Archer gained access to the Spanish court despite the rampant xenophobia which caused all foreigners, and especially non-Spanish Jesuits, to be looked on with suspicion. This left him well-placed when the King, the Pope and the Jesuit General — Claudius Aquaviva — at last all agreed that a positive response should be sent to the Irish bishops and chieftains who had begun to clamour for Jesuits to strengthen the faith and improve the education of the Catholic people. Interestingly, the educational objective seems to have arisen from fears that the newly founded Trinity College in Dublin would succeed in promoting the Reformation where physical force had failed. For the King of Spain the attraction was the offer of the crown of Ireland made on behalf of the Irish leaders by Hugh O'Neill, the Earl of Tyrone. Like many indecisive men, Philip II overplayed his hand when he eventually moved. His fleet of 98 ships, carrying many Irish exiles and a considerable army nearly 11,000 strong, was scattered by the wind like the Armada eight years before. The more realistic Jesuit General avoided grand schemes and gave Archer the limited brief to go to Ireland to raise money for his college in Salamanca and to report on the feasibility of reviving the Jesuit mission. The English authorities, alerted by spies and the preparations for the fleet, were waiting: they soon got word that the notorious Father Archer, S.J., had arrived in Waterford where he adopted the name Bowman. The impish bravado of his punning incognito tantalises us with an all-too-brief glimpse of attractive vivacity in the man whom his enemies would dub an 'Arch-Devil' and present as the stereotype of the Jesuit intriguer, the dark and menacing figure standing behind O'Neill or other chieftains whenever they came to parley.

Archer's activities in Ireland are to be noted rather than dwelt upon, for his importance lay in what he was thought to represent rather than in any ongoing achievement. Government agents pursued him relentlessly, with the result that he could make little or no communication with Rome. A tentative decision to appoint him superior of a new Irish mission had to be abandoned. Yet curiously enough, when the General sent Father Henry Fitzsimon to the Dublin area a year or two later, Mass was being openly celebrated and the Lord Deputy, Ormond, even invited Fitzsimon to engage in public disputation with Protestant ministers. The logic of these contradictory attitudes lay in the revolt spreading over large tracts of the provinces, the threat of Spanish invasion and the military successes of the forces led by O'Neill (especially at the Yellow Ford). Once again it was judged necessary to win the good-will of the townspeople while maximising the campaign against the insurgents. Hence the perceived wisdom of permitting Catholic worship in Dublin conducted by a Jesuit who could be treated as a pastor and an intellectual — Fitzsimon, a convert, was an Oxford graduate — while putting a price on the head of another Jesuit considered to be a subversive conspirator bent on fuelling rebellion. It was a distinction which perhaps could only have been made by somebody as sensitive to the abrasive co-habitation of the several traditions in Ireland as a Butler, to which ancient Hiberno-Norman family Ormond belonged. Some time later, however, when he had been briefly kidnapped by the midland chieftain Owny O'More, Ormond firmly put the blame on 'the most wicked villain and unnatural traitor, James Archer, the Jesuit', a phrasing which suggests he saw wickedness, villainy, treason and jesuitry as all of a piece. No doubt the fact that Archer, like Ormond himself, came from Kilkenny exacerbated the sense of injury.

Archer had indeed been involved in the kidnapping epi-sode, which was bad enough in the eyes of the government, but more damning still was his prominent place in the entourage of O'Neill, in the Irish camps (where, as a former chaplain, he must have felt at home) and ultimately, after visiting Rome and spending some time in Spain, among the Spanish forces which disembarked at Kinsale in 1601. His active role in that ill-fated expedition cannot be denied. Writing to Father White in Salamanca, he described a quarrel with the commander, Don Juan del Aguila: 'I begged him to keep twenty pieces of artillery but he was satisfied with only six, which was the cause of the loss of the port . . . we begged him to defend the trenches but he refused . . . O'Neill and O'Donnell came with a good army on the day appointed for him to sally out and meet them . . . but he refused to leave Kinsale.' And so on. It is hard not to feel some sympathy for del Aguila who, according to Archer, 'replied with disdain that it was my function to pray, teach doctrine and confess'! This, of course, was the campaign in which the Elizabethan commander, Mountjoy, defeated the Irish forces and definitively ended any hope that the old Gaelic world might find a fresh lease of life. After further adventures, Archer was withdrawn by his superiors and assigned to the overall supervision of the Irish Colleges in Spain and Portugal.

Notwithstanding his immersion in political and military matters, James Archer diligently discharged his duties as a priest. In August 1598, he wrote to the General: 'I have heard two thousand general confessions . . . instructed rough and barbarous persons in the faith; got some to abjure heresy and return to the Church.' He described how he had reconciled 'a noble person' with the wife whom he had put away when he took up with 'a harlot'. He spoke with evident emotion about the crowds who came to hear Mass and go to confession: 'a very rich harvest,' he claimed, would be gathered 'if many members of the Society were sent here'. In an interesting revelation of the state of the country, he said that 'the nobles, especially those of the North . . . promise for our fathers every protection and help.' Chieftains in the South were also asking for a Jesuit mission 'but they do not dare openly to undertake the protection of our fathers.' As for Archer himself, he had been administering the sacraments 'in the camp' (presumably the army encampments, although in the Italian and Spanish usage to which he was accustomed it could mean 'in the countryside') because he was not able to work 'among the subjects in the cities'. In Archer, therefore, we find a dedicated missionary priest ministering in hazardous circumstances, as well as a lobbyist at the Spanish court and an advisor in the politico-military deliberations of the Irish leaders.

The government made no distinction between the different facets of this dual role. They assumed that all Jesuits were not only dabblers but prime movers in the intrigues of England's enemies. Two years after Kinsale, the lord president of Munster offered a reward of £40 for every Jesuit killed as against a mere £6.3.4d for a 'seminary priest' (i.e. one trained on the continent) and £5 for a 'massing priest'. If the implication was dubious, the formidable renown of the Jesuits could not be doubted and in Munster its emergence was due above all to James Archer of Kilkenny, Louvain and

Salamanca. His story is important, paradoxically, because in its political aspects it was untypical of his contemporaries, the other Irish Jesuits who began to come home about this time in some numbers. If Archer had an influence on these men, it was through his pastoral work which they went on to emulate. In the eyes of the English authorities, however, Jesuits long continued to be tarred with the conspiratorial brush. As it happened, both Archer and the government officials who reacted so strongly to his known activities and legendary reputation were equally anachronistic. The Papacy was moving away from the futility of attempting to depose heretical princes.[53] The French Jesuits were already wriggling uncomfortably under the papalism of Bellarmine and Suarez, and they would soon be openly rejecting it.[54] Aquaviva, with a sure feel for Ignatian objectives, was holding the Society as firmly as he could to its spiritual role.[55] The dark-visaged, black-robed prompter at the elbow of Catholic statesmen and soldiers belonged more to Protestant nightmares than to the real world of hard decision-making. But Archer had done enough in his day to give the colour of credence to nightmare.

By force of circumstance rather than choice, Archer spent virtually his entire mission among the Gaelic Irish. He had to avoid the towns, where he might have been recognised, and clearly felt it necessary (although not so instructed by the General) to keep in contact with O'Neill and the other Irish nobles who lived beyond the reach of English garrisons. Unlike his predecessors, Broet and Salmeron, he established a rapport with the Celtic population among whom he found himself: so we may conclude from his encomium of the people's faith, the long time he stayed in their midst (he had every excuse to leave since his General was so anxious to hear from him) and his decision to return to Ireland with the Spanish fleet. He must have acquired a fluent grasp of the Irish language since he could not otherwise have heard all those confessions or even conversed with most of the people around him. The commitment was unusual in one of Old English stock and a distinct change from Wolfe's approach, which had deliberately focused on the towns. It may be that this carried the flavour of 'going native' or 'letting down the

side' in the judgment of his fellow-townsfolk since otherwise
it is hard to explain why Fitzsimon disparaged his work and
others objected to the relatively modest authority he enjoyed
for a time as a vicar general. Or else it may have been simply
that Fitzsimon wanted some of the money which Archer was
collecting for Salamanca to be diverted to support the Irish
College recently founded at Douai in Flanders by a secular
priest, Father Christopher Cusack.

The initiative of providing a service to the people of the
Gaelic country areas was maintained when Aquaviva reopened
the Irish Mission in 1598. Although the Superior, Father
Christopher Holywood, was another Old English Palesman
(from Artane near Dublin), he saw that a comprehensive
apostolate had to involve the Gaelic majority as well as the
half-anglicised urban population. Perhaps, as is thought to
have been true of Archer,[56] association with the Gaelic Irish
abroad mitigated any prejudices he may have harboured.
For whatever reason, Holywood wrote from Milan upon his
appointment, asking the General to assign Florence O'More
and Andrew Moroney to the mission specifically because
these Jesuits spoke the Irish language: Father Moroney
would be sent in due course as would others of Gaelic name
and background.

Not that it was easy at the outset of this mission to place
Jesuit priests in any part of Ireland. Fitzsimon, who had been
sent on ahead while news was awaited from Archer, presumed
too much on the tolerance of the authorities, continued to
carry out his pastoral duties openly in the Dublin area and
even spoke with admiration of O'Neill's successes in battle.[57]
By the end of 1599 he had been arrested and imprisoned.
Meanwhile, Holywood had been caught in England on his
way to take up his appointment as Irish Superior, and lodged
in a London jail, from where he was later sent to Wisbech in
East Anglia. The General named Father Richard Field,
already in Dublin, to be Superior in place of Holywood. To
him it fell to organise the early stages of the new mission. In
a letter which Archer delivered in Rome for him on his visit
in 1600, Field asked that more Fathers be sent not only for
'this more civilised part of the kingdom' but also to minister
in Gaelic districts to 'those raw people, who are indeed

nominally and in a general way fighting for the Faith, but who in their lives and manners are far removed from Christian perfection'.[58] He also added that it would help if the papal bull excommunicating the Queen were not renewed as it created problems of conscience for many who, to his discomfiture, came seeking his advice on the question. Although he was happy with the progress of the war, Father Field left little doubt that he preferred to be spared involvement in what he called 'matters of State'. Not for him Archer's role of *éminence grise*.

Association with Archer was a danger until he left Ireland. Dominic Collins, a Jesuit Brother who went with him on the fleet to Kinsale, was captured in the weeks after the debacle and interrogated by Mountjoy himself. The English commander may well have been curious to meet this scion of Gaelic nobility, whose immediate family were merchants and who had been an officer in both the French and Spanish services but chose to exchange a military career for what was seen as the humblest rank in a religious order. Mountjoy made repeated efforts to persuade him to join both the English army and the Established Church. Collins refused all blandishments and was brought for execution to Youghal. From the gallows he exhorted the people: 'be not unworthy of your ancestors who boldly professed the faith; do you, too, uphold it. . .'. Before he could say much more he was pushed from the ladder to hang before being drawn and quartered.[59] This was on 31 October 1602.

It may be taken for granted that the General in Rome, Father Aquaviva, heard of Brother Collins's death with sadness and pride. At the same time, it is likely to have hardened his resolve that Jesuits should keep themselves aloof from the diplomatic manoeuvres, alliances and enterprises of rulers and would-be rulers. He told Holywood when appointing him Superior: 'Above all things — and not only because our Institute requires it . . . but also because the times themselves and the preservation of the mission demand it — your Reverence is to see to it that Ours do not involve themselves in any way in matters of politics or of State, but let them attend only to matters concerned with the saving of souls.'[60] The emphasis left no room for quibbling interpretation and the reference to 'the times themselves' suggests that Aquaviva, a philosopher by training, had detected the emerging shift towards co-existence and away from war *à outrance* as the proper comportment to be adopted towards one another by Christian states of different religious denomination. The arrival on their respective thrones within the same decade of Pope Clement VIII, Henri IV of France and James I of England had much to do with this, as also did the end of religious conflict in France and the calm that settled over Germany before the storm of the Thirty Years War. The new century began in dawning recognition that the Reformation and the Counter-Reformation alike were great movements of the human spirit which had to be lived with and could not be expunged.

Such considerations, of course, concerned the highest level of policy-making. They did not mean that Catholics or Protestants could everywhere count on greater tolerance in states professing adherence to a religion other than their own, and still less on automatic acknowledgment that they might have a right to live and worship God in accordance with their conscientious beliefs. 'Liberty of conscience . . . is the worst thing in the world,' said the pious and ascetic peacemaker, Clement VIII.[61] He was, however, commenting on the Edict of Nantes which allowed Protestants considerable freedom in France and which he did not oppose. In the same way, others read the signs of the times and eased in some degree the out-and-out effort to suppress religious deviation. James I, who succeeded Queen Elizabeth in 1603, preferred to convert rather than to persecute[62] but could only fitfully relieve the pressure on Catholics because of intransigence on the part of some of his advisors, including some in his Irish administration, who did not forget the papal claim of authority to dispense subjects from their allegiance. The claim, although allowed to lapse, was not revoked and its theoretical continuance left Protestants unconvinced by the distinction which Catholics were beginning to make again between temporal and spiritual allegiance. Father Wolfe, after all, had made that distinction until the Pope asserted his claim by excommunicating the Queen.

Some Catholics also, by their own actions, obstructed relaxation of the laws against them. In Ireland, it was thought that

James, as the son of Mary Queen of Scots, would be lenient to those who professed his mother's faith. Upon hearing of his accession they at once seized the churches in a number of the towns and revived the public celebration of Catholic worship. An army had to be sent out by the authorities to restore order — order in its Jacobean sense, meaning repossession of ecclesiastical buildings by the Established Church and the reinstatement of Anglican worship as the public norm. If Irish revolt alarmed the Protestants, it was nothing to the discovery two years later of the Gunpowder Plot in London itself. Rigorous implementation of the penal laws tended to follow such events, ensuring the continuance of Catholic disaffection, while in Ireland the plantation policy — involving the transfer of land in Gaelic areas to Protestant settlers, English or Scottish — did nothing at all to advance the conversion on which the King had set his heart. The overall result was that not much more could be claimed for the new reign and the opening decades of the new century than that unpredictability had replaced relentless hostility as the government's stance vis-à-vis Irish Catholics. There was no official change on the part of the state, which continued to be uncompromisingly Protestant, while the great majority of the people (Gaelic and Old English alike) remained steadfast in their Catholicism.

Interestingly, the Jesuits drew criticism on their heads by refusing to participate in the so-called Revolt of the Cities at the time of King James's accession. They stood aside from this public assertion of the Catholic religion because 'they were most strictly forbidden to meddle in matters of State, such as this movement was likely to end in,' the Superior later reported.[63] Several more Jesuits had now arrived and were already carrying out the more positive aspects of the General's instructions by attending to 'the saving of souls'. Father Field informed Aquaviva in early 1603 that 'Fathers Moroney and Lynch are working zealously in West Munster, Father Lane and myself devote our labours to Leinster . . . Father Fitzsimon is still held captive. . . . Our efforts are chiefly directed to confirm the Catholics in the Faith, to bring back to the fold any whom we find to have fallen away, and to extinguish mortal enmities and discords between many leading men.'[64] This somewhat dry and businesslike summary must have covered quite a few adventures of the kind recorded more graphically later on by Father Holywood. Holywood had been banished from England (which is to say, the government chose to be rid of him as the best option after the death of Elizabeth) and he promptly made his way to Ireland where Father Field handed over his responsibilities as Superior of the mission. Thus began an impressive pastorate of more than twenty years.

The new Superior held a conference in Clonmel during Lent, 1604, with the five other Jesuits then in Ireland. This was a risky undertaking: a similar number of Jesuits in England had escaped a priest-hunting posse literally by minutes when they came together to renew their vows some years earlier.[65] The Clonmel meeting took place in the immediate aftermath of the revolt of the cities, and in the province where a Jesuit's head was being valued at £40. No whit deterred, and presumably encouraged by the reunion with their confrères, the Fathers set about their work with fresh vigour. One of them converted a man 'of rank' in County Cork, who had been providing a refuge for highwaymen but who now built three gallows on his estate and proceeded to hang such robbers as came his way! A less dramatic but perhaps more Christian outcome was recorded in Limerick, where the Fathers preached twice a week for a month, reconciled three wives to their husbands and persuaded the municipality to open a hospice for the poor. In Tipperary the Jesuits put an end to cattle rustling and in another county (possibly Kerry) induced a penitent to make restitution of no fewer than 446 horses and cows.[66]

The mission was soon moving out from its bases in Munster and Dublin. Within months of his arrival, Holywood had received approaches from the North and he asked the General once again to send him 'Florence More' who, as a native of Armagh, spoke the Northern dialect of Irish. O'More, he was to say later, would also have been able to advise him on the possibility of a mission to the Orkneys, which the General had asked the Irish to consider. In fact O'More was never sent home because the Austrian Jesuits blocked his transfer from Bohemia, where he was ministering in the footsteps of Peter Canisius. But two Fathers went from Tipperary into the Western province of Connacht, 'where they visited Bishop Malachy, who dwelt on the banks of the Shannon River' (Malachy O'Queely, vicar apostolic of Killaloe and afterwards Archbishop of Tuam? Or Malachy O'Molony, Bishop of Kilmacduagh?), and they made their way to Galway, doing 'solid work' there 'in spite of the heretics and the Protestant garrison'. Another crossed to the Aran Islands to teach catechism and administer the sacraments, succeeding at the same time in converting 'a celebrated septuagenarian gambler' — whether from heresy or gambling the Memorials do not make clear. In Holywood's time Jesuits were found as well in Longford, Leitrim and parts of Ulster. In 1619 Father David Galway, a Jesuit from Cork, conducted a mission single-handed through the islands of the Inner Hebrides and the Clyde, celebrating the first Mass ever attended by the people then living on Islay, baptising children on Jura and converting so many inhabitants of Kintyre that a body of armed soldiers was sent in pursuit of him by a Protestant minister.

With his penchant for a good story, his racy narrative powers and his manifest enthusiasm for implementing Gospel values and Christian charity among the people, Christopher Holywood's reports can leave an impression of busy piosity which distorts a very considerable achievement. The *mise en scène* must never be forgotten. In the towns a resentful majority of Catholics had to suffer the presence of a garrison and an administration dedicated to the destruction of the religion they professed and the Church which embodied it, but which could not be dispensed with if order was to be maintained, commerce facilitated and protection provided against domestic warfare or foreign invasion. The country-side, especially in the West and the North but also in much of Munster and Leinster, still comprised great tracts of forest and bogland where the Gaelic people lived within their own culture, speaking their own language and clinging with a growing sense of doom to those elements of self-identity coming under threat everywhere from a rampaging foreign army, settlers speaking a foreign tongue and parcelling out the land in an alien manner, and each bringing with them what in the people's eyes was a foreign Church.

> Any worthless crew that thought to cross the sea to the
> fair, gold, age-old *lios* of Cobhthach 'the just' — theirs
> without struggle of hands our mighty mansions and the
> choicest swards of our lovely-bordered places.[67]

It is possible to argue that the Old Irish would have done
better to compromise with the Renaissance values springing
up unasked among them rather than seek to prolong a civilisation advanced in decadence and withering on the bough;
it might have been the way to secure more than fitful tolerance
for their religion, at least in the decades between Elizabeth
and Cromwell. It can certainly be argued that the New English
would have done better to trust the townsfolk, who wanted
only that their loyalty be spared the cruel test of religious
allegiance — better, also, to have seen in the Gaelic Irish
lifestyle the survival of a different (rather than inferior)
Weltanschauung meriting respect instead of thoughtless
contempt. There was room for co-existence and not solely in
matters religious. But such was not the temper of the times
in Ireland, whatever developments may have taken place
elsewhere. Too many for too long had been making religion
a political label, after the model of sixteenth-century Europe.
Wolfe, Sanders and Archer had all done so with the best
intentions and unwittingly contributed thereby to the civic
turmoil in which loyalty to a religious banner superseded
active Christianity as the prime expression of faith. We need
not stress it overmuch. Wolfe's and Archer's concern to
advance their truly religious mission has been noticed. The
Tudor government did far more in Ireland than any Jesuits
to attach the political label to religion. And anyway, all were
acting out the roles in which they were cast by the age in
which they lived.

What matters is that the Field/Holywood mission, while
overlapping with the end of Archer's, differed radically from
his, and it can hardly be doubted that the new emphasis was
entirely deliberate. Its object was to re-awaken regard for the
commandments, the sacraments, the duties of spouses to
one another, of each to his neighbour, of creature to Creator:
what today we would call Christian renewal . . . and all, of
course, within the context of Catholic faith and practice. No

politics. No conspiracies. No tramping around with armies or
scurrying off to continental courts in search of funds for
insurrection. Just priests serving the people in priestly ways.
Sermons of quality had been less than common, so let there
be preaching. People were loyal to the religious banner while
knowing little of what their religion taught, so let them be
instructed. Many lived scandalous lives, not least the wealthy,
so let them be told the errors of their ways and be persuaded
to repent. Some had grown rich by theft and violence under
the cover of anarchy, so let them be warned of the retri-
bution the God of Justice would exact if they neglected to
restore what they had unlawfully taken. Such was the agenda
of Fathers Field and Holywood, urged on from a distance by
Father General Aquaviva. Is it too much to describe the
ambition as saintly in a country torn by a generation of
domestic strife, foreign invasion, racial and confessional
antipathy, social upheaval, recurrent famine, the breakdown
of order. . . .?

The small band of Jesuits, it must be acknowledged,
worked within a support system which had two elements. The
people remained Catholic, which guaranteed protection and
hiding-places even when persecution flared up again, as it
did more than once without warning. And there were many
other priests in Ireland, with some thirty or forty returning
every year from their studies on the continent,[68] secular and
regular (Franciscans, Capuchins, Augustinians, Carmelites,
Dominicans and others). The structure of the Irish Church
also remained in place, however much disrupted by oppression. The succession of bishops continued in the greater
number of dioceses virtually without interruption and they
were able to exercise their jurisdiction to a considerable
degree. Where a chieftaincy or lordship survived for a time —
in Donegal, in West Munster — an open church life was
possible, with friaries functioning and church buildings kept
in use for worship. For all that, the picture remained patchy
at best and the conduct of any sacred ministry by Catholic
priests was an activity fraught with danger, for priest-hunters
were everywhere. During a Jesuit's three-hour sermon on the
Passion in Clonmel, we learn, 'the door was held by a sturdy
band of "Tipperary boys", who prevented the soldiers from

entering'. Reports survive from Jesuits working in the countryside: 'Whatever is to be done must be done in the night time. No place is safe for us on account of the number of our pursuers.' And again, cheerfully, 'we are well, though we can never sleep securely without fear of our pursuers, who are hunting for us day and night. . . . We are most secure when we are in the mountains, or in bogs, lakes, caves and such places.' In an almost laconic note to the General, Holywood apologises for a delay in writing, 'as I was obliged to go to remote parts in order to keep clear of the more than usually troublesome presence of our adversaries'.

Although some friction arose on the continent over what was seen by secular clergy as excessive control of seminary facilities for Irish students by the Jesuits,[69] there was no local antagonism against them in Ireland. On the contrary, the campaign for renewal — for reviving Catholics' personal commitment to Christian truth and values — seems to have been recognised as their special vocation, the sustenance they could give to a spiritually undernourished people. A constant feature of the reports to Rome and other records of Jesuit activities is the account of crowds flocking for their counsel when they arrived in a neighbourhood. In Carrick-on-Suir: 'The crowds who come to Mass and to hear the sermons swarm about the doors and the windows, as there is not room in the chapel. . .'. In Connacht: '[the Jesuits] received an extraordinary welcome [and] explained the truths of religion according as the crowds came to them, and sometimes preached four or five times a day. . .'. In Munster: '[our Fathers] heard confessions and preached, and in performing these and other functions of their ministry they had scarcely time to breathe. . .'. In Leinster: 'crowds came to hear [one of the Fathers]; the sick were brought in carts, some not able to travel were carried on the shoulders of their neighbours, and many remained four or five days in one place waiting for their turn to go to confession. . .'. Elsewhere: 'the inhabitants of twelve villages assembled to hear a Father preaching a mission . . .', and 'People everywhere show the greatest respect and veneration for our Fathers, come out to meet them on the roads, and welcome them as they ride along.' When the Jesuits 'return to their residences after a mission they are greeted with the acclamations of the people, and with such wishes as "May God increase your numbers," "May God restore to you your rights.'"

No propagandist intent should be read into these accounts of the need met by what effectively were parish 'missions' or 'retreats'. They were compiled for the most part to keep the General informed and were not designed for publication. Those quoted extend over a period of some fifteen years between 1605 and 1620. They reveal not only a consistent pattern of service in which the Irish Jesuits were clearly expert but also a consistent pattern of the Irish shortcomings which they endeavoured to cure without much permanent success. Robbers and adulterers require shriving throughout these years. Catholics who have fallen into 'schism' or 'heresy' have to be re-admitted to the fold. A particular problem, destined to have a long history in Ireland, begins to loom in 'the foul habit of drinking which the English soldiers had introduced into this island', as Holywood himself described it in 1605. In later years he referred to the abolition in one parish of '"treating" or drinking bouts' and refers to a family of otherwise good Catholics who were unfortunately 'too much devoted to the English practice of challenging each other to contests in drinking, to see who would hold out the longest'. No blame is attributed to perfidious Albion, however, for the Cork tradesman who left his earnings by will to be spent on drink at his wake!

It is surely a measure of the worth attached to this apostolate that the number of Jesuits sent to Ireland — or, to be precise, sent home, since all were Irish themselves — grew considerably. Five had come together to welcome Holywood at Clonmel, the entire complement then in the country. By 1609 there were eighteen and when the aged Superior died in 1626 there were forty-two to mourn his passing. The names of most of them have been preserved but except in a few cases we cannot be certain what work each was engaged upon. Because of the fear of interception, letters to Rome more often mentioned 'our Fathers' or 'one of our Fathers' than named members of the Society. Those of exceptional merit, nonetheless, were sometimes singled out. Father Walter Wall was 'a man of great eloquence' and when he preached on the Passion 'he was interrupted so often by the sobs and cries of the faithful, that he had to give up preaching, as his voice could not be heard'. Another famous preacher, perhaps less charismatic but certainly not wanting in pragmatism, was Father Barnaby O'Kearney whose hell-fire sermons proved remarkably effective in scaring the wits out of cattle-stealers. Whether the Superior altogether approved of these preaching styles may be questioned, for he once wrote that, in addition to Wall and O'Kearney, 'Fathers Moroney and Lynch do great things also but with more moderation and prudence.' Various calamities befell a number of the Jesuits. In Waterford Father Maurice Wise was reduced to penury by 'exactions and fines'. Father Nicholas Nugent spent four years imprisoned in Dublin Castle, where he composed hymns in Irish. And some, unnamed, were not above tweaking the noses of the government officials: 'they contrived to smuggle in through the gates of Cork a magnificent statue of the Blessed Virgin, which had been purchased in Portugal, and which it took eight strong men to carry.'

The distinguishing characteristic of the Jesuits was the extended spiritual formation they underwent and the high level of education they attained. While Aquaviva was 'most anxious that Irishmen should be admitted into the Society',[70] he stressed that they had to be men of sufficient ability and the right temperament.[71] The 'innate aversion for any lack of thoroughness' which had been so remarkable a quality in Ignatius Loyola,[72] found reflection among the Jesuits in Jacobean Ireland. Describing Father Patrick Lenan as one of 'the great sinews of our mission', Holywood outlined his *curriculum vitae*. 'Patrick studied his humanity here and at Oxford. He was Master of Arts in Douay and Bachelor of Divinity in Louvain, where he studied five or six years under Father Leonard Lessius and Dr Stapleton . . .'. Training was not suspended merely because of the vicissitudes of the Irish ministry. Henry Cusack, reported Holywood, was 'resting from work this year and going over subjects which he had studied in the schools so as to be better prepared for every kind of labour'. The Superiors of the mission came themselves with formidable qualifications. Field had studied in the Jesuit College in Paris and at the prestigious new University of

Pont-à-Mousson in Lorraine — a powerhouse of Counter-Reformation scholarship where the Chancellor about this time was Richard Fleming, another Jesuit from Dublin.[73] Holywood had an even more distinguished career, having taught philosophy in Italy, been Professor of Theology at Dôle and Pont-à-Mousson, and Professor of Scripture at Padua. It could not be said that the Society of Jesus short-changed Irish Catholics in the calibre of the men they sent to serve them.

The formidable intellectual background of the Jesuits caused concern among Protestants too intelligent to worry about conspiratorial stereotypes. Objectively speaking, it cannot be denied that the Reformation was negligently handled in Ireland during its initial decades. As has been accurately said, 'Protestantism was not only the religion of conquest, but was typically purveyed in the language of the conqueror by men who were too sure of their own superiority to excite interest or support. . .'.[74] This, of course, would change and in time Irish Protestantism would acquire its own distinctive high quality and its place in national life. In its beginnings, however, with its English divines and English-rooted doctrinal approach, it could mount no effective challenge to win the minds and hearts of the Catholic Irish. The 'seminary priests' deprived it of credibility, as the poet Edmund Spenser acknowledged when he wrote in his *View of the state of Ireland* about the 'great wonder to see the odds which is between the zeal of popish priests and the ministers of the gospel; for they spare not to come out of Spain, from Rome, from Rheims, by long toil and dangerous travel hither, where they know peril of death awaiteth them and no reward nor riches. . .'.[75] Dedication was copper-fastened by evident learning — always admired by the Gaelic Irish — and was not effectively countered by the mere printing of biblical texts in Irish by the established Church. Again Spenser saw to the core of the Protestant dilemma: 'The speech being Irish, the heart must needs be Irish.'[76]

Theological learning was the special province of the Jesuits. It quite possibly explained the conversion to Catholicism of more than one Protestant minister recorded by Holywood. It certainly helped to confirm the faith of the people. 'Our Fathers', he told the General, '. . . won the ears even of those who were accustomed to hear the polished and laboured discourses of the ministers.' And this was conceded from the other side: 'The Protestant ministers sometimes praise our Fathers for their learning, for teaching the catechism in the native tongue, preventing robberies, causing restitutions to be made and reforming abuses all over the kingdom.' Perhaps the ultimate accolade came from James Ussher, the most respected of the Anglican clergy, afterwards Archbishop of Armagh but at this time Professor of Theological Controversies (almost the same title as Bellarmine's) at Dublin University. The Memorials tell us that in 1609, 'Ussher delivered a series of lectures in Trinity College partly with a view of refuting the "errors" of the Jesuit Holywood.' Ussher was far too wise to rest his laurels upon an assumption of his own superiority.

The trouble, of course, with a reputation for keeping the people faithful to the Catholic religion was that it amounted to a reputation for frustrating government policy. Accordingly, on 24 January 1623, it was decreed from Dublin Castle that all Jesuits were at once to quit Ireland under pain of death. It was the full turn of the wheel. Nearly twenty years earlier the President of Munster had issued a similar edict. That had been provoked by James Archer's involvement in matters of state. Christopher Holywood had done nothing with the faintest political tinge. But since conformity in matters religious was a yardstick of allegiance, total concentration on the things of the spirit offered no protection against those determined to sniff out — and snuff out — treason. The Jesuits probably sighed at another frustration. They did not quit, but rather set about establishing more firm bases for their Irish mission than had been possible up to then.

2

FALSE DAWN

WHEN Christopher Holywood died in 1626 the Society of Jesus had more than 15,000 members, with numerous colleges and other institutions throughout Europe, and major missionary enterprises flourishing in India, the Far East and Latin America. Irish Jesuits were found as widely disseminated as the order itself, whether as college heads in Spain, university professors in France and Italy, chaplains in the Low Countries, preachers in Bohemia. In the same year as Father Holywood, Father Thomas Filde died far from his native Limerick: he had been among the first to bring the Gospel to Paraguay[1] and was therefore almost certainly one of the small band of Jesuits who set up the villages which developed into the famous Paraguayan Reductions[2] where the indigenous people were protected against the hazards of a nomadic life and exploitation by slave-traders.

Not surprisingly for so large and far-flung an order, the Jesuits became involved in a number of contemporary controversies. In France a revival of the argument over the rights of the Pope as against the rights of the King resulted in a further move by the French Jesuits in the direction of Gallicanism, or royal supremacy in matters short of the Church's dogmatic teaching.[3] In the terrible Thirty Years War, by which Germany was being ravaged, there were Jesuits who favoured toleration for Protestants[4] and others who wanted them forcibly converted or expelled from the territories held by Catholic princes.[5] The English Jesuits, despite the ongoing state campaign to eliminate Catholicism, had to defend their methods against the criticism of secular priests and at least one of the vicars apostolic appointed by Rome to carry out episcopal functions in the absence of a diocesan hierarchy.[6] A serious quarrel broke out in Spain between Jesuit and Dominican theologians over the nature of grace and free will.[7]

There had been much activity farther afield as well. Savage persecution and expulsion had all but terminated the Xavierian mission in Japan — the fault in part, it must be said, of inept dabbling by some of the Jesuits in local politics, contrary to the wish of the General and not mitigated by ongoing rivalry in the Far East with other orders, especially the Franciscans.[8] By contrast, China was proving a fertile field through the novel approach of Jesuits profoundly respectful towards the country's ancient culture and passion for scientific learning: in 1618, at the missionaries' request, the General sent out a platoon of Jesuit astronomers and mathematicians, a telescope and a science library of 7,000 books.[9] Without pretending to compare like with like, it makes sad reading to contrast this perception and willingness to comprehend with the virtual flight from a far less alien culture by Salmeron and Broet when they visited Ireland in the days of Ignatius Loyola. . . .

The Irish Mission, of course, had come a long way since then through the efforts of Wolfe, Archer, Field and Holywood but it needs to be remembered that it remained an integral part of the international Jesuit apostolate. Not only did it receive more attention from successive Fathers General than might have been expected of men burdened with immense and multifarious responsibilities, but it reflected in some degree the character of the order and drew upon itself some of the wary reaction which Jesuits met elsewhere in Europe and in places distant from the Old World.

The ubiquity of the Jesuits, their dominance in Catholic universities, seminaries and colleges, their special commitment to serve the Holy See, and their actual or supposed presence around Catholic statesmen and princes convinced every Protestant government of the early seventeenth century that they were the ultimate enemy — popery incarnate, moulders of the Catholic mentality, fanatical in religious belief, without scruple in politics. Protestants whose learning kept them aloof from such populist prejudice recognised the thorough training that went into Jesuit formation and the consequently formidable status of Jesuit scholarship; this awareness, however, tended to harden Protestant resolve to guard against the Jesuits since it implied they were far more insidious and influential than mere machiavellian conspirators. This resistance sometimes took the form of theological controversy, with the publication of treatises to refute the positions adopted by individual Jesuits. Thus King James I wrote a book against Bellarmine,[10] and the Church of Ireland Archbishop Ussher, having already responded to Holywood, returned to the fray in 1625 with an answer to a book by William Malone, an Irish Jesuit then living in Douai of whom more would be heard (although Ussher called Rome 'a dung-heap of errors', he sent a copy of his book to Malone in the best tradition of academic courtesy!).[11]

Among the Catholic laity the Jesuits seem to have been universally admired, whether as counsellors in time of trouble, stiffeners of faith or teachers of the young. Many clergy saw them in a different light. The Society of Jesus had emerged a generation after Luther nailed his theses to the door. It represented the new age, the Council of Trent, the Catholic Reformation — to use the phrase of Henri Daniel-Rops which describes the phenomenon more accurately than the familiar but negative 'Counter-Reformation'. They saw no need to wear clerical dress, or to force converts to worship in exactly the same manner as the West European norm, or to assume that Saint Thomas Aquinas had spoken the last word on the theological issues confronting the Church four centuries later. The older orders and the secular priests, who could perhaps loosely be considered the oldest 'order' of all, often found it hard to envisage an answer to the Protestant Reformation other than a return to medieval practices and attitudes. Some of them simply resented the Jesuits as johnnies-come-lately, others genuinely viewed their experiments and open thinking as unacceptably superficial. This combination of nostalgia and suspicion lay behind a lot of the tension which developed between the Jesuits and other clerics on the continent and in England. Together with

Protestant animosity, it would show itself in Ireland too, although to a lesser extent than in other countries. The biggest quarrel in Ireland would prove to be essentially home-grown.

Father Robert Nugent became Superior in succession to Father Holywood in 1627 at the age of 49 and in the seventeenth year of his service on the Irish Mission. The Nugents were a County Meath family, described as 'very distinguished'[12] and socially well-connected, being related to Lord Inchiquin and apparently on friendly terms with the Leinster Fitz-Geralds: Nugent resided with some of his companions for much of his Superiorship in Kilkea Castle, thirty miles west of Dublin, where accommodation was provided for them by the Dowager Countess of Kildare.[13] Lady Kildare in fact made the castle over to the Jesuits, contrary to law, but continued to live there herself until her death in 1645 when the mansion became effectively Jesuit property for the short time left before the Cromwellian invasion swept everything away. The Countess, wrote Nugent to Rome when she died, was 'truly the mother of our Society in this realm'.[14]

To be able to lodge in a great house typified comforts available to English priests rather than Irish during the reign of Charles I, which commenced in 1625. This reflected the relative peace and order of England, where many gentry and nobility retained not only their Catholic religion but also their baronial homes, at least until the Civil War began in earnest in 1642. At the same time it has to be said that for much of this period it was easier to function openly as a priest in Ireland than in England. The royal authorities were desperately short of money. In mainly Protestant England this inhibited them from overt concessions to Catholics which would have alienated the puritans who were coming increasingly to the fore in parliament. In mainly Catholic Ireland the reverse was the case. As late as 1641 the Irish House of Commons had a majority of Roman Catholics and included Gaelic representatives as well as Old English in its membership. To raise substantial funds in Ireland the government had to act leniently towards Catholics, for it dared not alienate them into stubborn parsimony, nor, still less, provoke them into a rebellion which could be suppressed only at enormous cost.

When Nugent took over, therefore, Irish Catholics had begun to bask in something of an Indian Summer. Orders decreeing banishment for various types of clergy were revoked or left unenforced. The Discalced Carmelites opened a friary and chapel in Dublin. The King offered a range of concessions in return for financial contributions to the up-keep of the army. Protestant protests against the toleration of Catholics were ignored.[15] The Dominicans were promoting the rosary and importing statues of the Blessed Virgin.[16] Cynics could identify the return of full Catholic life in a controversy which broke out in Dublin over the respective jurisdictions of the seculars and the religious orders.[17] In 1628 the King granted an expanded package of concessions, called the 'graces', which amounted to extensive toleration of the Catholic religion. In the optimistic spirit of the times, Nugent set up a chapel near Christ Church Cathedral in Dublin together with a college to serve Jesuit novices and lay students: a donation from the ever-generous Lady Kildare helped the project towards speedy realisation.[18]

Almost as speedy was the reaction of the government. Toleration of Catholicism was one thing. The flaunting of popery, not least in the capital city, was quite another: in particular, because, it might be reported back to the English puritans. Orders went out for religious houses to be dissolved, and when nothing happened seventeen Mass houses in Dublin were raided and forcibly closed together with their attached friaries, schools and other church premises. A major riot followed when thousands of indignant Catholic citizens attacked the government officials — not sparing the Church of Ireland Archbishop.[19] It did no good, for the chapels remained closed, or, rather, were given over to other purposes. Trinity College acquired the commodious Jesuit premises; in the eighteenth century the Tailors' Hall would be built on its site. Suppressions took place also in a few other towns but, except in Dublin, Cork and Drogheda, Catholic life had been too firmly re-established to be seriously disrupted by the government action.

Oddly enough, in Rome the Father General of the Jesuits, Muzio Vitelleschi, received the news of this set-back with equanimity. Like his predecessor Aquaviva, Vitelleschi had responded sympathetically to the pastoral thrust of the Mission under Holywood. Christian renewal was, after all, the ultimate objective of the Council of Trent. He also favoured Jesuits living in community, the provision of education in colleges established by the Society and the maintenance of public churches for worship and preaching — but only where it was feasible to undertake these activities. He did not consider circumstances in Ireland to be suitable, fearing that the blatancy of community houses, colleges and churches would draw the wrath of the Protestant government down on the Mission and thereby put at risk the special pastoral vocation of the Society in its service to the faithful. He had voiced his doubts to Nugent who, he felt, should have consulted Rome before taking the decisions in question.[20] While Nugent had his own problems in finding a reliable means of communicating with Rome, the General was certainly vindicated by the turn of events.

Nugent was what we would call today a management type. He sought to define his targets, devise a strategy for attaining them and organise his resources to achieve his goals. Contact with the General being patchy at best (as if to disrupt further an already erratic messenger service, King Charles had gone to war with France), the Superior had a relatively free hand. He chose education as the distinctive service to be offered by the Irish Jesuits. Within two years he had colleges functioning in Dublin, Drogheda and Waterford, with schools — or at least school-classes — being provided in Kilkenny, Cashel and other towns. It was not that pastoral work had been abandoned (indeed sometimes, as in Carrick-on-Suir and Galway, its demands on the small number of Jesuits available were too great to permit the organisation of teaching as well) but there seems to have been a cut-back in the number of retreats given in country areas or places where the Fathers were not normally resident. Pastoral activity was arranged so as to facilitate teaching activity if possible. This meant a greater concentration on towns, with enhanced opportunities for living in community rather than as individuals in private houses. Chapels for public worship were opened and, in association with them, branches of the Sodality of the Blessed Virgin were founded.[21]

Although this evolution of the Mission ran counter to what the General thought prudent, by the time he got to hear of it he was faced with a *fait accompli*. Nugent had in fact gone some distance towards creating in Ireland the conditions of living and working familiar to the Jesuits of Catholic countries on the continent. Much of it was illusory, for neither the colleges nor the schools could be seriously compared with the highly developed institutions in, say, France or Flanders: classes (in grammar and the humanities) were simply on offer for those who wanted to avail themselves of them. No doubt the novices in the short-lived Dublin novitiate had an organised course of study, but elsewhere it seems to have been more a case of setting up facilities before deciding on the details of their use. Yet the facilities were impressive enough for a country in which Catholics enjoyed no more than a precarious toleration. The Dublin college had twenty-six bedrooms. Its well appointed public chapel had seventeen sets of vestments. Drogheda and Waterford were adequately equipped also, proportionately to their size: each had a library. The brief outburst of anti-papist ire by the government in 1629 and 1630 terminated the more advanced of these initiatives but left the Irish Mission still energetically active in its restructured form in a number of the small towns of Leinster and Munster.

It is tempting to wonder whether Nugent hoped that the Mission might be turned into a Province. A Province had the important right to be represented in the General Congregation, the Society's legislative assembly, and it enjoyed somewhat more autonomy in ordering its affairs than a Mission. The Superior of a Mission was in theory required to refer to the General in Rome regarding major matters of policy. In practice, Mission Superiors in faraway countries or in countries where the government was inimical to Catholicism had frequently to make decisions at their own discretion. This was the case in Ireland and it would certainly have clarified the authority actually exercised by Father Nugent if he had been named the Provincial of an Irish Province. Provincial status, however, assumed that the order was securely established in the country or region concerned and that it was able to conduct its affairs in a regular manner in accordance with the Constitutions. Indicators that it was functioning in this orderly way might be the number of community houses and other foundations, like colleges, which it maintained, its intake of new recruits and — especially — whether it trained them in its own novitiate. Nugent clearly did much to give the Irish Mission the appearance of a potential Province.[22]

A precedent near to home would have given him reasonable cause to be hopeful. In 1623 the General constituted the English Jesuits a Province of the Society. True, they were nearly three times as numerous as the Irish, having 152 members working in England or Wales in 1625 and 115 abroad[23] (as against some 50 Irish in Ireland about the same time with another 50 on the continent).[24] On the other hand, the laws against Catholics in England were more stringent than in Ireland and were being more diligently implemented. Although the Jesuits in England were assigned to 'colleges' and 'residences', these were fictitious entities and merely identified the regions of the country in which they carried out their ministry.[25] Thus a Jesuit working in Wales was attached to the College of Saint Francis Xavier and another in Lancashire to Aloysius College. In reality each of these Fathers would be living in the 'priest's hole' of a stately home or perhaps in a cottage attic from which he ventured forth disguised as a shepherd or a market gardener bringing produce to the fair.[26] In Ireland, their counterparts — who had indeed known similar conditions and worse a decade earlier — might now be living in community, saying Mass in a modest but real chapel and teaching the rudiments of Latin in a proper classroom (probably using the Latin textbook, published in Salamanca by William Bathe, S.J., of Dublin, which was widely adopted in continental schools).[27]

Their nationality, however, gave the English an advantage. The Tudors had made England a major European power. The arrival of the Stuarts had kindled the hope in Rome, which long persisted for no logical reason at all, that the country might be reconverted to Catholicism. The continuing covert but practical support for the Old Faith provided by the network of Catholic landed families had made possible the establishment of continental colleges of high repute at Reims, Douai and St-Omer (or St Omers, as the

English insisted on calling it), with all of which the Jesuits were closely involved. The interest of the French and Spanish authorities in helping such colleges had more to do with politics than religion but helped to enhance the standing of English Catholics in Roman eyes. Compared to recognisable mainstream European connections of this kind, the Irish with their Gaelic chieftains and small-town Old English merchant families, their conspiratorial plotting on the continent and their initially less distinguished little colleges in Spain and the Low Countries, must have seemed worthy but minor players on the post-Reformation stage.

If a Jesuit Province was going to be erected in one or other country in the 1620s, therefore, it was inevitable that it would be in England rather than Ireland despite the fact that the Irish population remained overwhelmingly Catholic, the diocesan structure of the local Church remained intact and the Jesuits under Father Nugent engaged in ministries more like those of their continental confrères than could be undertaken in England. Indeed, the difficulty of functioning at the level of a Province soon became apparent when the English novitiate set up in Clerkenwell was raided in 1628, seven Jesuits were arrested and the attempt to train novices in England had to be abandoned.[28] Still, the overall situation looked satisfactory from Rome since the *Annual Letters* or Reports to the General gave an optimistic picture, with conversions to Catholicism featuring prominently. As a historian of the English Province notes about these years, 'a charming feature of all *Annual Letters* is that all undertakings always succeed.'[29]

The word reaching Rome from Ireland was rather different. Although problems of communication meant that the Superior's comments were infrequent, Nugent's critics — including some of his Jesuit colleagues — succeeded in conveying complaints about the Mission to the General. Vitelleschi responded with instructions from which the alleged shortcomings can be deduced. Jesuits were to stop playing cards, avoid dressing too well and be less arrogant in claiming their rights. If they lived in community they were to observe the appropriate rules, like maintaining silence at meals, and limit the number of lay guests invited to dine with them. Novices were to be allowed fewer visitors and the furnishing of rooms in community houses was to be kept simple. In the following years, curial officials had to sort out quarrels between the Irish Jesuits and other religious orders. Some of these were very trivial, such as an argument over the Dominicans' insistence on holding meetings of their Rosary Confraternity in town parishes at the same time as the Jesuit Sodality was meeting. Another dispute concerned the Franciscans, who were said to be claiming that Saint Francis visited Purgatory every day to release people who had died wearing the order's habit! A suggestion that the Jesuits were setting up new houses without observing the relevant Church regulations was disposed of in the Society's favour.[30]

What needs to be said in the light of such incidents is that they show how little the Church had to trouble it in the Ireland of the 1630s, or at any rate how little by comparison with the persecution of earlier years. The clergy's 'problems were those of success'[31] — arguments over the various orders' rights and the jurisdiction of the diocesan clerics. When the four Archbishops came together in 1635 to regulate these matters, they had to meet in 'a hut in a remote part of Leinster',[32] which suggests continuing caution despite the general relaxation of anti-Catholic measures, but the hazard was small enough as long as Viscount Wentworth was Lord Deputy. Wentworth's brief was to extract the maximum benefit from the 'graces' and from the general accommodation of Irish wishes by the government.

In crude terms this meant trading leniency towards Catholics for financial contributions to the royal treasury. Occasionally the arrangement came under stress, with Wentworth threatening to reimpose fines for non-attendance at Protestant services if the subsidy for the army fell short,[33] or the Catholic-dominated Irish parliament blocking proposed legislation because the Lord Deputy was falling down on some of his promises.[34] But Wentworth quite genuinely hoped to avoid confrontation. He recoiled against extreme positions in religion or politics, believing in a 'live-and-let-live' approach which he thought would be possible if all parties were to minimise their demands and refrain from provocative public display of their activities. By meeting discreetly, the Archbishops showed their understanding of this very English appeal to compromise. Curiously enough, Wentworth's attitude also matched the instinct of Vitelleschi, the Jesuit Father General in Rome, but of this he was unaware. The Lord Deputy knew only the burgeoning Catholic church life around him, including the work of Robert Nugent's confident Jesuit Mission, and its increasing conspicuousness annoyed him. He blamed the 'friars and Jesuits' for rocking his carefully balanced boat.[35]

There was truth of a kind in this beyond his understanding. Where he suspected conspiracy he was in fact faced with a recovery of Irish self-identity pegged on the religious orders. The Irish members of these international organisations included many who came from well-known families, both Gaelic and Old English — the families to whom the Irish had been accustomed to look for leadership. To speak of the Jesuits alone, we have already noticed the family connections of the Nugents. Jesuit Nettervilles, Plunketts, Dillons and Bathes enjoyed cousinship with the Old English aristocracy. On the Gaelic side, Maurice O'Connell's background was as distinguished as that of Dominic Collins before him. Thady O'Sullivan and Brian MacDavett were other Jesuit names that would be respected in Gaelic Ireland. There were Lynches from Galway, and the Waddings of Waterford boasted five Jesuits as well as the famous Franciscan. At that, the Jesuits were among the smaller orders in Ireland. When the predominantly Gaelic Franciscans and Dominicans, the predominantly Old English Capuchins and Discalced Carmelites, the Augustinians and the rest were added, all with their own links into the network of clans synonymous with the two strands of Irish Catholicism, the significance of the orders can be appreciated. They represented Catholic Ireland refurbished into a proud new image, part of the vibrant Church that had grown from Trent, part of revivified Catholic Europe.[36]

Neither English oppression nor English tolerance had much bearing on this evolution. It was Irish and continental. To the English Lord Deputy it was alien and cause for suspicion. He came upon half the truth in recognising the involvement of 'friars and Jesuits' but he missed their significance as the mirrors in which the Catholic Irish saw themselves restored. There was in fact no room in their vision for a New English or Protestant presence at all: hence the futility of Wentworth's appeal to the English concept of reasonableness, of compromise. This was a prescription for a country divided in itself, as Reformation England had been (and indeed as modern Ireland now is). It made no sense in a country where the compromise was to be effected between the status quo and a double intrusion upon it by the introduction of a foreign religion and foreign planters, both unwanted. The Catholic Irish, of course, were themselves divided between the Celtic Gaels and the Old English but that, by now, was a family affair, as it were: although it would soon acquire critical significance in the Confederation of Kilkenny, it had no bearing on Wentworth's wheeling and dealing since he made no effort to exploit the Old English loyalty to the Crown by contrast with Gaelic disaffection. He actually caused particular concern to the Old English by threatening seizure of some of their lands for the benefit of the English and Scots Protestant settlers offered holdings in Ireland by the government.[37]

Irish Catholics thus found many reasons to coalesce against English pretension. Wentworth unwittingly helped them do so by his leniency, and the religious orders, linking Ireland and Europe, convinced them of their own worthiness to stand as a people apart. Beyond religion and politics, cultural elements played a role as well in distancing the Irish from things English, a role abetted by the orders. Robert Nugent, the Jesuit Superior, was 'by no means unskilled as a musician, for he was able to do much towards the improvement of that national instrument, the Irish harp.'[38] His brother, Father Nicholas Nugent, as we saw, spent his time in prison composing hymns in Irish. Irish was the spoken language outside Dublin and its immediate hinterland. Townspeople had English also but nobody could get very far without the Gaelic vernacular. It loomed large in the Superior's administration of the Mission. Jesuits who spoke no Irish were of limited use to him since they could work only near Dublin.[39] A Welsh Jesuit, landed in Ireland by a pirate who had captured him at sea, could not take part in any organised apostolate because of his 'Englishness'.[40]

When Vitelleschi responded to Nugent's request for rein-
forcements by offering him some priests from the English
Province who had difficulty in getting into their own country,
the Irish Superior was less than pleased: he always resisted
the mingling of Irish with English Jesuits,[41] sensing a divisive
incompatibility. Perhaps significantly also, in the 1640s *every*
Irish Jesuit spoke one or other of the four major Romance
languages[42] but at least two of them spoke no English —
these were of Gaelic stock[43] and their want of English does
not appear to have occasioned the same frustration as others'
lack of Irish. Clearly, self-identity was as much a factor in the
Irish Jesuit community as elsewhere in Irish Catholicism.

Nugent was nonetheless much criticised for favouring the
Old English over the Gaelic members of the Mission.
Examples cited were his alleged preference for Leinstermen
as against natives of other parts of Ireland[44] and his allocation
of senior posts on the Mission to Old English Fathers.[45] The
allegation could be unfair, a pointer to the prejudice of
Nugent's critics, not his own. His interest in Irish music and
in the Irish language (if only for pragmatic reasons) has been
noted. At the end of his superiorship in 1646, three of the
ten local superiors were Gaelic,[46] a higher proportion than
Gaelic Jesuits would have been entitled to on numbers alone.
In the Confederation's greatest crisis, as narrated below, he
took the side favoured by the Gaelic clergy rather than the
Old English. The reality may be that his forceful personality
reflected, or was thought to reflect, the superiority complex
which sometimes marked Old English attitudes towards 'the
mere Irish'. When he gave the Mission an educational bias, it
involved of necessity concentration on the towns, which for
the most part were bastions of the Old English tradition. His
friendship with Lady Kildare would also have created the
impression of a man keeping his distance from the Gaelic
heartland. Such factors were enough for Irish imagination
and cynicism to turn into a defect of character more extreme
than may have been the case.

Oddly, and sadly, we have more information about the
quarrels and tensions of Nugent's superiorship than about
the day-to-day work of the Mission under his guidance. The
reason for this, by a further paradox, lies in his very success.

Change brought about by authority always provokes complaint, and complaints reached the General accordingly. Expansion of effort requires manpower, and Nugent's demands for more men landed on the General's desk. The General's responses involved chiding as well as expressions of support, and requests for more information to be sent more frequently as well as satisfaction over what had been done well. A degree of muscle-flexing resulted in protests from other religious orders and from the secular clergy. We are left with more disputes and reprimands on the record than actual achievement. That the achievement was there we need not doubt. By 1640 the Jesuits were established in thirteen residences, mostly in Leinster and Munster — and mostly real *places* of residence, with two or more Jesuits living in community, although some continued to lodge in private houses. The residences usually had small schools attached, which provided free education, and despite some of the complaints to Rome all the evidence suggests that these priests lived in considerable poverty, often on the alms of the faithful. The preaching continued also: in 1633 Barnaby O'Kearney's second volume of sermons appeared in Paris, with introductory material by younger members of the Irish Mission;[47] the Sodality continued to spread (a new branch was inaugurated in Wexford in 1640) and steps were being taken to attract more recruits from the North into the Society — 'your Ulster is very dear to me,' wrote Vitelleschi.[48]

For a time after the loss of the Dublin novitiate, Irish Jesuit novices had to go to the continent for their training. In 1635 the Jesuits were given charge of the Irish College in Rome, the students of which took their theology lectures at the prestigious Jesuit-administered Collegio Romano.[49] Seminaries for Irish students in Spain and Portugal (Lisbon, Salamanca, Santiago, Seville) had earlier been founded by, or given to, Irish Jesuits — who of course had been established in the peninsula since the days of James Archer and Thomas White.[50] Running a College in Spain had become something of a personal vocation. Having founded Salamanca, White went on to become first Vice-Rector successively at Santiago (1612) and Seville (1619). Father Richard Conway emulated the achievement by serving in turn as Vice-Rector of both these colleges and Salamanca as well. The title 'Vice-Rector', it should be noted, referred to the actual head of the house: for diplomatic reasons arising from Spanish chauvinism the Rectorship was held by a Spanish Jesuit, usually the Rector of a local Spanish College. National sensitivities in fact played a large part in the emergence of these institutions. In 1592, while still a secular priest, White had come upon a number of Irish youngsters in Valladolid. These were boys who had been educated to grammar-school level by individual lay or clerical teachers, not unlike the 'hedge-school' teachers of a later period, and who had come to Europe to find the higher learning unavailable to Catholics at home. The famous Jesuit, Robert Persons, whom we have already met befriending James Archer, had opened an English College in the town. Persons refused to accept Irish students, being already aware of the problems which could arise from mixing two nationalities — there had been much trouble at the English College in Rome between the English and the Welsh.

White, therefore, with the support of the Spanish King, set up the separate Irish College in Salamanca which was put under Jesuit auspices, with Archer as Vice-Rector. The students attended Salamanca University, then among the most distinguished in Europe, and lived by rules taken in part from the English College in Rome but modified to accommodate the Irish temperament. Thus in behaviour 'a certain informality and spaciousness' was accepted (which to English observers was mere indiscipline!). Leniency did no harm to the students' academic attainments. In 1596 a report from 'the Rector and Masters of the University' said that the Irish gave 'a good account of their studies in Theology and Philosophy'. The Irish taste for argument was surely reflected in the comment in the same document that they attended to their lectures with great care 'as appears from the difficulties they propose to the lecturers, and from the public disputations. . .'.

The students were not charged fees. Finance came from a somewhat inadequate royal subsidy, alms collected both in Spain and Ireland, and donations from Irish nobility or other well-wishers. But the purpose being to train candidates for the priesthood, the students had to promise to recoup the

College financially if they failed to take Holy Orders — a hint, perhaps, that some entered solely for the education and with no intention of becoming priests. After four months it was normal to require them to take an oath analogous to that of the English College, whereby they undertook to embrace the ecclesiastical life and 'go into Ireland to save souls'. Being under Jesuit direction, their spiritual formation reflected the Exercises of Saint Ignatius, and their intellectual formation the *Ratio Studiorum* (a compilation of norms on which the Jesuit approach to learning was based).

None of these colleges was intended exclusively for Jesuit students. The greater number of their *alumni* were expected to be secular priests although students from various orders, including the Jesuits, were taught there too. In theory Jesuit supervision was approved both by the Iberian authorities and by Archbishop David O'Kearney of Cashel (Barnaby's brother) in the hope of maintaining a balance between the competing interests of other orders and the secular priesthood as well as guarding against the Irish parochialism which sometimes resulted in Kerry families or Leinster dioceses trying to monopolise specific colleges for their own use. From an early date, however, the Jesuits found themselves under attack for supposedly luring the best of the students into the Society and discriminating against the Gaelic Irish. The test case on the latter charge concerned an applicant called Maurice Ultona — from Ulster, as his nickname implied — who was refused a place. Maurice turned out to have plans for a career in medicine! The allegations nonetheless endured for many years. The saintly Oliver Plunkett believed some of them as late as the 1670s. The record in fact failed to sustain a case against the Jesuits.

Of the colleges, Salamanca remained outstanding but Spain became less popular for a number of reasons: the reputation of Spanish theology declined rapidly in the seventeenth century;[51] from Bordeaux to Nantes and Paris, institutions were established for the Irish with French support;[52] and the Low Countries offered the attraction of major foundations at Louvain and Douai (then in Flanders) to which Irish colleges were attached and which had the added lure of a climate more congenial for young Irishmen than the heat of Spain.[53] A steady inflow of recruits to the Irish Jesuits came from these French and Netherlands centres, none of which were under Jesuit direction (apart from an Irish College opened at Poitiers in 1674, more than twenty years after Father Nugent's time), which suggests that the Society needed no special advantage to draw Irish students into its ranks.

Nugent, as it happened, was not particularly anxious to continue any longer than necessary with training abroad, and by 1640 was looking into the possibility of opening a novitiate in Ireland again.[54] He feared that Irish students in foreign countries might be tempted to join continental Provinces of the Society[55] — as happened often enough — and the Irish Mission could in fact exercise little real control over houses theoretically in its charge: a foreign Jesuit might be appointed Rector[56] or other dispositions be made by the General since a Mission Superior's authority was so limited. The retrieval of Irish Jesuits from continental assignments was never easy. Father Ambrose Wadding, whom Holywood tried to recall, found it impossible to abandon his professorship of logic and metaphysics at Dilingen when the Germans had brought pressure on the General to leave him there, while his cousin (and cousin of the Franciscan scholar of the same name), Father Luke Wadding, spent his whole priesthood in academic posts in Spain. [57] There were other hazards too. Father John Meagh (*recte* Meagher?) from Cork was preparing to return to Ireland from a brief spell of pastoral work in Bohemia when he was shot dead by a band of Swedish soldiers at the height of the Thirty Years War.[58] Father Nugent would, of course, always have had in mind the value of a local novitiate in making the case for creation of an Irish Province.

The live-and-let-live circumstances in which an Irish self-identity and the discreetly free practice of the Catholic religion had grown apace and side by side came to a dramatic end in 1641. Wentworth was gone and, although elevated to the Earldom of Strafford, would soon be executed following impeachment by the anti-royalist Long Parliament in London. In the absence of a Lord Deputy, the

government of Ireland was consigned to Lord Justices—local
Protestants much less concerned than any representative of
the King to placate the papists, who were seen as a threat to
their own interests. The mood of the English parliament and
the Irish administration prevailed over that of the Catholic-
dominated but subordinate Irish parliament. By mid-
summer the authorities were drawing up plans to restrict the
activities of Catholic priests. The atmosphere of menace
emanating from London and Dublin, however, spurred the
Catholics to pre-empt any action against them. In October
an uprising in Ulster resulted in the Gaelic Irish taking
control of most of the province. It also resulted in the
massacre of thousands of Protestant planters: an event terrible enough in itself, God knows, but grossly exaggerated in
puritan propaganda during the following years . . . and,
indeed, centuries.

In a matter of months the greater part of the country,
except Dublin and a few coastal towns, had gone over to the
insurgents. Most significantly, the Old English joined them
once they were satisfied that the objective of the rising was
not only to protect the Catholic religion but also to defend
the King against his domestic opponents. In May 1642, the
Catholic bishops, a number of clergy, Gaelic chieftains and
Old English gentry met formally in Kilkenny to approve the
rising and set in motion the process which resulted in the
creation of interlocking institutions under the collective
name, the 'Confederate Catholics of Ireland' — known to
history as the Catholic Confederacy or the Confederation of
Kilkenny. It was not in fact a confederation but a unitary and
autonomous state which functioned under the motto *Pro
Deo, Pro Rege, Pro Patria* — for God, for King, for Homeland.
A 300-member assembly analogous to a single-chamber
parliament (in which the bishops would sit as Lords
Spiritual), a 24-member Supreme Council analogous to an
administration, regional councils and a judiciary were established in due course in accordance with proposals drawn up
by the lawyer, Patrick Darcy, in his *Model of Civil Government*,[59]
which has a serious claim to be considered the first written
constitution of a European country. It was an extraordinary
achievement for a people so recently oppressed, even if what

could be implemented was patchy at best since the Confederates never controlled the whole country and never enjoyed a prolonged period of peace during which the regime could take root and flourish.

The Jesuits took no part in the plotting which led to the 1641 rising, although the Protestants were not easily persuaded of this. As early as 1640 the citizens of London had been warned of a 'grand conspiracy of the Pope and his Jesuited instruments to extirpate the Protestant religion. . .'.[60] The Lord Justices reported that the rebellion had been incited by 'Jesuits, priests and friars'.[61] In his *History of the Irish Rebellion* Sir Richard Cox, a future Lord Chancellor, alleged that the day of the rising, 23 October, was 'dedicated to Saint Ignatius (a fit patron for such a villainy)'.[62] These charges must be seen as the pavlovian response to any papist stirrings, real or imaginary. In those unecumenical times the word 'Jesuit' was used much as 'communist' would be in MacCarthyite America or Verwoerd's South Africa. No evidence was quoted to link the Jesuits with the plot, nor was it likely that any could have been found since the rising originated in Ulster, where the Society had no residences and few contacts. The Father General's directive against political involvement still stood and would have been obeyed. Also, for all his interest in Gaelic music and in ensuring that the Society's pastorate could be carried out in the Irish language, Robert Nugent was far too much imbued with Old English instincts to participate in a purely Old Irish revolt.

Once the Old English chose sides, however, and the bishops' support became clear, Nugent and his brethren inevitably found themselves committed as members of what looked like an emergent Catholic nation. The Superior welcomed this, to judge from his presence as a representative of the clergy at the proceedings in Kilkenny.[63] With typical energy, he soon set new projects in train throughout the area where the writ of the Confederation ran. Paralleling the retrieval of cathedrals, churches and religious houses for Catholic use, Jesuits were conspicuous in the restoration of public worship, spiritual direction and schools for the Catholic people: so much so that in places — Kilkenny, Waterford, Galway — fresh disputes broke out with other orders, usually when the Jesuits acquired possession of buildings which had belonged to the friars before the Reformation. Nugent had grander plans too, including, at the behest of the Supreme Council, the establishment of a university, possibly in the diocese of Meath where Bishop Thomas Dease was favourably disposed, and especially the reopening of a novitiate in Ireland. So much enthusiasm alarmed the aged General, Vitelleschi, who had always urged caution in the conduct of the Irish Mission and now, but only with reluctance, agreed to the novitiate which Nugent promptly set up in Kilkenny in 1645.

The General, as it happened, had reason to be cautious. Viewing Ireland objectively and from a distance — and he was well-informed about Irish affairs — he must have noted a degree of recklessness in the Superior's hyper-activity. Not only was Nugent stretching his resources to a dangerous extent, given their limited numbers (some 60 at the most, including novices) and the fact that many of the Fathers were more than middle-aged by the standards of the seventeenth century. There was also the fact that the Confederation had been formed unilaterally, without the approval of the King, despite its own protestations of loyalty. By 1642 a Scottish army, well-disposed to the English parliament, had landed in Ulster and subdued much of it. Another army, initially royalist and commanded by Father Nugent's Protestant relative, Murrough O'Brien, Lord Inchiquin, controlled Cork and its hinterland, while the old Pale from Dublin to Drogheda was held for the King by the Earl of Ormond, soon to become Marquis and Lord Lieutenant as well. Civil war had broken out between king and parliament in England; after some hesitation, Inchiquin went over to the puritan parliamentarians while the Scots entered into a treaty with them. As a result, armies in Ulster and Munster were ranged against the confederates and royalists; the royal forces faced puritan and confederate opposition; and the confederates were threatened on three sides by actual or potential enemies: potential in the case of Ormond once he concluded a truce with the Confederation.

The Jesuit General in Rome can scarcely be blamed for seeing this as a highly unstable situation, in which it was almost ludicrous for Nugent to behave as if Ireland were a

Catholic entity as solidly secured as Flanders or Portugal. To the instability was added unavoidable involvement of the Irish Mission in politics. The Confederation was a *political* structure devised to aid the Catholic *religion*. Pope Urban VIII had recognised it as such and sent not only a papal envoy but also money for the purchase of arms[64] to mark his support for its objectives. Vitelleschi could hardly reprimand Nugent in the circumstances for assigning Irish Jesuits to the confederate service, both as agents at foreign courts and as chaplains to the armies which the confederates had quickly recruited to resist the English and Scottish threats. Indeed, whether intentionally or not, Nugent had ensured that Jesuits were located in all the nerve-centres of the Confederation. Father Brian MacDavett, one of the few natives of Ulster to join the Society, was attached as chaplain to the famed commander of the northern army, Owen Roe O'Neill, a scion of the foremost family of Ulster Gaelic stock. Father William St Leger belonged to the entourage of the Old English leaders, Thomas Preston and Sir Richard Bellings. Father Matthew O'Hartegan represented the Confederation in Paris and was the channel for many communications between Ireland and Rome. In Brussels, Father Henry Plunkett bought weapons for the confederate armies.

Quite suddenly, therefore, the Irish Jesuits had become more deeply implicated in politics than at any time since the days of James Archer, and would be totally compromised if the confederates were to lose and be treated as rebels. Nugent would probably have answered that it made no difference. No priests, and least of all Jesuits, received much quarter in places under Protestant control after the rising had begun — and even before the Confederation was formed. Soldiers severely beat Father Henry Cavell, who suffered from paralysis in the legs, and then deported him from Dublin to France (he insisted on returning but the journey was too much for him; he died shortly after his arrival in Ireland).[65] The once flamboyant Father Henry Fitzsimon had to sleep on straw in a damp and draughty hut on the Dublin mountains: from here he kept up his ministry until he could make his way with some of his flock to confederate-controlled countryside (he too died from his exertions after reaching

Kilkenny in 1643). It was the same story in Cork and Drogheda, from which priests were also expelled.

Survival under persecution was by now an ingrained habit among the Jesuits and Dublin was not left without their ministrations. Father Thomas Quin moved around the city disguised as a 'bearded soldier, cobbler, merchant or, at times, a baker with a tray of steaming loaves'. Father James Latin apparently spoke in a brogue and could not pass as a Dublinman so he played the part of 'a rustic selling plants' (he was captured, imprisoned and finally deported when caught saying Mass for visitors to the jail). The brothers John and Robert Bathe, both Jesuits, stayed on in Drogheda while others kept catechism classes going in Cork as well as a ministry to prisoners. It was magnificent but not calculated to convince the General that Ireland was a haven of Catholic tranquillity in which the Society could hope to emulate the work of the continental Provinces. Had the old man lived, he would have seen his worst fears come to fruition in 1647 when, in renewed fighting, Lord Inchiquin's troops captured Cashel and in taking the famous Rock killed seven priests who had taken refuge in the cathedral. One of them was a Jesuit, William Boynton. Only a few years earlier the Society had regained possession of its house in the town and the Fathers had welcomed there the papal envoy, Paolo Scarampi, in whose honour one of their students had written a poem. Cashel gave warning of the fragile ground on which the Confederation was built.

By then much had happened. Pope Urban had died and his successor sent a fully accredited nuncio to Ireland in 1645. This was Archbishop Giovanni Battista Rinuccini, with whom Father Nugent established an unwisely close rapport. He entertained him at Kilkea Castle (as he also entertained Owen Roe and Preston). He gave him advice which so impressed the Nuncio that he tried unsuccessfully to have Nugent appointed his whole-time assistant when, in 1646, the Mission heard it was to receive a new Superior. Nugent, as it happened, was glad enough to be relieved of the burden but the reason for the change showed up further deficiencies in the organisation of the Irish Jesuits. The new Pope, with the loyal support of the new General (for Vitelleschi had also died), decreed that Jesuit superiors should hold office for only three years at a time.[66] The instruction applied to all superiors — heads of houses as well as of missions and provinces. In Ireland there were now so many residences, most of them thinly staffed, that finding more than a dozen competent new superiors in a short time proved inordinately difficult. But this structural problem soon disappeared from sight as the Nuncio launched upon a course of intervention in the complicated political situation which provoked a major cleavage in the Confederation and a not insignificant one in the Irish Jesuit Mission even as, unknown to the participants in the quarrel, Armageddon loomed.

Rinuccini was, quite simply, a foreigner insensitive to the balance of relationships in Ireland between the basically royalist Old English and the culturally more detached Gaelic population, between both these Catholic groups united in the Confederation and the Protestant settlers, between the Anglican and puritan Protestants and between the British military forces on the island who supported the King and those who supported the parliamentarians. And that was only to phrase the Irish complexities, which in turn could be affected by the outcome of the civil war in England where the balance was tilting against the King. Whether the Nuncio was infected by Nugent's expansionist ideas, or emboldened by the news of Owen Roe's victory over the Scots at Benburb, or simply believed that intransigence was the best policy against Protestants (of whom he can have had little experience) is difficult to say with certainty. For whatever reason, he rejected any proposal for a peace agreement which did not declare Roman Catholicism to be the state religion of Ireland. It was altogether improbable that any English faction, even the beleaguered King, would accept so extreme an abandonment of the Reformation — it was not even being imposed on defeated Protestant rulers in the Thirty Years War now drawing to its close in Europe, although Rome would protest ineffectually against the formula *cujus regio, ejus religio*[67] — but the Gaelic Irish were willing, by and large, to support the Nuncio in what perhaps they saw as an all-out bid to assert the survival of their weakened culture through its most distinctive feature, their religion.

It was surprising to find Father Nugent on the Nuncio's side of the argument. The Old English relationship with the Crown had been built on compromise as long as anyone could remember. They valued the royal connection as part of *their* distinctive identity. They dominated the Supreme Council in Kilkenny and so were able to negotiate a treaty with Ormond in 1646 which guaranteed Catholic rights but stopped short of Rinuccini's requirements. The Nuncio's opposition secured repudiation of the agreement and replacement of the Council members who had supported it. With Rinuccini mixing politics and religion so thoroughly the new Jesuit General in Rome, Father Vincenzo Carafa, might as well have saved his ink when he wrote to urge the Irish Mission to 'teach, preach and administer the sacraments' rather than dabble in political questions (he was troubled to learn that Nugent had arranged for the Jesuits to make their printing press available for confederate needs). The actual outcome of the Nuncio's policy was the repulse of a confederate move against Dublin followed by Ormond's submission to *force majeure* when he abandoned the capital to the parliamentarians. Less seriously, Nugent's former base, Kilkea Castle, had to be abandoned at the same time. Meanwhile Inchiquin, spurred to action, descended on Cashel with the appalling consequences we have already seen — and, of course, the loss of the Jesuit residence there.

In 1648 Inchiquin unexpectedly reverted to his allegiance to King Charles. The Confederates seized the opportunity to conclude a truce with him. Rinuccini, undeterred by warnings from Rome not to go too far, responded by excommunicating everybody who supported the peace move and the subsequent treaty concluded with Ormond, who had returned to Ireland.[68] Those affected by the Nuncio's censures included the majority of the Supreme Council, eventually some eleven bishops and the greater number of the Jesuits — among them, their new Superior, Father William Malone, the learned theologian who had earlier been in dispute with the Anglican Archbishop Ussher. An appeal to Rome against Rinuccini was immediately set in motion but could not prevent the most bitter and widespread division that ever took place in the ranks of the Irish clergy. The excommunication had involved an interdict (essentially a prohibition on the celebration of church services and the normal administration of the sacraments) until the Confederation relented. Priests and bishops loyal to the Nuncio shut their churches. A number of bishops — Limerick, Tuam, Ossory — kept their cathedrals open to indicate that they considered the censures suspended pending the answer to their appeal. Others, like the Bishop of Waterford, closed their doors in literal obedience. Although the division took place largely along Gaelic and Old English lines, it was not completely so. The 'confederate' Bishop of Limerick was an O'Dwyer; the 'nuncioist' in Waterford was a Comerford. It may have been relevant that Bishop Comerford was an Augustinian: the Augustinians, Franciscans and Dominicans, with some exceptions, took Rinuccini's side. Other orders, again with exceptions, tended to back the Supreme Council. The bitterness spread to the continent. As late as 1652 Gaelic Franciscans were trying to have Luke Wadding, a critic of the Nuncio, removed from office at St Isidore's College in Rome.

Despite his own strong feelings on the subject, Malone tried to ensure that the Jesuits, as a religious order, remained outside the nuncioist controversy. He adopted the simple expedient of instructing the various houses to be guided by the example of the local bishop: if the cathedral was open, they were to continue working as usual; if not, they were to suspend their services. The instruction failed in its purpose. Not only was the Superior sometimes disobeyed — notoriously in Limerick, where the head of the Jesuit house, Father William Hurley, insisted on upholding the interdict, Bishop and Superior notwithstanding — but his search for a middle way merely roused suspicion on all sides. The greater number of the Jesuit houses, because of their location in 'confederate' dioceses, continued to function. This was enough to confirm the Nuncio in his quite accurate belief that most of the Jesuit Fathers personally favoured the stance of the Supreme Council. The Supreme Council, however, was none too sure. Knowing that some houses were closed, remembering the friendship between Rinuccini and Nugent, and seeing Malone go out of his way to visit the Nuncio in Galway (in fact a nugatory meeting at which neither man could persuade the other of his *bona fides*) the confederate authorities seized the printing press and warned the Jesuits that any ambiguity in their attitude would lose them the Council's protection. Worst of all, however, was the reaction in Rome.

However mistaken the curia officials thought Rinuccini's policy to be, they could not accept the right of any Catholic to disown the Pope's representative. Carafa, the Jesuit General, held this view strongly, which made sense in Rome but grossly over-simplified the Irish reality. Acting on the limited information available to him — contact with Ireland was becoming more difficult by the week — the General took the extraordinary step of ordering Malone to proceed at once to Bordeaux without telling anyone and to submit himself there to the Provincial of the Jesuit Province of Aquitaine (south-western France). That Provincial in turn was to send a Visitor to Ireland with the General's authority to examine the situation at first hand, see the Nuncio and be guided by him as to what should be done. It was grossly unfair to Malone, who had not been heard in the matter, but the turn of events had one happy feature. Father Mercure Verdier was chosen as Visitor, a man humane, urbane and judicious, who was able, with no disloyalty to those who sent him, to deal equitably with all sides, obtain a clear picture of the Nuncio's and Malone's opinions alike and incredibly, in a war-torn and dissentious country, travel to widely separated Jesuit houses and speak with most members of the Society other than the few ministering in disguise in Dublin and Drogheda.

Verdier acted with circumspection regarding the primary purpose of his Visit. With his interpreter, a scholastic from Limerick named John Stritch,[69] he landed conveniently at Galway where Rinuccini was at hand. The Nuncio consented to ordain Stritch and went on to tell the Visitor of his outrage over the attitude of the Jesuit Superior and many of his subjects. But there was also a Jesuit residence in the town where opinions were mainly anti-nuncioist. This was scarcely surprising, given the views of the Hon. Father George Dillon, a son of the Earl of Roscommon, who for years had personified the Galway Jesuits: he had by now been transferred to Kilkenny, perhaps because the anti-nuncioist Bishop of

Ardagh had made him his proxy for a meeting in Galway on the crisis before Rinuccini arrived there and while the Collegiate Church of Saint Nicholas was still open by direction of the equally anti-nuncioist Archbishop of Tuam. Dillon later wrote to the General pointing out that a directive to close the churches could not be expected to have much impact in a country where they had not been permitted to open for a hundred years!

This Jesuit comment fairly enough underscored the Nuncio's tactlessness in ordering Irish Catholics, so recently come into their own, to revert to the spiritual deprivation they had long sought to overcome. That he did so in consequence of an essentially civil matter raised the question whether he was exceeding his powers. He could, of course, argue that the extent of religious toleration to be granted in any peace arrangement directly concerned the papacy and that, in any event, bishops and clergy were in duty bound to obey an envoy acting with the Pope's authority. Verdier held firmly to the latter belief. Without endorsing Rinuccini's case for imposing the interdict, the Visitor refused to condone the action of those Jesuits who had not obeyed it. At the same time, he heard what they had to tell him in Galway, Kilkenny, Limerick and elsewhere. He quickly concluded that the circumstances called for damage-limitation rather than condemnation. The non-arrival of correspondence from Rome as well as some ambiguity in his instructions enabled Verdier to leave Malone (who had not yet gone to France) in charge of the Mission rather than risk injuring 'the Church and . . . our Society' by removing him from office: a clear indication that the Visitor recognised the strength of feeling aroused by the Nuncio's stance. He also extracted from Rinuccini, by what charm and diplomacy we can only imagine, the power to absolve the technically excommunicated Jesuits. The departure of the Nuncio from Ireland in February 1649 then eased the tension a little so that Verdier could concentrate on examining the state of the Irish Mission. But the same month brought news that the King had been executed in London. This boded ill.

Verdier's reports have left us with a vividly etched picture of the Irish Mission as it was moments, historically speaking, before its near-annihilation: like a panoramic photograph of Hiroshima taken when the drone of a B-29 bomber could be heard growing louder below the horizon. The Mission consisted of fifty-three Fathers, three Brothers and eleven novices. The Kilkenny novitiate, under the direction of Father John Young, whose piety and frankness much impressed the Visitor, was the hope for the future. Since at least thirteen of the priests on the Mission were over the age of sixty and only twelve were under forty, the assurance of worthy replacements mattered greatly: it was a measure of their difficulties that the revived apostolate in Cashel had to be consigned to a 'very old' priest and an epileptic assistant. Kilkenny was the major residence with twenty-five members of the Society, including the novices. Galway had nine Jesuits, Waterford seven and Limerick six. Clonmel, like Cashel, got by with two, and their lifestyle showed how irregular the ministry in Ireland could be by comparison with a Jesuit community on the continent. The two priests in Clonmel lived on the same premises as three nephews of one of them, and two maid-servants had been engaged to take care of the household. Even in the more normal conditions of Galway, four of the nine Jesuits — including the local superior — lived in lodgings rather than in the community house.

Oddities of behaviour came to light as well. Dillon liked fashionable clothes, a taste he could indulge since the Irish Fathers did not wear clerical dress (originally for security reasons and then as a matter of tradition). He had a bias against the Gaelic Irish and disapproved of admitting them to the Society. Father Stephen Browne also dressed well and allowed his beard to grow too long. Father Robert Bathe was a scholar and knew it: 'he thinks very well of himself,' wrote Verdier. Several of the Fathers carried watches, which seemed to conflict with their vow of poverty. They all observed the Irish practice of greeting ladies with a kiss, which perhaps was less distressing in the Visitor's judgment than the prayers offered in public by the Wexford community for the welfare of a pirate who was kind enough to share his loot with them! In fairness to the Wexford Fathers, it should be added that Verdier found them so poor that nobody could be added to their number — presumably since the paucity of alms meant that one more man could not be supported. This certainly was the case in nearby New Ross where the three Jesuits were so impoverished that 'they often lacked bread at meals'.

Notwithstanding the elegant clothes and watches of some of the priests (who may well have received them as gifts), poverty struck Verdier as characteristic of the Mission and he found every house of the Society, with the exception of Kilkenny, to be a less than adequate building. One reason for this poverty was doubtless the refusal to take payment for teaching, and teaching had been made more and more the prime activity of the Mission under Nugent. Holiness, too, was a quality he noted in many of the Irish Jesuits as well as a willingness to work hard. Their commitment was certainly remarkable: when Father James Everard died in Cashel in 1647, mercifully before the town was sacked, he had spent forty years on the Irish Mission.[70] It was easy to understand how men so long cut off from community life developed habits elsewhere unknown. The Irish Jesuits' irregularities of organisation and personal quirks, which the Visitor felt in duty bound to report, he did not denounce as as degenerate or wilfully wayward. He treated the Mission for what it was, a segment of the Society which had weathered much obstruction and outright persecution. He appreciated that, if its way of life did not conform to Jesuit custom on the continent, this was because for a century the Mission had had to make do as best it could. He was so understanding, indeed, that he may have been less critical than he should have been. The plethora of small houses, in which only one or two men were competent teachers, showed up the illusions of Robert Nugent in launching out on an educational apostolate the scale of which far exceeded his resources. The welcome of the Gaelic Fathers for the three-year limit on superiorships since it gave them some hope of more say in decision-making and running the affairs of the Mission, together with the attitude attributed to Dillon and the fact that Malone spoke no Irish, suggested that Gaelic complaints — even if exaggerated — might have borne investigation.

It would be interesting to know a little more about the spirituality of Irish Jesuits at this time, the content of their preaching, the pastoral services they carried out and the subjects taught in the schools. We may assume, but cannot say with certainty, that the Irish Fathers made an annual retreat, as their counterparts in England contrived to do from an early stage.[71] In their schools we know that they were unable to follow the letter of the *Ratio Studiorum*, but tantalisingly Verdier simply noted that the hours of teaching (five hours a day) were too long. When, however, we recollect the bogs and forests of that virtually roadless Ireland in which it took five days to ride from Kilkenny to Galway, the sporadic warfare liable to break out at any moment and Verdier's lack of the English language — not to mention Irish — the perception, diligence and sympathy of the Visitor can only be wondered at. Is it fanciful to imagine him sitting on a bench in the corner of a back-street shebeen, note-taking by candlelight as he listens to the story whispered in halting French or stilted Latin by the poor but upright old man beside him? And checking with young Father Stritch when the aged priest cannot find the foreign words for a thought or a phrase? It must have been done like that more than once, as well as in the slightly more tolerable setting of a community house or, perhaps, the home of a small-town family who kept a room for their Jesuit cousin so that his needs would not deplete the limited supplies on which his brethren had to depend.

The Visitor would have puzzled a little over stories of Kilkea Castle, which was no shebeen . . . but which, in its way, was part of Father Nugent's illusion. The former Superior could never have hoped to enjoy it freely, for the Countess of Kildare's relatives disputed his right of possession, and he could not have sold the place for he would have been unable to give clear title to a purchaser. It may be that illusion was necessary to the sane survival of an Irish Jesuit in the mid-seventeenth century. At least it would have helped if the future looked brighter and more hopeful than the grim reality. It was looking hopeful enough when Verdier departed in the early summer of 1649. The rift in the Catholic camp could be ignored for the moment as Ormond, Inchiquin and the confederate armies began to whittle down the territory in parliamentary hands. Tragically, as it would turn out, Drogheda was among the towns liberated in July. But within weeks Ormond had been routed at Rathmines outside Dublin. The parliamentary Commander-in-Chief (and effectively dictator of England), Oliver Cromwell, was able to land with a seasoned army of 12,000 men at Ringsend.

Having issued edicts against swearing and drunkenness, Cromwell made his way to Drogheda. What happened there between 11 and 13 September he justified on two grounds: first, by the rules of war a garrison which refused to surrender after being summoned to do so and its defences had been breached had no claim to 'quarter', that is, to have the lives of its officers and men spared; secondly, by refusing quarter for this reason he would strike such terror into his enemies that they would hasten to submit and further bloodshed would be minimal.[72] The savage slaughter of the 3,000-man garrison, which he ordered, took place after summons, breach and refusal to surrender. It could therefore be explained, if not excused, by the rule-book. What was altogether abominable was the simultaneous killing of non-combatant civilians, including women and children. Cromwell would afterwards allege that they had paid the merited price for the mob violence of 1641 in which thousands of innocent Protestants had undoubtedly, and horribly, died. Drogheda, however, was *permitted* by the senior officer who could have stopped it. Also, the unfortunate citizens had nothing to do with the events of 1641 or afterwards, for until a few weeks before Cromwell arrived the town had been held throughout by English forces. Rather than add to the Irish recriminations that echo banefully down the centuries, let us simply note what a great English leader, considered to be no great friend of Ireland, had to say of Cromwell at Drogheda. Wrote Winston Churchill:

> There followed a massacre so all-effacing as to startle even the opinion of those fierce times. All were put to the sword. None escaped; every priest and friar was butchered. . . . Cromwell in Ireland, disposing of overwhelming strength and using it with merciless wickedness, debased the standards of human conduct and sensibly darkened the

journey of mankind. . . . Upon all of us there still lies 'the curse of Cromwell'.[73]

Among the butchered priests were two Jesuits. Soldiers dragged the sick and elderly Father Robert Netterville from his bed, clubbed him severely and left him to die in the roadway.[74] They also seized Father John Bathe together with his brother, a secular priest, hustled them down to the market-place, abused them, beat them and finally shot them.[75] The Jesuits in Wexford and New Ross either hid or escaped when Cromwell descended in turn on these towns, but of course the residences were lost and open activity of any kind had to be abandoned. The puritan commander then headed for Waterford but dysentery caused havoc in the army and he had to lift his siege of the city on 2 December, a decision attributed by some to the intercession of Saint Francis Xavier since this was the eve of his feast day. A brief respite followed as campaigning came to a halt for the winter but early in the new year another calamity began to show itself in the towns of Ireland. A Spanish ship brought bubonic plague to Galway and the virulent epidemic spread rapidly.

The plague reached Kilkenny in March, just ahead of Cromwell. Despite their requests to be allowed tend the victims, the novices were sent to Galway — more to spare them from Cromwell than from the sickness. A number of the priests remained in disguise, but their house was ransacked and burned down by the Cromwellians. 'It seems that the devil himself wants us to be destroyed, so there is nothing of us left on earth,' wrote Father Young to Rome. Father Malone, the Superior, was with the Waterford community when the plague broke out. The Jesuits threw themselves into the work of caring for the stricken. Inevitably, some of them caught the disease. Father James Walshe, himself a native of Waterford, died there in June.[76] The disease brought 'immense suffering, which he bore with heroic patience' to the redoubtable Father George Dillon before it carried him off in August.[77] The enemy were closing in on the city again but Malone managed to send Father Gregory Dowdall to minister in and around New Ross, 'disguised as a gardener, selling fruit and vegetables':[78] the plague was to kill Dowdall also a few months later. Another Jesuit took over from him before his death, probably Father Stephen Gellow who was certainly working in the area for most of the Cromwellian period and for many years afterwards. He was four times arrested but always escaped. His disguises during the worst of the persecution included those of 'a dealer in faggots' and 'a seller of rabbit-skins' and he was said to have 'continued to offer up the Holy Sacrifice each day'.[79]

Waterford eventually fell to the puritans, as did Clonmel after a brave resistance, and many other towns both before and after Cromwell went back to England in May. Malone had already made contact with Rome and advised that Father Robert Nugent be recalled as Superior to cope with the most serious crisis which had ever arisen for the Mission. Nugent, by now in Galway, proved to be the man for the hour. He applied his management skills to control the contraction of the order as effectively as he had used them in the days of expansion. Typically he left no record of the pain he must have suffered to see the edifice collapsing which he had worked so diligently to construct: there was a job to be done and he did it. He was already busy finding berths on ships out of Galway to take the novices (some of whom had completed their novitiate and were now scholastics) to the continent. He sent Father Young to Rome with reports on the situation, showing that at the end of 1650 there were still forty-seven Jesuits in the country, including seven scholastics, but only three residences: Galway, Limerick and Athlone. Athlone seems to have been a temporary refuge rather than a foundation consciously planned. The Jesuits in Athlone and Limerick had only such alms as they could collect on which to live.

A further list in May 1651 showed the total numbers down to forty. Individual priests were scattered about the provinces of Munster and Leinster, mainly in hiding near former residences — Waterford, Wexford — and discharging whatever clandestine ministries were possible. Nugent hoped that the western province of Connacht could hold out but he took no chances. Father Thomas Quin, the veteran of persecution in Dublin down the years, was dispatched to Flanders with the archives of the Mission. It was a wise move, for Limerick was taken in November 1651 and finally, last of the major towns, Galway in May 1652. A General Congregation of the Society happened to be in session in Rome at this time and was persuaded, perhaps by Young, to agree that the European provinces would each take an Irish novice for training until he should be able to return home. A number likewise undertook to accept aged Irish Fathers who could not be expected to survive the hardship of living in the woods and mountains. As one of his first tasks, the seventy-year-old German, Father Goswin Nickel, who was eventually elected General and served for nine years,[80] wrote to the Fathers of the Irish Mission and told them, 'the sudden change from such prosperity to such hardship affects me deeply'. It was indeed a sudden change, dramatically underlined by the news that Robert Nugent had taken ship from Galway only to come ashore on the remote western island of Inishboffin, where he died in May 1652, far from the company of the titled and powerful to which he had been accustomed a mere five years before.

Talk of living in the woods and mountains, like the secret pastorate of Father Gellow in New Ross, revived memories of the worst oppression of Elizabethan times. It was indeed so, and still worse. Under the dictate long remembered in the phrase 'To Hell or to Connacht', Catholic landowners were expelled from the southern and eastern areas where the Jesuits had been most active. This in many cases deprived the remaining Fathers of the shelter they had been able to count on in the past from their relatives and friends. Not only was the shelter gone but the prospect of alms, for those sent to Connacht brought little with them. Fear Dorcha Ó Meallain may have been a priest. At any rate, the personal tone in his lines on what he called 'An Díbirt go Connachta' (The Exodus to Connacht) suggest that he walked westward with one of the trudging evicted families:

> Our sole possessions: Michael of miracles,
>   the virgin Mary, the twelve apostles,
> Brigid, Patrick and Saint John
>   — and [for] fine rations: faith in God.[81]

When the puritan authorities ordered all 'Jesuits, seminary priests and persons in popish orders' to leave the country in

1653 they also made it a felony punishable by imprisonment to be caught harbouring such indicted persons. Nor was it easy to come by the basic means of subsistence. At least four armies had been ravaging the countryside and for long afterwards gangs of disbanded soldiers and deserters seized what they could find for their own needs. 'Patriots' they may have been in that they kept up sporadic attacks on the parliamentary forces,[82] but like guerrillas everywhere they lived off the land and thus depleted what little food was left in the huts and cabins of the poor. Father John O'Carolan, formerly of the Jesuit house in Galway, died of hunger 'some time between the years 1652 and 1656'.[83] Father Christopher Netterville made his home in a family vault. Others lived in caves. Piaras Feiritéar, the Kerry poet who was himself hanged by the Cromwellians, could have had in mind a Jesuit huddled in a dripping cave (perhaps Father Maurice O'Connell, who was working in Kerry) when he wrote the quatrain:

> O God up there, do you pity me now as I am,
> A desolate waif scarce seeing the light of day?
> A drop up there, on high, from the rocky roof,
> Falls into my ear . . . and the waves sound at my heels.[84]

Such was the condition of the fewer than twenty Jesuits thought by Father Young to be still in Ireland by the end of 1653. All would have been in disguise when they moved about and most can have been able to do no more than celebrate the sacraments in places far from the prying eyes of informers: the 'Mass Rock' tradition probably dates from this time. The Jesuits, of course, shared their sufferings with all the Catholic clergy. Of the twenty-seven bishops, three (those of Ross, Clogher and Emly) had been executed, others were deported or forced into exile, some died and by 1655 only one, Eugene Sweeney of Kilmore, was still in Ireland. Priests were deported in large numbers and any who returned were liable to be sent as slaves to the West Indies: few enough incurred this penalty, as it happened, for the Caribbean planters did not want them since they formed a focus for discontent around which other Irish deportees could rally; also, Cromwell had no great liking for slave-traders and he obstructed their activities whenever he could.[85] Father Malone, whose fate immediately after the fall of Waterford is uncertain, was captured in 1654 and sentenced to be transported to the Barbados but was put instead on a ship bound for Cadiz.[86] Two Irish Jesuits volunteered for pastoral service in the West Indies. Matthew O'Hartegan, once the envoy to Paris, offered to settle in St Kitt's when the General of the Society expressed concern for the spiritual welfare of the Irish on the island.[87] He does not in fact appear to have gone. But Verdier's translator, John Stritch, certainly worked in Martinique and Guadeloupe.[88] He was to return to Ireland after years of service among his expatriate countrymen.

By the mid-1650s the Commonwealth, England's only experiment in republican government, had been apparently well-established and had absorbed Ireland and Scotland into a premature union of the former three kingdoms. No doubt feeling that the realm was pacified, the paranoic oppression of popery and papists was eased a little so that priests, still incognito, found it possible to enter Ireland again. Some new bishops were named in 1657 and there were rumours of Mass being celebrated in Dublin's Marshalsea Prison.[89] The Jesuit General, Father Nickel, wanted the Mission to continue, as did the Irish Fathers themselves, and he encouraged the discreet transfer of men from the continent. One of the first to go back was the intrepid master of disguise and survival, Thomas Quin, who was made Superior. But almost everything achieved in Ireland since the days of Archer had been shattered beyond repair. Nothing was left but continuity of pastoral service here and there, in a mountain pass, in a wooded glen: that, and a memory which a pair of brave Jesuits kept alive by reopening school-classes, Father James Ford in a cabin on the Bog of Allen and a nameless colleague (surely Father Gellow?) at New Ross.[90]

We can but guess at what would have become of the vision inspiring Nugent and Malone had the Confederation been victorious. Assuming that the quarrel with the Nuncio could have been patched up, the infusion of fresh blood via the Kilkenny novitiate would have strengthened the smaller houses and made them more like the vigorous institutions in Galway and Waterford. This was all the more likely because permission had been sent from Rome, but never arrived because of the Cromwellian war, to ordain the young men when they completed their novitiate — a major concession running counter to Jesuit practice but designed to meet Irish circumstances. Continuing the tradition of Holywood's superiorship, a number of the Irish Fathers — Fitzsimon, Nicholas Nugent, Malone himself, Christopher Sedgrave, William St Leger — were men of high educational attainment, beyond the average achieved by Irish priests in the continental seminaries; of Father Stephen White, who had been professor of divinity at the university of Diligen[91] and died in Galway in 1649, the Anglican Archbishop Ussher — ever ready to acknowledge Jesuit scholarship — wrote that he was 'a man of exquisite knowledge in the antiquities not only of Ireland but also of other nations'.[92] If the country were at peace, such reputations, allied to a successful novitiate and the provision of a solid base for the precarious expansion undertaken by Nugent, should sooner rather than later have resulted in the creation of an Irish Province: successive Generals, after all, were sympathetic, restrained only by their caution in the light of the news from Ireland. As a Province of the Society, the Irish would have had less trouble in securing the return of their best men from the continent — at any rate, those who had not joined a continental Province — for a Provincial could have ordered what a Superior could only request. And with that, the cherished idea of a university might have been implemented.

But that is to speculate. Too many of the prerequisites for a Province were never acquired by the Irish Mission and the Cromwellian debacle destroyed what had been put in place. The disaster did not mean, however, that the service of the Jesuits to the Irish Church had been reduced to the minimal pastorate they carried on within the country. They still had charge of the major Irish colleges in Spain and the Irish College in Rome as well as holding lectureships in colleges elsewhere. Father Francis White, for example, was teaching moral theology at Lisbon in the 1650s,[93] Father William Ryan was lecturer in philosophy at Amiens[94] and Father Nicholas Netterville was teaching philosophy and theology at an unrecorded college in France.[95] The Jesuit Luke Wadding was professor of jurisprudence at the Imperial College of

Madrid until his death at the end of 1651[96] while William Malone, upon his eventual arrival in Spain, became rector of the Irish College at Seville in 1655.[97] Malone's appointment, incidentally, confirmed the rehabilitation of the famous opponent of Rinuccini's interdict. While, in the manner so common among exiles, controversy raged for years between nuncioists and anti-nuncioists on the continent, Rinuccini himself fell into disfavour. Pope Alexander VII, who had been Nuncio in Cologne when the treaties ending the Thirty Years War were signed in the face of strong papal disapproval, had refrained from imposing censures in Germany and he felt that Rinuccini should have been equally judicious in Ireland.[98]

The Jesuits were left with one item of unfinished business. In the days when the Mission was flourishing Father Nugent, as Superior, had lent a substantial sum of money to Rinuccini. In the dire straits of the Cromwellian era, the Irish members of the Society at home and abroad needed every penny they could find but the former Nuncio never repaid his debt. It was a small matter, however, by comparison with the survival of the Mission. And the Mission did survive. Notwithstanding the appalling conditions in which they lived as well as the arrest and deportation of several Superiors,[99] Jesuits in Ireland even found the opportunity to make their solemn profession of four vows: Father Richard Shelton in Dublin in 1652[100] and Father Andrew Sall in Waterford in 1654.[101] But the Mission's pulse was beating low.

3

DE PROFUNDIS

A T first sight the collapse of the Commonwealth in 1660 and the return of the King in the person of the so-called Merry Monarch, Charles II, promised reversal of the Cromwellian disaster. The Confederation, before extinction, had made its peace with him in 1649 and many of its soldiers had battled in his cause. He inherited also the tolerant Stuart sentiment towards Catholicism. Was his brother James, Duke of York, not already leaning towards conversion? But Charles, as he himself stressed, had no wish to go on his travels again. Not only Catholic but Protestant royalist hopes in Ireland were sadly disappointed. Some of the land seized by the Cromwellians to reward their officers and troopers was given back, Catholic worship was allowed to resume if conducted discreetly, and after a time (the delay, it must be said in fairness, arose from caution in Rome rather than English opposition) Catholic bishops were able to reside in their dioceses and administer them, provided that they in their turn acted discreetly. That was all. The King simply had no intention of aggravating former parliament-men or Protestants who leaned towards puritan views. For the most part they remained in place, in town and country. They would set down roots and in time become a major element in the Protestant part of the Irish nation. This growth of a Protestant Ireland had major implications for Catholic Ireland too.

In 1662 the indestructible Ormond, now a Duke, returned as Lord Lieutenant to head the royal administration. The country then bore little resemblance to the Ireland of the

Confederation or even of Wentworth before it. By the time claims and counterclaims were settled, Catholics were left with not much more than one fifth of the land as against the three fifths they had held in 1641.[1] Much the same had happened in the towns, where membership of corporations and guilds as well as the control of trade had fallen largely into Protestant hands, especially where Catholics had been expelled from within the walls as in Cork.[2] For the most part, however, these changes represented a shift of power rather than of people. Only Catholic owners of land and their retainers or others who chose to go with them were involved in the 'Exodus to Connacht'. Catholic labourers, townsfolk and the poor generally remained in or near where they had always lived. In the north-east alone did Protestants become the dominant population. Limerick, Waterford and Galway had substantial bodies of Catholic citizens, as Cork had in its suburbs,[3] and Dublin even found a way to to admit them to a kind of associate membership in the guilds,[4] which indicates how prominent they must have been among the capital's inhabitants. Indeed, Dublin in these years was absorbing many immigrants, some from England but considerable numbers also from rural Ireland[5] who would, of course, have been almost all Catholic.

The shift of power had the dramatic consequence of eliminating totally, forever and almost overnight the distinction between the Gaelic and Old English Catholics. Sentimental imaginings about Anglo-Norman families in the provincial lordships having become 'more Irish than the Irish themselves' had counted for nothing in the rifts opened up by the Papal Nuncio and in any event had not been a noticeable feature of the Old English in the towns. It had taken Cromwell to fuse virtually all Irish Catholics into a common status through a common disaster of apocalyptic proportions. This survived the return of the King and the centuries that followed. By the same token, what the shift of power entirely failed to do was to diminish Irish Catholics' commitment to their religion. A negligible number converted to Protestantism. The rest retained a serenity of Catholic belief most beautifully phrased by Dáibhí Ó Bruadair in the Gaelic hymn to which he gave the title *Adoramus Te, Christe.*

Ghost of our blood, I worship You,
 Hero on Heaven's rampart,
who left for love a mighty Father
 — by Mary's grace — to save us . . .

We regard Your nurse the more, God's son,
 that she was of David's line . . .

Bright, noble and fair to nurture You,
 Child, in a holy nook.
Pure like her never grew in womb
 Nor will till the end of time.[6]

So assured a faith despite so many tribulations was a siren call
to the deported ministers of the Gospel and the younger men
ordained on the continent during the years when no Irish
priest abroad could easily or safely make his way home. It could
have been one of these exiles who wrote the nostalgic lines:

Awake, I am here in France.
When I sleep I'm in the Ireland of Conn.[7]

And home they came. It has been estimated that by the
1670s a thousand secular priests were in the country and six
hundred regulars.[8] Of these, perhaps some thirty-five were
Jesuits: this was the maximum size of the Mission between
1660 and 1690.[9] By 1664, a mere four years after the end of
the Commonwealth regime, the Mission had revived ten residences: in Dublin, Drogheda, Kilkenny, Cashel, New Ross,
Waterford, Clonmel, Cork, Limerick and Galway. As these
were all places where the Society had been established in the
past we may deduce that the handful of Fathers who kept the
Mission alive under Cromwellian persecution had taken care,
when they could, not to abandon the people to whom the
Society of Jesus had been providing educational and spiritual
services.

As always after a period when only a fitful and secret
ministry could be carried out, the immediate requirements
were pastoral. There were Catholics who needed to learn the
elements of their faith and others hungry for the sacraments
of which they had long been deprived. The Mission therefore
concentrated on preaching, retreats and the Jesuits' own

focus for popular spirituality, the Sodality of the Blessed Virgin, branches of which were inaugurated wherever a residence was opened. The Society's educational apostolate so loomed in its members' consciousness, however, that schools were soon functioning in New Ross, Kilkenny, Dublin and Drogheda. Archbishop Oliver Plunkett had invited the Jesuits to open not one but two schools in Drogheda, to be attended by clerical students as well as lay boys.[10] Whatever his views on the Jesuits' administration of Irish Colleges on the continent, Plunkett never doubted their pastoral and teaching talents: 'They have not their equals in this kingdom,' he wrote in 1672, 'they labour incessantly.'

It should be stressed that the religious toleration of these years was relative only, a welcome improvement on Cromwellian times and occasionally even involving co-operation between the government and the Catholic bishops,[11] but always liable to be rescinded if Protestant fears were aroused by rumour-mongering: we may reasonably suppose that their memory of 1641 died hard, or rather did not die at all. Catholic schools were consequently as often closed down as opened. Brief episodes of renewed persecution took place, most notably in the aftermath of the 'Popish Plot', allegedly discovered by Titus Oates in England in 1678, one of the consequences of which was the martyrdom of Saint Oliver Plunkett; the Jesuit Superior at this time, Father William Ryan, was arrested as well as Father Nicholas Netterville and a former Superior, Father Richard Burke. A number of the Fathers were expelled from the country, including Ryan and the head of the Dublin house, Father Stephen Rice. Rice was especially admired by Plunkett,[12] whose schools in Drogheda he had run after scoring a legal victory when he resisted prosecution for teaching in New Ross without taking the oath of supremacy as the law laid down; he pleaded successfully that the law meant teaching for a fee, and of course he took no fees, so. . . .[13]

The retention of anti-Catholic legislation on the statute-book left every enterprise open to proceedings of this kind and few clergy, if hauled before a judge, had the wit or good fortune to win like Father Rice. The survival of a school depended on the willingness of the local authorities to turn

A near contemporary print shows Father James Archer (left) with his friend, the chieftain Owny O'More, at the kidnapping of the Earl of Ormond. Ormond spoke of him afterwards as 'the most wicked villain and unnatural traitor, James Archer, the Jesuit'.

*Very few physical belongings of the pre-Suppression Society in Ireland have been preserved, apart from books like the missals which belonged to the Clonmel residence **(top)** and three chalices in Galway, of which the 'Birmingham Chalice' **(above, left)** is one. Father John Young **(above, right)** was Novice-Master at Kilkenny in the 1640s. The French Visitor, Father Verdier, was impressed by his 'piety and frankness'.*

*Letters concerning the Irish Jesuits were written to the General of the Society in 1673 by Saint Oliver Plunkett, Archbishop of Armagh **(top)**, and in 1689 by the exiled King James II. The Archbishop had much praise for the work done by Father Stephen Rice. The King wanted the General to find a suitable Irish Father to be Rector of the Irish College in Rome.*

A martyrology published in Prague in the late 17th century carried engravings of the deaths of the Irish Jesuit martyrs. Some of the details are fanciful and some of the dates a little wayward, even allowing for the difference between the Julian and Gregorian calendars, but the executions are depicted with substantial accuracy. These illustrations testify to an enduring tradition at the time they were made and could be important evidence in a canonisation process. (Above) Brother Dominic Collins; (opposite) Father John Bathe.

Father Philip Mulcaille, who died in 1801, kept a school in St Michan's parish, Dublin. Bishop Michael Blake of Dromore recalled 'the classic elegance, the attic taste, the chaste refinement, the placid virtue and the Gospel simplicity of...the learned and venerable Mulcaille'.

'The likeness of the Very Rev Thomas Betagh, S.J., Vicar-General of the Archdiocese of Dublin and during more than twenty years the excellent and most vigorous pastor of this parish' said the inscription on the marble monument by Turnerelli in the Church of SS Michael and John. '... His chief delight and happiness it was to instruct the young, especially the needy and the orphan...' Father Betagh died in 1811 before the Restoration of the Society.

1491 SAINT IGNATIUS OF LOYOLA **1991**
1540 SOCIETY OF JESUS **1990**

COMMEMORATIVE MASS

ST PATRICK'S CHURCH
WATERFORD

June 16, 1991 - 3.30 p.m.

The special association of the Jesuits with the city of Waterford throughout the penal days was remembered in the Ignatian Year.

a blind eye to what was going on. One stratagem used by the Jesuits was to take in Protestant pupils as well as Catholics. The general scarcity of schools and the Jesuits' reputation as teachers ensured that Protestant boys were sent to them from time to time. This might avert prosecution for a while but invariably, in the end, other Protestants took fright, protested and as often as not secured the closure of the school. Sometimes it was possible (as at Cashel) to keep the Jesuit school open by promising *not* to admit Protestants and seeing to it that the pupils paid fees to a local *Protestant* schoolmaster![14] Thus here and there, for a time, two or three Jesuit Fathers would give elementary or secondary education, covering perhaps the classics, philosophy or even (at Drogheda, for the four years the schools lasted) theology and the art of preaching. A school might have over a hundred students (Drogheda again, and New Ross), some of them boarders (Cashel),[15] but nobody could guarantee that it would last from one week to the next for it had neither legal status nor solid financial underpinning. Alms, gifts, contributions from a bishop, himself dependent on the generosity of his deeply impoverished people, were all that the Jesuits could rely upon.

Although the Jesuits enjoyed a special reputation in teaching, the other orders also had schools, and freelance schoolmasters were at work, but all educational endeavour for Catholics risked suppression without warning. The miracle was that this stop-go system managed to inculcate a noticeable level of literacy and, to an extent, of learning among many of the general population. More than a hundred years earlier the young Edmund Campion had recorded that 'the mere Irish . . . speake Latine like a vulgar tongue, learned in their common schools of leech-craft and law'.[16] The post-Cromwellian schools, despite their insubstantial existence, must surely be credited with keeping this tradition alive in the later seventeenth century. An English traveller, Sir Henry Piers, noted in 1683 that 'the inhabitants of the county of Kerry, I mean those of them that are downright Irish, are remarkable . . . for their gaming, speaking of Latin and inclination to philosophy and disputes therein. . .'.[17] That the Jesuits had a hand in preserving or developing the more academic of these characteristics in young Irishmen we cannot doubt. We saw in the previous chapter how the professors at Salamanca University identified competence in philosophy and disputation as praiseworthy qualities in the students from the Irish Jesuit College. It may be significant, too, that Father Rice, the successful defendant at New Ross and headmaster at Drogheda, was a Kerryman from Dingle![18]

Be that as it may, the insecurity and the pressing demands for priests simply to celebrate the Eucharist, confess the people and preach the faith prevented the consolidation of Jesuit activity between 1660 and 1690 into a coherent policy for the future such as Nugent had been working towards before the cataclysm. The Jesuits now featured less than they had in the faction-fighting between various elements among the clergy which sadly broke out in the Irish Church whenever persecution eased: this time it mainly took the form of arguments over jurisdiction between sundry bishops and vicars apostolic. The Jesuits took a prominent part in one argument only. Fathers Shelton, Quin and Sall were among those who led the opposition to the 'schismatical Remonstrance' of the Franciscan, Father Peter Walsh.[19] This was in fact a not unreasonable attempt by Father Walsh, who was friendly with Ormond, to draw up a statement of loyalty to be addressed by the Irish clergy to the King, which might induce the royal government and parliament to grant more freedom to Catholics. His document would have denied that the Pope had power to absolve subjects from allegiance to their prince:[20] an authority which for over seventy years Rome had not been anxious to aver. To have it publicly rejected by bishops and priests was a different matter, far too close for Rome's liking to the evolving Gallicanism — emphasising the rights of the Crown and minimising those of the Pope — which was growing ever more dominant in the Church of France and (with qualifications) among French Jesuits.[21] Rome denounced the move in Ireland, even in the modified form found acceptable by Plunkett's predecessor, Archbishop Edmund O'Reilly of Armagh.

Ormond in turn rejected the modified Remonstrance, so the question ceased to be relevant in Ireland. The Jesuit position was interesting nonetheless. Since the days of Father Holywell, the Mission had taken care to avoid the kind of political involvement which required the juxtaposition of allegiance to the Pope on the one hand and to the King on the other. The Society in Ireland had produced no disciples of Bellarmine since Archer. Neither had it shown any signs of Gallican influence, although some might have wished to represent the dispute with Rinuccini in that light. No realistic comparison could actually be made between the embattled Confederation's quarrel over practicalities with a stubborn Nuncio and the precisely phrased propositions touching royal and papal authority drafted by the Sorbonne (the University of Paris) for the concurrence of the French Church.[22] The firm stance of the Irish Jesuits on Friar Walsh's proposals showed itself in the refusal by the Superior of the Mission, Father Andrew Sall, to sign the 'Sorbonne Propositions' offered in 1666 as part of the modified Remonstrance.[23] It seems reasonable to conclude that the Jesuits recognised the issue of principle at stake in a quasi-theological formula which had originated as a statement drafted to meet the political needs of the French monarchy.

While it has been said[24] that the Jesuit Fathers in Ireland had to combat Jansenism as well as Gallicanism at this time, it is hard to find much evidence of Jansenist theory at large in the country. The esoteric doctrine of grace at the heart of Jansenist theology was unlikely to spark enthusiasm or even interest in an Irish Church struggling to achieve the minimal freedom in which to worship and organise without fear of oppression. A misuse of the word 'Jansenism', which confuses it with the English puritan ethos, still bedevils discussion of Irish Church history. Jansenism was in fact a highly sophisticated deviation from accepted Catholic belief, and condemned by Rome as such, but it stimulated much debate among theologians in Paris and Louvain during the mid-seventeenth century. Irish priests were found on both sides of the argument on the continent[25] but would have found little scope for this concern at home in Ireland.

A more pressing hazard was the danger that Catholic priests would be lured into the Protestant fold. This reversed the trend in Father Holywood's time when, as we saw, Protestant pastors were drawn into the Roman Church by the advocacy of Jesuits trained in the Irish Colleges abroad. We need not doubt that the training was just as good in the later period but the sheer strain of the Catholic ministry, the uncertain future and the persuasiveness of Anglican divines, whose quality as evangelists and controversialists had noticeably improved,[26] combined to weaken the commitment of more than one priest to his inherited faith. It was an occasional rather than common phenomenon and in the post-Cromwellian era appears to have involved only one member of the Society in Ireland. To quote a modern historian, 'Some polemical writing came from Andrew Sall, an ex-Jesuit who had been head of the Irish College in Salamanca; he entered the Church of Ireland in 1674 and became prebendary of Cashel.'[27] This Sall must be distinguished from his contemporary of the same name who took his vows in Cromwellian-occupied Waterford and later, as Superior, rejected Friar Walsh's Gallican Remonstrance. *In a Chronological List of Jesuits connected with the Irish Mission from 1550 to 1799*[28] the Superior can be identified by his patronymic 'Fitzbennet', as we know that his father was Bennet Sall of Cashel;[29] he entered the Society in 1635. The apostate Sall, as his brethren would have judged him, entered in 1641. It is recorded that Father Ignatius Brown, first Rector of the Irish Jesuit House of Studies at Poitiers, 'wrote several learned works, among which are *The Unerring and Unerrable Church*, a reply to a sermon by Andrew Sall, preached at Christ's Church, Dublin, in 1674. . .'.[30]

The foundation at Poitiers was unusual in several respects. In the first place it came much later than the Colleges in Spain and Rome, being established only in 1674. It differed from these institutions because it was specifically an Irish Jesuit house, not a college maintained by Irish Jesuits for the benefit of clerical students destined for the secular priesthood or other orders as well as members of the Society itself. Its purpose has been variously described, not only as a House of Studies but also as 'a house of refuge for old, infirm or exiled missioners'[31] and as 'a grammar school, an Irish St Omer . . . the Collège Petit'.[32] It would seem in fact to have discharged all these functions — much as a Jesuit boarding school does today, in which the community consists not only of men actively engaged in teaching but also of those for whom accommodation can be provided while they complete a special study project, and some older Fathers who have retired from full-time ministry but can still do useful work in a busy house where substitutes are required from time to time in the classroom or at the altar. It may not be too much to say that the Collège Petit was the first modern house of the Irish Jesuits, the first which would be recognisable to anybody familiar with Rathfarnham, Clongowes or Gardiner Street. The pity was that it had not been established much sooner for the education of Irish laity on the model of the English Colleges at St Omer and Douai.

Father Brown, its founder as well as first Rector, came from Waterford. He studied at Santiago and achieved a high reputation for scholarship (apparently in what we would call apologetics) but he spent ten years as a preacher among the poor in the towns of southern Ireland before going to Paris. He clearly had excellent connections since he raised the necessary resources to found the Irish College of Poitiers through the influence of Louis XIV's confessor and Catherine of Braganza, the Portuguese wife of King Charles of England! When his term as Rector ended he became confessor to the Queen of Spain.[33] Later Rectors moved in less exalted circles but a number had not only a scholarly background but had served as Superiors of the Irish Mission. These included Father Ryan (who had been *inter alia* professor of scholastic theology at Bourges)[34] and Father James Relly (who had taught philosophy in Perugia and held a chair of theology in Siena).[35] Father Richard Burke, another former Superior, worked there for a time[36] as also did Father Stephen Rice,[37] the friend of Saint Oliver Plunkett. If the Irish Mission depended on the older colleges for much of its manpower, Poitiers clearly depended on the Mission for its staffing and direction. It was, as it were, a witness to the Mission's status as a meritorious work of the Society, distinguished for its members' learning and their ceaseless promotion of the faith despite their trials. Soon it would only be through such foundations abroad that the Irish Church would be able to express itself and ensure that its true character could be seen and understood.

Charles II died in February 1685. His brother, the Duke of York, succeeded him as James II. James had become a Catholic in 1669 and was expected to grant further relief to his precariously tolerated co-religionists. Those who knew him admired his considerable intelligence, his competence as a naval commander and his personal courage. These virtues loomed less in his brief reign than his shortcomings of arrogance, insensitivity, stubbornness and poor judgment of persons. It would not be grossly inaccurate to say he was too blatantly Catholic in England and insufficiently so in Ireland, thereby ensuring that he caused maximum offence in both countries. In England he flaunted his religion — it was unnecessary to visit the Catholic chapels of country towns on a Royal Progress;[38] it was imprudent to appoint a Jesuit to the Privy Council;[39] it was provocative to bring over largely Catholic regiments from Ireland to strengthen the army.[40] Although the Father General of the Society in Rome had reservations about allowing Father Edward Petre to become the King's confidant, the English Jesuits soon enough and willingly enough threw themselves into a very public promotion of the Catholic religion. A Victorian Jesuit summarised what was done under James: 'nearly throughout the entire Kingdom, by great efforts in which the fathers of the English Province were conspicuous, sacred edifices were seen to rise in most of the principal cities. Some of the fathers preached in them once, twice or thrice a week. Others gave catechetical instructions and controversial lectures . . . they visited both towns and villages and were everywhere successful in confirming those who had always held the faith and in bringing back Protestants to the fold of Christ.'

It can be argued that this, like the schools which they also opened at the time, was what Jesuits were meant to do. The account conveys more than a hint of *blitzkrieg*, however, which suggests that the methods employed and the prominence assumed by the Society lacked the caution that should have marked Catholic evangelism among a people not only virulently Protestant but specifically anti-Roman and anti-Jesuit, accustomed for generations to believe that the Pope and the Order dedicated to his service posed a permanent threat to the safety of the realm. The indiscretion of the

English Province in the circumstances differed so much from the normally sophisticated approach of the Society — not least in England — that it prompts speculation on how it came about. The answer seems clear enough: the King wanted it. He certainly favoured the Jesuits. He donated a large sum to their new London chapel in The Savoy, where they also opened a community house (which for a contemporary Catholic critic was 'over-reaching'), and compelled the secular clergy to surrender another chapel to the Society in the centre of London. These buildings provided convenient focal points for mob violence when William of Orange supplanted King James in 1688.

While he coat-trailed his religion in England, James appeared primarily concerned in Ireland to mollify Protestant opinion.[41] True, he granted 'liberty of conscience' to Catholics and modest stipends to their bishops but he gave their Church no special position in the State: it was the Anglican, not the Catholic, bishops whom he summoned to attend the Irish parliament. He resisted as long as he could the Catholic demand for a root-and-branch redistribution of land to redress the injustice of the Cromwellian settlement; when, in desperation (because he needed money like his father before him), he yielded to the largely Catholic parliament's pressure on the land question in the end, he took refuge in a stalling tactic that would still be a feature of Irish politics in the late twentieth century — he appointed a commission to look into the matter. Ironically, while the King's attitude left the Catholics very dissatisfied, it did little to allay the anxiety of Protestants. They saw the army filled up with Catholic recruits, commissions and the military command itself given to Catholics and, rather oddly, Catholic priests appointed deans of two Protestant cathedrals. The King further directed that Jesuits be put in charge of government-controlled schools whenever vacancies occurred for headmasters. This last was probably the only measure which would have been of real benefit to Catholics, but it was unlikely to commend itself to those Protestants who already objected to Jesuits teaching Protestant children; there is no evidence that any member of the Irish Mission accepted an appointment under this provision.

Meanwhile, much had been happening in England. Many Irish Protestants had taken fright early in the reign and had fled there or to the Protestant parts of Ulster. The alarm of these refugees stoked further the resentment against James. When his Queen bore him a son and the Catholic succession looked thereby secured, the plot was launched to bring over the Prince of Orange in his place. It succeeded; James fled to France and came thence to Ireland. William came too. Great sieges and battles followed, for the French (on the side of James) and William's Dutch, Danes and Germans ensured that the struggle took on a European dimension. After encounters at Derry, the Boyne and Athlone, at Aughrim and at Limerick twice over, William's forces triumphed. James, the French and the flower of the Irish soldiery left for the continent and Ireland was subdued.

So, by the autumn of 1691 the Catholic monarchy was no more. Perhaps it was doomed from the start. It was too sudden a change. The Protestant people of England could not have slept easily knowing that a papist sat upon the throne. James had paid the price for reminding them daily of his religion, while his belief in the divine right of kings stamped him as a backward-looking prince on the threshold of the Age of Enlightenment. Yet, in his going something was lost. When James invoked 'liberty of conscience' he did not speak lightly. 'Endeavour to settle Liberty of Conscience by a Law . . . 'he wrote in his testament to his son. 'Be not persuaded to depart from that. Our Blessed Saviour whipt people out of the Temple, but I never heard he commanded any should be forced into it.'[42] He intended to govern all his subjects by this principle, Anglicans and Catholics, Presbyterians and Quakers.[43] The so-called 'Glorious Revolution' which replaced him may indeed have moved an inch or two out on the long road to representative government but, unlike James Stuart, it prefigured nothing in the distant recognition of the rights of the person. Irish and English Catholics were about to bear witness to that.

Throughout the turbulent years the Jesuit Mission in Ireland avoided the high profile adopted by their English contemporaries. They were urged to set up colleges but the only initiative they took was to open a chapel in Dublin:[44]

whether caution or paucity of numbers lay behind this reticence we are left to speculate. More significantly, by September 1690 the course of the Williamite war had forced the Superior, Father Patrick Lynch, to retire to his native Galway. He reported that four of the Jesuit houses had been destroyed, the Fathers dispersed and several of them arrested.[45] It was a foretaste of what was to come.

The Treaty of Limerick, which ended the war the following year, promised Catholics such freedom of worship as was 'consistent with the laws of Ireland or as they did enjoy in the reign of King Charles II'.[46] The intention of the military officers who negotiated the Treaty was to guarantee reasonable tolerance to Catholics but 'the laws of Ireland' could be readily amended and the spirit of the Treaty thus broken. This was precisely what happened. Between 1695 and 1728 the Protestants, back in the Dublin parliament in force, passed the body of legislation known collectively in Ireland as the 'Penal Laws'.[47] These laws purported to banish Catholic bishops, senior church officials and all regular clergy from Ireland; prohibited the entry of priests from foreign countries; forbade Catholics to teach or to be sent abroad to be taught; required parish priests to be registered and to carry out their duties without the assistance of curates. Wide-ranging limitations on careers, office-holding and the ownership of property were also enacted, some of which applied to nonconformist Protestants as well but they bore most heavily on Catholics. No Catholic could hold land absolutely or on a long lease, be a member of parliament or of a municipal corporation, vote in a parliamentary election, be a magistrate or join the legal profession, carry arms or (in the least important but longest remembered property disqualification) own a horse worth more than £5.

At this distance in time it is possible — and desirable — to understand the fears which evoked these draconian measures. The threat posed by King James to property and offices held by Protestants amounted to a threat to Protestant power in Ireland, to Protestant control of the country. The catholicisation of the army revived something close to panic when the massacre of 1641 was recalled (and it was never forgotten; instead, it was increasingly exaggerated). The sheer number of Irish Catholics was felt as a constant menace — not least, it may be, because the revocation in 1685 of the Edict of Nantes in France, which resulted in the expulsion of the Protestant Huguenots, was seen as a warning of the fate which awaited Protestants at the hands of a Catholic majority. Much libellous pamphleteering and rumour-mongering in England,[48] abetted by injudicious public activity there on the part of a number of Catholics (including the Jesuits, the *bêtes noires* of every Protestant nightmare), left little doubt in the minds of the fearful that the supposed sources of malign influence in the body politic would have to be removed. So much can be understood. Unhappily, there was also an unreasoned hatred of 'popery', as there was of 'heretics' on the other side, which may have been typical of the age but was no less baneful or unchristian for that. It was the first aspect of the mentality behind the penal laws to show itself, as it would also be the first to abate.

Father Lynch died in Dublin in 1694. Father Anthony Knoles succeeded him as Superior and served for the lengthy term of thirty-three years: fortunately, given the problems of the Mission, the three-years-at-a-time limitation on post-holding in the Society was rescinded about now. The problems were indeed immense. The letters he succeeded in sending out of the country provide unconnected vignettes of the perils facing the Irish Jesuits — and other priests too.[49] In 1695 he wrote about a manhunt set up by the magistrates of Kilkenny to find three Jesuits who had been teaching children in the town. At the end of 1696 his letter came from Waterford prison, in which he and a number of diocesan clergy had been locked up. He was kept incarcerated for thirteen months. How he came to be released we do not know but, regardless of the law, he remained in the country. In 1712 he reported: 'all our chapels are closed; the pastors have fled; in some places the laity are dragged into court to swear what priest's Mass they have heard during the last six months. . .'. The next year he told how he had been a fugitive for three months and said that, in spite of the persecution, there were still eleven Jesuits in Ireland. What work they could do must have been very limited. 'My brethren are obliged to desist from their usual labours, and keep in their hiding holes,' wrote the Superior in 1714, 'for no priest can be seen in public.' Especially not a Jesuit. The scale of reward to a priest-hunter just then, as a Bishop of Kerry later remembered it, was:

£30.00 . . . for a simple priest;
£50.00   for a bishop;
£40.00   for a vicar-general;
£50.00   for a Jesuit.[50]

Father Knoles seems to have based himself in or close to Waterford for most of his superiorship, perhaps because Dublin was particularly hazardous and as a Waterfordman he could function best — and find hiding-places — in the countryside he knew. He brought the Mission through its darkest hour, worse than the Cromwellian persecution because it was more prolonged. What he described was a rigid, even literal, enforcement of the penal laws: he and the other Jesuits were harried, because they were regulars; secular priests were pursued, most probably because they were not registered; chapels were closed, as was legally permitted, under the pretext of a threat of war: the pretext could be readily invoked in the years before 1720, during which the Jacobites on the continent more than once plotted an invasion of Ireland[51] and carried out a major invasion of Scotland and England. Despite the rigours under which he had to discharge his pastorate, the hounded Superior did not lack resources of his own. He had lectured on theology and philosophy in a number of Spanish colleges before his return to Ireland and he was a personal friend of the General, Father Tirso Gonzalez, who had been professor of theology at Salamanca.[52] Knoles was able to bring sufficient foreign pressure to bear to ensure that the royal assent was withheld from 'a shameful bill passed by the Irish Parliament against the Catholic clergy'.[53] This probably refers to proposed legislation for the flogging of nuns and branding of unregistered priests.[54]

The possibility that a Jesuit residing in Ireland contrary to law could, from his hiding-place, influence the decisions of the King's advisers in London is less fanciful than it seems. English administrations never felt as strongly as did the Irish parliament about restrictions on the Roman Church in

Ireland, for the Irish parliament was drawn from a people most conscious of a resentful Catholic population outnumbering them several times over in three of the four provinces. The social and political clauses of the penal laws in large part met London's concern that Catholic, and therefore Jacobite, interests should have no access to power. London had wider policies to consider, too. The first half of the eighteenth century saw a shifting pattern of alliances between the European powers, who no longer chose sides on the basis of religion. England was particularly anxious to cultivate the friendship of Austria and not to alienate the Spaniards if it could be avoided: in this way French ambitions might be contained. The Papacy was none too happy, either, that Gallican France should dominate Europe. Against this background, British ministries — which had the ultimate say in the government of Ireland, regardless of the pretensions of the Dublin parliament — were sensitive to suggestions that certain continental countries would like to see moderation in the treatment of Catholics. The Jesuit international network was well placed to encourage such nudging of the English, and was available to even an Irish Superior acting through his General. The Jesuit ability to exercise this kind of influence was not the least of the factors which gave the Order an importance beyond its numbers or local circumstances in any one country, Ireland included. It was also not the least of the factors which roused Protestant suspicions, as well as political and clerical resentment, in Catholic countries, and which in the end brought about the suppression of the Society. But this is to anticipate.

In fact by 1720, with the Crown of England fairly firmly settled on the Hanoverian King George and with the Jacobites for the moment in disarray, a general improvement was becoming noticeable in Ireland in the application of the penal laws. Although priest-hunters might still lay information against unregistered priests, and 'discoverers' would, for many years to come, acquire landed property for themselves by uncovering illegal Catholic owners behind seemingly Protestant trusts, the more obnoxious provisions against the Catholic religion were increasingly being ignored by the state authorities. Bishops resumed the administration of their dioceses, often registering themselves as parish priests; friars were coming into the country from the continent; Dominican, Carmelite and Poor Clare nuns established convents; [55] and at some time before 1718 two Jesuits, Fathers Michael Murphy and Milo Byrne, were able to open a school in the Mary's Lane district of Dublin just north of the river.[56] The mere existence of this school must have brought joy to Father Knoles but there is little evidence that the Jesuits were able to expand their activities as much as the secular clergy and other religious orders. Their numbers were so few that a little teaching, some parish work and the more specialised apostolate of giving retreats to priests must have been as much as they could take upon themselves. But two events under Knoles's successor, Father Ignatius Kelly, could hardly have happened if the climate were not becoming a little brighter for the Mission as well as the Irish Church as a whole. In the summer of 1731 a Jesuit residence was opened once more in Galway[57] and shortly afterwards Father Kelly undertook a visitation of the Irish College in Poitiers where financial problems had to be sorted out.[58] A residence and a visitation were aspects of very normal Jesuit life and we may take it that any need for concealment was over before either could be put in hand.

The 1730s were a period of transition for the Irish Church from a time of oppression to one of new life quite different from what it had known before the Williamite upheaval. Its repudiation by the state left it free to develop in its own way as long as it avoided provoking the state into active opposition. Discretion took simple but effective forms. Priests dressed as the laity did. Chapels were mostly mere 'Mass-houses' — barns, inns, outhouses or, if custom-built as places of worship, constructed to be as unobtrusive as the ordinary buildings in a city side-street or back-yard or on a farm. Public statements from clerical sources eschewed any sentiment that could be condemned as politically disloyal. Such restraint must have been a burden to many Irish men and women, but it hugely facilitated the emergence of a vibrant Catholicism. A survey of the whole country in 1731 found 892 Mass-houses, not counting the open-sided huts used in poor country places to shelter a movable altar; there were 1,700 priests, of whom 254 were said to be regulars; there were thought to be 51 friaries.[59] From the statistics, we can see that the Church was still (or again) a formidable institution, yet the statistics are the lesser part of the story. The Irish Church, the *Pobal Dé* or People of God in Ireland, underwent a spiritual awakening too,[60] which corresponded to the cultural lyricism of Gaelic verse-making among the same impoverished populace. They would listen enraptured by the fireside to the poet's envisioning of their country as a beautiful apparition:

> Brightness most bright I beheld on the way, forlorn.
> Crystal of crystal her eye, blue touched with green.
> Sweetness most sweet her voice, not stern with age.
> Colour and pallor appeared on her flushed cheeks.[61]

They would set off for the Mass-house next morning, reciting on the way:

> We walk together with the Virgin Mary
> and the other holy people who accompanied her only Son
> on the Hill of Calvary.[62]

And at the Consecration of the Host they would welcome their Saviour with the acclamation:

> A hundred thousand welcomes, thou Body of the Lord,
> Thou Son of her the Virgin, the brightest, most adorned . . .[63]

The spiritual and the secular thus readily mingled in the Gaelic culture. But were the Jesuits much involved in this distinctive form of Irish penal Catholicism? We simply do not know and therefore might too readily suppose that their association with the towns cut them off from a rural phenomenon. This is to make more than one unwarranted assumption. At the worst of the penal times, in Father Knoles's day, rural areas may well have been the only places in which Jesuits could conduct an active pastorate; indeed, at the worst of times Catholic townsfolk had to go outside the town walls to find a Mass-house.[64] It needs also to be said that Irish towns were small, not rigidly cut off from their hinterland, its language or culture. Father Kelly came from Dungarvan; his successor, Father Thomas Hennessy, came from Clonmel.[65] Both would have been fully acquainted with the dominant religious tradition. Tradition included pilgrimages, which remained highly popular despite growing episcopal disapproval,[66] and the Jesuits had an early association with these: back in 1609 the English authorities received a complaint that Jesuits came annually to Inis Cealtra on the Shannon 'to give absolution and pardons' — allegedly 'making a yearly revenue of rich and poor' therefrom![67]

Perhaps the most intimate identification an eighteenth-century Jesuit would have felt with popular Irish religion arose from the fact that 'devotion to the Blessed Virgin had an important role in Counter-Reformation spirituality, and strikingly marked off the Catholic from the Protestant'.[68] The Jesuit Sodality of the Blessed Virgin was dedicated to this devotion and the same emphasis comes shining through the folk-prayers of the people. Another feature of eighteenth-century prayer throughout the Irish Church can be traced directly to Jesuit inspiration. This was the cult of the Sacred Heart,[69] which was strongly promoted at Salamanca and in the other Spanish colleges administered by the Irish Jesuits. It seems to have reached Ireland through the former students of these colleges, especially some of the Irish bishops and, of course, Jesuits who came home to serve on the Mission. Father Leonard Sweetman, an alumnus of Seville and future Rector of Salamanca, worked in Clonmel from 1735 to 1742 and was said to have been zealous in encouraging devotion to the Sacred Heart wherever he went. Father Edward Lisward of the Waterford community set up a Sacred Heart confraternity in Dungarvan during the 1750s, one member of which was the poet, Tadhg Gaelach Ó Súilleabháin, who composed the much loved hymn *Gile mo chroí do chroí-se, a Shlánaitheoir.*

> The light in my heart, O Saviour, is Thy heart,
> the wealth of my heart, Thy heart poured out for me.[70]

Father Lisward ministered mainly in the Decies and the Nire Valley,[71] the mountainous and coastal parts of west Waterford where the Gaelic tradition would still have been fully alive at mid-century. But his base was in Waterford city, where the Jesuits were given charge of Saint Patrick's chapel[72] in one of the old parishes dating from the Middle Ages; they also took responsibility for the Clonmel parish of St Mary's[73] in the same diocese. This concentration of activity in the Waterford 'catchment area', to which New Ross also belonged, strengthens the likelihood that Waterford continued to be the Mission's administrative centre until 1760. Whether by coincidence or otherwise, not only were Father Knoles and Father Kelly natives of this part of Ireland but so were the next two Superiors, Father Thomas Hennessy (from Clonmel) and Father Michael FitzGerald (from Dungarvan).[74] Father Hennessy was in Clonmel when he died; the other three died in Waterford. It seems reasonable to assume that the Superior normally resided in the city.

Father Hennessy was once mistaken for a cardinal by an over-imaginative priest-hunter, who did not realise that every priest vested in a cope for the ceremony of Benediction. There must have been something of an episcopal aura about Hennessy, since shortly after this episode (and long before he became Superior) he was named to act as Vicar-General for Bishop Richard Piers of Waterford and Lismore, who was exiled under the penal laws. Father FitzGerald had a more conventional but distinguished career. After studying and teaching in Languedoc, Roussillon and the Auvergne, he returned to Ireland in 1727, was given the task of re-opening the residence in Galway, went back to France as Rector of Poitiers, on to Rome as Rector of the Irish College and then home again to be Superior from 1750 to 1759. As ever, the Society did not stint in the quality of the men it chose to head its Irish Mission, even in the years when the Mission was no more than a handful of beleaguered preachers and teachers.

Despite the penal pressures and the particular problems of working in proximity to an inimical government, its garrison and its prolific agents, the Jesuits had never deserted Dublin. The chapel which they had opened in Lucy Lane (now Chancery Place, beside the Four Courts) seems to have survived the Williamite occupation of the city; the local branch of the Sodality still existed in 1696.[75] The immediate fate of a classical school which the Fathers had conducted nearby — with a future Archbishop of Dublin, John Linegar, among the pupils — is less certain. It would have been difficult to keep it going, even in secret, while two of the Jesuits were imprisoned for a year. Whatever property they had must have been plundered since by 1692 they were reporting their extreme poverty and in 1694 Father Knoles wrote of the whole Mission that 'Wee are in great want, all our substance being lost in this countri and our best men not in a condition to shift for themselves.' But in Dublin somehow they made shift. A survey[76] drawn up early in 1698 to assist enforcement of the Act decreeing the banishment of all regular clergy, and specifically Jesuits, uncovered four members of the Society in the capital: Edward Chamberlain was 'liveing neere the Convent in Cooke Street', Bryan McTernon was found in Saint Catherine's parish, and it was noted that 'Father Netervil a Jesuit lodges on the Key at Dr Cruise house'; there was also 'Johnson a Jesuit who did live att Mr Synotts on Merchants Key' but was 'now wthdrawne and supposed to be skulking about the towne'.

Implementation of the banishment law abruptly ended the last vestige of overt activity by the Jesuits and several decades would pass before more than two or three were able to stay in the city at a time. They mainly helped the secular clergy and were sometimes registered as parish priests, like Father James Gibbon who lived at Grangegorman in 1704. A clever device was now thought up to increase the number of priests permitted by law: medieval parishes were revived which had long been absorbed into bigger units.[77] If parish priests could not have curates, curates could be made pastors of parishes! Some at least of the regular clergy were able to function through this arrangement. By about 1720 there were at least six Mass-houses in the city run by religious orders, as well as nine served by diocesan priests.[78] The few Jesuits available became associated with Saint Michan's parish — that is, the Mary's Lane area — in the same way as their colleagues in Waterford and Clonmel had a special relationship with individual parishes in those places. We have to speak vaguely of a 'relationship' since the Jesuits themselves thought it safer not to have a place of worship openly connected with so notorious an order. Their caution failed to prevent the parishioners of Saint Michan's from referring to their local Mass-house as 'the Jesuit chapel': being relatively large, it had a side-altar and this was dedicated to Saint Francis Xavier, so the connection was obvious anyway.

It must have been a lively parish in which to work. The parish priest (a diocesan, of course, not a Jesuit) from 1703 to 1738 was Father Cornelius Nary, a Doctor of Laws of Paris University and an inveterate writer.[79] He debated with Protestant scholars, wrote a *New History of the World*, a catechism and a translation of the New Testament. In 1731 it was reported of Saint Michan's that 'there have been several conferences held in the said parish in order to pervert the Protestants' and it can hardly be doubted that Dr Nary involved his Jesuit helpers in this activity. The Jesuits' principal occupation, however, was probably running the revived classical school. Father Knoles reported to Rome in 1717 that 'Father Michael Murphy is taking the risks of giving education to young people in the capital of the country. He has taught Greek and Latin throughout the last five years and is doing so at present.' This was hazardous. John Garzia, a priest-hunter, had Father Murphy arrested in 1718 and told the judge that the Jesuit 'kept school in Dublin and taught Grammar and Philosophy'. Since Murphy resumed his work upon his release and at least one other Jesuit, Father Milo Byrne, was engaged in the same apostolate it is interesting that in 1722, when Garzia compiled a list of 'all the popish Bishops and clergimen in the City of Dublin',[80] he failed to identify any Jesuits although he named a number of members of other orders; he noted 'Doctor Nery' at Mary's Lane but did not say that he had any assistants. Not all priests in the list are named and the Jesuits may, of course, be hidden under the loose entry, 'two priests', used by the informer several times when he could not discover his victim's names. But clearly it was not only in country districts that Jesuits had to go to ground.

Schools mattered. As early as 1730 the diocesan statutes of Dublin required every parish priest to engage a schoolmaster to teach Catholic doctrine.[81] This directive quickly acquired enhanced importance when a royal charter was granted in 1733 to the 'Incorporated Society in Dublin for

Promoting English Protestant Schools' in which 'the children of the popish and other poor natives . . . may be instructed . . . in the principles of true religion'.[82] Only in retrospect can it be said that these 'charter schools' largely failed in their purpose. At a time when not a few Catholics of wealth and position were conforming to the Established Church in order to protect their property, how were the poor to be persuaded to avoid the lure of a good education for their children if they allowed them to be instructed in the Protestant faith? A necessary part of the answer had to be extensive provision of Catholic schools, the law on the statute-book banning them notwithstanding. But how were schools for impoverished Catholics to match institutions sustained by large donations, an annual royal bounty and the proceeds of sundry taxes?

Rome supported proposals for setting up schools in the major towns, with financial assistance from the laity, and also urged the religious orders to establish schools; the Congregation of Propaganda Fide — the department of the Roman Curia responsible for Irish affairs — undertook eventually to provide an annual grant for Catholic schools in Ireland,[83] a counterpoint to the charter schools' bounty. By 1750 1,400 children, including 400 in Dublin, were attending these schools established by the bishops; the figures did not take account of 200 youngsters apprenticed to trades.[84] All these returns seem to have referred to boys only, since it was separately noted that girls were educated by nuns. The statistics look modest enough, given a total population of more than three million in 1750,[85] but it has to be remembered that the number of parents who would consider sending their children to a school of any kind, or at least to a school which taught more than reading, writing and simple arithmetic, was unlikely to be large. Also, at this time there were numerous 'hedge-schools' providing education of varying (but sometimes high) standard throughout the country. Although not under episcopal jurisdiction, these were in most cases, and for all practical purposes, Catholic schools conducted with the approval of the local clergy.[86] In the diocese of Ossory, it was reported that nearly every parish had one by the 1730s.[87]

Catholic life was coming into its own again outside the boundaries of an establishment unable, and increasingly unwilling to try, to destroy what a Church of Ireland bishop called 'the mild and harmless superstition'[88] that was popery as long as it involved no acquisition of political control by papists. An unnamed Jesuit wrote in 1747, 'Never was a city better provided with learned and zealous instructors than Dublin is at present; we now begin to have vespers sung and sermons preached in the afternoons. You see hereby how peaceable times we enjoy.'[89] Whatever about those vespers (the divine office in choir was one of the traditional features of religious life dropped by the early Jesuits),[90] the sense of winter passing infuses the comment. The charter schools were almost the last fling in the spirit of the penal code to interfere with the religious belief of Catholics, although it has sadly to be said that attempts at proselytising through education were to continue in Ireland for another hundred years as a chosen instrument of evangelical Protestantism. Lest this remark be considered lacking in ecumenical charity, it must freely be admitted that the Jesuits, as well as other Catholic clergy, were only too pleased if they could attract Protestants into the Church of Rome, as we have seen from the account of Dr Nary's parish conference. Attitudes simply reflected the confrontational and unfraternal spirit of the age. That said, the penal laws, combined with establishment wealth and power, obliged Catholics to work doubly hard to protect their own against the threat of sectarian seduction.

Needless to say, the Jesuits threw themselves into the educational apostolate with much enthusiasm and nowhere more than in Dublin. Their numbers were now increasing. By 1750 they had some ten or twelve men in the capital and its vicinity. An additional effort beyond that of the school in St Michan's parish became possible. It was undertaken by a very remarkable member of the Society, Father John Austin,[91] of whom it was said that as a boy he so impressed Jonathan Swift that the Dean advised his parents 'to send him to the Jesuits, who would make a man of him'. After training, teaching and ordination in Champagne, he returned to Dublin as assistant priest in the parish of St Michael and St

John's south of the river. Here in Saul's Court, off Fishamble Street, he founded a classical school about 1750 which attained such high standards that it was used as the diocesan school of Meath as well as Dublin for the training of priests prior to the foundation of proper seminaries at Carlow, Maynooth and elsewhere late in the century. By 1770, with the help of Father James Philip Mulcaile and one of his former pupils, Father Thomas Betagh, both Jesuits, he opened a boarding school beside the original foundation. Father Austin not only built up a prestigious academy but somehow found the time to carry on a mission of mercy among the deprived people of the district for more than thirty years. He died in 1784, and in the 1790s Charles Bowden, an English visitor, came upon stories of his extraordinary exertions. He was told that Father Austin had been dedicated to the poor, 'visiting them in cellars and garrets, never a day happy that he did not give food to numbers'. The better-off helped him and 'while the means lasted [he] was constantly on foot administering relief to innumerable poor wretches, never resting while he had a single guinea'. He was also famous as a confessor and preacher. Among his initiatives was the 'charity sermon', which would be still a feature of Catholic life in nineteenth century Dublin as a means of raising money for good causes.

Father Betagh, destined to be even more renowned than his mentor, took over the school after Father Austin's death and extended the project by providing evening, day and Sunday classes for the very poor in the same teeming area of the old city. He was a man of outstanding personal qualities. William Reed, a Baptist minister from Gloucestershire, left a pleasing picture of him in old age, which illustrates both Father Betagh's reputation and his personality: 'I desired to be better acquainted with the real character of the Roman Catholic religion in Ireland. On arriving in Dublin, I was desired to consult Dr Betagh, who was said to be the most learned and best-informed man in Ireland, and who added to these accomplishments an amenity of manners that was almost enchanting. Accordingly, one morning I knocked on the door of this venerable monk, but could not have access to him then, as he was giving audience to two Bishops. The

next morning I found him alone. Requesting to know my
business, he desired me to draw my chair nearer to the fire;
and we soon entered into the depths of the most serious
conversation. I questioned him on the subjects of Purgatory,
Indulgences, the use of Holy Water, Praying for the Dead,
Transubstantiation, Praying to the Saints, and particularly of
the Virgin Mary, whom they call the Mother of God. I found
him very eloquent. He defended every part of his system
with an acuteness and force, ingenuity and masterly address,
that astonished me. He had received me with the greatest
politeness.'

   When Father Betagh in turn died in 1811, Dr Michael
Blake, who was once his pupil and would later be Bishop of
Dromore, spoke of his achievement in founding 'that Free
School where three hundred boys, poor in everything but
genius and spirit, receive their education every evening and
where more than three thousand have already been educated'
and he recalled how Father Betagh 'at the age of seventy-
three, would sit in a cold damp cellar every night to hear the
lessons of these children, and contrive to clothe forty of the
most destitute of them every year at his own expense'. Dr
Blake used the same occasion to mention Father Mulcaile,
who had died ten years before, saying that none could forget
'the classic elegance, the attic taste, the chaste refinement,
the placid virtue and the Gospel simplicity of . . . the learned
and venerable Mulcaile'. Father Mulcaile had continued to
work in St Michan's, where in his own words, 'between a
confessional , a pulpit and a school, and the care of a parish
and a number of other daily avocations I am day after day at
the oar, rowing for life'. Among his concerns was the
promotion of education for poor girls and he played a large
part in encouraging the foundation of the Presentation
Convent for this purpose at George's Hill in his parish.

   Education, indeed, seems integral to the Jesuit story.
Almost from the beginning, teaching was, of course, a prominent element of the Society's mission but the conditions of
life and ministry in seventeenth and eighteenth century
Ireland did not allow the Jesuits to run their schools there in
the same way as those on the continent. Saint Ignatius had
laid it down in the Constitutions — the body of directives

which he drew up for the Society and which amount to its
basic law — that reading and writing should not ordinarily be
taught because, although it would be a work of charity, the
Society was limited in numbers and could not attend to
everything.[92] 'In a typical case, a boy might receive his
elementary education from tutors at the ages of 5 through 9,
then enter a Jesuit university and study languages from 10
through 13, arts from 14 through 16, and theology from 17
through 21. . .'.[93] Such a schema incorporated the concepts
of school, college and university proper, and would be elaborated in greater detail after the death of Saint Ignatius in the
Ratio Studiorum, the Jesuit plan of education, but even in its
general intention it clearly involved a system far more ordered
and sophisticated than was imaginable in a country where for
most of the time Catholics were prohibited by law from
having schools at all and Jesuits were not in theory, and often
enough not in practice, allowed by law even to exist. The
remoteness from Irish reality becomes more obvious still
when it is realised that for Saint Ignatius languages and arts,
or 'humane letters', covered grammar, rhetoric, poetry, history,
Latin, Greek and Hebrew.[94] To these should be added where
'necessary or useful' other languages 'such as Chaldaic, Arabic
and Indian'.[95] Obviously the additional languages offered as
examples would not be 'necessary or useful' in Ireland, but
the principle involved had equal application to instruction in
English and/or Irish. Nor was that all. 'Logic, physics, metaphysics and moral philosophy should be treated, and also
mathematics in the measure appropriate to the end which is
being sought.'[96]

It may be objected that the full range of studies was meant
only for members of the Society proceeding to the priesthood, charged with aiding 'our fellowmen to the knowledge
and love of God and to the salvation of souls',[97] and that the
other studies were really envisaged as prerequisites to 'both
the learning of theology and the use of it'.[98] True, Ignatius
saw the training of Jesuits in this light. Apart from the brief
establishment of novitiates in Dublin and Kilkenny, no
extended courses of study for Jesuits were provided in
Ireland before the nineteenth century and it might therefore
be supposed that the Ignatian principles did not arise. But

the Society had from the beginning much wider educational objectives than merely training its own members. Schools open to the public were to be established 'at least in humane letters, and in more advanced subjects in accordance with the possibility which obtains in the regions where such colleges are situated'.[99] It was on this basis that the provision of schools was undertaken with such persistence wherever the Society gained a foothold. And since the minimum objective of the schools was to be the provision of 'humane letters', the intended extent of the curriculum in them was formidable, to say the least. It was made no more easy by the further requirement that 'extern students' should be 'well instructed in what pertains to Christian doctrine' and that 'they acquire along with their letters the habits of conduct worthy of a Christian'.[100]

The sheer improbability that such directives could be substantially carried out in penal Ireland would surely have deterred the Jesuits from even trying, were it not for the practicality and pragmatism of their Founder. He took care to qualify his instructions by making extensive allowance for local circumstance. Thus, 'when there are some things in the service of the Lord which are more urgent, and others which are less pressing and can suffer postponement . . . the first ought to be preferred'[101] and 'when there are some things which are especially incumbent upon the Society or it is seen that there are no others to attend to them, and other things in regard to which others do have care . . . in choosing missions there is reason to prefer the first to the second'.[102] The urgency of making education available to Irish Catholics, identified as early as the Elizabethan era by the Gaelic chieftains, and the permanent shortage of trained teachers — especially of teachers trained to the remarkably high level of so many Jesuits — left no room to quibble when it came to choosing the primary mission to be carried out in Ireland. Certainly there were other schools, but never remotely enough, so when it came to doing what they could to serve the needs of the hard-pressed Irish Church, the single most important contribution which the small band of Irish Jesuits could make was in education. By the same token, the educational need embraced the whole spectrum from the most elementary to the most advanced parts of the curriculum. Among the poor children of Dublin we may take it for certain that Father Betagh's Free School taught reading and writing. In the classical school which he inherited, as it were, from Father Austin with its boarding department attached, we may be equally certain that logic, metaphysics and theology were covered as well as Latin and Greek: otherwise its courses would have been unlikely to satisfy the Archbishop of Dublin and the Bishop of Meath who used it for training some of their clerical students in the absence of a seminary. And finally, we need have no doubt that Saint Ignatius would have approved this response to the demands of Irish circumstances since flexible adaptation to meet actual needs took precedence in his thinking over guidelines intended to help but not to constrict.

It should not therefore surprise us to hear that Father Murphy, a little earlier, was teaching Latin and philosophy in Saint Michan's parish. That is to say, it should not surprise us to find that Father Murphy *aspired* to teach Latin and philosophy. How he did it remains something of a mystery, as also does the approach of Father Austin and Father Betagh to their various endeavours. For simple lessons in literacy, addition and subtraction, no doubt slates, chalk, a lead marking pencil sufficed, although reading would have required a chart or a few books which could be passed around. But Latin and Greek, more advanced mathematics, and even introductory courses in philosophy and theology, would have required text-books for study, some literary and spiritual works, paper, quills and ink for exercises, time and quiet for study, opportunities for tutorial sessions . . . the mind reels at the thought of how these basic requirements could be met in Fishamble Street or Mary's Lane. The answer *has* to be that there was a gradation among the students, the poor in the Free School getting by with slate and chalk, the sons of the merchant classes (trade being the activity in which Catholics were best able to prosper)[103] attending the equally free classical schools but providing themselves with the necessary text-books, writing requisites and so on. It is reasonable also to suppose that the parish priests helped; some of them accumulated good libraries[104] which we may suppose would have been at the disposal of senior pupils. But still more remains to be explained. There is reason to believe, for example, that Father Betagh used to reserve places in the classical school for the brightest boys among those who studied by night in cold cellars:[105] somehow, they had to be supported. How was it done?

In the end we can only stand in awe of the implications behind the simple sentence in the obituaries of so many Irish Jesuits, 'he opened a school'. The reality of doing so, and especially of achieving anything remotely resembling continental standards, was immense. It did not deter Fathers Austin, Betagh or Mulcaile. They responded to a need with all the dedication their Founder would have expected of them and they brought to the task certain personal characteristics which it may not be irrelevant to underline. Look back to the tributes paid them by visitors to Ireland and by Dr Blake in his sermon. Read again Father Mulcaile's brief note on his labours. Making every allowance for kindly reminiscence, the good habitually acknowledged in the dead and the determined cheerfulness of a man under severe pressure, the image left with us of these three Fathers is that of quintessential Jesuits. The best qualities of the Society can all be felt here: a slightly distant dignity, solid scholarship, assurance in controversy with precision of argument and clarity of speech; concern to advance the faith and to serve with controlled passion the cause of justice. By no means every Jesuit combines the totality of these characteristics, but the three remarkable priests so dedicated to the Church and people of Georgian Dublin combined them. And as it happens, every man of them had ceased to be a Jesuit long years before his Master called him home.

Pope Clement XIV suppressed the Society of Jesus in August, 1773. Such a momentous decision, involving some 23,000 Jesuits, hundreds of schools and colleges, many universities, foreign missions across three continents, charitable institutes and other work for the poor, not to mention a deep mine of scholarship at the Church's disposal for the elaboration of its message, has clamoured down the centuries for adequate explanation. That the root-and-branch abolition was ordered by the Pope, to whose service the Society was especially dedicated and in the service of whose predecessors so many spiritual sons of Saint Ignatius had died martyrs' deaths, makes what happened all the more incredible. It can easily enough be said that a weak papacy submitted to sustained pressure from the governments of leading Catholic countries which had fallen under the sway of atheists, agnostics and freethinkers, unbelievers bent on destroying the Catholic Church — and to that end, destroying the Jesuits as the most formidable embodiment of Catholic power and influence. There is truth in this. Such attitudes, abetted by public men who were themselves practising Catholics but who resented the prestige and independence of the Jesuits, brought about the preliminary moves against the Society, the expulsion of the Jesuits between 1759 and 1768 from Portugal, France, Spain (yes, Spain!), from the Kingdom of Naples and the little Italian duchy of Parma.

It cannot be denied that leading personalities in the Age of Enlightenment saw the elimination of the Jesuits as the major step to be taken in undermining the Church, in shaking off 'the yoke which in the centuries of barbarism had been imposed by the court of Rome on the childish credulity of princes and peoples'.[106] Voltaire said that 'once we have destroyed the Jesuits we shall have the game in our hands'.[107] After the Society had been thrown out of France, the Voltairean d'Alembert wrote: 'The Jesuits were the regular troops, recruited and disciplined under the standard of superstition. They were the Macedonian phalanx which it behoved Reason to see broken up and destroyed'.[108] Nor can it be denied that some at least of the politicians involved intended ultimately the demolition of the Church itself, or at least its containment under their control as a department of state. Pombal, the Portuguese chief minister, claimed that by attacking the Jesuits he was showing the Bourbons 'how to negotiate with Rome':[109] various branches of the Bourbons ruled France, Spain, Naples and Parma, so his boast was quickly borne out. Significantly, in Spain once the Jesuits were gone the King ordered that all papal bulls, edicts and other messages addressed to his subjects had to be cleared by his council before they could be published.[110] Nor were these governments satisfied to be rid of the Jesuits from their monarchs' dominions. They relentlessly badgered the Pope to suppress the order completely. And so inexorably to *Dominus ac Redemptor*, the decree of 1773.

It came about thus, but the story cannot really be told in terms of scapegoats. The Suppression of the Jesuits was the culmination of an illness within the Church itself, a kind of paralysis, the onset of which can be traced back to the early seventeenth century and even to the Catholic Reformation — the Counter-Reformation, if you will. It was as if the great effort of renewal had so fatigued the Church that it felt it could rest on its oars with the Protestants confounded, the faults of the old Church cleared away, the Tridentine formulas defining the faith and obligations of Catholics with precision. Of course, the energy took time to slacken. Great theologians took up the themes of the day, great missionaries preached salvation beyond the oceans, institutes of learning were set up and Trent was eighty years gone before the boundaries of Catholic and Protestant Europe were finally settled. But the slackening began early enough. We have noticed the stultification of Spanish theology. France replaced Spain as the centre of vibrant Catholicism. But France was soon producing mutants of Roman belief. We have noticed the nationalism of the Gallicans, the puritanism of the Jansenists, the pragmatism of *cujus regio, ejus religio* which gave religious liberty to rulers but not to the ruled. Rome condemned and solemnly protested but, perhaps fearing to provoke another cataclysmic revolt on the scale of Luther's, failed to keep up its resistance.

The Gallicans, the Jansenists, the indifferentists, should have been answered in their own coin with a case equally well presented, offering contemporary thoughts on contemporary questions. To accommodate to the latest intellectual or popular fashion would, of course, have been no way to cope with the new attitudes emerging in philosophy from Descartes to Kant or stimulated by the discoveries of physical science associated with Galileo, Newton, Lavoisier. But neither was it helpful to atrophy, as if the last word had been said and the Church had only to repeat its inherited wisdom to satisfy the questing spirit of the age. It left its response to plodding, sub-standard apologists. 'The fact that Holy Church had no one like Pascal, Bossuet or Fénelon to defend her against Voltaire, Diderot and Rousseau was undoubtedly her most serious defect in the Age of Enlightenment, and the principal cause of her eclipse.'[111] The eighteenth-century Church thus fell behind the world for it failed to delve into its repository of truth to find the relevant aspects to stress, to explore for itself the wider meaning of its beliefs, so that it could speak to contemporary men and women in the language of the time. That neglect virtually invited thinking people to look elsewhere for their answers or to work out answers for themselves without the aid of faith. In this way the Catholic Church was in no small measure a progenitor of the Enlightenment.

Corresponding to the Church's failure to match the needs of the age, the absolutist monarchies of Europe, with their extensions in Asia, Africa and the Americas, failed also to allow for the more thoughtful among their subjects. In Spain and France, not to mention the American colonies under the British crown, impatience grew among the intelligent, the ambitious, the seekers after justice, who saw themselves frozen out from the right to make decisions affecting their own welfare by the unmerited privileges of aristocracy, or the baseless claims of autocrats to unquestioning loyalty, or the selfishness of people with access to patronage. Late in the day, too late to avert revolution in the last decade of the century, some of the autocrats sensed the need for reform and looked to men of modern outlook to save their regimes for them. The modern men were men of the Enlightenment, and they measured the situation they found by Enlightenment standards. To see these standards as evil is to forget the part played by the Church in bringing them about. If men made Reason their measure it was at least in part because faith — or rather, the custodian of faith — had failed them. Today we can see that the freethinkers, the Deists, hit upon truths touching the freedom of the individual — freedom of speech, freedom of worship, freedom of conscience — that could and should have been advanced by the Church but were not. Instead, the Church bolstered up the outdated autocracies and drew upon itself the contumely of those determined to expunge from the body politic what they saw — in most cases, honestly if mistakenly saw — as the cause of its corruption.

Because France was intellectually the most alive, this coincidence of tendencies went further in France than anywhere else. Where others became anticlerical, French thinkers became antichristian. 'The spirit of Voltaire had already been long in the world: but Voltaire, in truth, could never have attained his supremacy, except in the eighteenth century and in France'.[112] Elsewhere, systems were to be reformed; in France the cult of Reason was building up the case for blowing apart the system itself. The crisis would not come for another quarter century but already the French Church stood exposed to the logic of Enlightenment philosophers:

> The Church rested principally upon tradition; they professed great contempt for all institutions based upon respect for the past. The Church recognised an authority superior to individual reason; they appealed to nothing but that reason. The Church was founded upon a hierarchy; they aimed at an entire subversion of ranks. To have come to a common understanding it would have been necessary for both sides to have recognised the fact that political and religious society, being by nature essentially different, cannot be regulated by analogous laws. But at that time they were far enough from any such conclusion; and it was fancied that, in order to attack the institutions of the State, those of the Church must be destroyed which served as their foundation and their model.[113]

The Society of Jesus invited attack sooner than other institutions. It was the most forward bulwark of the Church, the champion of faith against unqualified reason, of authority against incipient revolution. The indolent King Louis XV defended it, but the powerful magistracy — shot through with Enlightenment values — defied him and pulled it down.[114] They had the help of Church elements long opposed by the Jesuits: the Jansenists whom the Jesuits had indicted for heresy; the Gallicans whom, foolishly, they had sought to placate while denying them the intimate alliance of Throne and Altar which alone would satisfy the advocates of a national church. In throwing their weight behind the destruction of the Jesuits these Catholic forces only advanced the day of their own downfall. 'Let the Jansenist rabble rid us of the Jesuit blackguards,' wrote d'Alembert to Voltaire, 'do not put anything in the way of these spiders gobbling one another up.'[115] And after the Jesuits were gone: 'The Jansenists are merely the Cossacks and the Pandours whom Reason will make cheap work of once they have to fight alone.'[116] So, over the long haul, it would happen. It can fairly be argued that in the expulsion of the Jesuits from France we hear the first rumble of the French Revolution, the first downward swish of the guillotine blade.

How far were the Jesuits to blame for their own misfortune? They can certainly be said to have been the victims of their very success. Their proximity to kings and princes, who liked to have them as confessors;[117] their installation in so many university chairs,[118] their pre-eminence on the foreign missions where they enjoyed access to potentates like the Emperor of China[119] and organised 'small republics'[120] in Paraguay to protect the local people from exploitation, did nothing to make them popular with the friars or the secular priesthood or civil administrators. Neither did their presence in many offices of the Roman Curia,[121] nor the fact that as the eighteenth century progressed they were among the very few religious orders to be still growing in number.[122] In their time of trial they had few influential friends other, it must be acknowledged, than the bishops of France[123] and oddly — but providentially, as will be seen — the Protestant King of Prussia and the Orthodox (but really agnostic) Empress of All the Russias. It was the widespread dislike and suspicion directed against the Jesuits, and born of an inchoate jealousy, which made it easy for the Portuguese to take the first step towards the Suppression: they found their pretext in a re-alignment of Latin-American colonial frontiers where the Jesuits were conducting their most imaginative experiments in creating self-sufficient Christian communities.[124]

It may be that the Society overall by the mid-eighteenth century was wanting in discretion, unable to see the enmity it was engendering against itself. But in its character and in its good works it gave no cause for condemnation, nor much

ground for criticism. It was not the griping of the less successful which toppled the Society. It was the spirit of the age,
the Age of Enlightenment, of Reason. Because the Church
as a whole had abdicated any part in the evolution of ideas
going on around it, it lacked the power and ultimately the
will to save the Jesuits to whom it owed so much for their
loyalty even unto death. That the Bourbon powers —
France, Spain and Naples — continued mercilessly to bully
Pope Clement cannot be denied, nor that he apprehended
the danger of schismatic churches emerging in these
countries as had happened in England long before. The
papal brief suppressing the Society of Jesus therefore spoke
of the disharmony which troubled the Church and which
centred on the very existence of the Jesuits; but it did not,
for it could not, blame the Jesuit Fathers for bringing this
disharmony about. They were in fact to be sacrificed to
buy time for a Church beset by rampant infidelity. 'The
whole history of the Papacy can show no other example of
such craven cowardice.'[125] No, indeed. But distant echoes
could be heard. 'Truth? What is that? . . . . I can find no case
against him. . . . If you set him free you are no friend of
Caesar's. . . '.[126]

The expelled and suppressed Jesuits suffered many tribulations. They were forcibly removed in their hundreds from
Portugal and Spain, to be dumped upon the shores of the
Papal States. In France and elsewhere, including Rome, they
had the option of becoming secular priests. Some, including
Father Lorenzo Ricci, the General, were imprisoned without
charge. Everywhere their property was seized and retained
by the state, handed over to other orders or given to the
local bishop. For many, if not most, of the Fathers, suppression meant destitution. There was neither employment
nor money to sustain such a sudden influx to the secular
priesthood; for the Brothers it was even worse, since they
had fewer opportunities to find means of support. In France
it became fashionable to take an ex-Jesuit into one's family:
Voltaire, surprisingly, provided a home for Father Antoine
Adam.[127] The English Jesuits underwent a series of migra-
tions.[128] Their principal activity had become the provision of
education for Catholic boys from England in their highly-

regarded college at St-Omer. This they lost at the time of the
expulsion from France, although the college continued under
English secular priests. The Jesuits and most of their pupils
set up house at Bruges, then in the Austrian Netherlands,
only to be expelled again when the order was suppressed, the
boys having first rioted in protest! The Prince-Bishop of Liège
allowed them to keep the school in being, attached to a seminary with English Jesuit associations in his little statelet. The
respite was welcome, although the Jesuits were now secular
priests and other seculars were mingled in with them. In the
1790s, as the French revolutionary armies approached Liège,
the entire assemblage of boys, seminarists, ex-Jesuits and
seculars made their way back to England and a new home at
Stonyhurst in Lancashire where enduring fame all unknown
awaited them. . . .

The momentous happenings on the continent affected the
Irish Mission together with their Jesuit brethren everywhere.[129] The first blow came when the Society was expelled
from Spain and France. The Irish Jesuits lost their college
appointments and their own college at Poitiers. These
developments disrupted the supply of Jesuits for service in
Ireland — not least because the number of Irish Jesuits
working at home was limited to as many as could be supported
from funds abroad, and the funds were in France and Spain.
Even if they had the means of supporting a local novitiate,
the Mission could not now open one as the Holy See had
issued an instruction that the Irish entrants to religious orders
were to undergo their training in continental novitiates — a
decision intended to regulate the affairs of the friars[130] but
binding, accidentally as it were, on the Society. As a result,
the number of Jesuits on the Irish Mission fell and only
nineteen were to hand when the Brief of Suppression (technically involving two documents) was promulgated in 1773.
Archbishop John Carpenter of Dublin reported to the Nuncio
in Brussels that there were eleven Jesuits in Dublin, one each
in the dioceses of Ferns (Wexford), Meath (Drogheda) and
Limerick, two in Cork and three in Waterford.[131] Over the
early months of the new year, the Archbishop collected the
signatures of the eleven in Dublin to a document declaring

that they accepted the papal directive and put themselves at his disposal as secular priests; to these the Archbishop added the name of Father Edward Keating who had made his submission to Bishop Nicholas Sweetman of Ferns,[132] in whose diocese he served as a parish priest. Five submitted to the Bishop of Waterford and the others presumably to the Bishops of Limerick and Meath.

The pain of the Irish Fathers can well be imagined, with all their memories of student days and classroom duties in Spain or France, their dedication to the way of life of the order which they had embraced with such enthusiasm, and to the pastoral and educational work undertaken at home in Ireland for the greater glory of God in the spirit of Saint Ignatius. It so happened, however, that the Irish Mission was by now so thoroughly occupied with assisting the diocesan clergy that the Suppression raised few of the problems for its members that faced Jesuits in other countries. For the most part they remained at their posts, doing what they had been engaged upon before the tragic news arrived from Rome. Thus, Fathers Austin, Betagh and Mulcaile continued with their parochial and teaching activities, their colleagues in Waterford continued to serve the people of St Patrick's parish, Father Clement Kelly continued to be parish priest of Maynooth — against his will but by the Archbishop's directive at the request of the Duke of Leinster who, although a Protestant, seems to have enjoyed having a resident Jesuit on his estate. Apart from personal anguish, therefore, the transition from Jesuit to diocesan status should have come about more smoothly in Ireland than anywhere else. So it might, had there been no question of property.

It was not that the Irish Jesuits owned very much. But they got occasional donations and benefactions which they managed to retain despite the particularly severe provisions of the penal code. They sometimes made loans out of these funds to trustworthy Catholics, who accepted the moral obligation to discharge the debt and commonly went through the motions of securing it by granting the Fathers a mortgage on the borrower's house. A mortgage between Catholics was legally unenforceable but the Jesuits were happy to rely on the borrower's honesty in return for the convenience of being able to put money aside against a rainy day, beyond the reach of 'discoverers' sniffing around in search of trusts or legacies made contrary to law. At the time of the Suppression the Irish Mission held such a mortgage on the estate of Castlebrowne in County Kildare (a place with which, as it happened, the Jesuits were destined to have a much closer and longer association in the future). The mortgagee, the owner of Castlebrowne, was dying and he owed the Mission £1,600. He was prevailed upon to compound the debt with Archbishop Carpenter for £300, on the representation that what had belonged to the Jesuits now belonged to the bishop to whom they were subject. The Archbishop refused a request from the ex-Jesuits that he give them some part of this sum — so much less than what they had been owed — and instead asked Rome to approve his using it for the benefit of the Irish Colleges abroad;[133] Rome agreed and suggested that it be sent on for the use of the Irish College in that city. The Archbishop replied that he would transmit the money when it was prudent to do so; he had to be on his guard against spies who might start a legal process, he said.

The Castlebrowne debt makes a sad little story. Here was a handful of hardworking priests, shattered by what had just been done to the order to which they had dedicated their lives, quite unsure of their future, anxious only to secure themselves a pittance (as would become clear from what they did next) and see that funds donated to them were put to the kind of use which the donors would have approved. Instead of showing them the sympathy which in all justice (not to mention charity) they were entitled to expect, the Archbishop pursued a debt they had not even called in, agreed to its liquidation for a fraction of its value and denied them any part of the proceeds. It can be said in fairness to the Archbishop that he did not act out of greed: otherwise he would hardly have settled for so small a figure nor would he have offered to send the money abroad. His wish seems to have been rather to rid himself as quickly as possible of any troublesome consequences of the Suppression. The disposal of property in penal Ireland was particularly troublesome, and the nineteen ex-Jesuits had individual claims at least as valid as that which could be advanced by the diocese of

Dublin: neither body had legal corporate status, nor could the mortgage be foreclosed, but the return of the money owed might be sought as repayment of a simple loan. To avoid fuss with the Jesuits, the law, or both, the expedient approach was therefore to tackle the problem at once and dispose of whatever was disposable. The Archbishop may also have felt that by absorbing the Dublin Jesuits into his parochial clergy he was providing for them adequately; if this was his stance he forgot that he already had the benefit of their services, for which they were entitled to sensitive treatment, and that there were ex-Jesuits in other dioceses for whose security he could not answer.

Archbishop Carpenter's lack of concern for the ex-Jesuits' feelings was not uncommon among higher ecclesiastics. The Bishop of Bruges did nothing to help the English school, although he would not have annoyed the civil authorities had he come to their aid since the Empress Maria Theresa had affection for the order and personally deplored the Suppression. The Church authorities in Spain and Portugal offered little support, despite the harsh imprisonment of some members of the Society, and any who felt squeamish about turning their backs on the Fathers in their travail had on]y to look to Rome where the Pope held Father Ricci in a cell of the Castel Sant' Angelo until the ex-General died — having solemnly protested his own and the Society's innocence as the consecrated Host was held before him.[134] There were notable exceptions, however. The Bishop of Liège saved the English school-cum-seminary and in England itself the Vicars Apostolic — the bishops who administered the Catholic Church in the country without local title — showed the ex-Jesuits much kindness. Bishop Hornyold, one of the Vicars Apostolic, wrote to console a distressed Father of the Society and added, 'As to the temporalities which belong to your late body . . . those who have care or administration of them will go on in the same manner as they were used to do.'

Not all the Irish bishops shared the unfeeling attitude of their brother of Dublin. It is said that Archbishop Anthony Blake of Armagh and Bishop James O'Keeffe of Kildare (in whose diocese Castlebrowne was situated) remonstrated strongly with Carpenter over his seizure of the debt. The most sturdy defence of the Jesuits, however, was made by Bishop Nicholas Sweetman of Ferns. His letter to the Archbishop appears to have been destroyed but we can judge its temper from Carpenter's reply urging the Bishop to show 'respectful acquiescence' to the papal brief and saying that the ex-Jesuits had 'now become members of the most perfect and illustrious body of men that ever was or will be on the face of the earth, and one that has never suffered or will suffer either dissolution or suppression'.[135] Once more, the insensitivity strikes the reader: the Jesuits are to feel honoured that they have been accepted into the secular clergy, regardless of the fact that their God-given vocations had led them in another direction, now frustrated by the action of the Pope.

It makes unhappy reading, not least because of Archbishop Carpenter's excellence in other respects:[136] as a promoter of Catholic publishing, of sound expositions of the faith in Irish as well as English, of discipline among his priests (whom he ordered, *inter alia*, to keep out of 'public tap-rooms').[137] The ex-Jesuits, together with the proto-type trade unions of the day,[138] probably had the misfortune to run into the sterner side of his nature which left little room for normal human emotions when obedience was demanded to ecclesiastical rules, regulations and norms as interpreted by the Archbishop. He does not seem to have objected to ex-Jesuits as such: he favoured the appointment as Bishop of Limerick of Father Laurence Nihell, a former Jesuit who was parish priest of Rathkeale. To complicate matters, the Archbishop of Cashel's candidate was Father John Butler, another former Jesuit but of the English province although he belonged to an aristocratic Irish family. Father Butler turned down the appointment when it was offered to him, apparently because he felt he might then be prevented from re-entering the Society if it were restored.[139] Father Nihell became Bishop of Kilfenora.

The possibility of restoration was never far from the minds of the ex-Jesuits and in Ireland they took early steps to provide for it. The Archbishop's attitude, combined with the constant jeopardy in which the penal laws left the property of religious orders, called for some arrangement which would ensure that the remaining funds of the Mission were preserved for the benefit of a revived Society of Jesus in Ireland. Although no longer bound by Jesuit obedience or by the Society's Constitutions, the ex-Jesuits had maintained their links with one another. They looked upon the last Superior of the Mission, Father John Ward, as the leader of their informal group and with their approval he continued to administer the Mission's money. This had consisted mainly of a capital sum of £10,000 which the Mission had (presumably on some form of deposit) in Paris about the year 1760. This may have been money from French sources for the support of the College at Poitiers or it may simply have been donations to the Mission which had been transferred to the continent as a safer place to keep them than penal Ireland. In any event, the expulsion of the Jesuits from France in 1764, together with the sequestration of their property, left these Irish funds at risk and in fact half the money was lost. The remaining £5,000 was rescued through 'the activity and cleverness of a Mr Crookshanks': this seems to refer to Father Alexander Crookshanks, Rector of the Scots College at Douai. What exactly the resourceful Father Crookshanks did, we do not know, but he remitted the rescued funds to the Superior of the Irish Mission. Hence they were under the control of Father Ward at the Suppression.

Father Ward died in 1775 having made his former Jesuit colleague, Father John Fullam, his executor and residuary legatee. The Mission funds thus passed to Father Fullam, who proposed a very practical scheme for their preservation to the former members of the Mission. Under this arrangement, Father Fullam would retain control of the money and any donations which might be added to it with the possible restoration of the Society in mind. He would be answerable for the prudent administration of the funds to a committee of three Irish ex-Jesuits who would certify to the others that they were receiving satisfactory assurances from Father Fullam in the matter. Father Fullam, in turn, would transfer or bequeath the property eventually to a person approved by the committee who would then hold it on the same basis as Father Fullam. In this way the fund would be preserved, with few people having any detailed knowledge of its whereabouts. As to the disposition of the money, it was agreed that the capital would be retained intact to be handed over to the Superior-General of the restored Society of Jesus and used as he might direct. The interest was to be available for the incidental expenses of administering the fund and to provide an annuity for life to the former members of the Mission. Clearly, the annuities would be small at the outset, but as the ex-Jesuits died, the proportion going to each survivor would grow. A ceiling of £50 was therefore agreed as the maximum annuity to be paid; if that left interest over and above expenses, it was to go back to the main fund. When only three former members of the Mission were living, and if there then appeared to be no likelihood that the Society would soon be restored, they were empowered to apply the funds to 'such pious foundations' as seemed to them conducive to the greater glory of God and the spiritual advantage of the Irish Church.

It was a comprehensive, well-thought-out plan and it worked remarkably well. The fund in fact grew substantially, not least because as secular priests the ex-Jesuits were no longer bound by a vow of poverty and could acquire property themselves, which they were then able to pass on to the central fund. Father Fullam had a number of wealthy friends, through whose contributions he was able to double what was left of the fund when he received it. He also came into money in his own right, for he bequeathed the handsome sum of £50 per annum for ten years to the relief of the former Jesuits of the Province of Lyons, where he had studied, and made a similar bequest to the Jesuits of Russia where, as shall be explained, the Society survived. Father Ward, before his death, had already applied some of the Mission's funds to the assistance of Italian ex-Jesuits. Other good causes were helped as well. It is surely cause for admiration that the most impoverished, and for long the most persecuted, of the European branches of the Society was so ready to be generous out of the detritus of its own destruction. Meanwhile the capital, augmented from various sources, was passed on in accordance with the agreement, coming eventually into the care of Father Richard O'Callaghan. He was to live long enough to see the prospects of restoration greatly enhanced and he acted accordingly. . . .

Meanwhile, the ex-Jesuits came together in Dublin every six months or so if circumstances permitted, so that they might never drift too far apart from one another. Otherwise they got on with their appointed tasks as secular priests. For most, as we have seen, it involved no change and the greater number of them had completed many years of fruitful pastoral work when they passed away. Father Michael Fitz-Gerald reached the patriarchal age of 97 before he died in Waterford, where he had spent so much of his ministry. Father Lisward, the promoter of the Sacred Heart devotions, retired to the Augustinian house at John's Lane in Dublin. Fathers Austin, Betagh and Mulcaile, the Dublin education-alists, kept their schools in being and Father Betagh, the longest to survive of all the old Mission, became parish priest of St Michael and St John's and later Vicar General of Dublin under the Dominican Archbishop, John Thomas Troy. Dr Troy's successor, incidentally, would be Archbishop Daniel Murray, a former pupil of Father Austin's. An even more famous pupil of another ex-Jesuit was Daniel O'Connell who attended for a time the school run near the Cove of Cork (now Cobh) by Father James Harrington. At least, Father Harrington is said to have been a Jesuit secularised at the time of the Suppression.[140] His name does not appear on the chronological list of priests associated with the Irish Mission referred to earlier, and he was not among those who signed the submission to the papal brief in Ireland. But it happened from time to time that young Irishmen entered the novitiate of a foreign Province of the Society and remained attached to that Province. Upon the Suppression it would have been natural for such Irish priests to come home, and school-mastering would have been a natural occupation for them to take up.

By the mid-1790s the French Revolution was running its course in all its grandeur and horror. The worthy percep-tions of the Enlightenment had been given juridical form in the Constitution of the United States and the Declaration of the Rights of Man. Its shortcomings and arrogance were becoming patently visible in the egalitarianism which seemed to mean that all citizens were equally potential victims of the guillotine. The national Church had been set up in France, only to be overshadowed by the quasi-religion of Reason. Neither lasted long and it was becoming clear that Voltaire had deceived himself when he claimed to have done more in his time than Luther and Calvin: 'He wished, like them, to change the reigning religion, he acted the part of a founder of a sect',[141] but in fact his talent was that of the witty epigrammist who could 'put into handy little phrases the greatest discoveries and the greatest ideas of the human intellect, the theories of Descartes, Malebranche, Leibniz, Locke and Newton, the different religions of antiquity and modern times, all the known systems of physics, physiology, geology, morals, natural law, political economy. . .'.[142] As he bemused his age, the moving spirit of the Enlightenment bemused himself, but a brilliant way with words was no foundation for a new religion any more than was a competence in encapsulating other people's thoughts. It was as well the old philosopher did not live to see where his cult of Reason was to lead. There is a case for saying that what he hated was neither Christianity nor the Church but clericalism — the abuse by authoritarian priests of their role in the Church. Not that the Jesuits were the prime offenders in that regard, not by any means. . . . But they paid for the blindness of others.

The Enlightenment was waning, then, destroyed by the extreme application of its logic in the most logical nation on earth. It would be pleasing to say that the wisdom of centuries was reasserting itself and true religion, purged of its lassitude, was regaining its place in what used to be called Christendom. Of course, the pendulum did not so easily swing. The Catholic Church took much longer to recognise the elements of truth in the revolution, and the revolution took as long to acknowledge that faith was a reality in the hearts of men and women everywhere. But the tendency was there, the shoots of new growth, the possibility of religious renaissance. The Society of Jesus would have its part to play in this revival. But was the Society not dead, abolished, suppressed? The answer, miraculously, was that it had never been totally demolished. It lived on, its traditions unbroken, in the most unexpected corner of Europe. And elderly ex-Jesuits elsewhere were alert to what this meant. In England, they seized an opportunity.

In Ireland, Father O'Callaghan and Father Betagh agreed on what should be done. Like Moses, they were shown the promised land but not permitted to enter it. That privilege was reserved for the first Irish Jesuit in the modern mould, the first whose voice we can catch, whose mind we can enter, whose personality we can know in the round and not as an intriguing embodiment of biographical snippets.

4

NEW BEGINNINGS

IN 1772 the Empress Catherine II of Russia joined with King Frederick II of Prussia and the Empress Maria Theresa of Austria in the cynical exercise known as the First Partition of Poland. Each of the three monarchs annexed (i.e. stole) a large segment of the Kingdom of Poland adjoining his or her own dominions. Weak and divided among themselves, the Poles could not resist. Poland being largely a Catholic country (although it did have a number of Protestant and Orthodox subjects, to whom it had only very recently allowed political rights,)[1] this meant that the Russian Empire acquired over a million members of the Roman Church[2] — and 201 Jesuits, belonging to the Polish and Lithuanian Provinces of the Society, together with four Jesuit Colleges.[3] Although Jesuits were officially banned from Russia proper, the Empress was pleased with her acquisition because of the order's work in education and she decided that the Fathers should be encouraged to continue this apostolate in the former territories of Poland now attached to the region known as Byelorussia or White Russia. Interestingly, Frederick had the same opinion of the Jesuits and supported them in Silesia, which he had obtained under an earlier treaty, as well as in the West Prussian territory ceded by Poland.

Both Frederick and Catherine were typical figures of the Enlightenment and adherents of Voltairean philosophy. Insofar as either had any religion (in each case a formality demanded by their position), the one was a Protestant and the other Russian Orthodox. Their interest in the Jesuits was therefore, on the face of it, surprising. It can only be explained by saying that two of the better aspects of the Enlightenment were the concern it stimulated in rulers to ensure the provision of good schools and the realism which enabled the so-called 'enlightened despots' to overlook mere inconsistency if it secured a benefit for the state. It was also, of course, easier for rulers to apply such norms to the Jesuits in countries where Catholics formed a relatively small minority of the total population. Anti-Catholic paranoia had little relevance where the Church neither exercised much influence nor could be alleged to do so.

The Brief of Suppression arrived in Russia and Prussia the year after the First Partition. In both countries the rulers immediately decreed that it was not to be promulgated (that is, officially communicated to Catholics by their bishops and declared to be in force). This raised a problem of conscience for the Jesuits in question. Their loyalty to the Pope impelled them to obey his clear wish that they should disband. But the self-same obedience towards the Holy See obliged them to remain in being and at their posts until the local bishop not only promulgated the document but notified each Jesuit community in his diocese that they were suppressed in accordance with the Brief: the instructions from Rome accompanying the document made this clear.[4] It was an important point. It can too readily be assumed — as some Jesuits, not to mention the members of other orders, assumed at the time — that a mere technicality of canon law was involved. The general canonical requirement that a papal instruction be promulgated before it becomes operative was strengthened in the case of the Suppression by a precise directive which had to be carried out before a Jesuit could consider himself released from his duties as a member of the Society. The superiors of the Jesuits in Russia and Prussia sought clarification from the Holy See, and the Prussian problem was speedily enough resolved. The King agreed to the suppression of the order when the Pope accepted that the former Jesuits could continue to function as before, and in particular to run their schools, but as secular priests under the bishops' control.[5]

Russia was another story. Catherine not only rejected all approaches but threatened to force Roman Catholics in the Russian Empire to join the Orthodox Church if 'her Jesuits' were interfered with![6] The new Pope, Pius VI, had no wish to provoke persecution, nor was he especially distressed to see the Jesuits surviving. Although he had to act with diplomatic care to avoid disturbing the Bourbon courts any more than could be helped, he made no attempt to dissuade the Jesuits of White Russia from teaching, preaching and living in accordance with the Jesuit Constitutions. He reprimanded the local bishop, to whom he had given authority over Latin-rite religious, for allowing the Jesuits to open a novitiate[7] but he refrained from forcing its closure, and while he told the Bourbons that he disapproved of the election of a vicar-general by the Russian Jesuits[8] he avoided telling the Jesuits themselves. The French Revolution followed, and the revolutionary wars. The King of France and his Queen were beheaded. Other Bourbons began to fear for the safety of their thrones. In the utterly changed world of 1801, Pope Pius VII, who had succeeded Pius VI, directed that the Jesuit superior in Russia be known as General of the Society of Jesus and no longer as only 'vicar-general'.[9]

It was not a restoration but it certainly amounted to a major act of recognition. The English ex-Jesuits, a number of them still members of the Stonyhurst community, wrote to the General in Russia seeking affiliation.[10] After some initial hesitation, this was granted with the Pope's cautious approval conveyed verbally to the General who, in 1803, appointed Father Marmaduke Stone as Provincial: Father Stone was President of the Liège College, so oddly situated in Lancashire. Just what he became Provincial of is less clear than might be supposed. As late as 1808 he was telling Archbishop Troy of Dublin that the English members of the Society were Jesuits in private but that in public they were secular priests![11] Whether this left the Archbishop much wiser is hard to say, but perhaps it was better not to insist on sharp definitions which might force the Pope to disown the goodwill he had shown towards the new development: Pope Pius had problems enough in the Europe of Napoleon, by whom he would soon be put under house-arrest and exiled to France. Meanwhile, a number of English ex-Jesuits had renewed their vows (with an Irishman, Father Peter O'Brien, in the first group) and a novitiate was opened at Hodder near Stonyhurst.

All this not only brought happiness to the two surviving ex-Jesuits in Ireland, Fathers Betagh and O'Callaghan, but it opened up important possibilities. Already they had picked out several young men at Father Betagh's school[12] who seemed to have vocations for the priesthood and sent them to the recently opened seminary for secular priests in Carlow.[13] Before they had completed their studies there, the Jesuit novitiate had been established at Hodder. Father Betagh and Father O'Callaghan transferred their students to the novitiate and arranged at the same time for a number of younger Irish boys to go to Stonyhurst in the expectation that they too would become novices. In this way, and even allowing for those who did not persevere, the nucleus of a new Irish Jesuit Mission was built up through the initiative of the two ageing men still toiling away in Dublin. Apparently because he held the office of Vicar-General, Father Betagh felt it would be inappropriate to re-join the Society; Father O'Callaghan renewed his vows and was re-admitted by Father Stone in England[14] but continued to live in Dublin, lodging with friends at Church Street; he was in his 77th year.

Before his death, Father O'Callaghan had one more task to perform. As the remaining trustee of the Mission funds he had to decide how they were to be disposed of. The original compact had preserved the money intact and it had been substantially augmented by a separate fund accumulated by Father Fullam and passed on by using his sister as executrix — a device for avoiding restrictions on bequests to religious orders. The proposed manner of dealing with the fund when only a few of the original Fathers were living had been reconsidered, altered and reconsidered again according as the prospects for restoration wavered. The net effect was to enable Father O'Callaghan to hand the entire fund to Father Stone, to hold in trust for the Irish Mission — which nobody, by 1804, doubted would be revived as soon as sufficient new Irish members of the Society had been ordained. As if to confirm the old man's optimism, a letter addressed to Father Betagh arrived from Russia in 1806. It was from the General, Father Tadeusz Brzozowski, who wrote of his pleasure at hearing about the good work 'which your Reverence, though advanced in years, is doing' and he urged him to 'prepare successors with your zeal and spirit from among those youths who are being educated in England'. The General went on to say that he thought the Society would be restored in Ireland 'though cautiously, prudently and without much ado'. If young men were prepared in good time, 'the Irish Church and the Society' would have 'labourers and soldiers prepared to fight the battles of the Lord'. And the General sent his regards 'to Father O'Callaghan, that apostolic man'. With this seal of approval and sign of hope, 'the apostolic man' could lay down his burden, satisfied that he had done right. Father O'Callaghan died in 1807 at the age of 79.

Already word had come from Father Stone that the Irish boys at Stonyhurst were, 'in general, doing very well, and some of them particularly so'. The English Provincial hoped that the more outstanding pupils would become 'learned and useful members in some future and flourishing College in Ireland'. But he could not say as much of all the Irish students, for he disliked receiving those 'advanced in age' or 'destitute of classical knowledge'. Whatever lack of discrimination there might have been in choosing boys for Stonyhurst, few doubts were expressed about the calibre of the students from Carlow sent to the novitiate at Hodder. Of these, none attracted more attention than Peter Kenney. The surviving Edwardian accounts of his early years blur with piosity a clear picture of how he came by his vocation. Perhaps, as is said, he used to address his friends with 'eloquence and unction, urging them on powerfully to the practice of virtue and the avoidance of vice', and perhaps also he used to repeat the sermon he heard at Sunday Mass for the benefit of his fellow-workers in the Dublin coachbuilder's yard where he worked as an apprentice. The administrative competence, pragmatism and practical spirituality which were to be characteristic of the mature man, however, suggest that these stories of his youth are legends which grew around his unquestionable power as an orator. If indeed he was dismissed by his master, allegedly for wasting the other apprentices' time with sermonising, the reason was more likely to have been the content of the sermon or the possible fear — strong among Dublin employers in those days — that a young man who could command an audience of workmates would next be forming a 'combination' or trade union. There would have had to be a substantial cause, sustainable in law, to justify the *prima facie* breach of contract involved in dismissing an apprentice.

Be that as it may, Father Betagh had noticed the young man's talents at the evening classes he attended and, suspecting he had a vocation, included him in the group chosen to go to Carlow and eventually to Hodder. It would be interesting to know how the prospective Jesuits were supported at these boarding establishments and it may not be unreasonable to suspect that Father O'Callaghan was able to help the more needy of them from the interest being earned by the Mission funds: there would certainly have been a surplus after the modest personal wants of Father Betagh and himself had been met. As a clerical student Kenney distinguished himself yet again in the art of public speaking. His address on the 'Dignity of the Priesthood' at Carlow was heard with 'rapt attention' while at Hodder he had to be dismissed from the refectory pulpit because he so distracted his listeners that they left their dinner uneaten! After his noviceship, he took courses in mathematics and physics for a spell at Stonyhurst and was then sent to study theology at the University of Palermo in Sicily. The Jesuits had been revived in the Kingdom of the Two Sicilies in 1804 at the request of the King and with the Pope's consent. The seizure of Naples by the French meant another expulsion shortly afterwards, but left the Society functioning on the island of Sicily which remained outside French control. Once again, Peter Kenney made his mark. Reports sent to Hodder referred to 'the incomparable Kenney' and recorded how even after only one year of the theology course he was speaking in the manner of a 'maestro'. When he completed his studies he was unable to take his doctorate because of the wartime difficulties in contacting the General, without whose permission Jesuits could not accept degrees, but the Chancellor of the University issued a formal document certifying that the Irish student had attained this standard and deserved the highest honours the University could confer.

Peter Kenney was ordained in 1808 and was sent to minister to Catholic British soldiers (no doubt mainly Irish) then stationed on the island as part of the alliance against Napoleon. This provoked a now-forgotten controversy of some importance. The nearest British civilian official was the Governor of Malta who, apparently thinking that papist priests had no business in or about the army, ordered Father Kenney to desist. Henry Grattan, Archbishop Troy and the British Prime Minister, Spencer Perceval, all became involved in the subsequent recriminations as a result of which the right of Catholic soldiers in the British army to have chaplains of their own religion was recognised: it is piquant to note that Richard More O'Ferrall, a boy then about to go to Stony-hurst who would later become one of the first pupils at the College to be founded in Ireland by Father Kenney, was destined in the course of a distinguished career to serve for a time as Governor of Malta.[15]

Father Kenney meanwhile become involved in a remark-able escapade designed to spirit the Pope out of Rome. With the French all around him, Pope Pius had little freedom of movement. Either King Ferdinand of the Two Sicilies or the British government (the accounts differ) determined that he should be rescued and brought either to Sicily or to England (again the accounts differ). What is certain is that a Sicilian Jesuit, Father Cajetan Angiolini, and Father Kenney were sent on a British man-of-war to the papal port of Civita Vecchia. Father Angiolini went ashore and reached the Pope, who said that he would leave Rome only under compulsion — which the French, as it turned out, soon forced him to do. Even if Father Kenney was intended merely to be an inter-preter between the Italians and the English captain of the vessel, which appears to have been the case since he did not go into Rome with Father Angiolini, it was a signal honour and mark of trust to have been chosen at all for such a delicate enterprise.

It was also dangerous, with Britain and France at war. About the same time as Father Kenney was sailing to Civita Vecchia, six more Irish scholastics from Stonyhurst had left Liverpool bound for Sicily. The youngest of them, nineteen-year-old Bartholomew Esmonde, wrote a lively account of the journey.[16] Once they had crossed the Bay of Biscay, the captain set up a training session in the use of muskets lest they should be attacked by an enemy privateer. Before they reached Gibraltar, and again while anchored there, they were boarded by British naval officers who on each occasion impressed a sailor from the crew (that is, forcibly seized him to serve on a warship). Then, as they sailed in convoy with some other vessels along the Algerian coast, a sleek and speedy ship approached from the direction of the shore. When the English captain had 'made use both of strong language and strong liquor' to encourage his men, and 'ordered a gun to be fired, in token of defiance', the stranger hauled down its Algerian flag, ran up the French tricolour and 'discharged her whole broadside upon us'. Crew and passengers alike blazed away with small-arms and cannon, their sails were holed and when some cartridges exploded young Esmonde 'got a good singeing but escaped unhurt'. The privateer eventually withdrew and the English ship made landfall at Palermo. . . .

Father Betagh, the last survivor of the old Mission, died in February 1811. In November of the same year Father Kenney arrived back in Dublin accompanied by two of his companions from Sicily, Fathers William Dinan and Matthew Gahan. This little group was constituted a new Irish Jesuit Mission of which Father Kenney was named Superior by the Sicilian Provincial. His appointment was ratified the next year by the General, Father Brzozowski, who managed to send a letter across war-torn Europe from Russia in which he added, 'I leave you joined with the Province of Sicily for the time being in conformity with the pleasure of the Holy See' — in other words, until the Pope declared the Society as a whole to be restored. The Mission took up residence in Saint Michan's parish at Number 3, George's Hill, where Father Mulcaile had lived in his day. As the historian of the diocese, Bishop Donnelly, was to put it, the Jesuits 'resumed their old occupation of assisting in Mary's Lane Chapel, as if nothing had happened in the meantime.'[17]

Much in fact had happened since 1773, not only regarding the Jesuits but also affecting the legal position of Catholics in Ireland and of Ireland in relation to Britain. Old fears had waned, the descendants of Elizabethan and Cromwellian settlers had become a distinctive part of the Irish nation, all

public offices had been so long under Protestant and government control that the possibility of papist usurpation no
longer seemed real. Accordingly a series of measures for the
relief of Catholic grievances was enacted in the later decades
of the eighteenth century. Catholics were permitted to take
long leases and to inherit property, to buy land, open schools,
take degrees at Dublin University, vote in parliamentary
elections, be called to the bar and be appointed to posts in
the army or civil service. Saint Patrick's College for higher
studies was opened in Carlow, as were Saint Kieran's in
Kilkenny and a major seminary under royal patronage for
training future secular priests at Maynooth in County
Kildare. Other schools quickly followed, notably those of the
Presentation nuns for girls, and Mount Sion in Waterford,
where Edmund Ignatius Rice established the first school of
the Irish Christian Brothers to provide general education for
poor boys. The 'Protestant Nation' meanwhile had established
its legislative independence, which left the Irish parliament
free from interference by Westminster: a development which
proved commercially valuable as long as it lasted but was
politically largely vitiated by the continuing control of Irish
administration by the British government.

The French Revolution caused major repercussions in
Ireland with the foundation of the revolutionary United
Irishmen, the attempted landing by a large French army at
Bantry Bay in 1796 and the insurrection of 1798 in Kildare
and Wexford, Antrim and Mayo. The insurrection, which
took the form of successive armed risings in these parts of
the country throughout the summer, was everywhere put
down with much brutality. The leaders in North Kildare
included a pair of neighbours from the Catholic gentry,
William Aylmer of Painstown near Kilcock,[18] whose brother
Charles would go to Palermo as a Jesuit novice with Bartholomew Esmonde, and Bartholomew's father, Dr John Esmonde
of Sallins,[19] who was captured and publicly hanged at Carlisle
Bridge (now O'Connell Bridge) in Dublin:[20] this accidental
association between Jesuits and rebellion would afterwards
be remembered by those who wished the Society no good.
The broader consequence of 1798 was the Act of Union
which abolished the Irish parliament and merged Ireland

with Great Britain in a United Kingdom. The Irish Catholic bishops favoured this development since they expected it would result in the removal of the remaining penal laws — as the British Prime Minister, William Pitt, had indeed suggested it would — but the young barrister, Daniel O'Connell, among others foresaw no benefit in the Union and vigorously opposed it from the outset. Unable to persuade King George III to approve the grant of emancipation (the full rights of citizenship) to Catholics, Pitt had to resign and the bishops faced a *fait accompli* without the immediate concession for which they had hoped.

In 1808 the 'Veto' controversy[21] arose over a British government proposal that emancipation might be enacted if Rome would permit the King to forbid (veto) the appointment of persons unacceptable to the government as Catholic bishops: a privilege enjoyed at the time by the rulers of many countries with large Catholic populations. Rome was agreeable and so at first were some of the Irish bishops, who also saw advantages in the related proposal that government salaries would be paid to the impoverished parish clergy. Vehement opposition among the laity, led by O'Connell, to any surrender of independence by a Church which had survived so much persecution helped persuade the bishops to abandon all support for the Veto and they sent Dr Daniel Murray, Archbishop Troy's coadjutor, to Rome in 1814 to stress their rejection of the British scheme notwithstanding Propaganda's approval of it. Among those who had encouraged resistance to the 'Veto' proposal was old Father Betagh[22] but the significance of the argument was that it showed how popular opinion among the Catholic people, voiced primarily by the emergent Catholic middle class, was a force to be reckoned with. In O'Connell's hands, it would become the instrument whereby the Catholics of Ireland would extract emancipation from a reluctant government and King. That was for the future but already it was becoming possible to think of an Ireland whose administration and public policies and comportment in the world would be determined by its own people. The Jesuit apostolate would have its place in this prospect.

The returned Jesuits' immediate commitment to the parish of Saint Michan's had been disrupted within months when

Dr Murray, the coadjutor bishop who had reluctantly under-taken the Presidency of Maynooth for one year in July 1812,[23] prevailed on Father Kenney to become his Vice-President. This, of course, was precisely the kind of post so often filled by scholarly Jesuits on the continent before the Suppression but the invitation to a College so manifestly a preserve of the secular clergy underscored the high regard in which Father Kenney was held as well, perhaps, as the paucity of priests of strong academic calibre in Ireland at that time: the revolu-tionary and Napoleonic wars had limited the opportunities to obtain a thorough grounding in the sacred sciences at the universities of France, Spain and Italy. Father Kenney, like Dr Murray before him, had to be persuaded against his will. 'Nothing could be more foreign to my intention and to the wishes of my religious brethren than a situation in Maynooth College,' he wrote to Archbishop Troy, stipulating like the coadjutor that he should serve for only a year and subject to the proviso that 'a duty more directly mine does not neces-sarily call me thence'.[24] He was chiefly remembered in May-nooth for the meditations which he composed and which were preached each evening throughout most of his term of office.[25] He was to return frequently to Maynooth in later years to visit the friends he made there and to give retreats.

The long hoped-for and prayed-for Restoration of the Society had to await the release of Pius VII from French captivity in 1814. The Pope did not then delay. Happily we have a first-hand Irish report of the Restoration ceremonies which took place in the Jesuit mother-church of the Gesù on the morning of 7 August. The recently ordained Fathers Esmonde, Aylmer and James Butler were there, on their way home from Sicily, as well as Bishop Murray, the coadjutor of Dublin, who had come to Rome to urge the case against the Veto. Father Aylmer described the scene in a letter to his former novice-master at Hodder, Father Charles Plowden.[26] The Pope arrived 'in state' to celebrate Mass at the tomb of Saint Ignatius, 'attended by almost all his cardinals, prelates and about seventy or eighty of the Society'. The Jesuits, together with the cardinals and the immediate papal entour-age, then repaired to the sodality chapel where 'the Bull which re-establishes the Society all over the world was read'. The

Jesuits went in line to kiss the Pope's feet. 'He continually smiled at the number of old men who came hobbling up to the throne, almost all with tears of joy in their eyes. . . . [It] was truly a day of jubilee and triumph for the Society. The people exulted with joy, and loaded us on every side with congratulations. I could not refrain from tears. Little did I hope or expect to be present at so consoling a ceremony in the Capital of the World. . . . Never was any Order established in this manner; never such marked attention paid by any Pope. . . .'

Back in Ireland Father Kenney eagerly awaited the arrival of Charles Aylmer and his companions, for he had need of as many Jesuits as could be assigned to him. He wanted their help in a truly audacious undertaking on which he had already embarked, more daring than anything done by an Irish Jesuit since the high noon of Father Nugent's superiorship.

Father Kenney being now the Superior of an Irish Jesuit Mission, he could claim the money which Father Stone held in trust. We are told that the funds had been cared for 'most faithfully and most honourably by Father Stone'.[27] This acknowledgment was no platitude, for 'attempts were made by certain persons to obtain control of these funds'[28] and at one stage a senior official at Stonyhurst suggested that they should be used for the purposes of the English Province.[29] Father Stone, however, left the funds safely invested in government stock and handed them over intact, with their accumulated interest, to Father Kenney.

The thought that the Irish funds could be tampered with probably arose from a certain confusion over jurisdiction in the Society which persisted even after the Restoration and still colours accounts of the period. The old Irish Mission had been directly attached to Rome; the Superior reported to, and took his instructions from, the Jesuit General or persons (such as the French Visitor, Father Verdier) designated to act for the General. The English Province, reconstituted by arrangement with the General in White Russia, offered a practicable means for Irish ex-Jesuits to rejoin the Society prior to the Restoration and, as we have seen, Father

O'Callaghan joyfully seized the opportunity. Whether he can be said to have joined the English Province is a moot point. He was very old and simply remained at his post in Dublin. More importantly, however, he and Father Betagh sent their new recruits to Stonyhurst and Hodder for training. This put the students under the direction of the English Province which, for example, decided to send the brightest of them to Sicily for higher studies. These young men, in turn, treated their former teachers and their novice-master with filial respect, reporting their activities and progress to them — as can be seen from Father Aylmer's letter to Father Plowden describing the Restoration ceremonies in Rome. It may be that some English Jesuits consequently came to think of the entrants from Ireland as subjects of the Province and — since these were the only Irish Jesuits of whom they were aware after the death of Father O'Callaghan — concluded that a *de facto* merger had occurred and that Irish Jesuit property had therefore devolved on the English Province to dispose of as it saw fit.

Father Stone, a saintly, cherubic and unassertive man, was wiser. He may indeed have been 'for a time Provincial of England, Ireland and Scotland, with power from the General to accept novices'[30] but other than Father O'Callaghan (who soon died) there were no Jesuits in Ireland prior to the return of Father Kenney in 1811, whose Mission was linked to the Province of Sicily — an arrangement which manifestly put an end to whatever jurisdiction Father Stone might have claimed. All along, the English Provincial seems to have sensed an ambiguity in the situation. His reports on the Irish students' progress to Father Betagh were like those of a headmaster to a parent or guardian, not at all of a superior to a subordinate. But, of course, Father Betagh was not then a Jesuit, as Father Stone and the students were . . . in which case why the reports? A mere courtesy? Perhaps, but their tone also had the ring of one Jesuit superior writing to another on a subject of common concern: 'your pupils' or, to be exact, '*your* élèves' (Father Stone's emphasis)[31] was the phrase used by the English Provincial to the Irish ex-member of the Society. It was the kind of phrase which, in more orderly times, a continental provincial might have employed in reporting to the Superior of the Mission on Irish students sent to study in some institute abroad.

How did the students themselves understand the chain of command? In a letter to Father Stone written in January 1813 by Father Aylmer while he was still studying in Palermo, the Irishman said he would like to undertake some pastoral work in Spain 'should Superiors here and you think it advisable. . . . Please let me know how you would approve of such an act of charity' and in the same letter he said that the Sicilian Provincial 'desires me to ask you what you have determined' about the examinations to be taken by the students from Stonyhurst.[32] So the jurisdiction of the English Provincial was certainly accepted — but was it the jurisdiction of a provincial or of the ultimate head of the seminary (Hodder/Stonyhurst) to which the students were temporarily attached? In his letter eighteen months later from Rome to Father Plowden, Father Aylmer — no longer a student — wrote about the uncertainty of his next assignment and whether one of his colleagues would or would not be going to America; he seemed to assume that these questions would be settled between the General and the Sicilian Provincial.[33] And while he recognised that Father Kenney had a call on him, he indicated no expectation that anybody in England would be telling him what to do.[34]

It is difficult to see why any doubts should have remained after the revival of the Irish Mission under the jurisdiction of the Province of Sicily,[35] as approved by the General in Russia.[36] The Irish Jesuits had every reason to be grateful to their English brethren but they owed them no obedience once they ceased to be students under the control of their seminary superiors. They were subject to the Superior of the Irish Mission, who in turn was subject to the Sicilian Provincial, and he was subject to the General of the Society. At some time after the Restoration and possibly before the return of the General to Rome, the Sicilian connection ceased and the Irish Mission resumed its old status as a direct responsibility of the General. It may be noted, even if it signifies little, that in 1819[37] and 1830,[38] when Father Kenney was sent on Visitations to America, he was chosen by the General himself — and not by a Provincial (either of Sicily or of England) in the way Verdier had been chosen at the General's request by the Provincial of Bordeaux. Be that as it may, the modern biographer of Father Jan Philip Roothaan, General in 1830, clarifies the matter. Upon his election in 1829 the General found that the Society consisted of nine Provinces and 'two independent missions. . . . These missions were not connected with any Province but came directly under the General. [They were] the mission of Missouri . . . [and] the Irish mission. . . '.[39]

Yet, clear as this may be, the Irish Jesuits of the Restoration still sometimes received directions from Stonyhurst, by which they were not surprisingly 'chafed',[40] and as late as the 1880s a compiler of Irish Jesuit records found it necessary to note that 'Ireland . . . never at any time was united with England'.[41] We may hazard a guess that the confusion survived because of the continuing close association between the Mission and the neighbouring Province. Irish entrants to the Society had still to be sent for their studies to the English houses until a proper novitiate and theologate could be provided in Ireland — although close examination of obituaries in the records[42] shows that Irish novices from the 1820s onwards increasingly went to the continent rather than England for some or all of their training according as the Society re-established itself in various countries, re-opened its colleges and resumed its university connections. As long as students were attending Stonyhurst and Hodder, however, comments and advice as well as specific instructions might quite reasonably be addressed from England to Ireland. It was particularly important from the Irish side to keep the English Province advised of developments so that the wishes and intentions of the Irish Mission should be understood; *pietas* anyway would have ensured that the first generation of Jesuits on the new Irish Mission would write regularly and deferentially to their former teachers, to whom they owed so much, and would receive letters back responding with the interest, approval and occasional criticism to be expected of former teachers everywhere. Such a relationship seems to have existed between Father Kenney and Father Stone and could easily give the impression of client-and-patron or trooper-and-officer in the absence of wider evidence.

Finally, Ireland and England shared a common civil government, but English Catholics viewed that government in an altogether different light from their Irish co-religionists. Catholics formed no more than a tiny proportion of the English population. They wished simply to secure the full rights of citizens and to be considered loyal subjects. Irish Catholics not only wanted their citizenship rights; they also wanted a major role in the formation of policies touching Ireland and in the administration of their country's affairs. Despite their recently-granted entitlement to hold certain offices, they were in fact excluded from the entire range of administrative posts — judgeships, the magistracy, positions as registrars and sheriffs, senior civil service appointments and so on. As for influencing policy, this had to await achievement of the right to sit in parliament. English Catholics thus sought simply to be accepted into the system. Irish Catholics — not as Catholics, but as citizens — aspired to an influence within and over the system from which they believed the majority element in their country's population should not be excluded. In 1814 this late-penal discontent at discrimination in Ireland was only beginning to harden into a political goal. But those who saw how the wind was blowing were already preparing for the future. Among them was Peter Kenney, S.J., and his very Irish priorities would cause a momentary rift between him and the very English Marmaduke Stone, S.J. This minor episode in a larger story pointed to a difference of approach which could hardly have arisen had Father Kenney been bound by obedience to Father Stone. It happened because of Father Kenney's audacious decision to buy Castle Browne.

Castle Browne was the same Castlebrowne which featured in Archbishop Carpenter's seizure of the debt owed to the Jesuits at the Suppression. It consisted of a farm, spacious parkland and a sturdy castellated mansion in County Kildare, some twenty miles from Dublin. An elegant ride, or grassy path for horse-riding, bordered by tall lime trees, ran straight as a Roman road from the public highway to the castle a thousand yards away: originally a fortified tower-house on the perimeter of the Pale (the hinterland of Dublin under English control during the Middle Ages), the mansion was always referred to as 'the castle'. The Brownes, a Catholic family, had succeeded in retaining it by various subterfuges throughout penal times but the owner in 1814, General Michael Wogan Browne, had reached a prestigious position on the continent in the service of the King of Saxony[43] and willingly sold the estate to Father Kenney for £16,000. Here the Irish Mission proposed to open a school under the original place-name of Castle Browne, which was Clongowes Wood.[44] Clongowes would be a world removed from the city cellar where Peter Kenney had sat in class under Father Betagh. Before it opened its doors, it was envisaged as a College in the old tradition of Jesuit schools on the European mainland and its students were expected to come from the families of the Catholic gentry, land-owners and better-off bourgeoisie. Its handsome buildings and gracious setting matched the élite status planned for the College; so did the fees, which were set at fifty pounds a year for younger boys and fifty guineas for those above the age of twelve.[45]

It was a startling decision, not least because it so contrasted with the earlier educational endeavours of the Jesuits in Ireland, which had been directed towards the children of city and small-town families of modest means — and often enough, of no means at all. Jesuits, however, differ from most religious orders in having no permanent objective other than doing what redounds to the greater glory of God. This norm they have always interpreted to mean that they should serve the needs of the people among whom they work or to whom they are sent, according as these needs show themselves at a given time. In particular, they have taken it to mean (with no false humility!) that they should seek out those needs which Jesuits are especially well equipped to meet. In penal Ireland the need had been so great for priests to administer the sacraments and preach the gospel, and for teachers to make some level of education available elsewhere than in the state-approved Protestant schools, that the Jesuits saw their task as supplementing the parish clergy, conducting missions and retreats if possible — and setting up local schools in urban centres, where they could hope to achieve the maximum effect with their limited numbers. By 1814, as we have noted, a new Ireland was beginning to loom in which emancipation could not be long delayed and Catholics hoped to take their rightful place among those who controlled the country's destiny. But Catholics, for generations, had been excluded from the least access to power. Would they be competent to seize the reins when the opportunity arose? To ensure their competence was the need which presented itself to Father Kenney and led to the foundation of Clongowes, from which it was intended that 'the gradual infiltration of the system by highly educated Irish Catholics would follow'.[46]

Few would dispute that the Jesuits could be relied upon to offer the standard of education required if Irish Catholics were not to be rejected as inferior to the alumni of English and Protestant schools. From what has been already said, it will be remembered that schools for Catholics under various auspices were beginning to spring up all over the country and accordingly there was no special occasion for the Jesuits to resume the kind of teaching they had carried out in the past.

It may still be said that they should not have blocked access to their quality education so that only the wealthy could avail themselves of it. One answer to this criticism is that it seeks to apply modern perceptions to the early nineteenth century. The ruling caste in a class-ridden society was drawn from a social stratum wide enough to include the professions but certainly not open to all-comers. If that caste were to be broken into, broken up and taken over, it could be done only by Catholics who belonged to the social stratum from which the caste was drawn. Hence, the education of upper-class and middle-class Catholics had a value for all their co-religionists since it was a necessary step to enable the national majority to take to itself a quantum of power: short of violent revolution, there was no other route to the promised land.

What could be done would be brilliantly demonstrated by Daniel O'Connell's political manoeuvring in the 1830s, the decade immediately after emancipation. 'At the beginning of 1835, Irish government was, practically speaking, an exclusive tory preserve. Six years later, at a rough estimate, about one third of the Irish judges, magistrates, sheriffs, assistant barristers and other important officers of national management, belonged to the 'anti-tory' camp. At a still rougher estimate, some 30–40 per cent of the new appointments were of Catholics.'[47] But even then, and later, O'Connell was found deploring the dearth of impressive Catholics to put before the voters at a parliamentary election.[48] The infiltration of the system was no easy stratagem, but it worked over the long haul. Said the famous Jesuit educationist, Father William Delany, in 1879: 'Most of our foremost Catholics at the bar and in parliament passed through Clongowes, and many won distinctions in Trinity College.'[49] The objective really was to provide Catholic leadership across the spectrum of interests in Ireland: in the institutes of learning; the medical, legal and scientific professions; in journalism and, of course, in parliament. Without such leadership, the fruits of emancipation could not have been culled and Ascendancy privilege might have survived much longer. The same leadership provided the solid foundation on which Home Rule would be nearly achieved and the break-up of the landlord interest would be totally accomplished.

These considerations bring us to the threshold of the twentieth century with its very different values and priorities. It surely says a lot for Father Kenney's daring that his project for a College in 1814 can lead us at once into looking so far down the road that lay ahead of him. He was not, as it happened, the only one then reading the signs of the times. In Dublin Castle the Chief Secretary for Ireland, the future Prime Minister Sir Robert Peel, came under bombardment from anti-Catholic elements who claimed that this blatantly public assertion of popery threatened enormous (if unspecified) perils. Peel thought it prudent to invite Father Kenney to call and explain himself. Father Kenney skilfully parried the Chief Secretary's cross-examination,[50] insisting that the £16,000 purchase money belonged to him personally (as in law it did, since it had been made over to him in his own name); that the school he proposed to open was for the laity (i.e. it was not a seminary, as some opponents had suggested); that he was acting on his own behalf (i.e. not as an agent for anyone else — again, the legal position). Peel was little disposed to pick up the more bigoted objections or to invoke long-unenforced penal legislation. He simply cautioned Father Kenney not to jump to conclusions; the government was giving him no approval and he should watch his step. No doubt, as a good Dublinman, Father Kenney could catch the nuance in the Chief Secretary's comment and saw that he was free to proceed.

He must have wondered a little at some of Peel's other remarks, such as his query whether it was true that two Jesuits from Sicily named Wolfe and Esmonde, 'whose father and brother respectively had been hanged in Ireland as traitors,'[51] were to be employed as teachers in the College. The phrase comes from an indirect source, the Speaker of the House of Commons, who claimed he had his account from Peel himself.[52] Peel may not have been an accurate reporter, or he may have been using the kind of half-truth so often bought innocently from informers by the British authorities. Neither the list of Irish Jesuits in Sicily at that time[53] nor the early lists of Jesuits in the Clongowes community[54] refer to a Father Wolfe. Nor does any Wolfe appear in the standard modern work on the 1798 Rising.[55] Father Esmonde's father, as we know, was hanged and Father Aylmer's brother was certainly considered a traitor (he was spared execution in return for his surrender and went off to South America to join the forces of the patriot, Simon Bolivar).[56] Peel also hinted that the money at Father Kenney's disposal might be liable to seizure: a loose threat or an indication that he knew something about the history of the Mission funds? It did not apparently alarm Father Kenney at the time, but two months later it became clear that something of the story had got out, for Sir John Hippisley, a member of parliament, made a speech to the Commons in which he mentioned that £30,000 had been sent to Ireland, £16,000 of which had been used to establish a 'seminary' at Castle Browne.[57]

Father Kenney had intended to write to Hippisley 'defending myself on the broad grounds of equity & common justice . . . without entering into any explanation that would give him more knowledge than he had yet acquired'.[58] Before he acted, however, he learned to his fury that the English Provincial, Father Stone, had thought it proper to reveal for the guidance of some friends in parliament the whole story of the Mission funds — the manner in which they had been accumulated, passed on from one person to another, and finally to Father Kenney himself. Father Stone meant well, intending to counter Hippisley's statement by showing that the money had been bequeathed as personal property and not as that of a religious order. This reflected a typically English Catholic aim of the period: to establish one's good citizenship by telling all and showing there was nothing to hide. The Irish had more confidence in themselves and considerably less in the goodwill of government. They would give no hostages to fortune, and certainly none to those whose discriminatory rule they resented. As Father Kenney told his legal adviser:

> . . . I wrote to Mr Stone expressing my surprize that he should make such an avowal. . . . The cause might have been defended without telling friends & enemies that the Irish Ex Jesuits possessed at the suppression six or seven thousand pounds; and without admitting that it has since been amassed & bequeathed from one to another. This I feared would be taken as a proof that the property in question is the property of Ex Jesuits secreted and amassed for some superstitious purpose . . . it was publickly telling what I have refused to acknowledge & what I did not communicate [even] to those members [of parliament] who have so kindly spoken for me. . . . Mr Stone had no right to dictate to or to answer for me. . . .

It was spilt milk and the Irishman soon got over his annoyance, recognising that Father Stone had acted from the best of motives. But it served to demonstrate, first, that Father Kenney acknowledged no right in the English Provincial to speak on behalf of the Irish Mission's Superior and, secondly, that prudence required the Jesuits of the two countries to make their own dispositions in the light of their altogether different circumstances and attitudes.

Father Kenney had already made his disposition. He opened Clongowes as a boarding school in May 1814. He did so without the licence of the local Church of Ireland bishop, then mistakenly supposed to be required by law. Much used to be made of this to illustrate the risks Father Kenney was prepared to take. In fact, like the apparently bigger hazard of proceeding with an overtly Jesuit undertaking, the risk was small enough. As has been suggested elsewhere, the failure of the bishop to issue the requested licence may have been due to a fortuitous argument within the Church of Ireland about the patronage of the parish of Clane adjacent to Clongowes; there was a precedent in favour of opening the school and Father Kenney was legally advised that he could safely do so.[59] On the general hazard, the tenor of Peel's remarks had amounted to an assurance that there would be no prosecution. Thus Clongowes Wood College was founded, with Father Peter Kenney as its first Rector. He remained at the same time Superior of the Irish Jesuit Mission. Over two more months were to pass before the radiant morning in the Gesù when Pope Pius VII would declare the Society of Jesus to be everywhere restored.

It would perhaps be churlish to insist that Clongowes was the first College of the revived Society in these islands, for it owed its community to the training provided at Stonyhurst, and Stonyhurst was Jesuit in its origin, ethos and the greater part of its administration. But the Lancashire College was a pontifical seminary as well as a school and it still lived with the anomaly of 'the Gentlemen of Liège,' now 'the Gentlemen of Stonyhurst,' by whom theoretically it was run and who consisted of Jesuits, ex-Jesuits and secular priests; it was because the rules of the house had had to be adapted in various ways to suit this *ad hoc* amalgam of clergy that Father Plowden had moved the novitiate to nearby Hodder, where it would be possible to have a Jesuit community.[60] Indeed, the presence of so many non-Jesuits encouraged a curious secrecy at Stonyhurst so that the re-admitted Jesuits met behind locked doors to transact their own business and took great care to avoid any public reference to their membership of the Society[61] — notwithstanding their more general openness as English Catholics vis-à-vis the government. The Irish Jesuits, being *sui generis*, suffered no such inhibition and it caused some distress to Father Stone to hear that Father Kenney had willingly declared himself to be a Jesuit in his conversation with Chief Secretary Peel[62] (telling him about his money would have been quite another matter, as any Irishman can appreciate!). Clongowes was therefore publicly known for what it was from the outset, a Jesuit College for the education of the laity. Its unambiguous status must have been envied by the oddly-situated Jesuits of the English Province.

When he became Rector of Clongowes Father Peter Kenney was not yet 35 years of age.[63] Father Aylmer was 28,[64] Father Esmonde only 25[65] — in the difficult circumstances of the time and the half-restored character of the Society, some curtailment of the scholasticate must have been considered unavoidable (although it seems likely that theological studies would have been completed before ordination). The audacity of opening Clongowes lay not so much in the possible impact of anti-Catholic opposition, against which the Rector had taken suitable soundings and precautions, but in the youth and inexperience of the men who launched the enterprise. Father Kenney quickly set about retrieving Irish Jesuits, ordained and unordained, from Sicily, Italy and England, but nearly all were his juniors and he alone had ever been responsible for running an institution. This dozen or so of young clerics undertook the housing, provisioning, disciplining and general care, as well as the education, of the sons of many wealthy and well-connected families. It remains a mystery that the scarcely unsophisticated parents of these boys were willing to relinquish their offspring to the custody of unprepared neophytes and it says much for the reputation of Jesuit teaching, even after forty years of suppression, that Clongowes attracted more than a hundred pupils in its second year and had two hundred by 1816.[66] The neophytes met every expectation. As well as the subjects normal in a classical school, they were soon providing classes in theology, logic, natural philosophy (physics) and experimental philosophy (chemistry). Fencing, dancing and music could be had for an additional fee and no complaints were recorded about the quality of life in the College for the boys who lived there through nearly eleven months of the year — a single annual vacation being as much as was possible in the days before railways.[67] The results justified the audacity.

The other side of the coin revealed itself in 1818 when a very serious epidemic — possibly typhus — broke out in the overcrowded school.[68] It had to close briefly and resumed with smaller numbers living in improved and extended buildings. Whether an excess of enthusiasm in accepting so many pupils caused the crisis cannot now be established, but the care of so many children and teenagers required skills of cooking, nursing and orderly accommodation which few of the bright young Jesuits were likely to possess. It was more than timely therefore that about now a very important expansion in the membership of the Irish Mission took place. This was the recruitment of 'temporal coadjutors' or Brothers, who were members of the Society without being priests, and who met the manifold temporal needs of Jesuit houses as tailors, carpenters, cooks, bakers, infirmarians and much else, including the care of community chapels as sacristans. Saint Ignatius himself had provided for such a grade[69] and their patron in Ireland should surely be Brother Dominic Collins, who declined the proposal that he study to be a priest and who died for his faith on the scaffold at Youghal in 1602. Father Kenney secured the repatriation of at least one Irish aspirant Brother, John Nolan of County Carlow, from Stonyhurst[70] and another from Sicily, Philip Reilly of Longford, who had already entered the order.[71] Diligent research would probably reveal more who served on the Mission from its re-establishment but the major intake of new coadjutors did not begin until 1817 with the admission of Brother John Nelson of Armagh.[72] No fewer than five entered on the same day in September 1819,[73] and the numbers grew steadily over the following years. Indeed, it is tempting to wonder whether the Irish did not have a special vocation to the coadjutorship: of the forty-five Irishmen in the Jesuit Vice-Province of Missouri in 1846 all but five were Brothers.[74]

By taking charge of the day-to-day upkeep of Clongowes and the other residences soon to be founded, the Brothers helped to free the Jesuit priests for their teaching and spiritual duties. As anybody who has lived in one of the Society's schools or colleges will bear out, the Brothers carry much of the responsibility for keeping these institutions running smoothly: Jesuit thoroughness and pursuit of excellence are attributes not confined to the ordained or the scholastics. The coadjutors' duties were sometimes extensive. In houses like Clongowes and Tullabeg which had farms attached, it was common to appoint a Brother with the appropriate experience as land steward or *villicus* (not the best chosen of the classical titles which Jesuits liked to use for offices in the Society; in ancient Rome it meant a head slave who enjoyed the right to marry!). Brother Reilly had an adventurous and alarming journey home from Sicily. Father Kenney arranged for him to bring three tons of books — three tons! — for the Clongowes library. The captain was a drunk who failed to provision the ship adequately so that passengers and crew were half-starving when Ireland came in sight; the ship stuck twice on sandbars — outside Youghal and in Dundrum Bay, County Down, neither of them its port of destination. The books had to be manhandled ashore and many were damaged. With remarkable diligence, Brother Reilly managed to get letters dispatched from each of these places to Father Kenney, reporting what happened in graphic detail and wondering with a Brother's practicality whether his Superior had taken out insurance.[75]

For Father Kenney and his energetic colleagues Clongowes was only the first step in setting the Irish Mission on a solid basis. He did not forget his native Dublin, from which he had been snatched to become Vice-President of Maynooth. At least two Jesuits were based there. Father Mathew Gahan was attached to the parish of Saint Nicholas,[76] south of the Liberties from Francis Street to the Grand Canal and beyond; Father John Ryan worked in Saint Paul's parish,[77] along and behind Arran Quay. But this was redolent of penal times and the Suppression. Jesuits felt they should now have their own residence in the capital, from which to exercise their own ministry. The Poor Clare nuns used to keep 'a neat chapel with eight cells over it,' hidden in the garden of a house in Dorset Street on the northern side of the city; the chapel had its own entrance from Hardwicke Street at the back of the garden.[78] When the traffic to and from the nearby new Anglican Church of Saint George in Hardwicke Place at the top of the street became too much of a distraction for the contemplative sisters, the nuns moved across the Liffey to the semi-rural Harold's cross in 1804. [79] A secular priest took a lease of the old building and said Mass there regularly until his death, whereupon Father Kenney bought it for £400 out of the balance of the funds still in his possession.[80] The Jesuits thus acquired their first public chapel in Ireland since the Restoration of the Society, together with a residence above it — against 'much opposition,' we read, 'by the priests of the parish': an enigmatic comment, left unexplained.[81] The ubiquitous Fathers Aylmer, Kenney and Esmonde served successively as Superiors here, aided by one or two fellow-Jesuits. Hardwicke Street chapel, as we shall see, was to be the origin of both Gardiner Street Church and Belvedere College, the Jesuit bastions of Victorian and twentieth-century Dublin. But first the Jesuits needed a novitiate. . . .

Perhaps with memories of Hodder in mind, Father Kenney decided to purchase a house in a remote country area and found what he wanted at Tullabeg near Rahan in King's County (now County Offaly), almost in the centre of Ireland, far from any city and close to one of the country's most extensive bogs. The property cost £3,600 (the Mission Funds were still adequate)[82] and opened as a Jesuit house dedicated to Saint Stanislaus in 1818. It is better to say 'house' than 'novitiate', for although the intention in acquiring it is clear, what happened next is mystifying. Father Robert St Leger, a gentlemanly and ascetic native of Waterford who had been one of the students sent to Sicily with the future Father Esmonde, was appointed Rector.[83] Instead of concentrating on the novitiate, he made Tullabeg a preparatory school for boys destined to go on to Clongowes. He could scarcely have done this without approval but it may be significant that Father Kenney was soon preoccupied with his Visitation to Maryland — for the Tullabeg development sat oddly with what the Superior had had in mind and was not manifestly related to contemporary needs. Since Clongowes accepted boys from the age of seven, the question arises why it had to have a preparatory school at all, especially when the numbers in the College had fallen and accommodation had been expanded in the wake of the 1818 epidemic. Again, some imitation of Hodder may have been intended since 'a small preparatory school' was run at the English novitiate 'to disguise the activities of the novices.'[84] But this was part of the English Jesuits' penchant for secrecy and may also have

reflected a wish to inculcate something of Jesuit educational
values in the boys before they went on to the still not-quite-
Jesuit Stonyhurst. Neither consideration applied in Ireland.
Yet Hodder remained primarily and unquestionably a novitiate. Tullabeg developed as a respected primary school, then
a grammar school and finally a serious rival to Clongowes.

   That process of growth would occupy the next sixty years
and more. The school was fortunate, however, to have survived its first decade. Robert St Leger must have had qualities
that commended him to Father Kenney but he was a hopeless
school manager. He seems to have been opinionated and
more sure of himself than his faulty judgment justified. Debts
accumulated so alarmingly that it was said he could not
venture out of doors lest he might be arrested. He looked to
his younger brother, Father John St Leger, whose Master of
Novices he had been, to sort out the problems. John adopted
a policy of fiscal rectitude which apparently involved austerities
on such a scale that word reached Rome, for an English Jesuit
was sent over as Visitor. He quickly removed Robert from the
rectorship and replaced him with his brother! What the boys
and their parents thought of these upheavals history does
not record but Tullabeg adjusted to the new regime and
attracted increasing numbers of pupils. The St Legers must
have had considerable personal charism. Despite the perils
to which they subjected Tullabeg, first through improvidence
and then through parsimony, the Society continued to appoint
them to positions of trust. When the Irish Mission was raised
to the status of a Vice-Province in 1830, Father Robert became
its first Vice-Provincial — that is, its Superior. He went to
India as Vicar-Apostolic in Calcutta four years later, where he
promptly quarrelled with the Rector of a school run by the
English Province; the Irishman thought the local mission
more important than the school. Once more the complaints
reached Rome. Back in Ireland Robert was surprisingly made
Rector of Clongowes at a time when the College was 'oppressed with debt': it is tempting to think that the authorities
thought it was the other St Leger who had come home, for
Father John had also gone to India (as an army chaplain).
Robert was transferred upwards yet again, becoming Vice-
Provincial now for the long term of nine years. John, after his

own stint abroad, served another term as Rector of Tullabeg. It was said of him, in an unusually frank obituary by a fellow-Jesuit, that he 'laboured more or less in the ministry' and that as a preacher he 'possessed the useful talent of introducing into his compositions the beautiful and forcible language of others without allowing it to be perceived'.

The creation of the Irish Vice-Province, with its greater degree of autonomy, marked the General's favourable impression of the progress made by Father Kenney and his little band in the sixteen years since the Restoration. With a college, a school and a city mission the order was firmly established in the country, discharging the ministries for which it was best qualified and well poised to take advantage of Catholic Emancipation, which had been at last enacted in 1829 as a result of the campaign — the first manifestation ever of Christian Democracy in action, inspired by true liberal Catholicism — which had been so skilfully mounted by Daniel O'Connell. The Roman Catholic Relief Act at first sight was worrying: it required all Jesuits (specifically) and members of other religious orders who were then in the country to be enrolled, forbade them to accept further recruits and prohibited religious from entering the United Kingdom.[85] O'Connell said he could 'drive a coach and six' through the provisions designed 'to prevent the *extension* of the Jesuits and other monastic orders',[86] and the government gave private assurances that these clauses were mere sops to Protestant prejudice which would never be enforced. Nonetheless, the friends of the Irish Jesuits got up no fewer than three petitions to parliament against the restrictions: a national petition, one from the mainly Protestant gentry of County Kildare on which the first name was that of the premier peer of Ireland, the Duke of Leinster, and one from seventy old Clongownians who rallied to the defence of their 'venerable and respected' college.[87] As a precaution, a number of senior boys still at school in Clongowes registered as Jesuits so that they could enter the order later if they felt they had vocations; contemporaries at Stonyhurst did the same.[88] The clauses passed into law, but the government was as good as its word and no prosecutions were ever undertaken in Ireland.[89]

Once again, though, the coin had another side. Well-established the Irish Jesuits might be and high in public favour, but what had been happening at Tullabeg pointed to irregularities still to be overcome by the Vice-Province. None of its members had known the old Society and to some extent they had to re-invent the Jesuit wheel. Their paucity of numbers at the outset did not help: Father Kenney was so often away (usually preaching sermons by invitation in various parts of the country) that responsibility was thrown back on less mature colleagues[90] and, as we have noted, this may explain the change of emphasis at Tullabeg. That change in turn left the Irish Jesuits still without a proper house of studies for training novices and scholastics. The case of John St Leger shows that some novices went to Tullabeg despite what must have been the noisy distraction of small boys at their lessons and play. Some scholastics studied theology from an early stage at Clongowes[91] although it is hard to imagine where they could find room to sleep, let alone to undertake serious reading, in that busy and populous establishment founded for a different purpose.

Why a greater effort was not made to create facilities for the training of Jesuits in Ireland during the half-century after the Restoration remains unexplained. The answer may have been psychological, with the enthusiasm of the young men of the revived Mission leading to a concentration on teaching and pastoral work rather than preparing for the ministry — on doing rather than learning. There may have been a tendency to argue the undoubted advantage, especially to potential school teachers, of exposure to a different intellectual climate through studying abroad. There was also, if anybody recalled it, the tradition of the old Mission which sent its students to continental colleges and administered a number of them but, except in the case of Poitiers, avoided burdening the Irish Society with foreign houses for its exclusive use: a practical mentality which saw no point in wasting resources on providing services that could be acquired elsewhere. Whatever the reason, the scope for training in Ireland remained very limited and the obituaries of Jesuits who joined the Society in Ireland up to the mid-nineteenth century suggest that it was easier to send them abroad for the greater part of their formation than to provide it at home. Entrants were sometimes assigned to foreign novitiates and Irish scholastics went more often than not to the continent for their philosophy and theology — and, in a reversal of the earlier trend, to England again when houses of study were opened at Roehampton near London and St Beuno's in North Wales. Adequate arrangements for training at home were not completed until the opening of Milltown Park (1860) and a novitiate at Dromore, County Down (1884) — which was shortly afterwards transferred to Tullabeg when the school there had been merged with Clongowes and the boys removed to County Kildare. Many Irish Jesuits still spend time in study abroad, of course, but this is for specific purposes determined by their superiors and does not now arise from necessity.

The ghost of Father Robert Nugent, who had given such priority to the establishment of a novitiate in pre-Cromwellian Ireland, first in Dublin and later in Kilkenny, must have stirred uneasily at the long delay in the opening of centres for Jesuit formation. Even more disturbing to a Jesuit of his time would have been the practice of charging fees for teaching. Saint Ignatius had strictly forbidden it and school-fees had never been exacted by Irish Jesuits before the Suppression. True, in 1771 Father Betagh (while still a Jesuit) was charging his boarders 20 guineas a year[92] but since local boys attending the same school were charged nothing it seems reasonable to suppose that the 20 guineas was for board only and not for tuition; and if the sum seems rather high for lodging expenses, it should be remembered that clerical students were among the boarders and it would not have been above Jesuit wit to extract a little more from sponsoring bishops to help fund the education of the really impoverished![93] The first congregation of the restored Society, held in Rome in 1820, decided that *all* the ordinances inherited from the original body were to remain intact[94] so, by this re-endorsement of the old requirements as well as by the old requirements themselves which had applied until then, tuition fees should not have been levied in Clongowes or Tullabeg. Even allowing for the substantial costs of lodging, the minimum £50 charged at Clongowes and 30 guineas[95] at Tullabeg clearly incorporated a fee for being allowed to study in these schools, i.e. for tuition. How was this possible?

The simplest, and possibly not inaccurate, answer is to repeat that irregularities were commonplace in the restored Society as the members gradually found their feet and absorbed the full implication of the guidelines originally set down by Saint Ignatius himself in the Jesuit Constitutions. For Father Kenney, the first duty would certainly have been to meet a perceived need: hence the provision of a school to inculcate the qualities of leadership. Another reason was the absence in Ireland of the patronage which made possible the major Jesuit schools and colleges on the continent in the past, where no tuition fees needed to be charged because of the massive support from princely and civic authorities. This had been partially, but only partially, revived in continental countries after the Restoration and soon the generalate in Rome was coming under pressure from a number of Jesuit provinces to abandon the prohibition of fees. British and American Jesuits were disturbed by a social factor: better-off Catholic parents increasingly disliked sending their children to schools which all social classes could attend because no fees were charged.[96] While certainly less than admirable, it was a tendency which could not be ignored if Catholics were to be dissuaded from resorting to Protestant schools and especially if the Jesuits hoped to continue the formation of those Catholics likely to have most influence in public affairs. With some reluctance, Father General Roothaan allowed English Jesuits in 1833 to take fees for this reason, but upon the understanding that no boy would be turned away for want of money; he also insisted that the fees were to be used for the purposes of the school and not be spent in any way on the Jesuits.[97] After 1848 exemption from the rule was allowed generally where no other means of support for a Jesuit school could be found.[98] The Irish Jesuits appear not to have troubled themselves about all this; they had no need to, having turned a blind eye to the rule from 1814 and escaped, as far as is known, without reprimand. But Ireland was included in the formal permission to accept fees granted to Jesuit schools in English-speaking countries in 1883 precisely to ensure that Catholics would not be tempted to use non-Catholic fee-charging schools.[99] It would be disingenuous to suppose that Irish Catholics were any less infected than those of other countries by the considerations of class-distinction which so unhappily blossomed in the Victorian age.

What remained of the prohibition against taking tuition fees was finally eliminated for the whole Society at the General Congregation of 1923.[100] Since the Second Vatican Council of the mid-1960s the maintenance of fee-charging schools has become a matter of dispute inside and outside the Society of Jesus. Without commenting here on this modern controversy, it may be no harm to note almost at random some facts regarding the fees actually charged in Irish Jesuit schools long ago. The fees at Clongowes were reduced in the mid-nineteenth century to 35 guineas,[101] only fractionally more than Tullabeg, and remained at that until the first World War (Tullabeg had gone up to 40 guineas by 1877[102] and would go higher). Despite great changes in the value of money, boys entering Clongowes under the age of 14 in 1945 were charged only £90.[103] In the 1950s, this figure was increased to 100 guineas and older boys were charged 110 guineas. It would be ludicrous and insensitive to suggest that this pattern represented unrestricted democratisation of the school: £90 was not easily set aside by the majority of Irish families in 1945 and, for many, a single sum of this scale would have represented the unattainable wealth of Croesus. Nonetheless, the very considerable reduction of the Clongowes fees in real terms between 1814 and 1945, combined with the growth of a middle class in Ireland earning reasonable (although rarely substantial) incomes, meant that, as the decades passed by, more and more parents in no sense rich were able to send their sons to the best, most renowned and most prestigious secondary school in the country.[104] Since over the same years successive hard-won concessions and eventual independence placed Irishmen of the Catholic tradition ever more widely in the leadership of the professions, the economy, the bureaucracy and the government, the widening of the base from which the pupils of Clongowes were drawn kept the school undeviatingly on the path chosen for it by Peter Kenney in the very different world of 1814.

Apart from the level of fee charged, 'quite a number of pupils' at Clongowes were 'received free'.[105] This was a feature also of the Jesuit schools founded later, the genesis of which

we have still to record. In some of these the fees were very
low at the outset. Belvedere, a day-school, charged two guineas
a term in the 1840s. This had risen by 18 shillings in the
1890s, and at that 'there was considerable scope for negotia-
tion. The fee books show a range of figures charged, depending on the family's circumstances. In one well-researched
class, that of James Joyce in 1893, only twenty-one of the
twenty-eight boys paid fees, and of these only twelve paid the
full amount, £3 a term (the Joyces, like many others, were
'free boys' throughout their time in Belvedere).'[106] At the
Crescent in Limerick, fees of £3 to £6 *a year* were charged in
the 1880s; the average fee actually received was less than £4
and 'many poor cases' were helped; the pecuniary loss to the
Jesuits was £200 a year, according to evidence given to the
Educational Endowments Commission by the Rector, Father
Timothy O'Keeffe, in 1887.[107] A similar picture could have
been presented of Saint Ignatius in Galway, while at Mungret
(a boarding school) thirty pupils paid a fee of £38 a year, all
found, and forty were 'free boys' at a cost to the Jesuits of
£1,000.[108] The Mungret fee, being little less than that for
Clongowes when allowance is made for the extras chargeable
at the older school, may prompt the question why boys were
sent to the less famous and less well-equipped establishment
in the County Limerick countryside but, as will be seen,
Mungret was a special case — being in fact two schools with
different objectives but sharing the same site. Clongowes
would not have suited half the boys at Mungret, who were
destined for the priesthood; the number of 'free boys' would
suggest that fees were negotiable, as at Belvedere, and it may
well be that the full fee was pitched at a level to ensure that
the minority of parents able to afford it made a contribution
which mitigated the charge falling on the Society for the rest.
Whatever else may be said about the Irish fee-charging
schools, the Jesuits cannot be accused of making money from
them, setting the bills excessively high or excluding boys
whose parents could not pay.

Whether or not the Irish Mission was revived and expanded
on an incomplete grasp of the Jesuit Constitutions (in the
matter of fees) or to the neglect of priorities adopted by the

Society elsewhere (in the matter of a novitiate), it stood in high regard with successive Generals following the Restoration. The appointment twice over of Father Kenney to be Visitor to the American Jesuits was an act of particular trust, for on each occasion he was sent to report on a situation of some delicacy.

The venerable Maryland Mission[109] established by priests of the English Province in 1634 was languishing on the edge of the partially constructed federal capital of Washington, where it had a college and novitiate at Georgetown but fewer than thirty members to service them and to minister to small groups of Catholics scattered throughout the states of Maryland, Pennsylvania and New York. As a result of misguided pressure from Archbishop John Carroll of Baltimore — the first diocesan bishop appointed in the United States and himself a former Jesuit of Irish descent — the opportunity was missed of developing a major college in New York city, where there were many Catholics and good hope of finding substantial support for a Jesuit institution. On the banks of the Potomac, nobody was interested. The few novices were reduced to living on potatoes and water and the Society would have faded away but for a trickle of recruits from Europe. Missouri, a decade later, was the Wild West of the day, where the Belgian Jesuits, who had left Maryland because the old Mission had no money to support them, had to contend with endemic lawlessness in a frontier zone between civilisation and the wilderness as well as between the 'free' North and the slave-owning South: on his first Visitation Father Kenney would have heard of the 'Missouri Compromise' of 1820 which permitted slavery in that state but in no other as far north beyond the Mississippi[110] (by coincidence, Maryland and its coastal neighbour, Delaware, were the most northerly slave-states of the original Union). In Missouri, despite the banditry, faction-fighting, gambling and drunkenness which they reported as the typical life-style of the region, the Belgians had opened a seminary, taken charge of the diocesan college and begun to think of expansion eastwards and northwards towards Kentucky, Ohio and Wisconsin.

Peter Kenney arrived somewhat as a poacher turned gamekeeper in these diverse, colourful but less than comfortable

places. The need for a Jesuit presence in the area served
from Maryland much impressed him: 'Were a man fit to do
no more than catechize the children and the slaves,' he
remarked in a letter to Father Aylmer, 'he ought to consider
his being on the spot, by the will of God, a proof that it is
most pleasing to God to remain among them. . .'.[111] Accordingly, he approved the arrangements sanctioned by Archbishop Carroll, which included retaining the novitiate for a
Mission much more impoverished than that of Ireland. He
seems to have spent much of his time settling arguments over
the direction in which the Maryland Jesuits should develop.
Father Leonard Edelen of New York State told him, 'Your
measures to regulate our Society in this country have been
approved by all of ours. They will long cherish the recollection
of your prudent and energetic endeavours to introduce
peace and harmony.'[112] This was the common reaction and
Father Anthony Kohlmann, Superior of the Maryland Mission,
wrote to him some time later, 'of all persons that ever visited
America, I know of none whose return is so universally wished
for as that of your Reverence.'[113]

He went back to America in 1830 for a three-year Visitation,
this time concentrating on Missouri, where he found the
weather intolerable: 'An affair that is called a carriage was
borrowed from one Irish Catholic, a horse from another. . . .
The wind became severe to an extent never before experienced by me . . . it was as full in our faces as it could be. . . .
We were forced to walk, though scarcely able to move. I had
repeatedly to stop and turn my back to gain my breath. I was
half an hour coming up the private road that leads to the
house, endeavouring to breathe for life, without the power of
uttering a syllable, and every limb shaking like the leaves in a
storm.'[114] The hurricane was not the only unpleasant novelty
for a man accustomed to the gentle gentility of Clongowes.
He deplored the bias of the school in St Louis towards
'mercantile education' at the expense of Latin and Greek,
believing it unacceptable to abandon the *Ratio Studiorum*.
The Missouri Jesuits protested, reasonably enough, that English
and French were the only languages which the the highly
mobile population wanted their sons to be taught. But the
Mission, which following his Visitation became a Vice-Province,

caught something of Peter Kenney's enthusiasm for action. It set up so many schools and other institutions that by the 1840s Father General Roothaan in Rome became alarmed and wrote to a bishop in Kentucky that 'the great plague of the Society in your part of the world is this, that we undertake too many things and do not leave time for the training of subjects. . . . I cannot help entertaining very great fears for that portion of the Society where the harvest is gathered before it is ripe and where one must look for grass instead of grain.'

The Irish had escaped such rebukes when they founded Clongowes with a very youthful community in 1814, as they also escaped any directive like the stern refusal of Father Roothaan's predecessor to allow the Missouri Jesuits to charge school-fees in 1827. The stolid Belgians had sought permission; the Irish, accustomed by generations of penal oppression not to trouble authority if authority did not trouble them, appear simply to have gone ahead on their own. Father Kenney gave as much satisfaction in Missouri as he had in Maryland. 'I had full confidence in you when I ordered you to undertake so difficult a task. . . . My confidence has been strengthened and increased by the way you have acted,' wrote Father Roothaan, who also reported that favourable comments had reached him from the Americans about their Irish Visitor.[115] Father Kenney himself received a number of letters in the same vein as before and so favourable was the impression he made that he had to fend off a serious effort from within the American hierarchy to have him made Coadjutor Bishop of Cincinnati (he pleaded that the American climate was bad for his asthma).[116]

The mitre, as it happens, was a hazard for more than one Irish Jesuit of the Restoration. We read that Father Paul Ferley, of the companions who went to Sicily, 'was very nearly made a Bishop,'[117] which would have been remarkable since he was only in his twenties at the time, but Father Aylmer was certainly named *dignus* — i.e. placed third on the list — by the clergy of Kildare and Leighlin when that diocese fell vacant in 1819[118] (Rome chose, instead, the famous James Doyle, who would become known from his episcopal signature as 'JKL'). Long before Cincinnati loomed, Father Kenney was proposed as Coadjutor Bishop of Kerry by the diocesan priests with the strong approval of their aged Bishop.[119] On that occasion he had been spared by the intervention of the Lord Lieutenant of Ireland, who let it be known in the right quarters that the appointment would not be favoured by the government: [120] an interesting example of the Veto, which the Irish Church had persuaded Rome to refuse to grant to the British Crown, being actually wielded in practice. 'It seems', wrote old Father Plowden from England, that 'your conference with Mr Peel terrified [the] Ministers.'[121] The confidence of the Irish clergy and hierarchy in the Jesuits contrasts with the circumstances in England immediately after the Restoration. With one exception, the Vicars Apostolic (the English bishops) were unhappy that the Society was revived; they felt that Protestant opinion would be antagonised and emancipation delayed.[122] They asked the government what it thought, making the same mistake as the Belgian Jesuits in Missouri. A question asked invites an answer, and the English government gave the only answer politically possible: it could not look with favour on the proposal to restore the Society. The Vicars Apostolic then decided it would be imprudent to recognise the Restoration in England, with the result that it became difficult to have scholastics ordained as Jesuit priests. They were diverted instead to the ranks of the secular clergy. It needed the intervention of Pope Leo XII in 1828 to persuade the Church authorities to acknowledge that the Society of Jesus had been restored in England.

What happened in England was doubly sad. It was unfortunate that a new beginning should have been delayed for an inadequate cause (emancipation was achieved, through Irish rather than English endeavour, by a popular leader who was openly friendly with the Jesuits — the young O'Connells were among the first boys sent to Clongowes). Even worse was the pain suffered by men now elderly who had brought the Jesuit tradition back to England from Liège, set up a fine Catholic school-cum-seminary, re-established the Society by means of the Russian expedient when all seemed lost and generously helped to form the members of a new Irish Mission. The Irish Jesuits appear to have responded to the problems of their old teachers. It is difficult otherwise to explain why Father Aylmer arranged for six English scholastics to complete their theology courses in Clongowes about 1820.[123] The English can scarcely have been feeling the lack of physical accommodation or of a school of theology, since they were well equipped in these respects themselves. But if they risked having to embark on courses leading to ordination as secular priests, the attraction of Ireland as a country where scholastics could complete their formation as Jesuits was obvious.

Ireland offered refuge to brethren from farther afield as well. Father Claude Jautard, a pre-Suppression Jesuit from Bordeaux, had come to Ireland during the French Revolution, and at the age of 74 was admitted to the restored Society; he served for a time as Spiritual Father (i.e. Spiritual Director) at Clongowes, where he died in 1821.[124] In the following year there arrived the exotically named Fathers Casimir Hlasko, Franciscus Stackhowski and Adam Petryzca. These were Polish Jesuits expelled from the White Russian Province which, having served its providential purpose, was suppressed about now by the Tsar: he had turned against the Jesuits because their allegiance to Rome prevented them from falling in with his plans to unify the various religions in his dominions.[125] The banishment of the Society began in 1820 after the death of Father General Brzozowski, who had given such encouragement to Father O'Callaghan and Father Betagh, approved the revival of the Irish Mission prior to the Restoration and nominated Father Kenney to undertake the Visitation to Maryland. Father Brzozowski was forbidden by the Tsar to leave Russia at the Restoration. The return of the General to Rome did not therefore take place until the General Congregation of 1820 elected Father Luigi Fortis to replace the doughty old Pole who had died in distant Russia. Father Aylmer represented Ireland at this Congregation and it was here that he picked up the exiled Polish Fathers.[126]

The story would be repeated forty years later, when the Garibaldian forces expelled the Jesuits from Sicily and Naples. No fewer than two Fathers, two Brothers and fifteen novices from these dispersed provinces were found places in the new novitiate at Milltown Park[127] in the southern suburbs of Dublin; it was an appropriate mark of gratitude for the hospitality extended in Sicily to the Irish during their time of tribulation in the past. One of the Sicilian priests, Father Aloysius Sturzo, was to be a distinguished member of the Irish Province (as the Vice-Province had become in 1860), serving successively as Rector of Milltown, Rector of Tullabeg, Provincial (1877-1880) and Superior of the Australian Mission.[128] The two Brothers from Sicily, Michael Azzopardi[129] and Salvator Spiteri,[130] must have left an impression as well. Both were cooks at Milltown; an idle thought summons up the picture of Irish novices struggling to cope with such unheard-of dishes as *tagliatelle carbonara* or *spaghetti napolitana*.

Major developments had taken place in Dublin long before the opening of Milltown. By the 1820s it had become clear that Hardwicke Street chapel was insufficiently commodious for a city church and the community attached to it. The Jesuits were on the point of acquiring a site in nearby Great Charles Street when the landlord discovered that a 'Mass-House' was to be built there by the purchasers; he refused to complete the sale[131] (the Church of Ireland Free Church was shortly afterwards opened on the site). A better location in the same neighbourhood was bought in Upper Gardiner Street and the foundation stone of the Church of Saint Francis Xavier was laid in 1829; Archbishop Murray said the first Mass in the unfinished building in 1832 and blessed it upon its completion in 1835.[132] Together with the adjacent residence, it cost some £6,500 — the balance of the old Mission Funds still in hand.[133] It was money well spent, primarily because of the addition it made to the Catholic life of the city with its facilities for frequent Masses and other devotions, sodality meetings, retreats and confessions, but also because of its aesthetic quality. Basically renaissance-classical in the 'Jesuit' style, it recalls many other public churches of the Society — the Gèsu in Rome, for example, or Saint Michael's in Munich. The wide single aisle, the transeptal altars, the sumptuous sanctuary — all these recur in many of these churches, but the architect tends to modify each to match its surroundings. Thus, Munich has rococco features while the mother-church in Rome, for all its baroque richness, has not totally shed the sobriety of the Counter-Reformation. In Dublin Saint Francis Xavier's, or 'Gardiner Street' as the people call it, is 'set with exemplary good-manners into the Georgian facades'[134] among which it stands: the four Ionic columns of its granite portico are as stately and restrained as any in this city of classical buildings, and the interior, while finely decorated, reveals an insular simplicity rather than continental exuberance.

Father Esmonde's obituary says that he 'built our Church in Gardiner-street, Dublin, and was in great part his own architect'.[135] Others have suggested this also[136] but the architect appears in fact to have been named Keane — whether T. B. Keane,[137] Joseph B. Keane[138] or John B. Keane[139] seems uncertain. John B. is most likely: this name, with an address at 19 Mabbot Street, is said to have been signed on specifications for a chapel in Upper Gardiner Street in 1829[140] and a 'John Keane, architect,' otherwise identified as 'John B. Keane', was residing at 29 Lower Mount Street in 1850.[141] This implies progression to a more genteel neighbourhood, such as a successful architect might have expected to achieve in early Victorian Dublin — and the architect of Gardiner Street Church deserved every success. It is arguably the only building of special aesthetic merit commissioned by the Jesuits in Ireland — at least until the construction of Andrew Devane's fine chapel at Gonzaga College, Dublin, in the 1960s and the dramatically effective central concourse of the Crescent Comprehensive put up in Limerick in the 1970s. Father Esmonde's involvement with Gardiner Street was probably that of a client of well-formed tastes, rather as John Henry Newman would be in the case of University Church 25 years later. It is interesting to note that the interior has 'capitals after the style of [the] Roman College, having alto-relievo cherubim on the abaci' and that 'Father Esmonde, during his stay in Rome, interested himself in the High Altar, which is made of very beautiful marbles'.[142] The inspiration in matters of detail, deriving from a Roman visit, foreshadows Newman's experience exactly.[143]

5

MANY MANSIONS

THE early 1830s marked a watershed in the history of the
Irish Mission. The previous year had brought Catholic
Emancipation — superficially, of little enough benefit except
to those Catholics who could afford, and wanted, to be
Members of Parliament; in reality, an enormous boost to the
morale of the Catholic people and their pastors. A plea for
justice had been phrased as a political objective, pursued
through the constitutional process and conceded by a reluctant government whom a popular movement had outfaced
under the guidance of a charismatic leader. No longer did
Catholics feel it necessary to keep their heads down for fear
of attracting attention which might result in the revival of
dormant laws against them.

The Jesuits had been precursors in this assertion of self-
confidence when they opened their college at Clongowes a
mere twenty miles from Dublin, the centre of Ascendancy
privilege and oligarchic rule. Now they were repeating the
exercise by building a handsome church with a dignified but
prominent façade on the still fashionable Gardiner Street,
around the corner from the even more fashionable Mountjoy Square, apparently oblivious to the clauses of the Emancipation Act designed to prohibit the expansion of the Society
in Ireland. Their own status was enhanced in 1830 when the
Mission became a Vice-Province, so close in autonomy to a
full province that its head was habitually referred to as the
'Provincial',[1] and the stability of their Irish foundation
seemed guaranteed by the number of Fathers attaining

prominence (like John St Leger and John Curtis) who had not yet entered the Society when Peter Kenney brought his little group home from Sicily. Although the old Mission Fund was now exhausted, the Jesuits' dynamism was not. Whatever resources they possessed, they determined to put to use.

With the consecration of Gardiner Street church, the chapel in Hardwicke Street was no longer needed for worship. Here was the opportunity to establish another school, a day-school this time, in the tradition of the Jesuits of penal Dublin. As Rector of Gardiner Street, Father Aylmer had the old chapel and the rooms attached to it duly adapted, had Father John Shine brought up from Clongowes to be Prefect of Studies and sent Father Robert O'Ferrall — brother to the future Governor of Malta[2] and only just ordained — over from the new church to assist him. Father Kenney was in America on his second Visitation; once again, his steadying influence would have been welcome. For all his energy, Father Aylmer possessed only 'moderate, but useful, talents'[3] and seems to have launched the enterprise without adequate preparation. St Francis Xavier's school, as it was called, had fifty-one pupils by the end of 1832 but this apparent success was nearly its undoing. The building was unsuitable for such numbers and the staff was grossly overstretched: Fathers Shine and O'Ferrall were primarily attached to Gardiner Street where they heard confessions, preached, said public Masses and undertook calls to attend the sick — as well as teaching in the school.[4] A cholera epidemic killed both of them in August 1834: Father Shine died in Dublin, Father O'Ferrall at the O'Ferrall family estate in County Kildare, whither he had been sent following his colleague's death.[5] Oddly enough, epidemics had a way of springing up in the vicinity of Father Aylmer. He had been Rector of Clongowes when the typhus struck, and an earlier outbreak of cholera had taken off Brother Terence O'Brien, a carpenter, during the construction of Gardiner Street church.[6] (Father Aylmer himself died of a heart attack in 1849).

The Hardwicke Street school limped on a few years more, but only inexperienced men were assigned to it: very likely, no others could be found. Father Aylmer admitted as much in 1839 when he wrote to the General that they had 'not enough workers to serve both church and school'.[7] He might have added that St Francis Xavier's was coming under assault from within the Irish Vice-Province since Father John Curtis, now Rector of Tullabeg, had been urging that one of the Hardwicke Street priests should be transferred to his college, even if this meant closing the Dublin school.[8] Reading between the lines of these and other comments, the impression comes across that the Jesuits were slightly ashamed of Hardwicke Street. Times were changing and premises more suitable to the age of the penal laws, run by priests who combined parochial with teaching duties, undermined the image of excellence which the Society was increasingly trying to convey — not, be it said, for its own sake but to show that Irish Catholics could match the sophistication of the Ascendancy who still retained so much control over the country's affairs. Perhaps this rationalises the Jesuit attitude at the time overmuch, but hindsight gives it substance. When one of the finest Ascendancy mansions in the city came on the market, the needs of St Francis Xavier's for better accommodation suddenly acquired a new importance. Charles Young, a scholastic soon to be ordained, renounced an inheritance in favour of the Society which made it possible to tender for the mansion;[9] he also made his brother, Sylvester Young, available to act as middleman in negotiating the purchase,[10] for bigotry could still prevent the sale of property to a religious order and the Jesuits had no wish to be frustrated again as they had been when they wanted the site in Great Charles Street eighteen years previously.

Thus the brothers Young between them secured Belvedere House in Great Denmark Street, only two blocks from Gardiner Street Church, as the new location for St Francis Xavier's school. It was quite magnificent, if somewhat dilapidated after lengthy want of occupation, and was a real bargain at the £1,800 which it cost the Jesuits.[11] The second Earl of Belvedere had built it as his town house in 1786, during the heyday of Grattan's Parliament and the high summer of Georgian Dublin. The dignified facade of brickwork and stone, four stories high, five windows wide, with broad steps leading up to its pillared and fan-lit doorway, looked southwards over the city and dominated the slope of North Great George's Street lined with lesser houses in the Georgian vogue. This was dramatic enough, but more astonishing was the almost decadently rich plasterwork of the hall and staircase and great rooms inside: the Apollo room, the Diana room, the Venus room, all named for the themes picked out in brightly-coloured plaster relief upon their ceilings.[12] The centrepiece of the Venus ceiling had to go before young boys could be permitted to study beneath it[13] — call it prudery or prudence as you will! — but otherwise the Jesuits proved to be good custodians of the splendour that came into their care.

It sat well with the purpose they adopted for the school, or rather for the College of St Francis Xavier as it had now become. An announcement in 1842 said that 'The System of Education in this Establishment comprises the full Classical Course, adapted to those who are destined for the Universities or the Learned Professions'[14] but provision was also made for 'Those who are not intended for the Learned Professions': no doubt a wise precaution to encourage enrolment in a city where many young men were destined for a lifetime of commercial activity. Again, it sounds to our modern ears elitist. Again, we have to avoid reading our perceptions into an earlier age. The object of Belvedere, the name popularly given to the college and quickly adopted by the Jesuits themselves, was certainly to educate a particular segment of the growing Catholic middle class. After the Jesuit manner, the work was undertaken to meet a need. The need now was partly an extended version of that which inspired the opening of Clongowes. Catholics were becoming more prominent in the life of the capital: in the legal and medical professions, in wholesale and retail trading, on the City Corporation. The same autumn that Belvedere was launched saw Daniel O'Connell elected Lord Mayor as a result of legislation for municipal reform which he himself had largely inspired: it was a significant development, for it brought a degree of governing authority — however small — within the reach of persons outside the tory oligarchy, and many of these were Catholics in the professional and commercial classes.[15] The need to equip their sons to benefit from the new opportunities opening up was evident.

Furthermore, a number of parents in these reasonably well-off classes had taken to sending their boys to Protestant schools, which, given the unecumenical temper of the times, was thought to put their Catholic faith at risk. It would be futile to deny that sheer snobbery often underlay this practice. It is also relevant to remember that parents who wanted their sons to succeed in a world of jealously protected privilege saw 'the right school' as a valuable asset. By providing a school as prestigious as any other in Dublin, the Jesuits pragmatically met two pressing requirements at once. They made quality education available to families who wanted it — as we have seen, ability to pay was not imperative — and they provided the means by which the faith of young Catholics could be safeguarded without prejudice to their future advancement. The motives of the parents in those early days may not always have been admirable but the Jesuits could scarcely be impugned for creating a cadre of educated Catholics capable of serving their fellow-citizens at any level in the life of the city. It may indeed be that the Society of Jesus should also have queried the whole idea of class structure and privilege, as it would be found doing in the late twentieth century. But prophetic insight is a gift of the Spirit and, if not granted, cannot be commissioned. It would, in any event, not have absolved the Jesuits from simultaneously preparing young men for the world as it was, rather than as it ideally should have been.

The result was a school socially more mixed than Clongowes had been at the outset, thereby reflecting the variety of its urban environment. That variety, though, was limited enough in the immediate neighbourhood of Belvedere. In the school's first decade the householders of Great Denmark Street and North Great George's Street, Gardiner Street and Mountjoy Square included an inordinate number of barristers and solicitors, with a few surgeons and wine-merchants to relieve the monotony.[16] Several professors of music, a baronet, the Spanish Consul and the Attorney-General made for one kind of variety; a baker, a shoemaker, a straw-bonnet maker and a dairyman made for another. The baker may well have sent his son to Belvedere, for it is said that 'a very fine lady' was much distressed to find that her baker's young-

ster shared the same classroom with *her* son; she begged the
Rector to prevent 'undue intimacy' between the boys; the
Rector reassured her by pointing out that since the baker's
boy was always at the top of the class and hers always at the
bottom, she had nothing to fear![17] In truth, however, these
streets were solidly middle-class in the 1840s and most of the
boys would have come from the professional background
which typified the residents of the area: in the days before
trustworthy public transport, the greater number on the roll
lived within easy walking distance of the school, so variety
was not to be sought in imports from across the river or the
outer suburbs. This was not to change until the 1880s, when
an imaginative Rector, Father Tom Finlay, would engage
coaches to collect boys from faraway homes and deliver them
back in the evening: an early example of the school bus.

The Jesuits were, of course, concerned with more than
mere appearances. High quality education demanded fully
committed teachers. Belvedere needed better than the part-
time services of Gardiner Street priests. The strain upon the
resources of the Vice-Province was evident from the fact that
it took four years to build up a community attached solely to
the school under its own Rector. Thereafter, the school
flourished. At least, it flourished in the numbers seeking
enrolment. Its output was another matter. As would be found
later in Limerick and Galway, a Jesuit day school was a very
convenient preparatory establishment for a city youngster to
attend before going on to the more daunting conditions of
a boarding school. Parents acted wisely in this: a boy who
had been to Belvedere or the Crescent, say, had the advantage
in Clongowes or Tullabeg over those who came from other
schools, however good, which gave no introduction to Jesuit
ways and emphases, devotions, standards, even language.
Usually he had known one or more of the boarding-school
masters at some time in his former school, and the second
school was in a real sense a continuation of the first. But
what was helpful for the boy could be disastrous for the day
school if too many of his contemporaries took the same
course. A modern commentator speaks of the 'nomads':
'Belvedere was but a stepping-stone to most of them, and the
eminent figures in the Old Boys' Union were frequently also

graduates of Stonyhurst, or Clongowes, or occasionally European institutions, or indeed might have served out the remainder of their schooldays under Pharaohs who knew not Ignatius.'[18] Not that all Belvedere boys proceeded to boarding school. Many were expected to take up what an early Rector called 'jobs in the city,' for which schooling to the age of fifteen or sixteen was considered sufficient by their parents.

The haemorrhage of senior pupils probably explains the exceptional deference paid to parents by the Belvedere authorities in the school's early years. Father General Roothaan in far-off Rome might sternly require that the *Ratio Studiorum*, which he had taken the trouble to update,[19] be applied so as 'to produce learned men rather than merchants,' but this was scarcely a norm to carry much weight in a centre of commerce, and the Rector in 1847, Father Patrick Meagher, had to make the embarrassing admission to the General that they had lost both copies of the revised *Ratio* which he had sent them. This is revealing. If the Belvedere community had been in the habit of consulting the Society's guidelines, their copies would hardly have been lost. It may be that the Rector had a practical bent traceable to his transatlantic background (he was a native of Newfoundland) [20] but in fact the demand for modern languages, modern history, geography, mathematics and science had to be conceded if parents were to be tempted to leave their boys in the school. A compromise was worked out whereby the mornings were given over to Latin and Greek — the traditional foundations of learning — and the afternoons to what Victorian parents considered 'practical' subjects. (Logic, metaphysics and moral philosophy were offered too, in conformity with the *Ratio*, but seem to have had few takers.) This qualified acceptance of functional education, and even an unprecedented visit to Ireland in 1849 by Father Roothaan himself (in exile from revolutionary Rome), must have left successive Generals unconverted since, nine years on, the Rector of the day was still — and somewhat desperately — justifying the system to the then head of the Society. And as late as 1884 Father Finlay would be found telling the General how parents had to be persuaded 'that their sons will get a better education here than in any boarding school'.

The utilitarian attitude of the parents in the late 1840s can be readily understood. These were the years of the Great Hunger. Father Meagher starkly described its consequences in 1847: 'in this climate of universal misery and calamity, where a quarter of our people are dying of famine, and another quarter forced to emigrate, parents choose an education not to make learned men of their sons, but to fit them to earn a living.' The sense of crisis must indeed have been pervasive. Although urban-dwellers generally, with a more varied diet that the peasantry, and in particular the middle classes who could afford to buy what food they wanted, managed to escape the direct consequences of the potato-blight, the horror of the Famine pressed in upon them daily.[21] Refugees from the stricken countryside crammed the city, some seeking passage on the 'coffin-ships' to America, many looking for no more than the harsh shelter of the workhouses. The New Model Soup Kitchen at the Royal Barracks was serving more than 8,000 meals a day. The epidemics so familiar in nineteenth-century Dublin resumed with unprecedented virulence: first typhus, then the cholera: marquees had to be put up to accommodate the overflow of patients from the fever hospitals. Then the army was reinforced to cope with anticipated rebellion. The remarkable fact was not that erudition was retired for a while as an educational priority but that schools remained open at all and that the work continued of preparing boys to take up useful roles in the crumbling world of Irish adulthood.

The Famine hit hardest in the South, the West and the Midlands. William Francis Butler, then a schoolboy at Tullabeg, wrote later that 'the winter of 1848-49 dwells in my memory as one long night of sorrow'.[22] In the aftermath of this terrible disaster paralysis gripped the whole of Ireland and infected the Jesuits also. The expansionism last embodied in the opening of Belvedere College ground to a halt. No new house was founded until a residence was opened in Killiney, County Dublin, in 1852 — and that was closed a year later.[23] The pessimism of the times can be caught in the advice which Father Curtis gave in 1854 to John Henry Newman, whom Archbishop Cullen of Dublin had brought over from England to set up a Catholic University: the class of youths did not exist in Ireland who would come to the University, Father Curtis said, and Newman should tell the Archbishop to abandon the idea.[24] The shortage of manpower cannot have helped morale. The Jesuits received numerous requests to establish schools or churches in various parts of the country. Before the Famine, they had been unable to act upon invitations from the Bishops of Waterford[25] and Galway,[26] and the national calamity struck before any decision could have been reached on an alleged proposal that they should take charge of the new missionary college of All Hallows in Dublin.[27] In the 1850s invitations came from the Bishops of Down and Connor and of Kerry, from Glasgow and from Sydney,[28] none of which were proceeded with. The approaches from abroad indicate the status enjoyed by the Irish Vice-Province. As well as the request to open a school and church in Glasgow, it was suggested that Glasgow should be attached 'to Province (*sic*) of Ireland, and Edinburgh to Province of England'. The Sydney request was 'to take charge of the University' — the General decided the Irish Jesuits were too few in number at this time to undertake the task.

Not surprisingly, however, a Vice-Province in such demand could not long remain dormant. In 1854 Father Patrick Duffy and Father William Ronan went as military chaplains to the Crimea.[29] Both would be heard of again. A House of Studies for Jesuit students of theology was opened in North Frederick Street, Dublin, in 1857. Like the Killiney project, this had to be closed within a year[30] but negotiations were soon under way for property at Milltown Park in the southern suburbs of the capital to accommodate an Irish novitiate and a residence where lay groups could come for retreats. And in 1859 the Jesuits returned to two bastions of the old Irish Mission, the cities of Galway and Limerick.

In the opinion of the future Cardinal Newman, Dr John Ryan of Limerick was 'the cleverest Bishop' he met in Ireland 'and certainly to me the kindest'.[31] It was Bishop Ryan who invited the Jesuits back to Limerick, having first consulted Father Edmund O'Reilly,[32] a former priest of the diocese who had been a Maynooth professor before joining the Society of Jesus — he had later been nominated to the chair of theology at the Catholic University by Newman.[33] The Bishop wanted the Jesuits to take over the diocesan seminary of St Munchin's, run it as a boarding as well as a day school, and open a public church. Father Joseph Lentaigne, the Vice-Provincial, could not contemplate another boarding school at the time, given the demands of the Society's houses already established or contemplated, but he agreed to the day school. The Bishop was happy with this and after a fortnight's closure to facilitate the transfer from a staff of secular priests (who had become too involved in politics for Dr Ryan's liking) St Munchin's resumed in March, 1859, under Jesuit administration. The seminary, it should be noted, was not a college for the training of priests but rather a secondary school from which it was hoped to recruit some of the well-educated senior boys to proceed to the priesthood at the end of their schooldays. Classes at first did not go beyond what was called Humanities in the Jesuit system, i.e. Fifth Year. Father O'Reilly's influence could be detected in the six Jesuits appointed to the Limerick community: no fewer than three of them were Maynooth men, which was calculated to placate the diocesan clergy; as well as these, there was Father Edmund Hogan, a Celtic scholar of repute, which was bound to please the Bishop, and Father Thomas Kelly who had been a pupil at Hardwicke Street and Belvedere[34] and could therefore be counted on to understand the needs of a day school, as also could his brother, Father Edward Kelly, whom Father Lentaigne made Rector.

As we shall see, the Galway community was being built up at the same time and with the same care, which led to grumblings of discontent elsewhere. Father Michael O'Ferrall, Rector of Belvedere, wrote to the General in 1861: 'Two or three new houses have been opened. We are left with the slower teachers . . . the younger and more industrious are sent to other places, such as Limerick.'[35] Clearly, the Irish Jesuits had not learned — perhaps, did not *want* to learn — how to avoid the risks of expanding to the very limit of their resources. This trust in Providence, while getting on with the job which had to be done, dated back at least to the energetic Superiorship of Robert Nugent and endures to the present day as a particularly admirable trait of the Society in Ireland.

But stretched elastic sometimes snaps. We have already seen cases of ventures which lasted less than a year. It was to happen in Limerick too. Dr Ryan's successor, Bishop George Butler, asked the Jesuits to open a school specifically for poor boys in addition to St Munchin's. They went ahead, but St Patrick's School in Bedford Row lasted little more than a year, from March 1864 to June 1865: no additional staff were available and the St Munchin's community were simply overreaching themselves in trying to run two schools at the same time. It would be interesting to know how far the decision to abandon St Patrick's was influenced not only by the strain on the men involved but by the way in which its purpose was undermined from the outset, for it seems that a number of parents who were in no way poor sent their younger boys to the new school as preparation (at a nominal fee of five shillings a quarter) for eventual entry to the seminary — some from country districts even placed their youngsters in city lodgings so that they could benefit from early access to Jesuit education! Short of applying a means test, the Jesuits had no way of stopping this and it must have helped convince them that the project was scarcely worth the effort they had to put into it.

Meanwhile, the main enterprise in Limerick had been progressing well, especially after the Jesuits acquired the handsome Crescent House, so called from its dominant position in the Georgian circus known as the Crescent. Saint Munchin's moved here in 1862 from nearby Hartstonge Street and the Jesuits were now able to offer a full curriculum, including classical and modern languages, mathematics, physics, history, geography and elocution. The tone of the prospectus differed little from that of Belvedere: 'young gentlemen' were prepared 'for the University and the Ecclesiastical Colleges . . . the Learned Professions . . . the Public Service, civil and military'. But there was a more open admission that the world of business also existed. It could scarcely be ignored since, following the repeal of the Corn Laws, Limerick had become very active as one of the six major ports and railheads through which American grain was being brought into the country in quantity — largely to avert a repetition of the Famine by providing a cheap substitute for the blight-prone potato.[36] Accordingly, the school had a

'Mercantile Department' in which 'an extensive and accurate knowledge is imparted of Arithmetic, Book-keeping, Abstracts, and the other requirements of the Actuary's office'. Nor was the original objective of the school forgotten: several boys qualified each year to enter Maynooth as students for the priesthood. In 1867, however, the Bishop decided to re-establish his own seminary in Hartstonge Street. A temporary depletion of numbers followed, not helped by the fact that the Jesuit St Munchin's increasingly found itself exposed to the problem besetting Belvedere: many of the boys were removed at 13 or 14 years of age and sent off by their parents to boarding schools. The Jesuits' deliberate abstention from politics was also said to have done them some harm about this time in the most politically-conscious city of Ireland.

The decline was short-lived. A change of name, from St Munchin's to the Sacred Heart College, and the despatch of a new generation of teachers (notably Tom and Peter Finlay, then scholastics) brought new vigour to the Crescent in the 1870s. The Jesuits in these years became part of the fabric of Limerick life. From their arrival in the old St Munchin's, the Fathers had preached in city churches, given retreats for religious orders and probably — it is not certain — conducted missions in rural areas, both in Irish and English. They maintained a public oratory, first at Hartstonge Street and then in the Crescent. In 1869 the Church of the Sacred Heart, which the Jesuits built beside the College, was opened for public worship: its style might be described as modified Jesuit classical, distinguished by a profusion of Corinthian pilasters. Apart from providing the many Masses expected in those days of intensely practised Catholicism, the Jesuits soon set up the confraternities and sodalities through which the traditional devotions of the Society were propagated: the Sodality of the Blessed Virgin, the Confraternity of the Bona Mors, the Sacred Heart Confraternity. If none acquired the fame (or notoriety) of the corresponding Redemptorist organisations in the same city, the Jesuit retreats, sermons and spiritual guidance in the confessional had many devotees — not only among local people but in the country-side, and in Counties Clare and Tipperary too.[37] In our pluralist and ecumenical age, when faith finds expression in

ways unknown in the past, when also faith for many has withered on the bough, we cannot easily recapture the often
fierce commitment to religion normal in Ireland long ago.
This is not the place to discuss either the virtues or shortcomings of that commitment, the great good in it or the
harm which it sometimes brought about, but it should be
noted that the Jesuits played their part in sustaining and
serving popular faith, and they did so with a special expertise
developed through their long and diverse training and their
rigorous subjugation of self.

Paralleling that pastoral work, and indeed started sooner,
was the spiritual formation of the boys in the College. Features
common to all Jesuit schools were introduced at an early
stage in the history of the Crescent: the Sodality of the Blessed
Virgin, to which senior boys were elected by their peers, the
Berchmans Sodality for acolytes, the annual retreat (a modified form of the Spiritual Exercises of Saint Ignatius) at the
beginning of the academic year. Central to the curriculum
was religious knowledge. As the prospectus put it, the pupils
were 'instructed in the doctrines of the Catholic faith and
trained with great care to piety and virtue'. This phrasing,
dated 1863, demonstrates the growing inclination (some
might say, triumphal inclination) of Catholics to assert their
credal allegiance. The Belvedere prospectus, twenty years
before, had promised more vaguely that 'constant care'
would be taken 'to train the pupils in the precepts and
practice of Christian Morality' and that instruction would be
given 'at least once a week . . . on the principles of Religion'.[38]
It is not, of course, to be imagined that pre-Famine Belvedere
was in any way less diligent in the promotion of Catholic
teaching. It is rather that a hint of flaunting may be detected
in the reference to 'doctrines' and 'Catholic faith' by contrast
with 'precepts' and 'the principles of Religion'.

The point is not only semantic, for the Irish Catholic
mentality was changing in the decades following the Famine,
becoming more dependent on ecclesiastical authority as
ecclesiastical authority itself was becoming more dependent
on Rome. This centralising tendency typified the mid-
nineteenth century Church everywhere, but especially in
Ireland because there a demoralised people looked to the

Church for leadership in the void left by the death of O'Connell. This in turn led them to express their identity in stridently denominational terms instead of the democratic values bequeathed them by the Liberator. If this seems a lot to read into the wording of school prospectuses, it should be added that the wording chosen tells us something about the Jesuits who chose it. It tells us at least that they were not averse to swimming with the tide, and there is no reason to doubt they took pleasure in it.

If they did, it was not altogether to be wondered at. The Irish Jesuits belonged to an international religious order which had suffered a long suppression under the influence of the same forces which brought about the French Revolution. In continental Europe, where the Society was largely based and where many Irish Jesuits received their formation, few of the Fathers could see good in the contemporary ideas of liberty. They preferred to think that the clock might be turned back to the imagined better epoch before philosophies held sway that would dechristianise the state. 'The Jesuits as a whole — there were exceptions — found it a painful, anxious, and uneasy experience to adjust to the nineteenth century.'[39] They made little effort to understand the complex historical factors which brought about the new ideas: such factors, for example, as the neglect by the Church to enter into dialogue with the Enlightenment. Accordingly, the continental Jesuits in the decades after the Restoration were blind to 'the basically spiritual nature of the aspirations of the era of the French Revolution'[40] and the Society became associated in the public mind with reactionary politics which had nothing to do with the Gospel message. This caused the restored Jesuits from time to time to be expelled from one country or another, an experience which naturally did nothing to convert them to the modern age.

During these years also the 'temporal power' of the Pope as ruler of the Papal States and the city of Rome was whittled away and finally eliminated by the liberal advocates of a united Italy and their anti-clerical armies. Although the 'temporal power' had nothing to do with the Gospel, the assault upon it confirmed the unfortunate — dare one say, unIgnatian? — tendency of the continental Jesuits to look

Father Peter Kenney brought the Jesuits back to Ireland in 1811, served for a year as Vice-President of Maynooth and opened Clongowes in 1814.

The school band paraded through the grounds of Clongowes in the 1830s (above). As a scholastic, the future Father William Delany played the tuba in the Tullabeg band in 1865 (below).

*Father Bartholomew Esmonde **(left)** was one of the Irish Jesuits in Rome in 1814 when Pope Pius VII declared the Society restored. He had a major influence on the design of Gardiner Street Church **(below)**, which was 'set with exemplary good manners into the Georgian facades' – Craig, 292.*

(Above) The 'almost decadently rich plasterwork of the hall and staircase' in Belvedere. (Below, left) The college as it was in 1888 after Father Tom Finlay (below, right) had extended it during his rectorship. As a scholastic Father Finlay had helped to establish the high reputation of the Crescent. He became a Professor in the Royal and National Universities, champion of the co-operative movement and founder of Studies.

(Above) A 'bird's eye' view of Clongowes as it was about 1880. (Right) Father John Conmee in his later years. 'And they gave three groans for Baldyhead Dolan and three cheers for Conmee and they said he was the decentest rector that was ever in Clongowes' – Joyce, 53–54.

(Above, left) Father Joseph Lentaigne, who entered the Society at the age of 38, became the first Irish Provincial in 1860 and went to Australia to prepare the ground for the Mission. (Above, right) Father Joseph Dalton, formerly Rector of Tullabeg, was Superior of the Australian Mission from 1866 to 1883 and first Rector of Riverview College, Sydney. (Right) Father William Delany in 1901 during his second term as President of University College.

The calibre of Father Delany's University College can be gauged from this group of students and staff photographed about 1901. (Standing, from left) Father George O'Neill, S.J., Fellow of the Royal University, who would become Professor of English at U.C.D. after the establishment of the National University and later a famous preacher in Australia; James Joyce, destined to be 'the only author in the English language more written about than Shakespeare'; John Marcus O'Sullivan, a future Professor of History at U.C.D. and Minister for Education; Bob Kinahan, later an eminent K.C.; Séamus Clandillon, who would be Ireland's first Director of Broadcasting; Patrick Semple, Professor of Latin at U.C.D. from 1909 to 1947. (Seated, centre row, from left) George Clancy, who as Mayor of Limerick would be murdered by the Black-and-Tans; Father Edmund Hogan, S.J., Fellow of the Royal and a leading authority on the Irish language; Edouard Cadic, later Professor of French at U.C.D.; Father Joseph Darlington, S.J. (Father Delany's assistant). (Front row, from left) Felix Hackett, future Professor of Physics at U.C.D. and President of the Royal Dublin Society; Seamus O'Kelly, a Gaelic scholar who became a medical doctor and Lecturer in Obstetrics at U.C.D.; Michael Lennon, who became well-known both as a District Justice and as a critic of James Joyce; and Con Curran, renowned authority on the architecture of Dublin.

(Above) John Redmond, M.P., who had just won Home Rule for Ireland, speaking at the Clongowes centenary celebrations in 1914. The Great War broke out two months later. One of the Jesuit chaplains killed in the war would be Father Willie Doyle (below, left), whose reputation for sanctity has been equalled in the Province perhaps only by that of Father John Sullivan (below, right) who had been an Anglican before becoming a Catholic. Father Sullivan died in 1933.

backwards rather than ahead and to fail to discern the signs of the times. The 'spontaneity, therefore, sureness, and above all, freedom from the past with which the Society moved into the sixteenth century did not stamp the European Jesuits of the nineteenth century'.[41]

The Irish Jesuits, like their American counterparts, avoided much of this outlook: the penal age scarcely tempted nostalgia and O'Connell's liberalism had worked massively to the benefit of Catholics, not against them. The Irish Society could find an affinity with Father-General Roothaan. Despite his stern resistance to unthinking liberals, Father Roothaan's prudence and determination to revive the true spirit of Saint Ignatius made him very suspicious of those Jesuits who saw virtue in defending antiquated norms at every opportunity — and for whose indiscretions he was himself often held responsible. It was typical of him that he objected to the launch of the intellectual review *Civilta Cattolica*, the brainchild of an ultra-papalist Italian Jesuit, because it was bound to stir up unnecessary political controversy; the General in this instance was overruled by the Pope, who personally sponsored the first number of the journal.[42]

But if the Irish Jesuits occupied a middle-ground between the extremes of reaction and progress because of their own historical experience, they were still closer to continental Europe than the Americans. They were conscious of the Pope's travails, of the bitterness which marked the confrontation between the Church and the heirs of the Revolution, and were not immune in Ireland itself from the attacks of virulently fundamentalist Protestants who adopted the language of popular liberalism to denounce Catholic teaching and the Pope alike. In the clash of ideals it became more and more difficult to hold to the liberal-Catholic position which O'Connell had represented and which had been abandoned by the bishops under the powerful influence of Cardinal Cullen of Dublin. O'Connell and the continental Christian democrats whom he inspired would be vindicated by the Second Vatican Council, but that was far into the future.[43] In the 1860s it was a matter of choosing sides and the Irish Jesuits, for all their earlier restraint, had no problem in deciding which side they were on. For the next half-century they would remain embattled. A paragraph from the obituary of a colleague written by an unnamed Irish Jesuit in 1914 catches the flavour of the times:

> Father Keating was living in Rome in 1870. On September 20th of that years the troops of the robber King of Sardinia, Victor Emmanuel, laid siege to the city of the Popes, bombarded the walls of Rome, and entered into its streets as conquerors. While all this was going on, Mr Keating, as he then was, was not inactive. In the midst of balls and bombs, in the midst of whizzing bullets and falling masonry, at the risk of his own life, he went here and there and everywhere on his mission of assisting to the best of his power the wounded and dying soldiers and civilians. He was truly a martyr in desire. The same bandits that deprived the Pope of his dominions deprived the Society of their college. They were driven from the Roman College in 1870. In July, 1872, they were banished by the German Government from Maria-Laach, a college they had acquired only ten years before. If Father Keating had remained only a little longer, at Maria-Laach and St Acheul, he would doubtless have been driven out of house and home like so many of his brethren, at the point of a bayonet.[44]

Never mind that the fatalities in the fall of Rome totalled six papal and thirty-two Italian soldiers[45] or that no civilians actually died. The writer's concern was to present an allegory of good and evil, not a narrative of events.

Bishop George Browne of Galway was very anxious that the Jesuits should open a school in the city with which they had so long an association in the past. 'If going on my knees would get the good Fathers of the Society to come amongst us I would bend them,' he wrote to the Vice-Provincial, Father Patrick Bracken, in 1842.[46] 'A most worthy Bishop but his means are not great,' remarked the Jesuit, Father John Grene, the same year. The lack of means was a serious matter for the Society at a time when they had just undertaken the Belvedere project and Clongowes was 'in great difficulties and oppressed with debt'.[47] They had neither men nor money to take on another enterprise so soon. Nor were they much enamoured of the Bishop's proposal for dealing with his own and the Society's shortage of resources: he suggested that the Jesuits should live with him in the one house. Nothing came of his invitation in the end.

When the second-next successor to Dr Browne, Bishop John McEvilly, revived the appeal to the Society seventeen years later he put a much more firm proposition. He would sell them his own house and give them the small St Patrick's chapel to run until they could open a public church of their own. The Vice-Provincial, Father Lentaigne, agreed, bought the Bishop's house at Prospect Hill for £521.13.8d and in March — within a week of their return to Limerick — the Jesuits were established in Galway. Father Robert Haly, a Corkman and well-known preacher who had been Rector in several of the Irish houses,[48] was named Superior and had Fathers John Duffy and William Ronan, the former Crimean chaplain, to help him. After giving a Lenten mission by way of introducing themselves, the Jesuits settled in. Father Haly was soon writing to a cousin: 'My fingers grow stiff with age but my heart, I hope, retains its warmth . . . the air is salubrious but the people wretchedly poor . . . we have a very comfortable dwelling-house in perhaps the best part of the town. . . . Tho' Galway has become my headquarters I am still a rover — a regular gipsy. A short time ago I left Kinvarra and on next Sunday we open a Mission at Carrigaholt. My friends say Galway has added 20 years to my life . . .'. While Superior in Galway, Father Haly remained Director of the Missionary Staff (the Fathers who preached retreats in various parts of the country) and was already 63 years old;[49] hence the references to missions and age. As we shall see, the giving of missions and retreats was to be an important aspect of the work of the Galway community and a source of income for their house.

The important objective, however, as Father Haly noted at an early stage, was 'to do something for the gentry in helping to educate their children'. This was the Bishop's wish and it arose from the existence in the city of Queen's College, Galway (now University College, Galway). This was one of the so-called 'godless colleges' — the others were in Belfast and Cork — set up fifteen years before by the British government to provide university education in Ireland on an undenominational basis.

Although Dr McEvilly's predecessor, Bishop Laurence O'Donnell, had strongly favoured QCG,[50] the hierarchy as a whole had been weaned away from the Queen's Colleges after Rome declared them unsuitable for Catholics; the students' faith, it was argued, might be endangered if they attended institutions which excluded the teaching of religion and were not under episcopal control. Despite this warning, Catholics had not been forbidden to go to the Colleges and Bishop McEvilly decided that one way of guarding against any threat to the students' faith would be to have a good school in the city where young men likely to proceed to QCG would be well instructed in their religion. He calculated that the Jesuits could be counted on to meet the need as he perceived it.

The Jesuits made the school their first priority and by the Spring of 1860 were conducting classes in rooms they had acquired in Eyre Square on a somewhat tenuous lease. Within a year they had a hundred pupils and developments now took place at breakneck speed. The community grew rapidly and numbered eight priests by 1863 — a fair measure of the rapid expansion in teaching, parochial duties and requests for retreats which the Jesuits seemed to generate by their very presence in the West (and understandable cause for the mutterings at Belvedere over the removal of energetic young men for service in the new foundations!). They also undertook a major building programme in Galway, which meant finding funds. Money was 'collected' (no doubt politely begged from local business interests) by Father Haly and Father Ronan; some substantial donations came in; two Jesuits of a leading County Galway family — Fathers Christopher and Michael Bellew — raised £2,000 between them. The house purchased from the Bishop was sold (at a loss) and the proceeds pooled with the other sums so that by early 1861 the Jesuits were able to buy land at Sea Road near Salthill on which to build a church, a college and a community residence of their own. By the following February the residence and the College of St Ignatius were in use. St Ignatius' church, in Victorian-gothic style, was dedicated on its patron's feastday at the end of July 1863. Incidentally, the landlord of the ground which the Jesuits obtained to accommodate these buildings appears to have been one of the same Whaley family from whom, through intermediaries, the Catholic University had secured possession of 86 St Stephen's Green, Dublin, in the 1850s. The Galway purchase thus compounded an irony, for these Whaleys were of the same stock as the renowned priest-hunter, 'Burn-Chapel Whaley', who had been responsible in penal times for the demolition of a number of Mass-houses.[51]

Various problems arose in the course of the feverish activity undertaken by the Society in Galway. Anti-Catholic elements in the city muttered their dislike and seem to have prevented the Jesuits (by outbidding them) from buying a site in which they were interested before they chose Sea Road. Perhaps more distressing was the reaction of the Dominicans, already long established in Galway. Their Prior wrote to the Bishop to say that, while they 'welcomed with especial regard the Fathers of the illustrious Order of St Ignatius', the Jesuits' proposal to build a new church at Sea Road would result in 'ruin' for the Dominicans who already had a church in the same district and depended on local support; the Jesuits should build on the other side of Galway, where they had their house in the past. The Jesuits went ahead with their plans and the dispute must have been eventually patched over because Father Tom Burke, the great Dominican pulpit orator, preached at the dedication of the high altar at St Ignatius' in 1878 and in 1891 the Jesuits subscribed to the costs of a new Dominican church.

The Patrician Brothers had a different anxiety. Bishop McEvilly had invited them to establish a school which would suit many of the Catholic pupils who were attending the Model School (Model Schools were interdenominational as well as co-educational and were run by commissioners over whom the hierarchy had no control; they therefore attracted the same objection as the Queen's Colleges). The Patrician Superior, Brother Paul O'Connor, called on the Jesuits to ask whether they would disapprove if the Brothers were 'to undertake the education in classics of a few boys in humble circumstances who could not afford to pay the fees at St Ignatius'. Father Thomas Halpin 'replied "not at all," and left the Brother under the impression that the Jesuits were not the people to take umbrage at the efforts of others in the cause of education'. Some local families, however, took umbrage at the efforts of the Jesuits, who were expected to attract pupils from the Model School in cases where parents could afford the St Ignatius fees (which averaged £2.12.6d a year). 'The Model School had the confidence of the citizens,' says a note written some time later by an unnamed member of the Galway community. 'It was largely attended and there were people unfriendly who circulated unfavourable reports about the teaching given by the Jesuits.' This was perhaps a less than clever tactic to adopt against members of a Society universally held to be among the foremost authorities on education in Europe, but if the parents were satisfied with the inexpensive Model School their annoyance can be understood over the arrival of religious orders for the patent purpose of providing alternatives at the Bishop's behest.

The terminology of social distinction implied in phrases like Father Haly's reference to 'the gentry' and Brother O'Connor's to 'boys in humble circumstances' had connotations in Galway which were probably not quite the same as elsewhere in the country. Bishop McEvilly wrote to Father Lentaigne to tell him what he had in mind with regard to the Brothers: their school would be 'for the Middle Class which in Galway means the poor Shopkeepers whose children frequent the Model Schools'. In a letter to the people of the diocese announcing the establishment of the Brothers' school, he noted that 'ample provision has been already made for boys of the Upper Classes in the College of St Ignatius'. It would therefore seem that in Galway the gentry were those who sent their sons to the local university institution and the middle class were those who, although impoverished, determined that their children should have secondary schooling at least. The impression that nobody was very well off reflects the depressed state of the city's economy at the time. Despite its excellent harbour, Galway belonged to 'the ports of second rank along the west coast' which 'suffered a dramatic decline in their non-British trading contacts, both incoming and outgoing, in the 1850s and 1860s'.[52] The hope that it might become 'the terminus for a transatlantic steamship service' collapsed in 1861.[53]

The uncertain state of business for the rest of the century meant the Galway Jesuits could never be sure of what would accrue from school fees: in 1867–68 they got £246, in 1869–70 only £116; in February 1888, a note in the account book said 'nearly all the boys' pensions (fees) for this half year are still due'; the following year £131 came in; in 1893, £206. The number of pupils also varied, from an average of 90 in the 1860s to 50 or fewer in the 1880s and early 1890s, with periodic revivals — to 80 in 1882, to 90 at the turn of the century: the latter growth was attributed by some to canvassing for pupils who should have gone to the Patrician school! And there are earlier references to boys transferring from the Model School to St Ignatius. It would therefore be misleading to read too much into Bishop McEvilly's class distinctions. What is certain is that the Jesuits were left heavily dependent on church collections and what they could earn from giving retreats. Thus, in 1869-70 when school fees totalled £116, missions and retreats brought in £197, Mass intentions £169 and church collections £397. Legacies, donations and special collections (at Holy Week ceremonies, on St Patrick's Day and so on) helped to swell the receipts. They were needed. The labour, travel and small earnings involved in mission activity can be seen from a list of the retreats undertaken by named members of the Galway community in August 1892: 'Kenny at Roscrea £6, at Clonakilty £10. Kane at Mountrath £5. Lentaigne at Lurgan £5, at Tralee £8. Flynn at Enniskillen £2. Gallery at Dundalk £5. Donovan at Bantry £10.' This amounted to less than £50 in a vacation month when priests on the school staff would be relatively free to take on mission work! Yet overall the house seems to have been run with managerial efficiency — e.g. 'Total in 1891: Receipts £1,221; Expenses £1,053.' 'This year (1894) total Receipts £1,354; Expenses £1,365.'

Intense hard work lay behind the bland statistics. The retreats speak for themselves: Bantry and Enniskillen were not exactly the next parishes to Galway. Lurgan and Tralee were far distant and at opposite corners of the country, yet were covered by the same man in the one month. The many services provided in the church of St Ignatius had to be kept up, including from its first year 'all the approved devotions of the Society'. It was recorded in 1865 that 'Devotion to the Sacred Heart is especially flourishing. The Fathers are kept busy hearing Confessions. Penitents come to them from far and near.' Three years later Father James Tuite, a future Provincial, wrote: 'Though our College here (in Galway) is the smallest and the poorest of our Irish Colleges it is not to be despised. . . . Not only do we teach School every day but we labour by word and work. . . . Sermons are preached on Sundays and Holy Days, also during Lent and the Month of May. The Spiritual Exercises are given to men and women and to the Scholars.' They would not have thought it so, but in human terms these Jesuits must have been reduced to a kind of drudgery to keep it all going, and a quality school as well. Small wonder that at least once the series of Lenten sermons had to be abandoned for the sake of the community's health!

What manner of men were they who undertook so much in Galway and the other houses? 'As to food and clothing there is all that is absolutely necessary,' says the 1865 note about conditions at the St Ignatius residence. But what was considered necessary may not have amounted to much. Jesuits were disinclined to allow their asceticism to be seen by others and some of them even adopted an air of gracious living in public, like the Gardiner Street missionary whom a Galway colleague met on the way to Queenstown 'travelling *en gentilhomme*', or Father William Delany who encouraged 'acquaintance with good wines' at Tullabeg as 'part of an enlightened education'.[54] Such attitudes, however, were often no more than polite adaptation to the company in which the Jesuits found themselves or the promotion of standards which they wanted their pupils to emulate; it may even have been, in nineteenth-century Ireland, a conscious determination to show themselves socially no whit inferior to the Ascendancy class. In any case, their private lifestyle had little in common with their public image. When Bishop James Doyle of Kildare ('JKL') protested at the sumptuousness of a banquet given in his honour at Clongowes, Father Esmonde told him that the Jesuits' normal fare was 'widely different from that served upon a day that J.K.L. is expected.'[55] At Belvedere the 'founding fathers had no meal between breakfast at nine and dinner at five, except a *bicchierino* (small glass) of wine and a piece of bread for lunch, a custom they had brought from their Sicilian training'.[56] Such simplicity typified the Society. Father-General Roothaan visited his native Holland in 1849. The Dutch Jesuits treated him with the respect they considered proper: 'Roothaan showed some uneasiness about his splendidly furnished room. They tried to reassure him with the remark that it was the "Bishop's room". Nevertheless he asked for another, more ordinary room.'[57]

Having minimal personal requirements did not mean that the Jesuits suppressed every human reaction to their circumstances. The Belvedere lunch they could tolerate in its original form but when, in the name of poverty, a 'weak, acidy beer' was substituted for the wine it led to letters to the General. When Father Roothaan had been transferred to a suitably plain room, he joined the Fathers of the house and called for 'pipes of tobacco'. In all things, moderation . . . including asceticism! This, of course, is to speak of the typical Jesuit, not of those whose heightened sense of the spiritual drove them to an abstinence amounting to heroic virtue. They numbered more than the few, like Father Willie Doyle and Father John Sullivan, who have been especially remembered for their holiness. Brother David MacEvoy, who came from Banagher in County Offaly, can stand for many others. He worked as a cook in the various Irish houses for most of his forty-three years as a Jesuit, literally until his death in 1901. His personal and practical sanctity shines out from his obituary: 'For thirty years he never ate meat. On Christmas Day and Easter Sunday he would, indeed, to save appearances, take a piece of chicken on his plate, but he was never seen to eat it. After his death, there was found beneath the sheet the wooden board on which it had long been his custom to take his scanty and broken rest. His sleeping room (at the Crescent), which hardly deserved the name, was a sort of lumber room adjoining the organ loft of the public church to which he could, without difficulty, have recourse to visit the Blessed Sacrament at any hour of the day or night. . . . He was full of charity towards the poor. As cook and dispenser he pushed his generosity in this respect as far as ever obedience would allow him. . . . Shortly after dinner (at Mungret) you would find Brother MacEvoy, previous to distributing the broken remains, addressing a rather disreputable assembly of tramps at the back door, bidding them to keep from sin and say their prayers. . . . Another Brother, a good friend of his, used sometimes to remark, in a joking way, if you asked him at a certain time in the evening where Brother MacEvoy was: "Oh," nodding his head in the direction of the back yard, "he's round there *giving a mission* at the back door."'[58]

Apart from the saints, and perhaps including some of them, the Irish Jesuits of the Victorian era had their share of oddities.

The obituaries hint at characteristics of which the reader would like to know more. Father William O'Brien 'was an edifying religious, though somewhat peculiar and rather severe'.[59] Father John Hearne 'was of an ardent spirit, not always under sufficient control'.[60] Others were remembered as cheerful companions, good for a song or a yarn at recreation; Father Peter Kenny (not to be confused with his famous namesake of an earlier generation) was a magician. A member of the Galway community remembered how Father Kenny swallowed a carving knife: 'To my surprise and complete certainty he swallowed it — I was distant only a yard or two from him. To relieve my anxiety he [then] put his hand down by the side of the chair and showed me the knife.'

There were Jesuits who had unusual personal experiences. As a young layman, Christopher Bellew had been making a retreat at Clongowes before he was to wed a Protestant lady. Word arrived that her family insisted that the daughters of the marriage be reared in their mother's faith. Mr Bellew replied that in conscience he could not consent. Her people relented, agreed that all the children would be Catholics 'but the letter came too late, he had left Clongowes. No one knew where to send the letter. For some years he did not appear in Ireland again, and when he did return he came back as Rev. Christopher Bellew, S.J.' It turned out that he had entered a novitiate in Alsace![61] Father Matthew Saurin had to travel abroad for a different reason. His sister 'took an action against the Superioress and Community of the Mercy Convent at Hull for harsh treatment. It was thought prudent that Father Saurin should retire outside the jurisdiction of the courts lest he should be summoned as a witness. . .'.[62] And there were Jesuits who had been to war. As a secular priest, prior to entering the Society, Father John Bannon was working in America when the Civil War broke out and 'he cast in his lot with the Southern army, to whose memory he was ever loyal and true, and as chaplain to the Confederates he went through all the hardships and sacrifices of the campaign'.[63] Father Patrick Duffy, who had gone to the Crimea, 'was entirely military in his ideas'. Many years after the war, he met an Irish survivor of the Light Brigade in Australia and they reminisced about the famous charge. In a letter to his sister, Father Duffy told how he asked the veteran what he thought of this disastrous action. ' "Ah, Father," was his answer . . . "we did as we were bid — we obeyed at once, and without discussing the nature of the order, whether it was wise or foolish. That was no business of ours. That belonged to the commander; *execution* was our part, and *that* we did." "You are a soldier," said I as he ended, "every inch of you. You could not give me a better answer. Would that all we religious would do as you did — obey simply, promptly and cheerfully." '[64] Saint Ignatius would surely have approved. But it happened, of course, in the era before blind obedience to orders was seen sometimes to raise serious questions of morality.

Beyond their hyper-activity, plain living, private devoutness and often markedly individual qualities or shortcomings, almost all the priests of the Society in Ireland were highly educated. They were essentially *civilised*, distinguished by a breadth of vision which came from long training in a variety of different schools, universities, houses of study. After the mid-century every Irish residence was likely to have in its community a man who had studied at St Acheul in France, another who had been to the Roman College, a third who went to Tronchiennes in Belgium. Several would have done their theology in St Beuno's. Less expected places also crop up in the *curricula vitae* of the Irish Fathers: Issenheim, Paderborn, Laval, Montauban. It will be recalled that, with some differences of place-names, this had been the pattern in the old Irish Mission. Now, however, it served a new purpose. It infused the values and atmosphere of the five Jesuit colleges flourishing in the 1860s.

The diligence displayed and the expansion undertaken by the Irish Jesuits in setting up new houses in widely separated parts of the country, as well as opening their own novitiate at Milltown Park, had already brought about what Father Nugent dreamt of two hundred years earlier. In 1860 Ireland became a full Province of the Society and Father Joseph Lentaigne was promoted from Vice-Provincial to Provincial; the Province numbered 66 Fathers, 38 Brothers and 42 scholastics — 146 Jesuits in all.[65] (The total continued to grow steadily and in the Restoration Centenary Year of 1914 would be as high as 367;[66] it reached a peak of more than 700 in the 1950s and at the time of writing has slipped back to about 300.) The decision to grant provincial status would have been influenced not only by numbers but also by what might be called the Ignatian quality of the work carried out by the Irish Jesuits. Nowhere was this more evident than in their schools. Despite their divergence from the rather legalistic reading of the Society's educational ideals favoured by successive Generals, the Irish schools were modelled on continental norms and incorporated the flexibility which Saint Ignatius had always recommended.

A boy writing home to Derry from Tullabeg in the 1830s told his parents: 'In this college it is necessary to know well what we learn before we are allowed to go forward.'[67] While this would have been good pedagogic practice anywhere, the fact that a young boy noticed it showed the extent to which a prime principle of the *Ratio Studiorum* was being stressed. All the colleges retained Latin and Greek as 'the classical core of the curriculum'[68] but, as we have seen, provided many other subjects also, which the *Ratio* in fact permitted under the head of 'accidentals'.[69] They thereby met Ignatius' insistence on adapting to 'the circumstances of place and persons'.[70] The variety of subjects taught was remarkable. One merits special mention. 'Clongowes imported from the Continent the European tradition of teaching Natural Philosophy, as science was then called, . . . from the very beginnings of the college. This was unusual in these islands — such a subject was unheard of in English public schools until the end of the nineteenth century.'[71] The subject involved demonstrations and experiments: in 1817 an extra fee was charged for boys taking science 'to defray the extraordinary expenses of Instruments, Laboratory, etc.'. At first the classes in Natural Philosophy covered 'mechanics, optics, electricity, pneumatics and hydraulics, but eventually acoustics, heat, meteorology, magnetism and chemistry were all dealt with.' Every Jesuit college in Ireland followed this example and offered science on its curriculum[72] although Clongowes seems to have been alone, or at least the first, in having photographic equipment in the early 1850s.

It was possible to teach science and other subjects beyond what might have been expected, because of the Jesuits' continental training. Father Shine, later of Hardwicke Street, was a scientist and Father Hlasko from Poland had been a Professor of Natural Philosophy: Clongowes had the benefit of both. When textbooks were inadequate, the Jesuits wrote their own (as also did the Christian Brothers) — Father Thomas Halpin, whom we have already met in Galway, published a monograph on Plane and Spherical Trigonometry 'adapted to the Class of Rhetoric at Clongowes Wood College' in 1854. The Jesuits' training was reflected also in the wide availability of modern languages: French everywhere, Italian and German often — presumably depending on the experience of the men assigned to a given community at a particular time. All three were provided at the Crescent in the academic year 1862-63.[73] Father Humphrey Donovan of Tralee held the title of 'Professor of Irish' at Clongowes in the 1840s and was said to have taught the language there 'with great efficiency'.[74] This was more than thirty years before the Christian Brothers began teaching Irish anywhere (except, at Archbishop MacHale's request, in Tuam[75] which was then surrounded by a Gaeltacht or Gaelic-speaking district). The range of other subjects taught or made available by the Jesuits will have been noticed from the comments made on each of the colleges in previous sections of the present work.

Nor was learning confined to the classroom. Clongowes had a college society called the Academy to encourage the production of learned papers on non-classroom subjects and a debating society to promote ordered reading and public speaking: both of them founded with the enthusiastic sponsorship of Daniel O'Connell. These activities, taken up in one form or another by all the colleges, were firmly within the spirit of Saint Ignatius, who encouraged organised disputation, the public reading by students of their own compositions and an acquaintance with books other than those dealt with in class as means of progress in studying.[76] And there was theatre, an element in Jesuit education from the earliest days of the Society. 'For the Jesuits drama was not a trivial diversion, but rather a central feature of their school life. They used plays to dramatise the propagation of the faith, illustrating moral choices and heroic acts of faith with the aim of enlightening their students as well as diverting their guests.'[77] Diversion, it must be admitted, seems to have been the primary objective during the 1820s and 1830s at Clongowes with farces like *High Life Below Stairs* and *Fortune's Frolic*. This was understandable, if scarcely in the high didactic tradition of the Society's approach to drama. With the boys remaining in the College over Christmas and Easter, they had to be kept occupied and entertained! Goldsmith plays were being staged in the 1840s, however, and scenes from major dramas were commonly performed on Academy Day at all the schools.

Academy Day was another feature brought to Ireland from the continent, 'a genteel form of advertising in the days before PROs or school annuals or the publication of examination results.'[78] The boys demonstrated their knowledge and skills over the whole range of academic attainment before an audience not only of parents and community but also distinguished personages such as the Bishop, the Mayor of the city, university professors and the Irish Provincial. 'The Archbishop of Dublin . . . said to a nobleman sitting beside him,' goes a throwaway phrase from a Belvedere Rector's account of such an occasion. It was the outstanding day of the school year — indeed, sometimes of several school years, for the smaller colleges could not always put together so elaborate an event annually. The Crescent held its first Academy Day in 1863, when a display of elocution and a scene from Molière's *Médecin Malgré Lui* were particularly praised, an Italian 'oration' was delivered, examinations were held in mathematics, science and other subjects (which probably took much the same form as the television programme *Mastermind* today) and 'the College Choir sang several of Moore's Melodies.'[79] The last item must have come as something of a relief to the Limerick city dignitaries inundated by the deluge of erudition.

The presentation of papers on a chosen theme marked Academy Day in Galway — 'The Spirit of a Language' in 1868 and 'The Oratory of Demosthenes' in 1869.[80] Each year's papers were gathered together and published in booklet form; 'from the matter and style' these booklets seemed to be 'above the capacity of schoolboys and were prepared probably by Father John O'Carroll,' according to one slightly cynical member of the community.[81] Father O'Carroll was a noted linguist, said to have a fluent command of fourteen languages.[82] Whether any Jesuit had a hand in the long-famous event of one Clongowes Academy Day, a recital of Cicero's *Pro Milone*, translated into Greek by a boy from Rhetoric (Sixth Year),[83] history does not relate, but the demonstration of competence in languages and theatrical production both at Clongowes and Belvedere was interspersed with scientific experiments. At Clongowes, as might be expected, the ultimate in panache distinguished the annual event. Of no other college was it recorded that a Rector in the 1850s 'faithfully adhered to the custom of earlier times of wearing a Court suit on Academy Day'.[84] It is to be hoped that the good Rector did not skimp in this matter but put on full levee costume, including the dress sword!

These many aspects of teaching and learning, derived from centuries-old continental experience, gave the Irish Jesuit colleges their distinctive character until well into the 1870s. Contrary to a popular belief later fostered in the strongly nationalist atmosphere at the turn of the century, these schools were not founded in imitation of the English public schools of the period. True, the Jesuits intended to produce young men fitted educationally and in accordance with the social conventions of the day to match the best that England or the Anglo-Irish Ascendancy had to offer, but they planned to do so by their own well-tested norms and emphatically not by the adoption of alien formulae. It is never easy to prove a negative. Consequently, only an analysis of the Irish Jesuit concept of schooling, its application from the beginning in the several colleges founded in Ireland, and the source of these ideas in continental practice can lay to rest the assumptions still glibly made that the Jesuits set out to copy English models. Much more research needs to be done on the Irish schools, but hopefully what is outlined above and in the sources referred to in the notes to this section indicate how far the Irish Jesuit system was truly *sui generis*. The first prospectus for Clongowes stated in 1814 that 'it does not seem necessary to detail the actual plan of education adopted by Mr Kenney. The system is sufficiently known, and highly esteemed.'[85] This came as close as was safe to saying, in what were still penal times, that the school would be run on the principles which had made the Jesuits the great educators of Europe.

In no way could this Clongowes prospectus have been referring to the English system, if only because the English public schools of the day — and for a score of years to come — lacked any system recognisable to educationalists, being unreformed, narrow in their scope and often brutal in their administration.[86] Public schoolboys in England spent most of their time memorising Greek and Latin authors. Few other subjects were taught and textbooks were out of date. Order was maintained by force if it was maintained at all. 'When the Duke of Wellington talked about the playing-fields of Eton he had in mind not games but fighting. As late as 1818 two companies of soldiers with fixed bayonets were brought into the buildings at Winchester to put an end to a school "rebellion".' Among the achievements in later years of the famous reforming headmaster, Dr Thomas Arnold, would be his practice of asking questions 'about the subject-matter as well as the syntax of the books read by his boys', the provision of 'French and mathematics as regular subjects at Rugby . . . [where] they had been "extras"' and a decision 'to make the chapel a centre of school life'. The Irish Jesuits had nothing to learn from any of this! Another reforming head, Edward Thring of Uppingham, divided the school day in the 1850s so that core subjects were studied in the morning and optional subjects in the afternoon; but as we have seen, they were doing just that in Belvedere ten years earlier.

The overall impression from such memoirs as survive (again a field for further research) is that the Jesuit colleges in Ireland at this time were happy schools, remembered long after by their pupils with affection. Not only did they offer a much broader and fulfilling education than would become general in English public schools before the later decades of the century but there was also a notable absence of unpleasant features common enough in England. The phenomenon of 'fagging', or requiring junior boys to perform menial chores for older boys, was unheard of, and would never be heard of, in an Irish Jesuit school. Records from the 1840s show that corporal punishment was then rarely employed in Clongowes[87] or Belvedere,[88] while a past pupil of Tullabeg in the 1870s recalled that Father William Delany 'ruled not by fear but affection. Physical punishment was almost unknown. He trusted to the honour of his boys.'[89]

If there was any English influence at mid-century, it came from Stonyhurst, so well known to the restored Jesuits. From Stonyhurst the boarding schools took the 'line' system of dividing the boys into two or three age-groups,[90] each with its own library, dormitory and playing field: this ensured protection against excessive bullying and other abuses of younger boys by their seniors. From Stonyhurst also came cricket and the primitive form of soccer known as 'gravel football'. But Stonyhurst was scarcely a typical English public school and all these aspects of its life (even the cricket!) had been familiar in the Jesuit school at St-Omer. The names of its classes, of course, were of continental Jesuit provenance: Elements, Rudiments, Grammar, Syntax, Poetry and Rhetoric (corresponding, with occasional variations, to First Year, Second Year and so on up to Sixth Year), which were also adopted in the Irish schools. An Etonian, Harrovian or Wykehamist of the day would have been quite lost in any of these colleges — but would probably have been a lot happier than at his English school and, when his schooldays ended, much better educated.

None of this is recorded in a defensive or chauvinistic spirit. There were, inevitably, exceptions to the general picture. William Francis Butler disliked Tullabeg. He was 'thin and delicate', he wrote, and the cold of the bogland winter 'seemed to strike into the heart and soul of a frame such as mine. All the more did the climatic conditions tell against a small boy because the majority of the other boys were strong. Many of them were rough, and, it is needless to say, were as merciless to their smaller and weaker fry as though the school had been of pilchards.'[91] It would have brought him little consolation to know that the Jesuits shared his opinion of the Tullabeg climate, calling it 'Siberia' and disliking the long journey to get there by canal-boat.[92] The future Archbishop Edward Byrne of Dublin resented the corporal punishment which came into use during his time at Belvedere.[93] And the English public schools would undergo a transformation in the Victorian age, making them superlative institutions in their own right.

The Irish Jesuit colleges were to go through a transformation also but in their case it would not be for the better. The imitation of English public schools which had long been avoided began to show itself in the 1870s and to some extent would infiltrate all the schools thereafter. The best features of the reformed English system might have merited adoption for educational reasons, but sadly what seems to have happened is that the Irish parents observed the growing status — social status — of the leading English schools and increasingly sought it from the Jesuits in Ireland. If the word to describe this attitude is 'snobbery', so be it, and insofar as the Jesuits pandered to parents (it will be recalled that this was an established tradition at Belvedere for other reasons) they have to accept the blame for permitting a dilution of their own tried and distinctive values. There was something demeaning about the use of the phrase 'in accordance with the rule of Eton College' when merely instructing the Tullabeg boys that they had to be able to swim if they wanted to row a boat on the canal.[94] Clongowes had got by perfectly well without a School Captain, yet it was decided to have one from 1862, elected by the boys[95] (but in later years chosen by the Rector, upon whose advice the boys never knew). Clongowes in fact long held out against too much copying of others, but by the 1890s 'the sports, games, blazers, caps, coat of arms, all the trappings of an Eton or Winchester were added on. This was not because the Jesuits wished to emulate Eton or Winchester, but because they knew that this was what so many parents were impressed by.'[96]

One Jesuit, however, seems consciously to have wished to emulate the English. At Tullabeg in the 1870s Father William Delany took stock of the state of education in the United

Kingdom, of which Ireland was then part: 'All over Britain, as the empire entered on its final stages of expansion and openings in the public service increased — at home, in India, and in the army — more and more schools modelled themselves on Eton, Harrow and Winchester, the alleged moulders of the élite who managed the empire. Delany, too, looked to the more celebrated of the English public schools for points of comparison, and planned to make his neglected institution amidst the midland bogs into the leading college in the country.'[97] Being at once pushful and imaginative, he chose the most difficult characteristic of the English public schools to emulate: their influential connections. By instituting competitive sports, he lured many well-placed Protestants to stay in the college overnight as the members of military or gentlemen's cricket teams, and took care to entertain them not only hospitably but graciously (remember the fine wines!). He welcomed courtesy visits or visits of inspection to the college by senior personages of the then establishment, including professors of Trinity College and the Lord Lieutenant, the Duke of Marlborough — with whose son, Lord Randolph Churchill, Father Delany struck up a personal friendship which he exploited to get the maximum concessions for Catholic education in Ireland that he could extract from the English Tory Party, of which Churchill was a prominent member.[98]

The good impression of Tullabeg and its Rector formed by these elevated personages underscored the mirror-image of their own schools which they saw in Tullabeg, although it must be stressed that Father Delany succeeded in retaining much of the Jesuit liberal-humanist spirit beneath the 'public school' overlay. Of itself, the approximation (and it was never more than proximate) of the Jesuit boarding schools to the English public schools, and the Jesuit day schools to the English grammar schools, was harmless. The games played and the matches fought were as exciting or as tiresome, depending on the individual's disposition, as any other activity that might have been decreed to occupy his leisure-time, and the Jesuits thankfully were never to go to the lengths of other 'rugby schools' — or 'GAA schools', for that matter — in turning sport into a quasi-religion. In more important matters, a boy in a blazer needed as much teaching as his predecessor in a plain jacket and only a very foolish parent would take more pleasure from paying a bill because it was set out on a sheet of notepaper bearing a crest rather than on one without such embellishment. These harmless foibles, however, did not come into being in a vacuum, nor was their origin without significance.

Within the Irish middle class (it would be wrong to suppose it was true of everybody in a white collar) an element had developed with a severe inferiority complex which could be assuaged only by constant reassurance that it corresponded to the social category of accepted gentility in England. The result was to import into Ireland, with modifications but with the same essential defect, 'a system which had established itself in English life. Class distinctions existed outside the schools; the schools did nothing to mitigate them, and, in the course of time, a good deal to intensify them. From one point of view it may be said that the public schools performed a certain service in mixing the old aristocracy with the new professional middle class; on the other hand they separated both these classes from the poor. Thus . . . the richer classes of the country had become attached to certain schools, familiar with the segregation of their own class into these schools, and accustomed to a particular code of habits, manners, and social behaviour which, for better or worse, the children of the poor had no opportunity to learn.'[99]

Class distinctions may not have been quite so stark in Ireland: aristocracy, for example, was a negligible factor and it will be recalled that 'middle class' meant 'poor shop-keepers' to the Bishop of Galway. Developments had been taking place in the Irish Jesuit colleges, as we have seen, with Belvedere and the Crescent adapting their curricula for boys proceeding to occupations in commerce, with Clongowes drawing its pupils from a social base broadening out from the landed gentry to the professions, and from the professions to some at least of the self-employed and salaried middle class. The 'rough' boys at Tullabeg, of whom young Butler complained, can scarcely have been a very exclusive set; their successors, no doubt, were the boys whom thirty years later Father Delany tried to civilise by such stratagems as hanging 'Roman paintings' in the corridors 'so that youngsters coming (as they usually did) from utterly artless homes, towns and wilds would gain a tolerable idea of what a Raphael or a Titian looked like'.[100] The potential for development, for further broadening of the base, for the successive removal of class barriers, therefore existed, and such development would have facilitated the Jesuit objective of training future leaders by paralleling the growth of democracy, the emergence of trade unions and ultimately the achievement of Irish independence. Instead, a bottom line was drawn, socially and economically defining the colleges as middle-class preserves. To the extent that the middle class itself expanded, Jesuit education continued to become available to more people, but the ethos as well as the fees, however modest, froze out what was called the 'working class' and the poor. The better part of a century would pass before the Irish Jesuits adapted some of their schools fully to serve popular educational needs and decided to reserve a substantial number of places for the underprivileged in their other schools.[101]

The middle-class colleges in fact did sterling work, producing thousands of *alumni* who served their neighbours and their country well, and among them more than one of the visionaries who saw the need to resume development of the Jesuit schools beyond the artificial barricades. Once again, no purpose is served by waxing indignant over the delay in the growth of prophetic awareness. It remains possible to regret that it took so long to show itself. We may therefore concede that, as the nineteenth century drew to its close, the Society in Ireland allowed its schools to settle a little too comfortably into their social niche — a reflection, perhaps, of the self-protective palisades being raised by Catholics who had achieved the security which eluded many of their coreligionists, the worst side of which would be seen in the Dublin employers' lock-out of workers in 1913 as well as in the antipathy shown by farmers who owned their holdings towards landless agricultural labourers.

We should be much slower to accept the criticism beginning to appear at that time and couched in such clichés as 'un-Irish' or 'anti-national'. Journals like D. P. Moran's *Leader* and Arthur Griffith's *United Irishman* resorted to extreme vituperation.[102] 'That den of Catholic shoneenism', 'West

British hatcheries' and 'that cricket and ping-pong college' typified the terminology used. The burden of complaint was often trivial: a British army band had been hired for a sports day, GAA games were not played, the teaching of the Irish language did not loom as prominently on the curriculum as it did in other schools. The Jesuits were not the only targets: schools conducted by the Vincentian, Holy Ghost and other orders came under the same attack, as also did some of the diocesan colleges. The Christian Brothers' schools were presented by contrast as truly Irish and nationalist in spirit. (It should be said straight away that, although they fought manfully for better recognition of the Irish language and Irish history within the public exam system, the Brothers themselves carried on their splendid work of education without embroiling other Orders in public controversy — and especially not the Jesuits whom they frequently engaged to preach retreats in their monasteries.) Seen in retrospect, the quite vicious campaign against the colleges appears to have been based upon a twin misunderstanding: the incidentals brought over from the English public schools were given greater weight than they merited as pointers to the schools' character and, far more serious, it was assumed that failure to share the principles of 'Irish-Ireland' nationalism was to be servile to English interests. The inability of some nationalists to admit that other views might reasonably be held on good citizenship — on how best, indeed, to be 'national' — undermined the unity of those who looked forward to an independent Ireland. It is an attitude which still survives among the obstacles to achieving a pluralist state in which citizens can respect, without concurring in, one another's opinions.

What was the reality concerning the Jesuit schools and nationalism? Much was made by Griffith and other hypernationalist writers after him of remarks by the Young Irelander, Thomas Francis Meagher, who had been a pupil at Clongowes in the 1830s. His teachers 'never spoke of Ireland,' he wrote, 'never gave us, even what is left of it, her history to read . . . Ireland was the last nation we were taught to think of, to respect, to love and remember'.[103] (It should be noted that he went on: 'I can't bear to say anything against Clon-

gowes. It is to me a dear old spot.' Any expression of affection
was usually dropped by those who chose to make capital out of
criticism.) But these comments date from 1856. Meagher was
looking back through the haze of romantic nationalism that
swept Europe in the 1840s, not to mention the 1848 Rising in
Ireland which resulted in his own conviction for high treason,
sentence of death and eventual transportation to Van Diemen's
Land. Such experiences coloured his view of what a school
curriculum might embrace. When Daniel O'Connell sent his
sons to Clongowes in 1815 he asked that they be taught
classical languages, French and chemistry, thereby reflecting
his own understanding of education, acquired on the continent and associated especially with Jesuit theory; he also
expressed the hope that the boys would be 'strongly imbued
with the principles of the Catholic faith and national feeling'.[104]

What O'Connell meant by 'national feeling' was evident
from the political campaigns of his own long lifetime —
namely, that the Irish had the right to control the administration and development of their own country for its people's
betterment. He despised and resented those who attempted
to obstruct the attainment of this objective. Had he found the
Jesuits to be party to 'anti-national' feeling in this way he
would not have left his sons with them, shown an ongoing
interest in Clongowes and its academic institutions or, in a
moment of depression in 1839, written, 'I think of . . . going, if
I am received, to Clongowes, and to spend the rest of my life
there.'[105] The Liberator is an important witness, more
important than the Jesuit names or the names of ex-pupils of
the Jesuits which can be sifted out from the totality to
establish the Society's share of patriots in the revolutionary
tradition, more important than noting the foundation of
Irish-speaking clubs in the schools (e.g. at Galway in 1904)[106]
or the establishment of prizes for work in Irish history at
Clongowes (for which Patrick Pearse was an examiner).[107]
What O'Connell clearly understood was that the Jesuits aimed
to fit their pupils at least to survive, and preferably to excel,
wherever they might find themselves: such was the formative
influence expected of classical education.

It is quite true that the Jesuits did not set out to make
'nationalists' of the boys committed to their care. Neither did

they set out to produce 'loyalists' or 'Castle Catholics'. What they hoped to create was a corps of informed and believing Christians who would conduct themselves in their public activities as well as their private lives in accordance with the values of the Gospel. The service and example to be expected of these well-educated men would be provided by each within his chosen environment, which at the turn of the century might be Irish or colonial, nationalist or imperial, professional or political or bureaucratic. It would probably not be unfair to suggest that, had the Jesuits considered the question, they would have felt their system justified when those of their pupils who became rebels proved to be efficient and exemplary rebels! It is unnecessary, and would be an unwarranted distortion of history, to gloss over the fact that the Irish Jesuit schools produced many judges, generals and proconsuls in the days of empire: the Jesuits were proud of them, and rightly so, for these were the alumni who had chosen the environment of law or army or public administration and succeeded within the only establishment then existing. It is also true that they produced many Home Rule politicians; many scholars; medical men, churchmen and teachers; engineers and farmers and businessmen; a number of nation-builders before and after Irish independence: all these gave sterling service too in their chosen fields, and the Jesuits took pride in them. Whether or not they produced 'nationalists' is the wrong question to ask of the Jesuits. The question is whether they produced well-instructed Christians who behaved as Christians should. This, for them, was the purpose of education. It would be sadly blinkered to argue that it served the country, or its people, or peoples elsewhere, any less effectively than education designed to set young minds in a single historico-political mould before they could think for themselves.

Until the 1880s the Irish Jesuits kept faith with the spirit of the *Ratio Studiorum* although they might have found it a little difficult in practice to explain how the basic guideline for the Society's schools was met by taking cognizance so often of parental or episcopal wishes. Fathers, mothers and bishops could not be expected to have based their views on a close and sympathetic reading of the *Ratio* and, indeed, were normally motivated by immediate concerns like extricating Catholic children from Protestant schools or ensuring that boys were well versed in the subjects which would open doors for them to careers in commerce or the civil service. What the Jesuits succeeded in doing was to serve such objectives while sustaining the status of learning as a virtue in its own right. They plunged their pupils into an atmosphere where they were encouraged by many devices to explore the depth, the breadth and the sense of what they were learning, to discover how to expound it themselves in writing, in speech, in scientific demonstration, to arrive at their convictions through discernment. This was what the Academy Days were about, the debates, the reading of prepared papers, the presentation of a scene from Shakespeare or a whole play by Molière. To inculcate that kind of understanding was to create an educated man, not necessarily a scholar but one with a comprehension beyond the average of matters on which civilised people were supposed to be informed: among these matters for the Jesuits, of course, was an intimate appreciation of the content of Catholic belief, rooted in the individual's own faith. The manner in which they taught as well as the subjects covered, and the varied activities in the schools as well as the careers which might be envisaged for the boys, were part of the Jesuit system and reflected the spirit of the *Ratio Studiorum.*

Suddenly, it was put at risk . . . and surprisingly, with Jesuit connivance. If the change can be assigned to a moment in time, it happened on the September morning in 1879 when a crowd of cheering boys burst out of the Crescent College in Limerick, carrying one of their number on a chair shoulder high. He was Charlie Doyle, whose widowed mother lived a short distance away in George Street (now O'Connell Street) and his friends bore him home to her in triumph, for Charlie had won first place in Ireland in the Junior Grade of the new examinations held under the Intermediate Act passed in the previous year.[108] Charlie's achievement was indeed astounding. The Crescent was a small school of ninety pupils, respected but hardly famed, and the Intermediate Examinations were taken, as Charlie's sister graphically put it, by 'schools of all (or no) denominations all over Ireland'. He would repeat his success in the following years, taking first place in the Middle Grade and finally in the Senior Grade, securing money prizes *en route* as well as gold medals — including one for being best in the country in modern languages, an award attributed to the teaching of Father John O'Carroll,[109] the linguist accredited with putting a professional finish to the Galway Academy Day papers a few years earlier. For Charlie Doyle it was a triumph and the Jesuits had every reason to be proud of him. But for the Society in Ireland, it was a pyrrhic victory.

The Intermediate Act had been drafted as a devious means of providing state assistance to Catholic schools which would assure them roughly similar support to the endowments enjoyed by Protestant schools. A devious approach had been necessary because evangelical Protestants, then an influential body of opinion in England, would not tolerate the grant of public funds to Catholic institutions as such. Undenominational schools, even if attended mainly by Catholic children, would have been acceptable but these the Catholic bishops refused to sanction. Hence to the principle embodied in the Intermediate Act. For the declared purpose of promoting educational standards, a Board was set up to conduct annual examinations at the 'intermediate' level (the level between primary school and university or other professional studies . . . what we call secondary school). Certificates, money prizes and other rewards were granted to successful candidates on the basis of their results and fees were paid to the participating schools in respect of their pupils who passed the examinations. All schools could enter, whether Catholic, Protestant or undenominational. In practice, since most schools were Catholic, these earned most of the prizes and fees despite some unwarranted anxiety at the outset that Catholic establishments would prove inferior to their Protestant counterparts. In this way public money (derived ironically from the surplus revenues of the recently disestablished Church of Ireland, which meant it was no charge on British taxpayers) became available for the support of Catholic schools.[110]

Politically, the scheme had the powerful backing of Lord Randolph Churchill who cherished the Tory ambition of proving that the Conservatives could confer greater benefits on Ireland than the Liberals — traditionally seen by the Irish as the more sympathetic of the British parties. The views of Father Delany, Rector of Tullabeg, were known to carry weight with Churchill. Well-informed contemporaries such as Dr Mahaffy of Trinity and Judge Matthias Bodkin had little doubt that the Intermediate Act was largely shaped by the Jesuit educationalist. Father Delany had certainly been in close touch with Irish and English politicians while it was being drafted and was highly pleased with the measure as enacted. Within months he had brought about the establishment of the Catholic Headmasters' Association to represent Catholic interests in discussions with the commissioners set up by the Intermediate Board. Through the Association he made a major contribution to drafting the curriculum for the examinations as well as the recommended booklists for use in the schools. He was well satisfied with the outcome of the first Intermediate examinations, held in 1879. While the Holy Ghost college at Blackrock, County Dublin, won the largest number of prizes, Tullabeg came second and, of course, the Crescent produced the most successful individual candidate in the country.[111]

The sums received by the schools in 'results fees' were modest enough and seem to have varied considerably from year to year, no doubt reflecting the number of pupils sitting the examinations. This in turn went up or down in the smaller day schools in line with the state of business locally which, as we have seen, affected the number of boys staying on to take the senior course of studies. Just as the total roll at St Ignatius in Galway swung between a minimum of 40 and maximum of 90, so the Intermediate payments to the school in the first twenty years of the scheme swung between a minimum of £8.10.0d and a maximum of £96.17.0d.[112] Nor did a large enrolment always mean that more pupils would be taking the examinations. Numbers were up in 1885, for example, but the boys were 'most of them *valde juvenes*' (extremely young)[113] and this was in fact one of the worst years for results fees earned. Schools which perhaps needed the money less did better from the system, for these were the schools where classes of some size continued to the end of the senior cycle: Belvedere's annual examination earnings varied from £143 to £686 (the fluctuations of a day school showing up even when larger numbers were available to take the several grades than in the provincial towns) and Clongowes received, on average, £930 a year between 1887 and 1916.[114] But almost from the beginning, the financial asset to a school of good results in the Intermediate came to matter less than the promotional value of the prizes and high places won by the pupils. The system let loose a spirit of intense rivalry between Catholic secondary schools, and between the orders who ran them, to the detriment of true education.

Father Delany saw it otherwise, believing as he did in 'the manifest benefits of competition and emulation'.[115] Whether he counted the cost is less clear. Competition was all very well in the hands of a brilliant headmaster, as he was, who could hold the balance between hard work, recreation, sport and the appreciation of literature and the fine arts. In the hands of less visionary teachers, competition led straight to cramming, with corporal punishment to hustle on the laggards, and the down-grading of any and every activity not conducive to high examination results. The down-grading, of course, also touched the quality of teaching since the objective was no longer to produce cultivated minds and personalities but efficient examinees. 'The idea of paying pupils to learn instead of paying teachers to teach [is] surely detrimental to all higher education,' said a wise observer of the trend as early as 1882.[116] Cramming ran clean counter to Jesuit theory. The model of the continental college, with scope for music, the display of individual imagination in writing and rhetoric, the emphasis on drama as a didactic discipline, the stress on personal honour rather than the infliction of physical pain as the stimulus to study — all were destined to totter before the relentless demands of the Intermediate. It ushered in a tension-ridden era at Clongowes and no doubt in other Jesuit schools as well.

Clongowes fared alarmingly badly in the early years of the Intermediate, for it knew nothing of the competitive approach.[117] It soon rallied, however, especially after it absorbed the boys from Tullabeg when that school was suppressed without warning in 1886 and the boys transferred to Clon-

gowes. The fate of Tullabeg was ironic. Not only had Father
Delany run it heavily into debt to make the many improvements he undertook,[118] but his ideal of 'emulation' embodied
in the Intermediate system (which is to say, the pressure to
achieve better exam results than other schools) meant that
every Jesuit college was clamouring for the best teachers.[119]
This put the Irish Province under severe strain at a time
when it was going through another bout of the Irish Jesuit
instinct to expand beyond its resources: it had just opened
not one but two new schools at Mungret in County Limerick,
as we shall see, and had taken on responsibility for University
College in Dublin, the vestigial remnant of Newman's Catholic
University. With vocations temporarily in the doldrums,[120]
something had to yield and the Provincial chose Tullabeg
which thus became part of the cost which had to be paid for
the new system. It must have hurt Father Delany but did not
bear on him directly for he had been transferred to UCD
several years before.

Meanwhile, spurred on by parents' expectations, the Jesuits
put little restraint on the competitive spirit and its harmful
incidentals in their schools. Its typical representative was
Father James Daly, 'Father Dolan' in James Joyce's *Portrait of
the Artist* and, interestingly, the only Jesuit of whom that quirky
and rebellious Clongownian-Belvederian genius spoke ill.
Father Daly was briefly Prefect of Studies (headmaster) at the
Crescent, where he obtained impressive results by means
which have been charitably summarised in the comment that
'idling and evasion of work. . .just found no scope, with Father
Daly in control'.[121] What this meant in practice was described
by a boy at Clongowes who later became a distinguished
Jesuit himself. Describing the atmosphere in that once happy
school after Father Daly arrived from Limerick and took
charge as Prefect of Studies, the boy wrote about the 'torture
of the whistling cane and resounding pandybat . . . the constant, unnatural dread, unworthy of a human being, of being
beaten like a dog for the most trivial offence'.[122] By such
methods impressive results were achieved. 'But results for
what?. . . . Clongowes had become a college devoted to cramming for the needs of a government exam.'[123] And so, more
widely: '. . . the underlying assumption that to pass certain

stereotyped written tests was the main goal of a child's career had a stultifying effect upon good, if individualistic, teaching, and also put a premium on those schools (notably the establishments run by the Christian Brothers) which had brought examination technique to a fine art that had little to do with education.'[124]

It should be said at once that the Christian Brothers' objective was to put poor, or relatively poor, boys into gainful employment and to enable the brighter of them to take up careers in which they might be expected to advance on the strength of their talents. In other words, the Brothers were serving — and serving with impressive commitment — a social need which could not properly be defined by reference to the aims of education divorced from the real world. The Brothers were not to be blamed for using and perfecting the system to hand. The same imperative did not bind the Jesuit schools, whose pupils came from families generally spared the pressing needs of many who sent their boys to the Brothers. Why Jesuits took up the cramming system with such determination is hard to understand, even when allowance is made for the demands of parents who wanted their chosen school to be seen garnering the prizes whether or not their own offspring appeared among the exhibitioners. The Jesuits were better placed than most to be able to identify the deficiencies of an approach to schooling which rewarded memory-work and cleverness but gave little encouragement to teachers devoted to helping the backward child to do his or her best — and which was too inflexible to find room for true intelligence unable to adjust to a bureaucratic formula devised as a common denominator for a variety of schools and pupils.

Of course, all was not lost and the Intermediate had good consequences as well as less happy ones. Belvedere found coping with the system a stimulus (perhaps not unrelated to the fact that its famous Rector, Father Tom Finlay, spent thirty years as a member of the Intermediate Board): weekly examinations, for example, turned out to be a good teaching discipline over and above their use as training for the real thing.[125] In Galway evening study in the college became mandatory, at least for senior pupils, as a preparation for the next day's school[126] — another spur to tackling subjects in an ordered manner. But everywhere Academy Days died out, elocution ceased to matter, the pursuit of information was little encouraged if it got in the way of the exam curriculum and it took years for leisure activities like drama and sport to re-establish themselves. Hard judgment though it be, something of a philistine character made its way into Irish and Irish Jesuit education with the Intermediate. The Jesuits soon enough began to find ways to humanise the new approach: Clongowes recovered much of its old happy character, mainly through the cultural awareness of individual Jesuits who took care to direct the pupils' interest to a wider world than the examination hall.[127] The fruits of national independence included the replacement of rewards-for-results in the Irish Free State by a capitation grant for each school-going pupil,[128] thus shifting the basis of payment from the student's ability to the school's willingness to teach him. It would call for a degree of myopic vision, however, to claim that the priority of examinations over learning has even yet been eliminated from the Irish concept of schooling. If the writer may be permitted a short outburst of prejudice, he would say that the tyranny of the 'points system' of entrance to third level education today and the proliferation of grinding schools dedicated to the achievement of exam results are the baneful legacy of the old Intermediate and of those who could contrive no better way than 'competition and emulation' to promote educational standards in Ireland long ago.

The Rector of the Crescent who presided over Charlie Doyle's triumph in 1879 was Father William Ronan, an Ulsterman from County Down and one of those men who made the Irish Jesuits of the Victorian era look rather like the repertory companies of the day in which every actor could take on a succession of different roles with equal competence. The whimsy might indeed be stretched to suggest that the Irish Province was something of a stage army, marching around in ever-changing scenery so that the busy activity concealed the comparatively small numbers involved. Father Ronan, whom we have already come across as a Crimean chaplain (which earned him a place in the history of the Sisters of Mercy, with whom he worked in the army hospitals during the campaign) and as a founding father of Saint Ignatius, in Galway, seems to have been less concerned with Intermediate successes than with helping poor boys who showed an interest in serving as priests in America, Australia or the newly-opening British colonies in Africa and Asia. That a number of boys were thinking of devoting their lives to such service in the wider world of which they were becoming aware in the post-Famine era of emigration and expanding empire, Father Ronan was certain: he met them frequently while conducting missions and retreats around Ireland[129] which, as we have seen, occupied much of the time of the Galway community. But how were these youngsters to be brought together and given the appropriate education without which they could not take up their calling?

He found the answer in France, where institutions called 'apostolic schools' had been founded in the 1860s with financial support from the bishops and Catholic laity. They were designed for boys from poor families who wanted to become missionary priests and provided a solid basic education together with an introduction to philosophy and theology so that their pupils could go on to higher level training in senior colleges and novitiates. With the support of Archbishop Thomas William Croke of Cashel, Father Ronan opened an Apostolic School in Limerick next door to the Crescent in September 1880, and the students attended the Crescent for general classroom subjects. They enjoyed amenities similar to those in the Jesuit boarding schools of the day, with boating on the Shannon, a brass band, debates and essay competitions. But either the accommodation was inadequate or the combination of boarding and day establishments proved unsatisfactory. In any event, Father Ronan determined to find new premises for the Apostolic School. He set his sights on an agricultural training college at Mungret in County Limerick, a few miles downstream from the city, which had proved unsuccessful and for which its trustees were seeking new tenants. Happily for the Apostolic School, one of the trustees was Lord Emly.

Emly had been better known as William Monsell, M.P. A close friend of John Henry Newman, he belonged to a remarkable group of East Limerick gentry who had all converted to Catholicism under the influence of the Oxford Movement: others of them included the Earl of Dunraven and the De Vere brothers, Stephen, Vere and Aubrey, the poet. While still a member of the Church of Ireland Monsell, as he then was, had been very much involved in the founding of Saint Columba's College, which became the leading Anglican boarding school in the country.[130] He was a non-cabinet minister in Gladstone's first administration but increasingly made the welfare of his tenants and neighbours in County Limerick his main concern. He threw open his estate at Tervoe — the only place in Ireland where Newman had found peace and quiet[131] — 'for frequent festivities, pilgrimages (to a Lourdes grotto, the first in Ireland, set up by his wife Berthe), and even picnics, for the people of the area'.[132] The Lourdes Grotto may point to an earlier Jesuit connection: an altar in the Sacred Heart Church in Limerick, with which Lord Emly would have been familiar, was the first in the country to be dedicated to Our Lady of Lourdes.[133] Despite these associations and his affinity with local life, Emly suffered the sad fate of so many Anglo-Irish, being judged Irish in England and English elsewhere. 'He is not at all Irish,' wrote a continental visitor in 1881.[134] But Newman felt that Archbishop Manning would keep him off a certain committee about to be appointed: 'as to Monsell, he is Irish — and this is an English matter.'[135] He opposed Home Rule, which added to the confusion.

Emly's importance to the Mungret project was as a trustee of the failed agricultural college. He not only supported the grant of a lease to the Jesuits but saw to it in the following years that the unfavourable clauses which, in their legal capacity, the trustees had to insist upon, were never invoked. These empowered the trustees to dismiss the headmaster, for example, and required the lessees to train their pupils in methods of agriculture. With hindsight, it may be regretted that one of these clauses was not enforced, that which obliged the lessees to accept pupils of any religious denomination. It was, of course, unlikely that Protestant boys would be sent to a school where they would be prepared for the Catholic priesthood! But as we shall see, Mungret offered more general schooling as well and a Jesuit education had long been admired by perceptive Protestants. An opportunity therefore existed to bridge in some small way the deep and bitter sectarian divisions of the age. Sadly the Jesuits showed no more instinct to do so than the Limerick Protestants, who fought tooth and nail to extract the maximum settlement favourable to their interests when the ownership of Mungret was rationalised by a government commission towards the end of the 1880s and the use of the college for exclusively Catholic purposes was formally permitted. We may regret, but must not condemn, the failure to introduce a speck of pluralism into the prevailing climate. There was no wish and no will on any side to do so.

Meanwhile, the Apostolic School had moved to its new premises. Through July and August of 1882 the students trudged between Limerick and Mungret, hauling furniture from their old house to their new, until the day when with unconscious symbolism they rowed their boats down to Tervoe Point. No sooner were they installed than their numbers were doubled on 13 September, for the Limerick diocesan seminary was once again transferred to Jesuit care and on this occasion lodged at Mungret. The seminary, it will be remembered, was essentially a lay secondary school from which it was hoped that some of the pupils would be attracted to become diocesan clergy. Within a few years, as it happened, the new Bishop of Limerick, Edward Thomas O'Dwyer, removed the seminarists from Mungret. Although he had been among the first pupils at the Crescent, this formidable prelate harboured a curious antipathy to the Jesuits, which probably sprang less from any dislike for them than from a distaste for sharing authority with collaborators whom he might find it difficult to control: this was a recurrent attitude in many countries on the part of strong-minded bishops throughout the history of the Society. The Jesuits simply converted what had been the seminary section of Mungret into a normal boarding school and continued as before. Accordingly, from the beginning there were two schools in the college, with different quarters and a different discipline, sharing many facilities, activities and classes, but not all. This curious arrangement survived for more than eighty years and succeeded tolerably well, although conflicting arguments arose from time to time as to whether the Apostolic students, being by definition poor relations, or the secondary schoolboys, who lacked a clearly defined and noble purpose in life, were the second-class citizens of their common home. As a boy there the writer, Austin Clarke, felt the 'apostolics' were better positioned — perhaps because the college time-table was drawn up to suit their needs.

Mungret had seventy pupils in its first year, equally divided between its two sections. The balance remained roughly even at first as the numbers increased, although the lay school became the bigger later on. Lord Emly kept up a practical as well as benevolent interest in the college, allowing the boys access to his adjacent estate for recreation, raising money for the Apostolic School and attending the annual prize-giving, where he used to plead for a sense of proportion between science and 'spiritual culture' so that neither might down-grade the other. He also provided the college with its science teacher, who was his own chaplain, a French non-Jesuit priest called l'Abbé l'Heritier. As a friend of Montalembert, Dupan-loup and other liberal Catholics, whose thinking on Church affairs he completely made his own,[136] Emly was a Franco-phile. So was Father Ronan, who not only took the very idea of an apostolic school from France but lured a French Jesuit, Father Jean Baptiste René, to come to Ireland as Director of the school; he was subsequently appointed Rector of the college. Other members of the Society came from France as well: no fewer than nine French Jesuits served on the college staff during the 1880s — most of them *en route* to the Chinese or other foreign missions and therefore particularly appro-priate teachers for boys with similar destinations in mind.

The college as a whole was soon performing well in the public examinations and the Apostolic School began to achieve its special objective. In 1895 it had past pupils studying theology in Rome, Aix, Montreal, Cincinnati, Emmetsburg, Carlow and All Hallows in Dublin. In 1907 Mungret men were working as priests in the United States, Canada, Africa, Australia, Tasmania, India, Ceylon and China. Although some had become Jesuits, the great majority were members of other religious orders or secular clergy: a tribute to their Jesuit advisers who resisted any temptation to take unfair advantage of having the school under their control. Despite successive vicissitudes in the new century, by 1974 when Mungret was finally closed it had produced over 700 priests from its Apostolic School and more than 300 from its lay school; they included a cardinal, two archbishops and at least a dozen bishops. It thus revived for the better part of a century the Irish Jesuits' tradition of helping to maintain the supply of manpower to the Catholic ministry — serving now the Church universal as they had served the Irish Church in darker days. As might be expected of any Catholic school, of course, each of the Jesuit colleges in Ireland could count its share of priests. During the later nineteenth century, the number of Jesuits who had been pupils at Clongowes is noticeable from the Province obituaries; there seems to have been a falling off in the post-independence era, although it must be stressed that this is no more than an impression. Belvedere was *alma mater* to three Archbishops of Dublin[137] and Clongowes to a fourth.[138] 'A scanty list, only tentative,' drawn up in 1935, showed that by then St Ignatius' in Galway had at least forty-seven priests among its former students.[139]

The lay schools, however, had the primary function of preparing their pupils for adult life as laity, not as priests. Clongowes and Belvedere were big enough (although neither was *very* big, having a normal complement of fewer than 300 pupils apiece) and strongly enough established to weather the crises which befall schools everywhere from time to time for reasons as various as poor management, mounting debts, a shortage of good teachers or the departure of a charismatic figure on whom the establishment had perhaps been too dependent. Finding good teachers for all its colleges was a constant problem in the overstretched Irish Province as the new century dawned — the Australian Mission, with *its* colleges, was a major dependency of the Irish by now — and the smaller schools at home were each to suffer periods of decline. 'The story of the college from 1900 to 1925 contains many depressing pages so far as academic success is concerned,' writes the historian of the Crescent, who says bluntly that the Province had 'too few men for too many works'; the re-launching of college societies and the provision of new buildings brought about a renaissance under the guidance of Father John Barragry as prefect of studies and Father Edward Andrews, who followed him.[140] Galway fell into eclipse somewhat later, for reasons which are difficult to pinpoint with certainty; here the *deus ex machina* was Father John MacSheahan, during whose rectorship the school, which had closed for three years in the 1920s, achieved new fame as the Irish-speaking Coláiste Iognáid.[141]

Mungret seems to have suffered sooner than most. At the risk of oversimplifying, it might not be wrong to see history repeating itself when Father Ronan went to the United States for two years to raise funds and bring the Apostolic School to the attention of American bishops. As happened with Clongowes in its early days while Father Kenney was in America, Mungret ran into difficulties, once deprived of the founder's controlling hand. The supply of French Jesuits fell off, the boats were sold. Strains developed between the two schools in the college and a major source of encouragement was lost when Lord Emly died in 1894. It may be a little unjust to say that successive Provincials neglected Mungret, for they had the impossible task of making a fair allocation of resources. But right through the earlier decades of the twentieth century it saw its staff too often changed and its amenities too little cared for or expanded. Nor did it help that the Apostolic School was undermined by the establishment of the National University in 1908, which meant that it could no longer bring its students up to degree status since the affiliation it had enjoyed with the old Royal University was not allowed in the new circumstances: this in turn dissuaded Provincials from allocating their best lecturers to the school. The miracle of Mungret was that it soldiered on in both its parts through a kind of family collaboration between the Jesuits and the boys in coping with its shortcomings.

Eventually Mungret would also overcome its decline, achieve its own renaissance and become a superlative school. When the young Oliver St John Gogarty was sent there in the early 1890s, however, that lay far in the future. Gogarty had the unusual, possibly unique, distinction of having attended three Jesuit boarding schools. His boy's-eye view of each makes for lurid comparisons. Mungret was 'third-rate', a place of 'misery and servitude' where he was 'herded into chapel . . . at hours unsuited to a growing child' and 'fed on what the boys called "cow's udder", for there was no bone on that insipid flesh'. He next went to Stonyhurst, 'where the routine was much the same, but the food was somewhat better and the school was cleaner. I never complained . . . for I imagined that all schools were miserably similar'. Lastly, came Clongowes: 'The best of the lot. . . . All in all, I enjoyed this school, which was a great relief from my English education. They fed us well. They did not try to break your will and leave you spineless.' After what has already been said about the prefect of studies then reigning, it must in fairness be added that among the attractions of Clongowes for Gogarty was the fact that 'one of the prefects came from an old Galway family well known for their eccentricities, the mad Dalys'.[142]

Some twenty years after Gogarty another boy at Mungret, who seems to have been more bored than unhappy, simply ran away, eventually reached Australia and tried to get himself accepted as a pupil at the Jesuit college in Sydney by telling them that he had been to Clongowes. The ploy failed, for Australia was still a Mission of the Irish Province. One of the community was himself newly arrived from Clongowes and able to challenge the boy's claim without fear of contradiction![143] Not that it injured the young man's prospects, for he went on to become a famous politician, a British cabinet minister, owner of the *Financial Times* and a viscount. His name was Brendan Bracken.

One way of dealing with the damage caused to a Jesuit school by a shortage of competent Jesuit teachers was to employ competent lay teachers instead. This was done from the beginning at Belvedere, indeed as early as the days of the Hardwicke Street school. At first it was a matter of sheer necessity: enough Jesuits were not available and for a time (horror of horrors!) not even 'a suitable Catholic' could be found and 'a heretic' had to be engaged to teach Latin and Greek, as the Rector explained to the General.[144] But in time lay teachers became a significant and respected element on the staff. Respect was shown in a practical manner by paying them well. George Dempsey, who was James Joyce's English teacher at Belvedere, 'earned £124 per annum, at a time when the average wage of a lay teacher in Ireland was £80 for

men, £40 for women.'[145] Father Delany always had half-a-
dozen or more lay teachers at Tullabeg and was prepared to
pay the best of them, who taught at university level, £200 a
year.[146] At Galway, 'in those years there was usually one lay-
master — "Daddy" Quoyle was Tutor; Professor Higgins who
once taught at Mungret — MacNulty who lived next door —
etc etc were a few of the Professors and Tutors.' We must
sadly conclude, however, that the entry for 1896 cannot be
accurate which notes that 'In October Mr J. W. Lyons was
engaged to teach Mathematics 1½ hours a day for £10 a
week.'[147] The Jesuits may have been generous; they were not
profligate!

In one case they actively opposed the lay teachers. This was
in 1920, during strike action by ASTI (the Association of
Secondary Teachers, Ireland) against the Christian Brothers
in Limerick. The Brothers had pleaded inability to pay a £75
bonus agreed by the Catholic Headmasters Association.
Despite the Jesuit part in setting up the headmasters' body,
both Mungret and the Crescent joined the Brothers in
resisting the payment, saying that the resultant increase in
fees would be unfair to parents.[148] Objectively speaking, this
attitude can be judged only in the context of the day. It was a
time not only of great political upheaval, with 'the Troubles'
(the war of independence) raging, but also of social agitation,
and both movements were particularly active in Limerick.
The institutional instinct to preserve the *status quo* until calm
returned would have been strong, not least in schools which
drew many of their pupils from more conservative segments
of the local population — the families of tradesmen in the
town and of strong farmers in the countryside. The Jesuits
were also well aware that trade and farming were no guaran-
tees of wealth in early twentieth- century Ireland; the need to
overlook parents' neglect to pay even modest fees was ever-
present to the bursars of Jesuit schools. That said, and bearing
in mind their general willingness to pay their teachers well, it
has to be regretted that the Jesuits of 1920 appear to have
been unnecessarily suspicious of organised labour, sniffing
'socialism' or 'syndicalism' on the part of workers banding
together to get themselves a fair deal in circumstances where
they had little security and no prospect of promotion. Another

example from the same period was a servants' strike, firmly resisted at Clongowes.[149] Yet Clongowes, it would surprise some people to know, was where a radically new attitude had begun to take shape which would alter entirely the Jesuit position vis-à-vis labour, organised and unorganised alike, and provide a voice for the destitute unable to speak for themselves. On which, more later. . . .

By the opening years of the new century, the nature and location of Jesuit schools in Ireland had settled into a pattern which was not to change until two world wars had come and gone: two boarding schools in rural areas, three city day schools with public churches beside them or in their vicinity, a special school for training boys destined to become missionary priests. The complex of buildings making up each of these establishments needed constant maintenance, alteration and extension over the years. Belvedere got a new classroom block, Clongowes a new chapel, Mungret an adaptation to its special needs at an early stage — which Father Delany characterised as 'an act of infatuation' given the insecurity of the lease.[150] New buildings in Galway served a novel purpose 'when delicate members of other Communities came to St Ignatius to rest'.[151] A Belgian Jesuit, Father Jassart, spent the greater part of 1900 in Galway, for 'he was in delicate health'. The proximity to the seaside resort of Salthill, a bracing walk away, made it attractive to more than the delicate. The presumably healthy 'theologians from Milltown Park' and 'juniors from Tullabeg' arrived for their summer holidays in 1900 and 1901. Other interesting visitors to St Ignatius' included Father Carmenin, a French Jesuit, and Father Lemaire who was 'preparing for his work as a Bollandist' and was therefore most likely a Belgian, since the Bollandists were scholarly historians whose ongoing *Acts of the Saints* and other publications had been a particular work of the Belgian Jesuits for more than 300 years. Both of these continentals came to Galway to learn Irish; its value to a serious historian is obvious, but Father Carmenin's purpose in acquiring the language has not been recorded.

The Galway Jesuits themselves went elsewhere for their holidays. At first they seem simply to have taken an occasional day off. In 1894, 'Rector and Fathers Kane, Kenny, went on an excursion to Cong,' we read, and 'the priests had an "out-ing" from time to time and went to Lisdoonvarna' — what they did there is difficult to imagine, but perhaps the excitement was in the trip through the Burren and a pony-and-trap drive to the Cliffs of Moher. In 1896 they began the practice of going on a 'Villa' — i.e. taking a holiday — when they went to stay at a Franciscan Monastery in Roundstone. This was less than a success: 'The "Villa" to Roundstone was not highly praised.' Enigmatically, as so often in the jottings of busy men, we are left to wonder why. These tours around the West of Ireland must anyway have seemed small beer by contrast with the constantly mobile traffic passing through St Ignatius'. Not only were the foreigners coming, but the residents were going. In 1899 'the cook, Casey, went to America' — he had come from Milltown for wages of £20 a year. 'Father Anderson set off for Cairo'; a sad story, that, for Patrick Anderson from Portarlington was in poor health and would die twelve months later in Egypt.[152] No doubt they talked of him at recreation, as they talked of Father James Daly's brother Oliver, another Jesuit, who was said to have saved the life of Archbishop Goold of Melbourne when a madman drew a gun on him. . . . To be a Jesuit then, as now, was to be ever aware of far horizons.

6

MISSIONS ACCOMPLISHED

THE nineteenth-century annalist of the Irish Province, Father John Grene, wrote about 1880 that 'some years ago' a chapter on the writings of Irish Jesuits would have resembled 'a chapter on the snakes of Ireland'.[1] This was not a comment on the character of Irish Jesuit writers! It was rather to say that there were very few of them: just as, allegedly thanks to Saint Patrick, Ireland had no indigenous snakes. Whatever about the work of Irish scholars in the pre-Suppression Society, the first half-century following the Restoration saw very little in the way of high-level intellectual output by members of the Province. It can readily be understood. The hyper-activity of the Irish Jesuits in running their various schools and public churches, meeting the constant demand for their services as preachers of retreats and parish missions, the physical and mental mobility required of each of them in taking on a succession of different tasks up and down the country — and sometimes abroad, like the Crimean chaplains and the men sent to meet the needs of Catholics in England, America, India and eventually Australia — left no time for sustained research, reflection and serious writing. The instinct to expand to the limit of their resources deprived the Irish Jesuits of the opportunity in those years to contribute in the major way which might have been expected of them to Irish or ecclesiastical scholarship. Indeed, until the opening of Milltown Park in 1860, they were too busy to set up a house of their own conducive to study.

Perhaps it was for the good. The polemical nature of so many Catholic books and articles of the day, the efforts to repel what were seen as the pretensions of science or liberalism or anti-Roman prejudice, the defensive refusal to condone any philosophy not grounded in Thomas Aquinas, all featured in the works of continental Jesuits. These were the decades when the Society was still backward-looking, over-conscious of the forces which brought about its forty-year suppression and over-suspicious of the modern age in which it had its being. Most of the Irish Jesuits had received some of their training on the continent and had they turned to writing would very likely have reflected the dominant trend of the times in the Catholic Church, which was becoming increasingly centralised, increasingly conservative, increasingly authoritarian. They were better off teaching school and preaching salvation. It is still to be regretted that, on the narrower ground of English-language writing, they took so small a part in the vigorous discussion of contemporary topics in journals like *The Tablet*, the *Dublin Review* and the *Rambler*, not to mention the spate of books in which Victorian churchmen vigorously propounded their opinions and counter-opinions on matters religious. As was evident from Peter Kenney's dealings with Father Stone and John Curtis's comments to Newman, the Irish perspective and Irish experience differed from the English; Irish commentary would have added a further dimension to Catholic thought. Not that the Jesuits were alone in their reticence. Irish Catholics in general, as Father Grene put it, 'trusted too much for their religious literature to London and latterly to New York'.[2]

It was want of opportunity, not of competence, that so long deterred the Irish Jesuits. The scholarship of the theologian, Edmund O'Reilly, or the linguist, John O'Carroll, could not be doubted. The same was true of the historians, Edmund Hogan and Denis Murphy. The fact that such men had begun to publish brought joy to Father Grene, who felt that the tide at last was turning and that the Irish Province was set fair to make an impressive contribution to the corpus of Jesuit writing. No longer would 'Fr Robert Carbery's beautiful little treatise on the Devotion to the Sacred Heart' be 'the only contemporary Irish item in . . . Père de Backer's *Écrivains de la Compagnie de Jésus*.'[3] What seems to have encouraged these authors was the founding of a journal, *The Irish Monthly*, in 1873 under the auspices of the Province and edited by Father Matthew Russell,[4] one of the Maynooth-educated Jesuits who had earlier been sent to Limerick to help establish the Crescent and who was himself no mean writer. Father Grene also noted with approval an 'excellent historical romance of the time of Owen Roe O'Neill', carried as a serial in *The Irish Monthly* and attributed to 'A. Whitelock'. This Whitelock turned out to be a scholastic, Thomas Finlay,[5] the future Rector of Belvedere who would invent the school bus but would also become, for more important reasons, a thinker of outstanding influence in the new Ireland then being moulded.

The new Ireland was the Ireland of which its own people would finally take custody after their long preparation, political and educational, throughout the greater part of the nineteenth century. In the 1870s one aspect of their educational preparation remained unprovided for. The Catholic majority had no university suited to their needs. Dublin University, of which Trinity was the only constituent college, was Protestant in its origin and ethos. The Catholic bishops frowned on the undenominational Queen's Colleges in Belfast, Cork and Galway as secular institutions which they considered to be inimical to the faith of Catholic undergraduates. The Catholic University, founded in Dublin by John Henry Newman twenty years before, was poorly accommodated, unrecognised by the state, dependent on church collections for its funding and — its most serious defect — could not grant degrees; it was rapidly sinking into oblivion for want of students since it offered so little to attract any. It is possible to argue that the bishops should have accepted the Queen's Colleges: the alleged threat to students' beliefs was unproven and national schools, set up on a similar principle, had been found satisfactory from the Church's point of view.[6] Be that as it may, the Colleges remained condemned and, although Catholics were not forbidden to attend them, episcopal disapproval dissuaded many from doing so. More than thirty years would pass before the university question was finally resolved.

The provision of higher education for Catholics in a university ambience during this interim was the most remarkable achievement of a remarkable Jesuit, the same Father William Delany who had so doughtily championed the Intermediate system. However much his attitude touching school examinations may have invited criticism, his commitment to university education was beyond praise. Because of the undergraduates whom he served so well, he can rightly be ranked among the foremost of Irish nation-builders. Because of the reliance he placed on carefully chosen Jesuits to maintain the highest academic standards, he ensured that from his time onwards there would always be members of the Society involved in intellectual activity at the most elevated and influential level, to the benefit of Irish scholarship and the Irish people. It began in Tullabeg, where from 1875 Delany had been entering senior pupils with remarkable success for the matriculation exam which permitted them to be enrolled at London University.[7] The Crescent followed Tullabeg's example.[8] Delany soon went further. London not only had its own colleges but offered well-regarded university degrees to extern students who passed its examinations. Already St Mel's in Longford and other diocesan colleges, as well as the Holy Ghost College in Blackrock and the Vincentions in Castleknock, enabled pupils to remain at school beyond the secondary stage in order to study for the degrees of London University.[9] Clongowes, for a time disdainful, took up the practice in 1879.[10]

Although he was not to be involved in university education himself for some years to come, Delany had ideas, contacts through whom he could promote them, and an essentially practical turn of mind.[11] What happened next was far from what he considered the ideal solution to the university question for Irish Catholics, but it went a long way towards realising as much as he thought could be extracted from any British government disinclined to expose itself to the opposition of anti-Catholic public opinion. It also came close to the form which he considered best in the given situation. The establishment of the Royal University of Ireland[12] in 1880 effectively adapted the London system to suit evolving Irish circumstances. The Royal was an examining board to which colleges of any denomination or none might affiliate so that their students could sit for the degrees it was empowered to grant. This meant that students attending a Catholic college could now become graduates of an Irish university together with students of the Queen's Colleges, which in future were to be affiliate institutions of the Royal. Notwithstanding the fact that it is remembered as 'simply' or 'only' an examining body, the Royal University had a further important function which London University could not discharge. It acted as an agent of indirect endowment by maintaining well-paid fellowships in various subjects to which it appointed suitably qualified scholars to teach in one or other of the participating colleges. From an early stage it was accepted that at least thirteen of these fellowships (half the total at the outset) would be assigned to Catholic institutions. The bishops in turn decided that the 'Catholic' fellowships should all be concentrated within the 'Catholic University College',[13] as the arts and science faculties of the Catholic University housed on St Stephen's Green in Dublin were now termed.

In this way a central Catholic institution, supplied with professors at state expense and offering access to recognised university degrees, was created by rationalising the possibilities inherent in the new arrangement. Other colleges, including Blackrock and Mungret, might continue to prepare their own students for the degree examinations of the Royal because this met their particular needs (it did not suit the Apostolic School at Mungret, for example, to send its students to Dublin) but the tendency quickly spread of taking matriculation at the end of secondary school and proceeding to University College for undergraduate studies. Not the least of its attractions, apart from the student societies and other incidentals of university life, were the high standards quickly established.[14] This was not to be wondered at. Excellent staff could be recruited because, although examination prizes were offered, the fellowships ensured that the Royal University 'endowment' primarily took the form of paying the teacher to teach rather than the pupil to learn. In this the university system differed radically from the Intermediate. High standards had another source as well. From the end of 1883 the President of University College was Father William Delany, S.J.

The Jesuits had fumbled at first in response to the arrival of the Royal University. They opened the College of St Ignatius in Temple Street, Dublin, to function within the scheme under Delany's direction. Together with University College, the Dublin archdiocesan seminary at Clonliffe, Cecilia Street Medical School and Blackrock, among others, Temple Street became a college of the Catholic University and thereby affiliated to the Royal. Because of misunderstandings with Archbishop McCabe, however, it got little chance to flourish before the hierarchy decided, by twenty votes to four, to ask the Jesuits (rather than the Holy Ghost Fathers at Blackrock) to take charge of University College. Father Delany was named President and St Ignatius' was left to merge with Milltown — appropriately, since its student body consisted mainly of Jesuit scholastics. Under Delany's guidance, University College quickly took foremost place among the affiliated institutions in arts subjects and performed exceptionally well in science for an establishment which lacked virtually all laboratory equipment. This, of course, is to measure its quality by examination results, as the President and his Jesuit brethren were disposed to do.[15] A more impressive, if less pragmatic, measure may be to note the physical limitations within which a thriving university atmosphere was generated, some names among the staff who inculcated the sense of excellence, and some of the students who achieved the results.

The location of the College was prestigious enough: Burn-Chapel Whaley's old mansion at 86 St Stephen's Green, which had been St Patrick's House of the Catholic University, with its adjacent houses, hall (the *Aula Maxima*) and Newman's exquisite University Church. Sadly, the bishops decided that the Catholic University, which survived as a corporate body, could not make over the church or the hall to what was only one of its component institutions — even though it was the central college to which the Fellows were assigned and the only one situated in proximity to these facilities, able (and needing) to avail itself of them daily; indeed the church, being legally the property of the Archdiocese,[16] could have been leased to University College with no fuss at all, subject to availability for the occasional more general purposes of the Catholic University as a whole. Part of '86' was also with-held from College use, being the apartment of the Rector of the Catholic University, Monsignor Gerald Molloy, who lectured at the College in experimental physics; two of the other houses turned out to have immovable tenants and, worst of all, the Catholic University library was transferred to Clonliffe. Add the dilapidated state of repair into which the buildings had been allowed to fall and the fact that the Jesuits had to pay rent to the bishops, thus depleting the very lim-ited funds at their disposal (confined in practice to the salaries of Jesuit Fellows and Examiners, since matriculated students from other colleges of the Catholic University were dispensed from fees), and it sounds like something of a miracle that within two months of Father Delany's arrival the College had 109 students, nine of whom were resident, and that as early as the end of his first academic year they began to register the outstanding results which would characterise University College throughout its Jesuit occupancy.

Delany was President from 1883 to 1888 and again from 1897 until the establishment of the National University of Ireland in 1909 when the College became part of the new structure as one of its constituent colleges: a settlement at long last of the Irish university question, brought about in no small degree through the President's continuing plea that Catholics be given 'a fair deal' and his influence not only with Tory politicians but also with leading Liberals like the writers John Morley and Augustine Birrell, who both served as Chief Secretary for Ireland. With some justice did Father Joseph Darlington, Dean of the College and professor of English, suggest that the Jesuits at the College should be called 'Whigs on the Green'! Not all these Jesuits were Irish. Father Delany looked for the best scholars wherever he could find them to put forward for election as Fellows and obvious places to look were the provinces of the Society of Jesus. Father Kieffer came from Germany to teach electrical science, Father Mallac from France to teach philosophy. Darlington was English, as also was the member of the community who would be the most famous of them after his death, the poet, Father Gerard Manley Hopkins, who was appointed a Fellow in classics.

It is tempting to count the attractive if broody Hopkins among the Irish Jesuits, with whom he worked and in whose company he is buried at Glasnevin, but this would be unjust to his memory for he was intensely unhappy in Dublin, having no inclination for teaching and suffering real distress from the anti-English attitude of so many whom he met. He was in bad health, scarcely helped by the living conditions in '86': 'The house we are in, the College, is a sort of ruin and for purposes of study very nearly naked,' he wrote.[17] He was 'warmly welcomed and most kindly treated'[18] but he probably voiced his true feelings in 'a patriotic song for soldiers,'

> Call me England's fame's fond lover,
> Her fame to keep, her fame to recover,[19]

and he took gentle vengeance on his hosts by resorting to outrageous stage-Irishry in a letter to his sister: 'Me dear Miss Hopkins — Im intoirely ashamed o meself. Sure its a wonder I could lave your iligant corspondance so long onansered . . .'.[20]

It was not Hopkins, however, or any of the non-Irish Jesuits who made the reputation of the College. It was, rather, the members of the Irish Province given fellowships often at Delany's instigation: men like Robert Curtis, the mathematician whose serious epilepsy prevented him from being ordained;[21] Edmund Hogan, the historian and Celtic scholar named to a chair of Irish language and literature; John O'Carroll, who taught Irish as well as other languages and Matthew Russell of *The Irish Monthly*. The acquisition of academic posts released these scholars from the pressures of normal Jesuit life in Ireland, the grind of school-work or the incessant demands of the pastorate (although they tended to keep up a degree of strictly priestly activity; Father Delany himself retained his confessional in Gardiner Street when he undertook his second term as President). They could now do research, propound ideas, deliver public lectures . . . write, above all. The most dynamic of them, Father Thomas Finlay, who fitted in a memorable spell as Rector of Belvedere between his election as a Fellow in classics and his long spell at University College as an economics professor both in the days of the Royal and later of the N.U.I., saw the importance of what Father Russell had proved. He founded a monthly, *The Lyceum*, in which the College staff — among others — were encouraged to examine educational themes, social questions and contemporary developments abroad in science and literature. It covered a wide field of interest: from Father O'Carroll on the state of Russian and Scandinavian writing to Father Finlay himself on national economics, from articles on Zola, Pater and Whitman to the first publication of Douglas Hyde's *Love Songs of Connacht*. When the journal was expanded further in scope and retitled *The New Ireland Review*, it became more noticeably a forum for the exciting literary, artistic, political (but not *party* political, Finlay insisted), economic and historiographical ideas of the day: a reflection of burgeoning Irish self-identity and the consciousness that in one way or another Ireland would soon be an autonomous state, its affairs consigned to the hands of its own citizens.

The sense that they were preparing the ground for a 'new Ireland' and honing the perceptions of its likely leaders permeated Delany's College as well as Finlay's journals, and engaged the enthusiasm not only of the Jesuits but of the staff in general and the student body. Father Finlay himself showed how practical shape could be given to theory when he joined with Sir Horace Plunkett in founding the co-operative movement which was to have so profound an effect on the development of Irish agriculture. Meanwhile, extra-curricular activities encouraged by the President included scientific, philosophical and French societies as well as the provision of classes for the general public in Irish by Father John McErlean (a Jesuit historian), Patrick Pearse (who would instigate and lead the 1916 Rising) and Seamus Clandillon (who would become the first Director of Broadcasting in the Irish Free State). Pearse was a lecturer in the College, as was Eoin MacNeill who would countermand Pearse's mobilisation orders for the insurrection. Clandillon was a graduate; so were Tom Kettle and Arthur Clery, future N.U.I. professors, the first of whom would die at the Somme while the second would be an opponent of the Anglo-Irish Treaty. Frank Sheehy-Skeffington, the pacifist-socialist, attended the College in its Jesuit days too, as also did Con Curran, a most civilised man of letters and art historian. The list of graduates who took their envisaged role as leaders in the new Ireland was formidable indeed: Chief Justice Hugh Kennedy; Professor John Marcus O'Sullivan, a scholar-cum-politician like O'Neill; Dr Thomas Bodkin, Director of the National Gallery; Felix Hackett, the physicist; and numerous others, including 'a notable proportion of the men who . . . staffed our government after the Anglo-Irish treaty,'[22] among whom could be counted senior civil servants as well as members of cabinet.

It would be wrong to suppose that the only influence on this remarkable generation of students was that of the Jesuit Fathers in the College. From Thomas Arnold (brother of Matthew), who dated from Newman's time, and George Sigerson who had been on the staff of the old Catholic University, to W. P. Coyne, Arthur Conway and the lecturers mentioned above, the lay staff of the College both in arts and the sciences were of a calibre to match their often precocious students and played a major part in moulding the young men's outlook. The Jesuits' role was nonetheless central. Father Delany not only chose many of the staff but bound them into an efficient team. He established an Academic Council of six professors, five of whom were laymen elected triennially by the teaching staff. To the Jesuits, especially Father Finlay, were traceable certain moral values which marked many of the graduates. 'These varying types, philosophers, economists, men of letters and of law, had one common denominator, an unselfish instinct for public service. They got their impetus in great measure from Finlay and they had their baptism in ink in the papers Finlay founded, edited and in turn passed into their general control.'[23] The Jesuits encouraged an atmosphere of thought and discussion through the student societies, especially the Literary and Historical debating society (the 'L-and-H') and at a mundane but vital level kept the stop-gap substitution for a true university in being by contributing their own salaries to its expenses, and indeed topping up the finances as required from the Irish Province's own funds.

None of it was achieved without travail. Delany found himself again and again in tension with an old friend, Dr William Walsh of Maynooth, who became Archbishop of Dublin in 1885. Dr Walsh favoured the Holy Ghost Fathers over the

Jesuits, objected to the concentration of fellowships in University College, and instead of the new university for which Delany was campaigning urged the imposition of a Catholic college on Dublin University side by side with Trinity. Over time, the President rebuilt his relationship with the Archbishop and even wheedled out of him the right to use University Church and the Aula Maxima (the Aula proved convenient for lectures attended by the first women students, who could not conveniently be accommodated elsewhere in the College for reasons which probably had more to do with Victorian standards of propriety than the interior dimensions of the houses involved), but he then became embroiled with the student body. The mounting awareness of nationality brought conflicts between Delany and the students' journal, the debating society and what today would be seen as protest groups who judged him to be too deferential to the British authorities. They shouted him down at an L-and-H meeting in the presence of Birrell at the very time when the Chief Secretary had committed himself to support the greater part of the Irish case on the university question. Finlay had his problems, too. His promotion of the co-operative movement was thought by some Irish parliamentarians to be a dangerous diversion of the people's attention from the overriding objective of Home Rule — despite the fact that Finlay was not above arguing for a form of Home Rule himself: in 1905, exasperated by British delay, he suggested that Irish Catholics should resolve the university question on their own by re-establishing the old Catholic University as a teaching institution in its own right, supported by public subscription. Pearse and Kettle cheered him on. Father Delany must have wriggled in discomfort.

Notwithstanding such problems, Delany steered the College successfully into port and in 1909 handed it over to its new custodians as University College, Dublin, of the National University of Ireland. The Jesuits left St Stephen's Green, their trust discharged. They did not leave the University. Their involvement in higher studies had by now become an ingrained characteristic of the Irish Province. Father Finlay became Professor of Political Economy at the new College.

The New Ireland Review continued briefly until plans for a quarterly journal were completed and the first issue of

Studies appeared in March 1912, to carry 'contributions in various departments of Letters, Philosophical subjects and Science'.[24] Although a review for the new College, it was essentially a Jesuit publication, destined to become the most respected in the country for giving publicity 'to work of a scholarly type, extending over many important branches of study, and appealing to a wider circle of cultured readers than strictly specialist journals could be expected to reach'.[25] Editorial control lay with a committee chaired by Father Finlay but the actual editing was done by a fellow-Jesuit, Father Timothy Corcoran, Professor of Education at U.C.D. — in which capacity, oddly enough, 'he did a great deal to denigrate the teaching of Newman on the idea of a university'.[26] Under the extended editorships of Father Patrick J. Connolly (from 1914 to 1950) and Father Roland Burke Savage (in the '50s and '60s) awesome standards were set for their successors. Few Irish scholars of repute, literary or artistic critics, or commentators on social and economic issues, failed to appear in the pages of *Studies*.

On occasion it gave the stimulus to a national debate, as in 1968 when an article by the Assistant Secretary in the Department (Ministry) of Education, Mr Sean O'Connor, provided insights on Irish post-primary education which would be mulled over for years. One of his points, incidentally, was that: 'Public examinations . . . are achievement tests, or, more accurately, memory tests, and their form is totally unrealistic . . . they are almost useless as predictors of initiative and creativity.'[27] The shade of Father Delany must have shuddered at the blasphemy in a Jesuit journal. . . .

If University College academics and graduates have tended to predominate in *Studies*, this indicates the context to which it primarily belonged until recent years, just as the number of Jesuit contributors underscores its provenance. These Jesuit writers symbolise the breadth of learning found in the twentieth-century Irish Province. Between 1909 and the 1970s, numerous priests of the Society were appointed to chairs or lectureships at U.C.D. — in history (Aubrey Gwynn and John Ryan), in mathematics (Michael Egan and Richard Ingram), in Irish (Frank Shaw), in botany (John Moore), in education (Sean O Cathain as well as Timothy Corcoran), in psycho-biology (Martin Brennan), in English (Michael Paul Gallagher). Names of Jesuits abound among the Irish authorities of the century on subjects from Roentgen rays (Henry Gill) to John Henry Newman (Fergal McGrath . . . not Father Corcoran!), from the Dead Sea Scrolls (Kevin Smyth) to child guidance (Paul Andrews). Not surprisingly, there were distinguished theologians (John Hyde, James Healy) and distinguished Gaelic scholars (Seosamh Ó Muirthuile, Diarmuid Ó Laoghaire). Father Kevin Quinn became Professor of Sociology at the Gregorian University in Rome. At the time of writing, Father Bartholomew Kiely heads the Institute of Psychology, also at the Gregorian, and is a Consultor to the Congregation for the Doctrine of the Faith. Father Gallagher has left Ireland to join the staff of the Pontifical Council for Non-Believers. Father Laurence Murphy has just completed a term as Rector of the International College at the Gesù.

Perhaps a little more surprisingly, given the comparative lack of interest of the nineteenth-century Jesuits in the visual arts, the 1950s and 1960s saw Jesuits become prominent as connoisseurs whose judgment was well regarded (John C. Kelly, Cyril Barret); Father Donal O'Sullivan was appointed Chairman of the Arts Council. It should be added that, from the 1920s on, the Jesuits commissioned much work from leading Irish artists — in stained glass especially, from Michael Healy (for Clongowes), Evie Hone (Clongowes and Tullabeg), Frances Biggs (Gonzaga). Louis Le Brocquy did the mosaic for a shrine in Galway, where the setting was designed by Michael Scott. This awakened interest is significant, for it is difficult to believe that aesthetic appreciation was not a concomitant of the high standards set and pursued at the College on the Green.

Aesthetic standards were indeed not lacking in the College. While the dean of studies lays the fire in the physics theatre, Stephen Dedalus quotes Aquinas on beauty in the eye of the beholder.[28] As a student at the College, James Joyce followed no course in philosophy[29] yet was acquainted with the standard texts in general circulation, for it was 'Father Delany's dictum that the philosophy faculty should be the heart of any university. It was so in the University College I knew. None of us escaped its tincture.'[30] The texts dealt with values like clarity and unity which Aquinas considered important in the idea of the beautiful, and Joyce, 'keener than the rest on his special objective and quicker to claim his property when he found it, found here the starting point of his aesthetics'.[31] So wrote his closest friend at College. To catch some feeling of what this meant, we can turn to another fellow student of Joyce who heard him read a paper on James Clarence Mangan to the L-and-H. 'It had the structure of a symphony,' he recalled in 1957, as he described the sequence of argument in Joyce's approach to the subject, and the reading ended by 'soaring to a conclusion of musical and oracular utterance.' It was 'an early outburst of a literary Nova which, blazing to prominence forty years ago, has ever since illumined the skies of English literature.'[32]

If Joyce took an understanding of beauty from University College, he had begun at Clongowes and Belvedere to savour words and to respect orderliness of thought, to observe, to register impressions and to dredge from the smallest experience the last tangible sight and sound it had to offer.[33] Without taking it for autobiography, the *Portrait of the Artist* still leaves no possible doubt that his schooldays were ever-present in his mind, from the 'pale and chilly' air of an autumn evening on the gravel playground at Clongowes[34] to 'the smiling face of a priest' momentarily caught in the glow of a Chinese lantern as he arrived for a drama production at Belvedere.[35] The scrupulous authenticity of detail suggests things remembered which he had no desire to forget, a sign surely that he remembered with affection. He was indeed always grateful[36] to the Jesuits and fair[37] to them, yet he caused them great embarrassment because of his irreligion, the stridency of which only sounded the harsher the more he invoked Catholic terminology and concepts. 'His was a Catholic mind that rejected superstition and thought it had rejected the Faith.'[38] This made it understandably difficult for the Jesuits to appreciate, until distance brought objectivity, that Joyce was 'an advertisement for the nature and quality of the traditional Jesuit education, both religious and literary,'[39] as well as 'for that determined realisation of one's own proper

vocation which lies at the heart of the Jesuit ideal of education'.[40] He in fact exemplifed a proposition tentatively put
forward earlier in this book: namely, that the Jesuits' encouragement of the pursuit of excellence was vindicated when
former pupils who became rebels proved to be superlatively
effective in their rebellion!

Be that as it may, from the age of six-and-a-half to 20 Joyce
attended Jesuit schools and colleges in Ireland for all but
fifteen months. When every allowance has been made for his
own genius and personality, the Irish Jesuits can neither
disclaim responsibility nor be denied the credit for exercising
the major formative influence upon the only author in the
English language to be more written about than Shakespeare.[41] It would be difficult to show that Shakespeare's
plays or sonnets reflect much of Stratford grammar school in
theme or language or insight to the human condition. But
the lessons taught and standards set by the Jesuits of the Irish
Province are woven warp and woof through the writings of
James Augustine Joyce.

Broadbeamed, low-slung, high-masted: the elegant lines of
the steamship *Great Britain* can be admired today as she
reclines at Bristol in the very dock where she rested from
long voyages in her heyday. Her only incongruous feature is
the tall metal smoke-stack abaft the masts, a contradiction
upon a vessel so manifestly designed to cut smartly along
before any fresh breeze that might blow. But as James Joyce
remarked with Saint Thomas, beauty lies in the eye of the
beholder. To her contemporaries, that shining black chimney
made *Great Britain* the loveliest ship afloat, the ultimate
triumph of the industrial revolution, for she symbolised
man's escape by his own ingenuity from the thraldom of
nature. Her master could use the wind if he chose, but if it
were too slight or blew from the wrong quarter he had only
to order that the engine be brought to life and then steam
on regardless. For some, religion had little place in this
exciting new world where human destiny seemed to have
been brought so completely within human control. Yet,
oddly enough, *Great Britain* in 1865 and again in 1866 would
play a role in evangelisation by carrying two parties of Irish

Jesuits to Australia, and among them Father William Kelly who would be a champion of faith against the excessive claims of science — a stance he was all the more competent to adopt for being a scientist himself.

Not that contention had any any place on the journeys out. The three Fathers and two Brothers who travelled in 1866[42] were given 'a wide berth' by the other passengers until it was seen that at dinner 'all the fun appeared to be confined to our table', where they had the company of the Bishop of Hobart as well as 'five heretics'. Thereafter, everybody got on famously and the Masses celebrated in the Ladies' Saloon, in Steerage and at an altar on deck in front of the main mast were attended by many Protestants, either out of idleness or because (as they politely said) they liked the Jesuits' sermons. They experienced all the incidentals of a sea voyage: albatrosses, whales and flying fish, a great storm, shipboard deaths and conversions. The last Sunday brought an idyllic calm, when the *Great Britain* was 'as steady as Marlborough Street Church'. A mock trial was held, with Father Joseph Dalton in the chair, to determine whether a certain lady had been seen kissing a gentleman; another lady, 'bold as brass', said she had seen it happen and that the gentleman was the captain; the female jury discounted her evidence and found the witness guilty of slander! Father Edward Nolan heard 114 confessions but was, of course, debarred from saying whether one of them concerned the kissing of a gentleman. The captain produced champagne for Saint Patrick's Day and on the evening before disembarkation 'the greatest bigot on board proposed the toast of the "R.C. Clergy", regretting "he had not had the privilege of knowing them sooner".' This pleased the Jesuits, who felt they had succeeded in overcoming some people's prejudices. Father Dalton himself was chosen to propose the toast of the captain, which 'was received with loud applause'.

The voyage could be read as an allegory of what the Fathers and Brothers of the Irish Province achieved in Australia, overcoming Protestant suspicions, winning social acceptability for Catholics, demonstrating their competence and all the while vigorously discharging their pastoral duties. It was done under the dual mandate to teach and to preach, familiar to any member of the Society coming from Ireland. They came at the request of the Bishop (later Archbishop) of Melbourne, Dr Alcipius Goold, who had urged the Jesuit General, with more success than the Archbishop of Sydney a few years before, to persuade the Irish to set up a mission.[43] Otherwise it was very likely that, with Limerick, Galway and Milltown so recently opened, the Provincial, Father Edmund O'Reilly (yes, the stage army was still on the march), would have pleaded shortage of manpower and declined the invitation — even though Father John Joseph Therry, a secular priest who had virtually founded the Church in Australia, had left a substantial legacy to the Irish Province accompanied by a broad hint that they should take up where he had left off.[44] As it was, responding to a directive from the General, Father O'Reilly picked the men for Australia with care. First, to reconnoitre, he sent his predecessor as Provincial, Father Joseph Lentaigne, and the preacher-scientist, Father Kelly. Father Dalton and his companions followed. Dalton was appointed Superior; he had been an energetic Rector-cum-Prefect-of-Studies at Tullabeg, where he initiated a number of the improvements later brought to fruition by Delany.[45] Bishop Goold must have been well-satisfied with the quality of the Jesuits sent to him: on his very first night off the ship, Kelly preached at a parish mission he found in progress in the church of Saint Francis in Melbourne![46]

The Irish were not the first Jesuits in Australia. In the colony of South Australia the Austrian Province had established a mission some eighty miles from the city of Adelaide in 1848, where most of the Catholics scattered through the country districts were German-speaking.[47] After various vicissitudes, they acquired a residence at a place called Sevenhills where they opened a college and a public church. The Austrians, however, were too few in number to expand and in any event the many Catholics in the populous colonies of Victoria and New South Wales in the south-eastern corner of the continent were almost all Irish: hence Goold's specific request to the General for *Irish* Jesuits. He wanted them to take over his secondary school, St Patrick's College, in Melbourne (capital of Victoria) and the parish of Richmond on the edge of the city. On paper the proposal had echoes of

Limerick and Galway. In reality, the scale differed greatly. Richmond stretched far into the bush and the Catholics in remote parts were less than diligent in the practice of their religion. Missions had to be undertaken, local schools which could double as chapels had to be set up and a church had to be built in Richmond itself. While the crash programme of renewal went ahead, the same handful of Jesuits had to put St Patrick's on a sound footing. In 1865 it had 30 pupils, a year later 102 with classes up to Syntax (fourth year). This was the work for which the Bishop had primarily sought out the Society of Jesus. He wanted to create leaders for the Catholic Church who could be expected also to become leaders in the colonial administration, the professions, politics, farming and business. The objective sufficiently resembled what Father Kenney had in mind when he founded Clongowes for the Clongowes formula to be applied by Dalton and his colleagues.

A liberal education based on the classics was therefore provided, with physics, chemistry, mathematics and modern languages offered as well. Debating was encouraged, especially by Father Francis Murphy who had been the first president of the Clongowes Debating Society. As at the Irish school, prominent Catholic public figures were invited to participate in College activities (including the Young Irelander and former editor of *The Nation*, Charles Gavan Duffy, who became Prime Minister of Victoria in 1871, the same year as Father Murphy became Rector of St Patrick's). 'Speech Days' in Melbourne were ecumenical, with all the secondary schools of the city participating together, but the Jesuits managed to introduce an element of 'Academy Day' by offering Latin odes and the like to honour visiting dignitaries: in reality, of course, to impress the dignitaries with the standards prevailing at the Catholic establishment. When a Catholic Academy was founded at St Patrick's, involving both devotional exercises and intellectual discussion, it became something of a club for Catholic lawyers and members of other professions. The Sodality and annual retreats reinforced the common faith of school-pupils and their elders. It was magnificent, all the Bishop hoped for . . . yet not quite to the colonial taste. As at Belvedere, as in Limerick, the demand grew for commercial subjects; as in Missouri, a population still half-pioneer saw little value in Latin and Greek; as would happen in Ireland, parents looked for examination results to certify the level of education attained by their boys. Jesuits wedded to the Clongowes tradition tried to hold the line; others, significantly Father John Ryan who had been to the Crescent, favoured the more popular view. By the 1880s book-keeping and shorthand were being taught.

St Patrick's was a day school, although in Australian conditions provision for some boarders had to be made, given the distance to be travelled into town. The demand for Jesuit education made a proper boarding school necessary. A site was found, building commenced and in 1878 St Xavier's College opened in the Melbourne suburb of Kew. Or rather, what became a suburb, for at the opening ceremonies Kew was still in the countryside, gigantic gum trees surrounded the new college and Father Kelly was able to preach on the biblical theme of what they had come out to the desert to see. Boarding pupils had already been arriving from New Zealand and Tasmania as well as remote parts of Australia, and the Jesuits felt obliged to take on further projects. Now at last they went to Sydney, the capital of New South Wales, the 'mother-colony' of Australia to the north of Victoria, where they again accepted responsibility for a large parish, a day school (St Aloysius) and the construction of a boarding school (St Ignatius' College) at a particularly picturesque site called Riverview, high on a peninsula overlooking two bays in Sydney Harbour. Riverview soon became the most prestigious Catholic school in Australia, although the claim might well have been challenged by St Xavier's. These fine colleges contrasted sharply with the rough conditions faced by the Jesuits in the bush-parishes they served adjacent to the cities. Richmond, outside Melbourne, they divided into smaller units — one of which, Hawthorne, was administered by Father Oliver Daly, destined in Irish Province legend to save the life of Archbishop Goold. The parish of North Sydney was even more extensive and when Father Dalton took charge of it he had to live in a shanty hut built of tin cans used for carrying kerosene: the Jesuits' residence thereupon became known as 'Kerosene Lodge'. When they sought to hire a housekeeper, the elderly woman who presented herself took one look at the 'Lodge' and turned down the job because, she said, she was accustomed to working for decent people!

The strain on manpower was beginning to show. Several invitations to open houses had to be declined and a promising small mission in New Zealand withered on the bough. A mission to the aborigines had to be left for the Austrians to organise (after some years of devoted service to the tribes around Port Darwin in the Northern Territory, the Austrian Jesuits abandoned the enterprise which they found unsuited to a nomadic people). Worst of all, perhaps, for an Order expected to maintain high educational standards was the effect in Australia of the acquisition by the Jesuits of University College in Dublin; the intellectuals of the Irish Province were now needed at home. Thereafter, and perhaps until the establishment of the National University, the men sent out from Ireland 'were not of the calibre of those early Jesuits who had taken over Saint Patrick's in 1865' since, even if they were 'zealous missionaries,' they 'lacked scholarship'.[48] It was surely desperation alone that allowed Father Patrick Duffy, one of the Crimean chaplains, to sail for Australia in 1888 at the age of 74. He had gamely volunteered and would in fact put in prodigious work for more than ten years in preaching missions and retreats all over the eastern seaboard from Queensland to Tasmania,[49] but he was hardly the kind of recruit whom the hard-pressed Dalton hoped to receive. Archbishop (later Cardinal) Moran of Sydney was heard to complain about the Mission's lack of qualified teachers for higher studies.

It may be relevant to add that the Jesuits never established the same rapport with Cardinal Moran or his predecessor, Archbishop Vaughan, that they enjoyed with successive Archbishops of Melbourne: Dr Goold, Dr Thomas Carr who had known them well when he was Bishop of Galway, and the formidable Dr Daniel Mannix who might have been expected to be unhappy with an Order which displayed rather less Irish-nationalist ardour than he did himself. The Jesuit style of preaching, however, with its stress on the Mass, prayer and the sacraments rather than abstract theological discussion, appealed to these Church leaders, who saw that it also suited the practical mentality of the people: Melbourne Catholics preferred to integrate their beliefs into their daily lives rather than to undertake contemplative exercises. In Sydney, by contrast, an English Benedictine tradition, different in tone and emphasis, had been in favour before the Jesuits arrived and this, together with more entrenched Protestant interests, left the Irish Fathers for a time feeling somewhat at odds with the officialdom of Church and State alike. Although Cardinal Moran had been Bishop of Ossory (and was a nephew of Cardinal Cullen), he absorbed something of the vice-regal atmosphere of Sydney and with it a degree of reserve towards the Jesuits whom he reprimanded from time to time over minor matters of dress or non-attendance at diocesan functions. This may have accounted for the notice-ably 'imperialist' ethos adopted at Riverview, with loyalty to crown and empire given a priority less evident in the more Australian-oriented atmosphere of the Melbourne schools; the route to social acceptance for Catholics in Sydney lay through identification with the establishment, while in Melbourne it lay through identification with the people.

The Irish Jesuits were also staunch defenders of the Catholic interest against the 'liberal' forces which they detected at work in the government's promotion of secular schooling after the creation of the Commonwealth of Australia as an independent dominion of the British Empire in 1901. Like many exiles, they tended to hold fast to the views they held when they left home. More open thinking did not come to them easily and in fact it was only on the eve of the First World War that they began in some numbers to reason their way through social issues to their own conclusions instead of repeating stock attitudes. By then, it was clear that Australian Catholics leaned more towards the Labour Party than towards conservative political alignments: this called for a healthy, if overdue, reflection on the variety of liberal attitudes . . . and especially on the varieties of socialism. Jesuits like Isaac Moore, Michael Phelan and Richard Murphy had been nudging Australian Catholicism away from purely negative views and towards a recognition of the duty of the state to involve itself in rectifying social injustice.

These perceptions now came into their own and provided some at least of the driving force for an active lay apostolate conducted by pressure groups linked together in the Australian Catholic Federation. Father William Lockington, a New Zealand-born member of the Mission, at the same time organised the Catholic Women's Social Guild through which, he said, women might hope to get justice for themselves and their sisters.

Important influences in stirring this awareness were, obviously enough, the teachings of Leo XIII, but also the writings of Father Finlay which, with their emphasis on rural organisation, made sense to many Australians. Curiously, until well into the 1920s the new-found interest in stirring the conscience of government seems to have concentrated heavily on securing fair treatment for church schools and on other aspects of church-state conflict in education. One reason for this was the Catholics' need to bring the Labour Party round to their point of view, since Labour began with a strongly secularist opinion on such questions: Archbishop Mannix took the line that if the Catholic workers failed to win their campaign within the party they would have to fight it from outside.

Needless to say, the Jesuits were only a comparatively small group among the numerous religious congregations working in Australia, and even among those who came from Ireland. The teaching orders — in particular, the Christian Brothers and the Marist Brothers — had contributed much to the formation of Catholic attitudes. But these orders did not live in a vacuum and the Jesuits had more than once sought their help, as well as that of women's congregations, to run local schools in the unwieldy parishes assigned to the Society: without the brothers and the nuns the Jesuits would more than once have had to give up ambitious pastoral initiatives. Close contact arose also from the use of Jesuits by other orders and the diocesan clergy as preachers and confessors. Archbishop Carr always personally attended the annual retreat which they gave for the Melbourne priests. The relationships thus built up, together with the Jesuits' own reputation as educators and the connections they established with political, professional and business leadership (where increasingly their former pupils were to be found), ensured that their opinions carried more weight than their numbers might imply. By the same token they were open to influence from other quarters: the First World War brought some painful tensions within the Australian Mission when some of the Fathers adopted the anti-conscription stance common among the Irish (and offered theological argument to sustain it) while some of their colleagues involved with the middle-class colleges were content with conventional acceptance of what was deemed necessary for the successful prosecution of the war.

Meanwhile, expansion continued. In 1901 the remaining Austrian foundations in South Australia at Sevenhills and Norwood (outside Adelaide) were amalgamated with the Mission of the Irish Province, of which they became part. These were two substantial parishes, each with its Jesuit resi-dence: the college at Sevenhills had been closed because of its inconvenient location and an alternative intended for Norwood was never built as the Jesuits felt that the parochial need for churches and local schools was more pressing. Seven-hills had served as a temporary novitiate when Australian recruits began to join the Society. A proper novitiate was opened at Richmond, transferred to Kew and eventually to a house in Sydney which was given the name of Loyola. The first Master of Novices at Loyola was Father Sturzo, the exile from Sicily who had served terms as Rector of Milltown Park in Dublin and as Irish Provincial. A house at Brisbane, Queensland, was opened in 1916, and in 1923 the Regional Seminary of Werribee was entrusted to the Society by the bishops of the Melbourne ecclesiastical province — another mark of favour by Mannix and a revival of the service pro-vided to the region in the early days of St Patrick's when the Jesuits had undertaken the training of students for the dio-cesan priesthood until they acquired a seminary of their own.

Surprisingly, throughout their first half-century in Australia the Irish Jesuits had little involvement with university educa-tion, although they encouraged their pupils to go on to the Universities of Melbourne or Sydney when they left school. It would be wrong to say there were no anxieties over the sup-posed danger to faith in attendance at universities not under

Catholic control: this peculiar and obstructive paranoia was widespread through the Catholic world until the mid-twentieth century, and not least in Australia. In Australia, however, it was tempered by recognition of the reality that the state universities were the most suitable universities available to Catholics: Catholic bishops, in fact, were appointed to seats in the university senates. In Sydney a Catholic College, St John's, was affiliated to the University and provided tutors to supplement university lectures in particular subjects. Archbishop Vaughan blocked a proposal to give charge of the College to the Jesuits (effectively a revival of his predecessor's invitation to the Irish Vice-Province in 1858 'to take charge of the University', which had in fact been a reference to the University *College* of St John's) and when Father Daniel Clancy, S.J., was appointed Rector in 1884 opposition within the New South Wales Church forced him to resign within months. A Jesuit continued to lecture there in logic and some Catholic students at the University resided at Riverview, but that was as far as the Society's connection with third-level education went. The problem lay partly in the endemic shortage of manpower, and partly in a lack of quality, for these were the years when 'the Irish Province was sending out builders, teachers and preachers, not writers,'[50] which is to say, not the kind of men who were achieving so much at University College in Dublin.

After the Society relinquished the Dublin College in 1909, successive Irish Provincials assigned Jesuits of high intellectual calibre to the Australian Mission: George O'Neill, who had been a Fellow of the Royal University; Albert Power, a writer who had been Professor of Theology at Milltown Park; Jeremiah Murphy, who had studied antiquities at Oxford; Dominic Kelly, 'a very gifted man who taught practically all the subjects in the curriculum in Clongowes . . .'[51] (and who, as a boy at the school, had written the stern denunciation of corporal punishment quoted earlier). With such scholars at hand it became feasible for the Mission to accept an invitation to provide a University College. Embarrassingly, two offers were received at the same time, the first to take over and revitalise the run-down St John's in Sydney, the other to build and administer a projected Newman College which would be affiliated to Melbourne University. As usual in Sydney the Jesuits ran into obstacles when discussing the matter, so they happily chose Melbourne where the Society had always been made to feel at home. With a private bene- faction, they were able to put up a handsome college, 'the first break with the traditional architecture of Oxford and Cambridge'[52] in Australian collegiate building. Under a Coun- cil on which the bishops of the region were represented, the Jesuits had complete charge of studies and the management of the College. A well-endowed scholarship system enabled students from every economic background to attend. Jesuits associated with Newman College in its early years included Fathers Power, Murphy and Kelly, as well as a number of Australian-born colleagues.

Newman, which by 1927 had 90 resident students and 46 nonresidents, set the ultimate and appropriate seal on the Australian Mission of the Irish Province. The time had come to let go of the leading-strings. In 1931 Father Wladimir Ledochowski, General of the Society, issued a decree which said: 'The Mission of Australia, first undertaken by the Austrian Province in 1848, has since for over sixty years been so developed and increased under the diligent and active care of the Irish Province, that it now seems possible for it to become independent. It has its own Novitiate at Sydney, five flourishing colleges, eight residences situated in the chief cities of Australia, especially in the South, and the Regional Seminary at Melbourne, which their Lordships the Bishops of that Ecclesiastical Province recently entrusted to the Society. Wherefore. . . . We separate the Australian Mission from the Irish Province and set it up as an independent Vice- Province . . . according to the Institute of the Society.'[53] Thus ended in rich and complete fulfilment the task undertaken by the Irish Jesuits who made their landfall in Melbourne Harbour when ocean-going steamships were still the wonder of the age.

The preaching of the Gospel by European Catholics in what today we call the Third World countries of Latin America, Africa and Asia was commonly considered to be the work of 'the Foreign Missions', as distinct from activity among Europeans or people of European origin which was treated as an extension of the home mission. Secular clergy and religious going from Ireland to England, the United States, Australia or New Zealand were not thought of as 'foreign missionaries' although they might be assigned for a lifetime to 'the English Mission' or 'the Australian Mission' and, in the days before air travel, were unlikely to make many visits home if they were working in other continents. The old concept of the Foreign Missions was that they brought the faith to people who had never seen the light of Christ — to 'pagans', as they used to be called until the word acquired a pejorative connotation, meaning lost in a welter of malevolent and immoral superstition. In time it came to be seen that 'pagan' beliefs were often manifestations of an age-old culture, sometimes of a high civilisation and even of a profoundly meditated philosophy or way to truth, deserving respect from Christians rather than suppression. Thereafter the Foreign Missions became agencies of witness to Christ, ensuring that the message of his Gospel was available in these lands and that people who made it their own could assimilate the Christian faith into their culture without needing to reject anything of their inheritance, except insofar as it contradicted Christian doctrine or morality.

The Jesuits, as we have seen, made the Foreign Missions a primary part of their apostolate from the outset: Francis Xavier's mission to the Indies was contemporaneous with the first mission to Ireland. An outstanding feature of the Jesuit approach was to accept as much prevailing tradition as they considered compatible with Christianity. They did so in Japan, in South America, above all in China where existing dress, rites and even religious terminology were retained in a Catholic context.[54] This, it should be stressed, is to generalise; Jesuits were not alone in taking this view but it was conspicuously associated with them. Neither were all Jesuits able to go as far as some of their brethren in conceding the validity of cultures they found alien at first sight. Salmeron and Broet were unable to do so in Ireland and the same limitation showed itself in José de Acosta, a Jesuit who meant well when he argued in 1576 for the admissibility of American Indians to the priesthood but who was hardly perceptive in choosing the Irish as an example of how 'uncivilised' people could be educated to the point where they became fervent Christians![55] Adaptability nonetheless became characteristic of Jesuit missionary enterprise and the Society had to face much criticism as a consequence within the Church itself, where they were represented as tending towards schism or heresy because they allegedly made up their own rules as they went along.[56] It was not until the mid-twentieth century that the Church conceded the universal importance of deferring to local culture.

From an early date (perhaps unknown to Father Acosta!) Irish Jesuits became foreign missionaries. We have already met Thomas Filde (or Field) of Limerick among the Fathers setting up in Paraguay in the 1580s: a mission which developed over the following century into the famous Reductions where the Indians lived in self-sufficient settlements under Jesuit guidance and protection. Father Thomas Browne of Waterford spent thirty years in the Reductions along the Paraná river and from 1708 to 1711 was Superior of the region; he was one of the Jesuits who defended Indian rights against the Spaniards.[57] Miguel Godinez may not sound very Irish but his name was a Hispanicisation of Michael Wadding and he also came from Waterford (of course!); he was several times Rector of colleges in seventeenth-century Mexico, was a noted theologian and wrote a classic work on mystical theology. A hundred years later, Thomas Lynch of Galway was Rector of two Brazilian colleges and for a time Provincial of Brazil. Cornelius Guillereag (*recte* Mac Giolla Riabhaigh) of County Clare and another Galwayman, Stephen de la Fuente (*recte* Font) worked together among the Mexican Indians and were typical of a score more Fathers and Brothers of the Society from Ireland who gave their adult lives to serving the native peoples of Latin America. Some went to the West Indies, like John Stritch who had been ordained by Rinuccini in Galway in 1649. There were Irish Jesuits on the other side of the globe: at Goa (Francis Skerret from Galway; James Aylward of a Waterford family; Brother John Baptist from Clontarf, whose surname has not survived) and in the Philippine Islands (Francis O'Driscoll from Cork and a Charles O'Dwyer). In the Philippines also was one who had his tongue slit by less than friendly islanders. This was Richard O'Callaghan, the Dublinman who returned home and did so much to protect the Irish Mission funds during the Suppression.

In every case, however, these Irishmen were attached to non-Irish Missions or Provinces of the Society. For centuries, the Irish Mission had more than enough responsibilities of its own without establishing foreign missions as well: Ireland was *nostra Japonia*, 'our Japan', according to Father Holywood in a letter to the General at a time of persecution.[58] No assignment abroad was given to the Irish Fathers as a whole, apart from the administration of continental colleges for the benefit of the Irish Church, until the Australian Mission was set up in 1865. Of course, individuals still served in other countries. One of the early arrivals in Australia, who later became Superior of the Mission and first Rector of Xavier College, was Father Thomas Cahill who had been working with the Portuguese Mission at Macao in Southern China.[59]

It was at no great distance from Macao, in the British island-colony of Hong Kong (which also included the city of Kowloon on the mainland and some territory in the immediate hinterland), that the Irish Province set up its first 'Foreign Mission' when its Australian commitment was approaching completion. Fathers George Byrne and John Neary went out in 1926, to be followed shortly afterwards by Fathers Richard Gallagher, Patrick Joy and Daniel McDonald.[60] Father Daniel Finn joined them from Australia. They had come at the invitation of Bishop Henry Valtorta, Vicar Apostolic of Hong Kong, who had three objectives in mind — all to do with education. The Jesuits were to take charge of a regional seminary to train Chinese priests not only for Hong Kong but also for the adjacent Apostolic Vicariates (effectively dioceses) on the mainland. They were to build a hostel for Catholic and other students attending Hong Kong University. And they were to make plans to open a Catholic secondary school. Unlike Australia, this part of China had no substantial body of Catholics: little more than 100,000 in a population of more than 30 million. The population of Hong Kong (including Kowloon) totalled a million, of whom non-Chinese were fewer than 20,000; again Catholics formed no more than a very small proportion although there were some hundreds of Irish, who were mainly Catholics, and some Catholic English, Scots and Americans. With convent schools, public churches and several hospitals run by French, American and Italian priests and nuns, the need was less for a general Catholic presence than for specific services to the Chinese under headings inadequately met, or not met at all. Hence the educational emphasis in the brief given to the Jesuits. The speed of their success was phenomenal: in less than six years all three of the institutions which they were commissioned to set up were fully operational and flourishing.

The explanation for such rapid progress lay largely in the strength of the Irish Church during these years: the Jesuits, like other orders, benefited not only from a steady inflow of vocations but also from the unquantifiable but morale-boosting upsurge of triumphal Irish Catholicism (1932 was the year of the Eucharistic Congress in Dublin). It is difficult to measure the kind of enthusiasm generated by a mixture of practical and emotional factors but the sense of achievement and the determination to do more, which mark the published reports from the Jesuit houses in Hong Kong at this time, still have the power to excite. By 1935 some 30 Irish Jesuits had been attached to the Mission, of whom 21 were at work there and the rest completing their studies. Another factor — one suspects but cannot prove — was the missionary situation itself. The paucity of Catholics, and therefore the limited number of facilities they could provide, seems to have prevented the development of abrasive relations between secular and religious clergy, between different orders, between Jesuits and bishops, which arose in places where the Church was stronger. Here all were consciously engaged upon a common enterprise, or such at least is the impression left from the contemporary accounts. Instead of being dissuaded from undertaking additional activities, the Jesuits were sought out: thus the Vicar-Apostolic in the mainland city of Canton (now Guangzhou) talked them into providing secondary classes at his primary school, Bishop Valtorta got them to revive a defunct Catholic journal called *The Rock*, Father Finn became temporary Professor of Pedagogy (Education) at the University and more surprisingly a colleague, presumably Father Thomas Cooney, B.E. (the report is surprisingly coy about naming him), served as temporary Professor of Engineering.

Such ancillary activities, however, had to yield to the demands of running the new institutions as they came into use. Ricci Hall, the university hostel, opened in 1929 with a chapel, a branch of the Sodality, a Catholic Action Club to help the poor and a fine library largely donated by friends of the Society in Ireland. The Regional Seminary, built in traditional Chinese style with landscaping to match, stood on a little hill jutting into the sea above a fishing village and must have been the most beautiful house in the care of the Irish Province when it opened in 1931: it was apparently often mistaken for a Buddhist monastery. It soon had over sixty Chinese clerical students and its first priests were ordained in 1935. In September 1932, the Jesuits took over a large secondary school, Wah Yan College, in Hong Kong city which had 700 day boys and 100 boarders — with no more than 50 Catholics among them even three years later. The College had in fact been founded in 1913 by a Chinese Catholic, who himself decided to hand control over to the Society on his retirement: no doubt he was aware of the Bishop's wish to have a Jesuit school in the Vicariate. Nine of the Jesuits had to be assigned to this considerable under-taking, which they ran very satisfactorily with the aid of some 25 lay-teachers, most of them Chinese. It was highly important that Wah Yan should succeed; the acquisition by foreigners of a reputable Chinese school, intended for Chinese boys and conducted by Chinese staff, caused resentment which could be overcome only by proving that the new administration was able to maintain and improve the school's educational standards without undermining its Chinese character.

The good impression created by the Jesuits as educationalists was one thing. Their anxiety to convert the Chinese to Catholicism was quite another. Parents were happy to send their boys to the Jesuits to be educated. Students flocked to Ricci Hall because of its reputation as an excellent university hostel. But on the Jesuits' own admission, it was an uphill task to lure those who were not Catholics into the Church. True, and to the Jesuits' credit, no pressure was applied. If youngsters were not attracted by Catholic example and what they heard of the Word of God, so be it. At the same time, it is hard to avoid the impression that the attitudes of triumphalist Irish Catholicism did not greatly help. The initial reaction to Chinese tradition recorded by the Irish Fathers reads strangely, not alone by modern missionary norms (to apply which might be to read history backwards) but also when measured against the understanding of Chinese religion and culture arrived at by Matteo Ricci, the great Jesuit missionary of the late sixteenth century, and his successors. Consider the terms in which the Irish reported what they found: 'a hideous shrine or temple', 'grossest superstition, a mixture of Buddhism, ancestor-worship, devil cult, idolatry, magic', 'Canton is a black pagan city', 'superstitious pagans, materialists, even enemies of religion', 'the religion of fear and hopelessness which centres round their placating of devils'.[61] Was it altogether surprising, in the light of the Irish Jesuit view of Chinese tradition, if 'boys who have asked for baptism have been forbidden by their parents'? And was it entirely fair to say that 'ancestor worship, which may be truly called the religion of China, is the cause'?[62] Within a few years Pope Pius XII would lift the papal ban of 1704 which forbade Catholics to participate in Chinese 'ancestor-worship'. That ban, as it happened, never alleged that 'ancestor-worship' was more than a social rite, devoid of religious significance.[63] And it had been obtained by enemies of the Jesuits who were outraged that the Society had secured a formal statement from the Chinese Emperor 'that the Confucian and ancestral ceremonies were solely civic in character'.[64]

To be sure, the 1930s were a time of absolute certitude in matters religious, when few Catholics doubted that their Church had all the right answers, that it not only *possessed* the fullness of truth (which was of faith) but also that it correctly *saw* the truth in any and every situation to which it directed its attention (which was debatable, to say the least). By corollary, anything associated with non-Catholic religion or philosophy was to be rejected with the contempt shown by many Protestants of the same era for Catholic attitudes, or by atheists for the essentials of Christian belief. It was particularly easy to be dismissive when observing 'popular religion' from the far side of the fence, the practices by which unsophisticated adherents of another religion expressed their convictions: to take an obvious example, much-loved Catholic devotions were a corrupt mutation of Christianity in the eyes of some Protestants, while Protestants who said so were written off by some Catholics as 'bigots'. Few paused to wonder whether they had understood others correctly, while becoming more than a little indignant when they themselves were misunderstood. At the popular level, Chinese religion may well have been a 'religion of fear'; was it to be denounced on that account by ministers of a Church which relied on the hellfire sermon as a stimulus to personal renewal? Then again, we read how rumour within the Mission had it that, before they acquired Wah Yan, one of the holier Jesuits 'dropped a miraculous medal in some corner of the building where it was likely to bear fruit' and shortly afterwards 'the miracle happened'[65] when the College was given to the Society. And they denigrated Chinese religion for its superstitious practices! Too much, of course, should not be made of a light-hearted joke about a colleague, and it can readily be explained that Catholics often make use of 'pious objects' as aids to prayer. In short, Catholics can understand that little story and chuckle. What is hard to detect in the early comments from the Mission is recognition of any need similarly to enter the Chinese mind and endeavour to appreciate its values.

Once more, it must be stressed that the Irish Jesuits were not alone in sharing an attitude that was common to many missionaries and to many Catholics. Once more, it is important to say that prophetic awareness cannot be commissioned. It remains sad that the Jesuits, for all their phenomenal energy and selflessness in bringing to fruition the tasks they were given to do in Hong Kong, appear to have been tardy in adopting the long-established insights of their own order regarding China, and in utilising their own sophistication to rise above the limits of triumphal Catholicism when faced with the culture of the East. Yet, they were tardy only. Terence Sheridan, S.J., wrote movingly in 1941 on what the West had done to China: 'We have helped very little by all our inter-

ference, but we have stolen a lot. China has nothing for which
to thank us. We have robbed and muddled and strutted so
much that it is little wonder that we are not loved in the
Middle Kingdom. There was but one thing we had that we
might have given; one thing that some of us, thank God, still
have and can still give. That thing is Christianity. . .'. And he
went on to refer to 'a great cultured nation, a gentle lovable
people. They have art, they have literature, they have music.
Their laws are as good as ours. They have everything but the
One Thing necessary. In God's Name let us give them that.'
Like Xavier, like Ricci, the missionary would have to
overcome the people's justifiable suspicion of the foreigner.
'The Chinese, in their polite way, called him a "devil",
because they would not attribute such baseness to men.'[66]
Here was noble recognition of culture and civilisation, and
more than a hint of entering the Chinese mind. It was a huge
advance on the simpler assumptions of a mere half-dozen
years before.

Now, quite suddenly, came crisis. In December 1941, the
Japanese bombed Pearl Harbour. Within hours the Japanese
armies on the Chinese mainland (where the Sino-Japanese
War had long been in progress) marched against Hong
Kong. Virtually the first building they reached was Loyola, a
language school maintained by the Jesuits for newcomers
from Ireland and at the time functioning also as a 'minor
seminary'. Fathers Daniel Donnelly and Edmund Sullivan
bundled out the ten boarders, marched them off towards
Kowloon, stopped a crowded bus and somehow squashed
the whole party on board.[67] In Kowloon they went to an
extension of Wah Yan College, opened by the Jesuits only a
few months before. Distributed through Kowloon and the
island of Hong Kong, on which were located Ricci Hall, the
Regional Seminary and the main Wah Yan College, were
twenty-seven Irish Jesuits under the leadership of the Mission
Superior, Father Patrick Joy. They could do little to protect
their various properties as air-raids commenced almost at
once, followed by artillery shelling as the Japanese got near.
The Fathers were required to take charge of parish churches
which had been run by Italian priests, all of whom were
interned on 8 December. Hastily mobilised civil defence

units, together with British Army and Royal Navy detach-
ments, were rushed to man a variety of outposts or assigned
to keep the defenders supplied with food and amunition.
The Jesuits found themselves quickly drawn into the battle.
Some took charge of refugees, others went to hospitals and
to the military strongpoints to provide spiritual consolation
or to administer the last rites to the injured.

Perhaps the most vivid memory for every one of them was
the number of people who sought confession — in alley-ways,
in restaurants, in barrack-yards. There were Irish policemen,
English nurses, stray Americans and quite a number of
Chinese. Students rushing off from Ricci Hall to take up
defence duties asked for baptism; so did others in the streets.
In chaotic conditions — the defence of Hong Kong hardly
ranks among the more impressive achievements of British
arms — it became apparent that the colony harboured many
more Catholics and persons who had been considering
whether they should become Catholics than the Jesuits had
realised. The ministers of other Christian denominations
were kept busy also. The overall number of Christians still
formed only a very small proportion of a population swollen
to two millions by the influx of refugees from the Sino-
Japanese conflict. Nonetheless, after the uphill struggle to
promote the faith in peacetime, the surge of demand was
exhilarating for the Jesuits despite the dangers of warfare.
Oddly enough, the greatest threat to life came not from the
bombs and shells but from the looters who ravaged Kowloon
and killed everybody who resisted them when the army
withdrew to the island after a few days. Father Richard
Gallagher and a scholastic, Joseph McAsey, mounted guard
with some students in the Wah Yan extension where a
number of people had taken refuge. The Japanese restored
order but interned the Kowloon Jesuits pending the capture
of Hong Kong island. Irish passports and protestations
of neutrality had no effect: 'England, Ireland, Scotland all
one piece,' said the Japanese officer. The other internees,
mostly English, gallantly rallied to the Jesuits' defence and
insisted that Ireland was neutral, but the Japanese remained
unmoved until Tokyo assured them weeks later that this was
in fact the case.

The siege of Hong Kong went on until Christmas, the shelling all the time intensifying. Ricci Hall fell to looters; British soldiers and Portuguese volunteers sought the sacraments; Father John Moran was made an acting army chaplain; Father George Byrne offered himself for a hazardous assignment because, he said, 'as an old man' it did not matter if he got killed. The Jesuits were used by the authorities for every kind of work from the distribution of rice in the Central Market (by Father Tom Ryan) to finding quarters for bombed-out families (the job given to Father Albert Cooney). The fighting stopped on Christmas Day. Foreigners and Chinese alike were encouraged to leave Hong Kong by the invaders who felt they could control the colony better if the population were reduced. Some of the Jesuits made their way to 'Free China' beyond the Japanese front line but some seventeen remained under Father Joy to keep a restricted service going at the original Wah Yan and the Regional Seminary: all their other houses were taken from them.

An emaciated Jesuit community survived the war and soon undertook refurbishment of its various houses. Ricci Hall was restored to life, the two Wah Yans expanded rapidly. Pastoral work in Canton resumed but staggered to a halt when the Communist revolution, followed by oppression, made it increasingly difficult for any foreign enterprise — especially a religious enterprise — to function at all (Fathers Canice Egan, Richard Kennedy and John O'Meara had valiantly kept going as long as they could, and suffered for it). The same revolution, however, hugely increased not only the population of Hong Kong but the Catholic population too, as a new influx of refugees set up home in the colony. Institutions called 'Post-Secondary Colleges' mushroomed to meet the expanded needs in education and Irish Jesuits became lecturers in several of them, doubling as chaplains to Catholic students. By 1962 the Jesuits' own Colleges — the two Wah Yans — could count a thousand Catholic pupils between them. A Hong Kong novitiate was built on the site of the wrecked language school and soon also, in Missions spawned by a Mission, there were Irish Jesuit houses — two parishes — in Malaysia and a College in Singapore. In 1968 Hong Kong, like Australia earlier, became a Vice-Province of the Society of Jesus in its own right: sufficient in itself, yet hoping always to be the springboard for a Catholic and Jesuit return to South China proper, where Chinese Christians would be the most effective witnesses to Christ in the cultural ambience of their still xenophobic homeland.

Notwithstanding the easy hindsight which enables the writer to query at a distance in time and space the first reaction of the Irish Jesuits to the clash of cultures facing them in China, it has to be acknowledged that in what they undertook, what they survived and what they built, they accomplished a Herculean feat. They had not been asked simply to go and preach the faith. Many other missionaries were already at that: the work of the Maynooth Mission to China can stand as an impressive example of what had been put in hand. The Jesuits were required to train a segment of the potential leadership in Church and State — a Church which was no more than a speck on a vast ocean of humanity; a State which was in domestic upheaval, facing foreign aggression and inimically disposed towards the most alien feature of the European, his religion. A platoon of Irish priests and scholastics was expected, through the provision of education, somehow to ameliorate this unpropitious situation in the most populous country on the globe. Even the incidentals of that charge were excessively burdensome. The Jesuits had to learn Cantonese, said to be the most difficult of Chinese dialects, without the textbook and literary aids available for the more respected Mandarin form of the language. They had to endure the dangers and destruction of war, the hardships of occupation, and not long afterwards the loss to hardline Communism of the land intended as the ultimate beneficiary of their efforts. Yet they soldiered on, set up thriving institutions and, to judge from the evidence of growth in intra-cultural understanding, were already advancing down the right road when the fresh vision of the Second Vatican Council broke in upon them with its stress on the rights of the person and of peoples to their own identity[68] within the unity — but not uniformity — of the People of God. To the mind of an Irish Jesuit writing in 1974, a familiar Chinese phrase summed up the Christian purpose of the Society in Hong Kong: 'Our school is called Wah Yan. "Wah" means Chinese and "Yan" is the lofty ideal of Confucius and his followers — "to promote the welfare of mankind", "to serve the community".'[69] Thus was the Gospel mandate both given to, and found in, the Chinese system of values.

On the feast of St Ignatius, 31 July 1950, nine Irish Jesuits — eight Fathers and a Brother — set off on a rescue mission. Their destination was in south-central Africa, the country which is today the independent Republic of Zambia but was then the British protectorate of Northern Rhodesia.[70] To speak of a 'rescue mission' is almost to pun: the Irishmen's assignment was to rescue a Jesuit Mission in danger of collapse. Since 1927 the Polish Jesuits had been running a Mission based on Chikuni, a settlement founded as far back as 1905 by two Jesuits of the English Province, Fathers Moreau and Torrend, who had made their way north from the Zambesi River. As missionary activity developed, areas of responsibility were re-assigned. The Polish Jesuit Province took charge of Chikuni and an extensive range of bush country extending towards Livingstone in the south-west and as far as Lusaka, the capital city, to the north-east. Father Moreau remained Superior of the Mission for many years and continued to work in the villages of the region, where he became renowned not only for his sanctity but for his remarkable competence as an amateur dentist — although 'obstinacy' may have better described the quality he brought to the exercise of this talent: at the age of 85, 'a month before he died, a recalcitrant molar caused both patient and practitioner to roll together on the grass; but, pulling himself up, Father Moreau displayed in triumph the gory relic on his forceps'.[71]

Among the facilities developed at Chikuni under the English and Polish administrations were a church and the College of St Peter Canisius where primary education was provided as well as the only secondary classes and teacher training courses for Catholics in Northern Rhodesia. Teacher training was especially important since the Mission relied on local teachers to keep the faith alive in villages where often there were few other Catholics; they helped by example to protect some of their co-religionists against the common tendency to fall away from the Church for want of contact; these teachers were also the agents of conversion and instruction for would-be Catholics and they turned their schools into temporary chapels for Sunday Mass or other occasional visits by a priest from the Mission. In the spirit of the time, the Protestant Churches applied precisely the same missionary tactics, and in the countryside served by the Jesuits during the early 1950s over 140 of the 200 village schools were Protestant. Whatever might be said, resorting to hindsight, about Catholic-Protestant rivalry — not to mention the rivalry between the Protestant denominations — it must be acknowledged that the Batonga people, the Bantu tribe of the region, owed much to all these Christians who came among them, for the Government of the day provided no more than six of the 200 schools although it did make grants available to aid the church establishments. The Irish Sisters of Charity had come to Chikuni, too, to conduct a school for girls together with a small hospital: over the years they would expand both facilities into major institutions for the area. But in 1950 the Catholic missionary endeavour was seriously at risk for in the entire Vicariate of Lusaka, of which the Chikuni region was part and which stretched from the Zambesi to the then Belgian Congo, there were fewer than twenty priests.

The reason was simple. In the aftermath of the Second World War a Communist government had been installed in Poland and no Jesuits could leave the country to work on the Chikuni Mission. The same was true of the Czechs who had charge of another part of the Lusaka Vicariate. Since 1946, four Irish Fathers had joined the Poles to help them but it became increasingly obvious that Chikuni had to be transferred to the care of a Province with substantial manpower and no restrictions on its use. Hence the invitation to the Irish and the 'rescue mission' they sent out on the feast of St Ignatius. The Jesuits travelled via Rome, where Pope Pius XII blessed them, spoke of Ireland's missionary tradition and lauded the work they were embarking upon. At Chikuni they spent a few months learning the local language and then set about revivifying the Mission — encouraged, no doubt, by the successful Mission of the Irish Capuchins in the neighbouring Vicariate of Livingstone. They first placed resident priests in three mission-stations strategically situated in different directions, each thirty-five miles from Chikuni. They used a lorry to maintain contact along the bush-paths that served for roads in the maize-growing farmland. As a result, daily Mass was made available at four locations, with monthly Mass at some fifteen other centres. The Church's presence was thus firmly re-established. Church buildings followed and within a short time simple but adequate places of worship had been constructed in selected mission-stations. By 1952, twenty-seven Jesuits of the Irish Province were at work in Northern Rhodesia, including three scholastics and three Brothers.

As had become traditional at this time with the Jesuits, education was a priority. They naturally taught at various levels in Canisius College but also undertook a rationalisation of the services it offered. They hived off the primary school, giving it its own boarding accommodation under the name of St Ignatius'. They built a new Teacher Training College, which they called Charles Lwanga in honour of one of the Uganda martyrs. They added a science block and new dormitories to the original Canisius, which now became a secondary school in its own right with nearly 300 boarders — almost matching the Clongowes of those days in student numbers. Like an English public school, it was divided into four houses, but its Jesuit and Irish connections were evident from the introduction of the Sodality of Our Lady, the Pioneer Total Abstinence Association and a Praesidium of the Legion of Mary.[72] A girls' section was added which developed from the primary school run by the Sisters of Charity. Pupils were prepared for the equivalent of the modern Irish Intermediate and Leaving Certificate examinations — although, as at the Irish day schools a century earlier but for different reasons, some years were to pass before the greater number of pupils automatically sat the final exams. This was partly because African children used to start school at a late age and simply had not reached the higher standards when it was time to leave. It may also have been because keeping a child at Canisius meant finding the money for boarding fees; in 1962 it was noted that 'as often as not, it will be an elder brother rather than a parent who will provide, because the elder brother has experienced the benefit of education, however slender that education may have been'.[73]

The slightly-educated elder brother and the late start at school both underlined the comparatively primitive agricultural society from which the people were progressing rapidly — and determinedly — towards modernisation. The process involved political upheaval and the Irish Jesuits, in their first fourteen years, saw Northern Rhodesia change from a protectorate to a component of the Central African Federation, and then to a republic under the new name of Zambia. Education was vital to modernisation and consequently the nationalist movement favoured the Society's activities. The fact that Ireland had wrested independence from Britain was known and at least did the Mission no harm. But of particular significance must have been the outspoken stance of the Irish Jesuits regarding some vestiges of colonial tutelage. Writing in 1960, in the days of the less-than-liberal Federation headed by Sir Roy Welensky, Father Robert Thompson referred to the 'eight roomy churches' by then completed and remarked how 'both African family and Irish exile may be found, of a Sunday morning, kneeling side by side around these altars of sacrifice', thereby demonstrating 'a fellowship which rapidly reveals the injustice, error and inhumanity of racial segregation or apartheid'. And he linked this observation to schooling: 'Facts reveal truth and expose error and the Bantu people have been marching energetically, with modern methods of education to help them, towards racial emancipation.'[74] Kenneth Kaunda, who became President of the new republic, held the school and the Jesuits alike in high regard, and the Zambian Government helped to fund building expansion at Canisius.[75]

It is perhaps invidious to select names from the long list of men who served in Zambia but pioneers like Fathers Brian MacMahon, Sean McCarron, Colm O'Riordan and Thomas McGivern, as well as Brother Patrick McElduff, were among the builders of the Mission — sometimes literally. The most distinguished of the Irish Jesuits associated with the country remains Dr James Corboy, former Rector of Milltown Park, who in 1962 was named Bishop of Monze. The hierarchy had been instituted in Northern Rhodesia in 1960, replacing the vicariates apostolic with a number of dioceses under their own bishops: a mark of the rapid growth of the local Church. Chikuni was in the diocese of Monze so it was appropriate that it should be given an Irish Jesuit as its Bishop. For want of a residence in Monze town (which began as a halt on the railway line named after a chieftain who had befriended Father Moreau), Bishop Corboy in fact initially chose to live in Lwanga College. One of his early visitors was the Archbishop of Milan, who had some priests working near the Kariba Dam (the only non-Jesuit priests in the diocese at the time). The Archbishop was Cardinal Montini, who the following June succeeded John XXIII as Pope Paul VI.

These were the years of the Second Vatican Council, in the public sessions of which Dr Corboy participated more actively than many of his fellow bishops. He made at least six speeches at 'general congregations' of the Council (i.e. the full formal meetings in St Peter's) where he spoke on the liturgy, on the nature of the Church, twice on the Church in the modern world, and twice on the missionary activity of the Church — on one occasion, presenting the views of seventy African bishops.[76] He was also one of twenty-four bishops who signed a plea to the Council urging rejection of the final text of the decree on the mass media as an inadequate statement which would only bring the Council's authority into question. He was not the only Jesuit to criticise this anachronistic and misinformed document: a virulent protest by respected American journalists was endorsed by three of the Society's most eminent theologians, Fathers John Courtney Murray, Jean Daniélou and Jorge Mejia, as well as by the Redemptorist Father Bernard Häring.[77]

Bishop Corboy led his diocese, and with it the Chikuni Mission, from strength to strength. New parishes, new churches, a catechist training centre and a diocesan secondary school were added to the older foundations. With a Bishop sympathetic to the conciliar vision, a friendly Government, further Jesuits arriving from Ireland and a native African clergy beginning to take shape, the story of Chikuni becomes frankly boring, as unrelieved good news will always become! In 1971 the Father General declared the Mission to be the Jesuit

Vice-Province of Zambia. The Irish Jesuits might fairly ask themselves whether a rescue was ever so impressively effected.

The missions undertaken by Irish Jesuits have included not only major enterprises dependent on the energies of numerous members of the Province but also very personal initiatives by men acting on their own with their superiors' approval. Father Patrick Moran went from the old Hardwicke Street chapel to South America to care for the Irish who lived in and around Buenos Aires.[78] He was the first Jesuit of the restored Society in the Argentine and remained at his post until his death in 1830. Father Matthew Gahan, who had returned to Ireland with Father Kenney in 1811, left Ireland again in the 1820s for the Isle of Man where the Catholics had no priest. Despite much privation, he built chapels at Douglas and Castletown.[79] He also opened schools, 'not, we may be sure,' wrote Father Grene, 'from the resources supplied by the handful of indifferent Catholics he found on the island'.[80] When he fell fatally ill in February 1837, Father Gahan was still the only priest resident there and no doubt was reconciled to dying without the usual consolations of religion. Providentially, Father Aylmer, who knew nothing of his colleague's sickness, chose this very month to visit him and and arrived just in time to administer the last sacraments.[81]

Nor were all missions, in the sense of personal undertakings, discharged abroad. Among the more remarkable Irish Jesuits in the later part of the nineteenth century was Father James Cullen. Father Cullen, although a Clongownian, originally had no wish to be a Jesuit at all. He not only disliked the possibility of having to teach but also felt that Jesuit life was insufficiently pious and prayerful for his ardent spiritual inclinations![82] He became a secular priest and only after some years conceded there was more to Jesuit spirituality than had met his schoolboy eyes. He entered the Society but was even then an unusual type of Jesuit, indeed an unusual type of saint — for no one doubted his sanctity. He was of melancholy disposition and lugubrious voice,[83] had 'passed through a phase of fearing an early death'[84] and was given to morbid reflecting on what he described as 'the swarming pestilential brood of my faults'.[85] He almost certainly did *not* preach the hell-fire sermon of Joyce's *Portrait of the Artist*, although he *did* give the last Belvedere retreat attended by Joyce; as a preacher 'in his early years at least, [he] was given to "hammering" at such topics as "the punishments of sin" and it is likely that his "lurid style" heightened the dramatic quality of his material, however sober it may have been'.[86]

Father Cullen, in short, was a pessimist,[87] and his cast of mind suggests that he was the kind of Catholic who could benefit most from the traditional Jesuit devotion to the Sacred Heart. This we have seen being promoted by the pre-Suppression Society in County Waterford — as, we may be sure, it was promoted elsewhere. The devotion began on the continent as an antidote to the Jansenists and its particular significance in Father Cullen's Ireland was that it alleviated the puritanical tendencies which had infiltrated nineteenth-century Irish Catholicism. Those tendencies showed themselves in religious anxiety, legalistic morality, scrupulosity and an unhealthy sense of guilt.[88] Trust in the Sacred Heart, preached in conjunction with the encouragement of frequent communion and devotion to the Blessed Sacrament, countered the puritanism. The Sacred Heart, which symbolised Christ's infinite love,[89] stood 'between the fearful soul and a God who was remote and very stern'.[90] It is scarcely surprising, then, that Father Cullen, who must have felt within himself the need for a hopeful emphasis of this kind, should have become the outstanding promoter of the Sacred Heart devotion. In 1888 he founded the *Irish Messenger of the Sacred Heart*, a periodical intended for a wide readership on the model of Sacred Heart *Messengers* which had been appearing in other countries since the first was launched in France by Father Henri Ramière, S.J., to support the Apostleship of Prayer, a pious association (also called the League of the Sacred Heart) set up in 1844. The English Province began publishing its *Messenger* in 1886, the Australian Mission in 1887. By 1912 separate *Messengers* were appearing in twenty-six languages, in 1936 there were no fewer than sixty-five editions in more than thirty languages.[91]

It would be hard to point to any religious devotion which achieved a greater popular following than the cult of the Sacred Heart or was more successfully promoted over so many years by the use of the communications media in their simplest form. Proportionate to population, the Irish *Messenger* must surely have taken the palm amid all the other journals of the name. In 1970 it was still selling more than 200,000 copies a month.[92] Patrick Kavanagh in 'Tarry Flynn' caught well its place in rural Ireland: 'There sitting by the fire, keeping it stoked, he sat smoking and reading the *Messenger.* The *Messenger of the Sacred Heart* was bought every month, and with *Old Moore's Almanac* and the local newspaper constituted the literature of Flynn's as of nearly every other country house . . . he read the *Messenger*, all of it from the verses by Brian O'Higgins on the Sacred Heart — a serial poem which ran for a year or more — to the story of the good young girl who had a vocation, and who was being sabotaged by the bad man, right through to the Thanksgivings "for favours received", at the back.'[93]

Father Cullen's other remarkable achievement was the Pioneer Total Abstinence Association of the Sacred Heart, which he founded to combat the excessive drinking which had become a major social evil in rural and urban Ireland alike. He used the *Messenger* initially to advance this cause as well: by 1919 he could count more than 277,000 adult members in the 'Pioneers'.[94] The Association still thrives and is strong enough today to have a diocesan spiritual director in virtually every diocese of Ireland.

It has been said that in the early decades of the century the Australian *Messenger* was 'a most valuable instrument for instructing both young and old in simple piety . . . the journal retained that simplicity of style and spiritual fervour which, while it did little to uplift Catholics intellectually, did much to to foster Catholic devotional practices, in particular that of devotion to the Sacred Heart. It was of particular value in the country areas. . .'.[95] While allowance must be made for Australian conditions, especially with a Catholic population scattered thinly through remote areas, the comment might well fit the work of the Irish *Messenger* in the same years. To estimate its impact is difficult: circulation or even readership should never be confused with influence. One article in *Studies* read by one politician or senior civil servant could well have produced more consequences in public policy than a gross of

Messengers. The *Messenger,* on the other hand, had little concern with matters of public policy. If the devotional journal set troubled minds at rest, brought souls into closer contact with a loving Saviour, helped people to see beyond the burdens of daily living and to find God in all things, its influence was different in kind but close indeed to what Saint Ignatius most wanted his Society to bring about. Comparisons are invidious. Missions vary, but few of Christian worth are closed to Jesuit endeavour. It is salutary to know that Father Ramière, founder of the first *Messenger,* was also editor of *Études.*[96]

7

MODERN TIMES

HISTORY merges into current affairs. In a country still trying to resolve the consequences of the form in which Irish independence emerged through the sequence of events from 1916 to 1923, and in a Church which has still to reconcile the certainties inherited from the nineteenth century with the broader and deeper understandings of the Second Vatican Council, the historian walks warily. It is too easy to interpret, even to describe, events of the 1920s by the standards of the 1990s. This may be a useful exercise in explaining contemporary viewpoints. As an account of what happened in the past it risks distorting most unfairly the motives, actions and achievements of persons who were guided by their own lights in the only world they knew. The history of the Society of Jesus in Ireland during the years still within living memory demands cautious handling for these reasons and not least because it seems to invite criticism on more than one score.

By the end of the new century's first decade the colleges of the Irish Province had settled into tranquil routine, competently educating their mainly middle-class pupils (*Irish* middle-class, it should be stressed, whose parents often enough had to scrape to find the modest fees) in preparation for mainly professional careers or self-employment in their own businesses: a service, and intended as such, to the country as a whole which would have more need than ever for a cadre trained to leadership roles in the various segments of Irish life following what few doubted was impending Home Rule. That leaders might be moulded otherwise, not least in the ranks of the labour movement, had yet to be widely recognised by men striving to meet the norms of the age in which they had grown up. Clongowes consolidated its reputation as the foremost school in Ireland, notwithstanding the taunts of nationalist extremists. Its pre-eminence could not be challenged in June 1914, when the principal guest at the celebration of the college's centenary was its most distinguished *alumnus*, John Redmond, M.P., faithful Parnellite, leader of the Irish Party at Westminster, the man who had wrung Home Rule from the British and was the prospective prime minister of an Ireland broken loose at last from the trammels of the Union. Unlike Tullabeg, which Father Delany brought into an abnormally close relationship with Dublin Castle in the years before its suppression, and unlike Mungret where Father Edward Cahill as Rector was promoting attitudes closer to Sinn Féin than to the Irish Party,[1] Clongowes had long been solidly associated with the Home Rule movement[2] — the campaign conducted by constitutional means to obtain self-government for Ireland within the British Empire: a seemingly realistic and realisable objective which for forty years had embodied the hopes of mainstream Irish nationalism. That sunny summer of 1914 saw the apotheosis of Home Rule, for Westminster had conceded the Irish demand and the enabling legislation was to be implemented in the autumn. Clongowes and Ireland marched in step.

Within weeks, the Great War had broken out. Home Rule was put off until peace had been restored; Redmond urged his followers to join the British army; a minority of nationalists rejected his appeal and set up the Irish (or Sinn Féin) Volunteers as a breakaway group from the National Volunteers who remained loyal to the Home Rule leader. By winter, the hopes of summer had been at best deferred and for many had begun to evaporate in dissension and anxiety: anxiety, because young Irishmen were already dying in Flanders. It is difficult today to appreciate the extent to which Irish families suffered constant fear, and many of them tragic bereavement, by reason of the war. At a very conservative estimate,[3] some 100,000 men from the overwhelmingly Catholic-nationalist provinces of Leinster, Munster and Connacht served on the various fronts. Jesuit schools like Clongowes, Belvedere and the Crescent, imbued with the Home Rule tradition and answering Redmond's call, contributed more than a goodly share to these numbers. It has been calculated that 'proportionately, more Old Clongownians died in the Great War than Old Etonians'.[4] Of those killed, two were Jesuit chaplains to the forces; other Jesuit chaplains to die included the saintly Father Willie Doyle. Throughout the years 1914–1919 the dominant concern of the colleges and the Society alike was reflected in the rolls of honour published in the school annuals. The same concern must have been shared in thousands of Irish homes, and it can readily be understood why the wives and dependants of Munster Fusiliers attacked a parade of Irish Volunteers on a march through Limerick in 1915.[5] In the homes, as in the memory of school-fellows, the Catholic-nationalist deaths in the Great War (totalling perhaps 25,000) cannot have been quickly forgotten, although in one of the strangest and saddest turns of Irish history they have been expunged from the race-memory in our own time: 'a classic example of national amnesia,' says an eminent historian who went to school at Belvedere.[6]

What happened, of course, was the initially unpopular Easter Rising of 1916 in Dublin, which was followed by a massive shift of nationalist opinion away from Home Rule and over to the Republic proclaimed on that fateful Easter Monday. Dáil Eireann was established in 1919, more fighting followed, the Auxiliaries and the Black-and-Tans arrived, then the Treaty, the Irish Free State, the Civil War . . . enough, it might be argued, to overlay the memory of Flanders although the Jesuit schools, by and large, remained far more conscious of the Great War while it lasted than of the local disturbances and changing popular attitudes: the scale of their ex-pupils' involvement in the European conflagration made this inevitable. But home events impinged on them too, and in a very personal way. Not all their ex-pupils were in Flanders. Some were in the General Post Office, the Dublin headquarters of the insurrection. Others would soon be lodged in British jails. A few were destined to die — before a firing squad, on the gallows, in the clash of arms. Elements of Greek tragedy marked these troubled times as early as Easter Week. Tom Kettle, in British uniform, was in Dublin when his fellow-Clongownian, The O'Rahilly, joined the Irish Volunteers in the GPO. The O'Rahilly would fall as he led a gallant, futile charge up Moore Street, sword in hand;[7] Kettle was also to die bravely in a hopeless charge, on to no-man's-land at the Somme. Reg Cleary, a Belvederian in the British army, was shot dead in the fighting near Mount Street Bridge;[8] Joseph Plunkett, another Belvederian, signed the Proclamation of the Republic and was executed in Kilmainham Jail.

The greater number of Irish Jesuits, but not all, gave an impression of remaining serenely above these tensions. Their detachment probably derived from the Spiritual Exercises of Saint Ignatius, which induce a kind of distancing from, and scepticism about, human alarums and excursions. It may also have been simple obedience to the injunction in the Constitutions not to take sides among princes.[9] It may even have been because '. . . the Jesuits, knowing their own Society had once been abolished for all time, developed an extraordinary invisible yardstick. It was not simply an implication that the temporal world became of little account when considered *sub specie aeternitatis*; it was that a temporal sea which had smashed and destroyed them in its time was singularly irrelevant in its flows and ebbs after their Society had arisen from the dead'.[10] The biographer of Kevin Barry makes a similar point: 'Belvedere had exercised the strongest influence on him and, indeed, the temperate attitude of the Jesuits must have acted as a useful counterbalance to the ferment of revolution without the walls . . .'.[11]

Refusal to show partiality towards one or other side in the successive conflicts did not imply any lack of concern for those caught up in them. The Jesuits lauded no war, they urged no young men to take up arms, but they praised unstintingly both those who gave their lives and their companions who fought beside them.[12] At first this acknowledgment was confined to the soldiers of the Great War but gradually, and well before the change of regime in 1922, recognition was extended to their former pupils and others associated with the Society who committed themselves to the cause of independence at home.

In June 1916, *Studies* carried the first of four contributions about the 'Poets of the Insurrection', three of whom had been either students or lecturers at University College (Patrick Pearse, Joseph Plunkett and Thomas MacDonagh). The frontispiece to *The Belvederian* for 1917 was an elaborately engraved presentation of Plunkett's touching poem, 'I see his blood upon the rose'. Articles and notes began to appear about experiences during 'the terror' (in *The Clongownian*, from 1920). [13] The diary written by the boys and published annually in *The Belvederian* revealed sentiments of a new order: '29 Oct 1920 — No school today. We are in mourning for the great Lord Mayor of Cork (Terence McSwiney) whose spirit the greatest of the Empires could not enslave.' '1 Nov 1920 — Yet another day without school! Our pleasure in the free day is gone. Kevin Barry, our school-fellow scarcely a year ago, proving himself a patriot, meets a criminal's end at the hands of the freer of small nations.' The hanging of Kevin Barry for his part in an ambush in which some soldiers were killed deeply touched Belvedere, not only the pupils but the Jesuits as well. He had left the school the year before with an excellent matriculation result and was highly regarded in sporting circles, especially as a rugby player. At the time of his capture he was aged 18 and a medical student at U.C.D. The last friend to visit him in Mountjoy Jail on the night before his execution was the future Father Tom Counihan, than a scholastic in the school, who had been 'Kevin's maths and chemistry teacher, his rugby coach, and above all his friend in the Jesuit community'. The Rector, Father Charles Doyle, approved the visit by the scholastic, who recorded later how he found Kevin 'so calm and self-possessed', delighted with a telegram 'from Father John Fahy, S.J., then in Mungret College, Limerick, sending Masses and prayers and blessings. It was Father Fahy who had received him into Belvedere in 1916. He was overjoyed that such a man was with him in spirit . . .'. Kevin wanted Tom Counihan to keep him company in the morning, but this was not permitted: 'I told him I would be with him at Mass and prayer in the college he loved.'[14]

Again, no attitude should be attributed to the Province as a whole on foot of the admirable pastoral instincts of named Jesuits during these years of ordeal. Still less should the general body of Irish Jesuits be suspected of political leanings because Fathers Cahill, Corcoran and McErlean helped draft a historical case for Mr de Valera to be presented to the Peace Conference at Versailles in 1919.[15] By the same token, the continuing honour so rightly accorded to the memory of the dead of the Great War — especially at Clongowes — indicated no overall Jesuit position on the evolving pattern of Irish politics and national ideology. The Society in Ireland criticised the allegiance of none who had been in its charge, neither that of Sir Michael O'Dwyer, governor of the Punjab, nor of George Clancy, the Sinn Féin Mayor of Limerick killed by the Black-and-Tans; neither that of Rory O'Connor who held the Four Courts for the anti-Treaty forces in the Civil War, nor of Ginger O'Connell, a senior general of the Free State army. The Jesuits would be able accordingly to have good relations with the governments both of William T. Cosgrave and Eamon de Valera, in both of which former pupils of their colleges served as Ministers. It may be suspected that, on the whole, the Jesuits would have preferred the implementation of Home Rule without violent severance of the remaining imperial link, but that is nothing more than a reasonable supposition; it cannot be proved from the record. Their detachment long survived. When the Jubilee of the Easter Rising was celebrated in 1966, *Studies* refused to carry a finely crafted essay by the Gaelic scholar, Professor Francis Shaw, S.J., which rejected some of the historical and even religious assumptions underlying the insurrection and which blamed some of the shortcomings of independent Ireland on the resort to arms in 1916. The essay eventually appeared in the Summer 1972 issue of *Studies* when it was felt that the revival of violence in Northern Ireland gave it special topicality. The shrillness of the controversy provoked by the article served to show how wise the Province had been in the past to stand back from arguments which it had not raised and into which it was in no way obliged to enter.

One advantage of the Jesuits' detachment from political ideology during the 'Troubles' was their freedom subsequently to join in discussing the problems of self-government. Immune to accusations of being *parti pris*, they could command a hearing for considered views on the economic and social questions of the day. These sometimes came from

Jesuit writers, sometimes from other thinkers for whom they provided a platform. The most important platform under their control was *Studies*, not because it enjoyed a wide circulation but because issues of policy could be examined in its pages 'without the need to score party points'.[16] This gave it a special value for Ministers, civil servants and decision-makers generally in the 1920s and 1930s. Subjects from the future of the railways to a native currency, and from free trade to public expenditure thus all came under reasoned scrutiny by Father Edward Coyne, S.J., Professor George O'Brien and similar respected commentators,[17] not to mention the frequent, and frequently stimulating, articles by Professor Alfred O'Rahilly, himself a former Jesuit scholastic: *Studies* carried twenty-one contributions by Dr O'Rahilly between 1920 and 1940, of which nine bore directly on matters then in the public arena: among them, 'Wheat growing and flour milling', 'The constitution and the senate' and 'The case for philosophy in secondary education'.[18] The interest in economics continued after the Second World War and in the 1950s the balance of payments and capital investment policies were discussed 'less bad-temperedly than they were treated elsewhere'.[19] Later still came the pros and cons of the Common Market, when it was 'refreshing to note' that the *Studies* articles were 'concerned much less with economics than with the spread of the idea of one Europe'.[20] Contributors garnered in by Father Burke Savage included the future Taoiseach, Dr Garret FitzGerald, and Professor Patrick Lynch, who did much to elaborate the new economic thinking, while articles of literary analysis appeared over such distinguished names as Denis Donoghue and Sean O'Faolain. Not surprisingly, the debates on the future of Irish education had a prominent place also.

Studies functioned at one level of public discussion, the same level as that of most of the Jesuit academics in the university with which the quarterly was so closely associated. It performed a necessary service until the later 1960s when the proliferation of economic and management institutes, the growth of investigative reporting in the media and a new-found Church interest in the underlying causes of injustice took much of the Irish debate about public affairs into a more popular forum. It was a forum where some Jesuits had been active, not to say belligerent, for many years. Father Timothy Corcoran, whom we have met as a critic of Newman's ideas on education, was 'unofficial leader of the Sinn Féin caucus in U.C.D.'[21] notwithstanding the political neutrality of the Province as a whole, and had played a major part in securing the election of de Valera as Chancellor of the National University; he was thought to be much involved with the *Catholic Bulletin*,[22] 'an anti-Cosgrave journal pulsating with confessional prejudices'.[23] The *Bulletin* was kept alive 'largely on anti-Masonic propaganda'.[24] It was not Father Corcoran, however, but Father Edward Cahill who made the exposure of the Freemasons his prime objective. Like his contemporary, the Holy Ghost priest Father Denis Fahey, Father Cahill firmly believed in a 'conspiracy of Freemasons and Jews against the Church.'[25] His book *Freemasonry and the Anti-Christian Movement*, first published in 1929, was much read in its day and went into a second edition.

Faced with the defects of this unfortunate publication, we must take special care to avoid reading history backwards. It is not for its want of ecumenical charity or its insensitivity to human rights that the book invites criticism, for these were characteristic of the polemical atmosphere on every side in the 1920s and 1930s. It is for its want of reasoned analysis, of care to undertake objective inquiry, its sheer emptiness of *scholarship*. It stands logic on its head, assuming from the *presence* of Freemasons at certain historic junctions that Masonry was *responsible* for what happened. It fails to examine the validity of received suppositions: notwithstanding Father Cahill's assertions to the contrary, for example, Freemasons as such had little to do with the Suppression of the Jesuits[26] or with the French Revolution.[27] The book misses the equation between the political rights of Catholics and those of Jews which Daniel O'Connell, for one, had been happy to acknowledge in logic and justice.[28] Other and worse misrepresentations of fact can be pointed to, but easy refutation at this distance serves little purpose. The question to be asked is how Father Cahill was permitted to put about such damaging and poorly researched material which could be — and was — received as unquestionably reliable because it came from a Jesuit pen. That it happened marks a low point in the Irish Society's reputation for excellence.

The historical context helps to explain the few polemical Jesuits and their superiors, even if it does not excuse them. Other churchmen, and not only in Ireland, engaged in the same kind of propagandist advocacy of a predetermined viewpoint. So did politicians, not least Irish politicians. So did opponents of the Catholic Church. The ideologists of Fascism and Nazism, with whom it would be grossly unjust to align any Jesuit, indulged in far worse vituperation. Also, the fact that what Catholic propagandists said was wrong or un-proven at many points did not mean that others were always right. The employment practices of some Irish business firms in those days, for example, were seriously open to question: the paucity of Catholics in the senior management of certain leading commercial institutions as late as the 1950s was blatantly obvious — thirty years after Irish independence and more than 120 years after Emancipation! It gives no pleasure in an ecumenical age to recall these unhappy and now long-terminated 'closed shops', for which trade unions would be roundly denounced if they tried to impose the like on a discriminatory basis; but to gloss over them would omit factors which went a long way towards making understand-able the motives of sincere if misguided Catholics when they sniffed conspiracy in the circumstances of the world around them.

Nor did it help that the general body of Catholics had their own faults. The triumphalism in the Irish Church at that time infected both clergy and laity with a supposition of righteousness, of having all the answers, and consequently disposed them to dismiss with little respect the convictions of others. As we saw, this may have been the reason why Chinese parents in Hong Kong were even slower than they would have been in any event to allow their sons to adopt the Catholicism preached by the Irish Jesuits during their early years in the colony. Whatever about that, triumphalism did an injury in Ireland itself to the quality of public debate since it lured many who had the good of the Church at heart into the easy self-indulgence of attacking the perceived enemy — Commu-nists, Protestants, Freemasons — instead of querying the adequacy or validity of Catholic attitudes. With thousands of co-religionists to cheer them on, and nobody answering back except non-co-religionists silly enough to offer themselves as Aunt Sallies to be swiped down, Catholic publicists in press and pulpit had an easy time of it. It took an exceptionally thoughtful man or woman to wonder from within the Church whether those who spoke for the Church did not sometimes exaggerate, misrepresent, even err.

Jesuits were thought to be thoughtful. It was a pity that they allowed themselves to be caught up in the Irish Catholic mainstream. There was scope and need for the same detachment which they had so wisely shown on political issues during the Troubles. To be sure, only a few took part in public polemics just as only a few had become involved in nationalist politics earlier. But there were two differences. On what pertained to the Church, Jesuits had a much higher profile (that is, they were more readily listened to and quoted) than on what pertained to Irish political independence. And secondly, the Irish Church stood in quite desperate need of solid theology, cogently reasoned argument and minds open on every question that was not of faith. Had the Jesuits supplied the want, their credibility as scholars would have hugely helped to mitigate the worst excesses of triumphalism. It can only be recorded sadly that they did not do so. True, it would not have been easy. It would have called for minds of exceptional insight, the supply of which can never be guaranteed. And if such were found, they would have needed the support of perceptive authorities within the Society to encourage and protect the men prepared to swim against the prevailing tide.

Certain emphases within the universal Church were also unhelpful. The polemical case would have been more difficult to argue if Leo XIII had shown a better understanding of the State in his much admired social encyclical *Rerum Novarum.* Accepting the thesis of his earlier encyclical, *Immortale Dei,* Pope Leo equated the State with the Prince who was father to his people.[29] Leo — and to a degree Pius XI in *Quadragesimo Anno* — left men like Fathers Cahill and Corcoran, with their counterparts elsewhere, to look for a paternalist ideal in democratic regimes. When they failed to find it,

(Above) The Crescent, Limerick, showing the Church of the Sacred Heart beside the former College, now transferred to Dooradoyle. (Below) The Church was the appropriate setting for a Mass to honour the centenary of the Irish Messenger of the Sacred Heart in 1988.

Coláiste Iognáid and the Church of St Ignatius, Galway. From the beginning, a place of 'intense hard work'.

Father Francis Browne, who conducted missions in parishes throughout Ireland, was a skilled photographer. In 1934, after he had preached a sermon in St Patrick's Cathedral, Armagh, he managed somehow to get to a vantage point outside in time to take this picture of the congregation on its way home!

(Above) Gardiner Street Church and adjacent accommodation were so crowded for the 1948 Novena to St Francis Xavier that 2,000 Dubliners were left outside. (Below) Fathers Kevin Laheen, Niall O'Neill and Seamus Mac Amhlaoibh inspect the cross put up at Newmarket-on-Fergus, County Clare, to commemorate a mission conducted in the parish by their predecessors in 1856.

'The Sacred Heart with Jesuit Saints', a window by Evie Hone in the Chapel at Tullabeg. 'To Evie Hone every figure of Christ and the saints was necessarily a simple and tender description of those who had eschewed all aspects of grandeur or sophistication' – White and Wynne, 17.

(Above) The Regional Seminary in Hong Kong 'must have been the most beautiful house in the care of the Irish Province when it opened in 1931'. (Below) The Charles Lwanga Teacher Training College in Zambia was completed in 1959.

(Above) Archbishop John Charles McQuaid of Dublin ordained ten Jesuits in Milltown Park chapel on 31 July 1950. *(Below)* Gonzaga College in Ranelagh, Dublin, was founded in the same year.

(Above) When a Visitor, Father McMahon, was sent from America by the Father General in 1962 he met the Brothers of the Irish Province at Belvedere. (Below) Father Cecil McGarry was the Provincial on whom devolved the major responsibility for implementing the reforms required by the Second Vatican Council, the 31st General Congregation of the Society (1965–66) and the new emphases adopted by the General, Father Pedro Arrupe.

instead of concluding that the State was now the People and that it reflected popular wishes, they decided that only anti-Christian conspiracies could explain the State's refusal to impose Christian and Catholic norms in the way a strong-minded Prince would have done. When the square peg of papal teaching failed to fit the round hole of liberal political philosophy, it was easier to denounce the liberalism and argue to a brief than think beyond the papal document to new formulations which would have contributed to the mind of the Church as Catholic scholarship is intended to do. Perhaps this is hindsight and asks too much of a local Church that was living under the shadow of the modernist crisis (when severe measures were taken by Pius X in the first decade of the century against Catholics advocating reconciliation between the Church and certain modern philosophies). Be that as it may, serious research leading to fresh insights would have served the Church better and been of more assistance to the new, independent and democratic Irish State than tiresome warnings about Protestants, Freemasons and anti-Catholic alien influences around every corner. The polemics contrasted sadly with the standards set at Father Delany's College on the Green, the standards still maintained at an academic level by a number of Jesuit professors in its successor university, and the standards by which secular subjects were being assessed even then in *Studies*. As one commentator has put it, recalling Joyce's urbane Rector of Clongowes who later served as Provincial, there were a couple of Jesuits in the later 1920s who 'expressed opinions on Irish life which, in Father Conmee's day, would certainly have landed them on the next train to Tullabeg or, in extreme cases, on the next boat to Australia.'[30]

In the very years when Jesuit participation in Irish public debate gave (or should have given) cause for disquiet, the Province made important contributions to the people's betterment outside the area of Catholic attitudes concerning other Churches and organisations. It must be acknowledged that Father Cahill had a foremost place also in this happier development and deserved much credit for its achievements, some of which continue in the marked commitment of present-day

Irish Jesuits to the poor. As Rector of Mungret in 1913, he brought Father Finlay down to talk about the co-operative movement[31] which was doing so much to encourage farmers to improve their lot by the common marketing of produce, sharing of machinery and other forms of self-help. Both Father Cahill and Father Corcoran felt that agriculture, as the basic industry of the country and the major activity of its people, should loom larger in the educational system and not least in the Jesuit boarding schools. They regretted the bias in these schools towards preparing boys to take up the professions and thereby urging young men away from the land. 'It is technical education which is needed,' wrote Father Corcoran, and as early as 1915 Father Cahill was calling for the introduction of agricultural science as a subject in senior classes to make farming as attractive as any profession and at the same time to help modernise farming methods.[32] He was conscious of the fact that Clongowes had a farm which could be made into the basic instrument of instruction, a 'model farm,' and he would have been well aware that Mungret itself had been a possibly premature agricultural training centre before the Jesuits acquired it. The proposals for the colleges fell on deaf ears within the Province. It can be said in passing, however, that they might well have offered the means by which Clongowes could have continued to broaden the base from which it drew its pupils, a desirable development which, as we saw, seemed to stultify in the early years of the century.

Such thinking was novel in two respects. It predated the general awakening in Ireland to Catholic social thinking, which had been much promoted on the continent ever since the publication of *Rerum Novarum,* and it approached the subject from a rural perspective. The encyclical had been concerned to inculcate a sense of balance in a world dominated by the opposing socio-economic doctrines of socialism and capitalism. It supported the right to private property but not the unfair distribution of wealth; it condemned bad working conditions and favoured State intervention to rectify injustice. It particularly sought to overcome the class warfare explicit in socialism and implicit in untrammelled capitalism, seeing the pursuit of harmony between the various interests

in society as a Christian objective. Like many papal pronounce-
ments, the encyclical was properly long on principles and
short on specific examples: it was for Catholics in their local
circumstances to consider how the principles might be
applied. This called for study circles, exchanges of view through
special periodicals, experiments on the ground. Such conscious response was lacking in Ireland, as Father Cahill's
friend, Father Lambert McKenna, S.J., pointed out in 1913[33]
although, Father Cahill would argue later, it was scarcely to
be wondered at since the country's attention had been so
taken up with the consolidation of the post-Emancipation
Church, the struggle for the land and the national question.[34]
For want of a suitable university before 1908, Catholics had
failed to develop a sufficiently large intellectual élite to bring
informed opinion to bear on social issues; this was also a
factor.

A further consideration was that the issues raised by *Rerum
Novarum* related more immediately to industrialised societies.
While socialist thinking attracted some favourable comment
from Father McKenna, quizzical criticism from Father Finlay
and stern condemnation from Father Robert Kane, S.J., who
brought on his head the wrath of James Connolly, it was not
a subject to cause much stir outside the Dublin of the great
Lock-Out (in which, as between socialism and capitalism,
capitalism showed itself to be the worse of the two phenomena). There was a mini-Soviet revolution in Limerick
during the Troubles, but when the dust settled after the Civil
War and the new State had been established, the Left found
itself marginalised in Ireland. Some polemical muscle-flexing
was directed against communism, attacking which made an
escapist exercise for those who preferred negative platitude
to positive thought and action. Communism in fact had little
relevance outside the extreme wing of the Leftist margin —
although there were Catholics who might have learned from
the dedication of the reviled Irish Communists in their
lonely and isolated exclusion from the smallest place in their
country's affairs.

Father Cahill, however, had continued to write and lecture
on Catholic social principles when he transferred to a
teaching post at Milltown Park. In 1926 he was a co-founder

of *An Ríoghacht* (The League of the Kingship of Christ), a federation of study circles, which left him well-placed in 1931 to pick up the ideas of *Quadragesimo Anno*, published that year by Pope Pius XI to update the arguments set out forty years before in *Rerum Novarum*. The new encyclical was more specific than its predecessor and put forward suggestions on how class warfare might be avoided: its central proposal was that 'vocational groups' or 'corporations' be formed in each industry, profession or area of economic activity through which employers, workers and all involved in the common endeavour might collaborate to advance their common interests.[35] This sat well with the agricultural co-operatives and with the wider purposes of the parish-based *Muintir na Tíre* (People of the Land), recently founded by Father John Hayes, then a curate in County Tipperary. The concept of vocational organisation made much sense both as a means of working out the needs of the various segments of society and as a means of ensuring that the opinions of these segments were publicly aired. Trade unions had long been doing much the same but, of course, with each union representing workers only or (less often) employers only.

Unfortunately, vocationalism in the 1930s suffered from a version of the defect in the papal understanding of the State mentioned earlier. It was argued that the vocational groups should relieve government of many of its obligations, taking over the conduct of affairs within their spheres of interest on the principle of subsidiarity: i.e. that superior authority should not retain to itself powers which could be discharged by a lesser authority.[36] This was re-inventing the wheel. The evolution of the modern State had already taken place. The manner in which the exercise of excessive authority by government should be constrained had been fully worked out. Checks and balances, division of powers, judicial review, electoral representation, the responsibility of government to parliament, bicameral legislatures . . . the whole gamut of constitutional thinking in its various forms had been brought to bear on the question. A system had been adopted in Ireland to the reasonable satisfaction of the people. Parish councils, associations of doctors' and farmers' co-operatives obviously had their uses but did not feature in the system of

government, nor could they have been incorporated in it
without extensive disruption of the civil service, which kept
the country running, or without cutting across the defined
functions of the cabinet and the national parliament. There
was little provable need for such an upheaval. And to make
matters worse, forms of vocational organisation were promoted by the totalitarian regimes of Germany, Italy and the
Soviet Union to give an appearance of representative government under what were actually dictatorships. Some people
in Ireland — some politicians and some civil servants especially — were inclined to suspect, however unfairly, that the
advocates of 'corporatism' wanted to replace democracy with
continental-type totalitarianism. In 1938 Professor Alfred
O'Rahilly 'suggested that conciliarism should be used to
describe vocational organisation or functional democracy
instead of corporatism which had acquired some sinister
overtones "through bad associations and misunderstandings".'[37]

The taint of subversive intent would attach to the vocational
ideas championed by several Jesuits, among others, and to
this day gives a dubious reputation to the school of thought
from which these ideas emerged. It is a pity, for the study
circles, summer schools (those held at Clongowes between
1935 and 1940 were outstanding)[38] and serious publications
brought out under the aegis of the Catholic social movement
had a beneficial influence on Irish public policy which, in
justice, should be acknowledged. The room left for State
intervention on behalf of the common good facilitated
acceptance of the many State enterprises — far more than in
other democracies — upon which the modern Irish economy
was built. The recognition that the right to private prope. ty,
above all t'   .ivate property in land, did not justify excessive
accumulauon injected into the public mind a healthy suspicion of private monopoly and a concern (never waning,
however inadeq· ᵃᵗ ;y met) that the poor be provided for
before the rich.

Of course, Irish society was and is shot through with the
selfishness inseparable from the human condition, but when
certain meritorious priorities keep recurring it is fair to ask
where they began. When Father Edward Coyne, S.J., attacked

the Report of the State-appointed Banking Commission in 1938 because it failed to consider how the social welfare of the country was to be achieved,[39] he took a stance vis-à-vis traditional economic theory which survives today in the trenchant comments on government fiscal policy by the Irish Conference of Major Religious Superiors as well as by the Jesuits' own Centre for Faith and Justice. At the same time, Father Coyne protested against minority reports by some members of the Banking Commission because they failed to indicate the economic cost of meeting desirable social objectives[40] — a pragmatic reminder that it is never enough to lay down a principle without working out the means of implementing it. This commonsense approach has marked much of the thinking to emerge from the Catholic Workers' College set up in Dublin by the Jesuits in 1948 to promote Catholic social teaching. The confessional emphasis may sound a jarring note today, but only to those who forget the surely laudable search for harmony to replace class warfare which this teaching embodied.

The College began with the idea of providing courses for organised employees *and* employers.[41] By 1967 it had evolved into the College of Industrial Relations[42] for management and trade union studies. Today, with the support of major unions and firms in the private and public sectors alike, it functions as a forum for alternative views on the organisation of Irish industry and as an umbrella under which public policy can be scrutinised from a variety of perspectives: if not quite productive of harmony, at least it compels the recognition that workers, employers, consumers and government all need to find common ground if the common good of all is to be promoted. The impressive results for the Irish economy of National Agreements between these 'social partners' in recent years leave little room to doubt the significance of such common endeavour. Without making an exaggerated claim for the Society, it can fairly be said that Father Cahill, Father Coyne and other Jesuits stood with Father John Hayes and like-minded social thinkers at the head of the road leading to more positive achievements than ever accrued from the arid ideologies of extremists on the Right or Left.

The merits and limitations of the Catholic social movement, not to mention attitudes within the Province, were thrown sharply into focus by the Jesuit submission of October, 1936, when a new Constitution for Ireland was being considered by Mr de Valera, then President of the Executive Council (prime minister) of the Irish Free State.[43] The Province had apparently no intention of involving itself in the business of constitution-making but Father Cahill on his own initiative decided to offer the President some thoughts on a basic law which would 'make a definite break with the Liberal and non-Christian types of state' like that which had been 'forced upon us by a foreign, non-Catholic power'. Would de Valera like him to discuss what he had in mind with 'some few others of the fathers' and produce a revised draft? The President asked him to proceed and, in particular, to try phrasing a preamble. The Provincial had little choice in the circumstances but to allow the exercise to proceed. He did not, however, give Father Cahill *carte blanche* to consult whom he chose or to write the document. A Jesuit committee was formed, consisting of Fathers Cahill, Coyne and J. Canavan with the historian, Father McErlean, as secretary and Father P. Bartley as chairman. A document drafted and approved by this body would be sent to Mr de Valera as a formal submission from the Irish Province of the Society of Jesus.

The agreed submission was modest enough by the standards of the day. The Jesuits did not compose it off the top of their heads. They consulted the constitutions of Poland and Austria as well as the social encyclicals. It revealed no paranoia about the liberal State and suggested no substitution of new structures for the established form of parliamentary democracy, with a government responsible to a chamber of deputies elected on a universal franchise. It did include a number of features to make the Constitution conform to Catholic values. According to the proposed preamble, the people of Ireland 'as a united independent Christian Nation' would 'sanction' the Constitution 'in the Name of the Most Holy Trinity and of our Lord Jesus Christ, the Universal King'. The 'unique and preponderant position' of the Catholic Church was to be recognised, and a concordat with the Holy See was envisaged to regulate relations between that

Church and the State. Relations with other Churches were to be determined by agreement between the State and their official representatives. Divorce was to be banned and marriage would be governed by the regulations of the Catholic Church if one or both parties were Catholic. The family was recognised as the fundamental unit of civil society possessing 'natural, inalienable and imprescriptible rights, prior and superior to all positive law' and, while schools were to be in principle denominational (with adolescent boys and girls being educated separately), all citizens and associations of citizens were to have the right to found, own and administer schools.

However much these provisions may grate on sensitivities today, when the separation of Church and State is seen to be positively desirable and the implications of the right to religious freedom have been extensively elaborated, the Jesuits of half-a-century ago seem to have envisaged a State which would take steps to respect and protect all organised religions rather than impose the beliefs of one Church on everybody — except, admittedly, in the highly sensitive areas of divorce and 'mixed marriages', and the less important (but in terms of human dignity not irrelevant) matter of phraseology, where the Catholic triumphalism of the day comes trumpeting loudly down the decades. The submission displays, in short, very much the same defects as the Constitution actually enacted,[44] on the content of which it seems to have had more than a little influence.[45] It may, however, be judged to have laid down more equitable principles on the subject of property than was done in the de Valera Constitution. Here it wanted the State to be empowered to see to it that 'the use which owners make of their property, especially goods of a productive nature, is in accord with the common good and with social justice'. It went on to say that the State should 'so adjust property rights as to secure that these are duly developed and utilized in the interest of the common good' and should 'promote a wide distribution of private property, especially in land'. Had mandatory provisions of this kind been incorporated in the Constitution, the headache for the Courts called to interpret them might have been considerable. But the Courts would have coped and social justice would have been further advanced than proved possible under the vaguer provisions adopted.

The more extreme exponents of Catholic teaching would have gone further than the Jesuit committee or Mr de Valera. Some of them would have been happier if Catholicism had been declared the religion of the State, or at least if the Catholic Church had been recognised by the State as the one true Church founded by Jesus Christ.[46] Happily the Jesuits stopped far short of this but seem not to have appreciated that expressions redolent of credal allegiance, as in the proposed preamble quoted above and also the very similar preamble endorsed by the people, are gratuitously offensive to citizens of minority religious beliefs — and quite unnecessary, since they have no significant effect in law. The use of confessional phrasing for generally acceptable propositions, like the Jesuit references to the family and similar clauses of the Constitution itself,[47] cause problems for judges required to apply Roman absolutes and ecclesiastical terminology to issues raised under a common law system which does not readily accommodate such concepts.[48] It seems never to have occurred to Irish Church thinkers in the 1930s that their ignorance of political science and constitutional law should have dissuaded them from pronouncing on the subject: the sources consulted by the Jesuit committee included a number of constitutions then in force in various countries, the Code of Canon Law, papal encyclicals and books on social principles; not a single textbook on constitutional law or any other aspect of civil law is mentioned.[49] That mentality was the essence of triumphalism.

The unhappy fact that less-than-sophisticated assertive attitudes showed themselves within the Irish Province during the 1930s was not the only disturbing feature of the time. Among the Jesuits trained in those years were some who told Michael Viney in 1971 of 'a "brainwashing theology", a prevailing anti-intellectualism, and "a whole clerical world dominated by making reports on people"... they battled with... nervous depression....'[50] If this typified the system it would surely have contradicted the fine tuning of the mind and sensitivity to the needs of the people around them which had for centuries marked the Society of Jesus. It could hardly have been reconciled with the Ignatian ideal of finding God in all things and making him known. But the world-wide militant Catholicism of the age was conducive to such an atmosphere, as was the legalism of a Church exhausted from 150 years of refining its stance against the excesses of liberal ideology; it would have matched the censorious mood of newly-independent Ireland seeking to establish its difference from, and superiority to, countries allegedly lacking in the moral fibre of Christianity; and it might have reflected the want of imagination inherent in a system built on the supposition that it had all the answers.

But how far is the era accurately represented in a few stark memories of its narrower aspects? A Jesuit who underwent his formation in pre-war and wartime Ireland vehemently challeges[51] the picture evoked in the comments reported by Mr Viney. 'A dispassionate and rigorous evaluation of the Roman-prescribed theological education of those times remains to be written,' he says, but 'it was not a "brain-washing theology". . . . It was arid. It was intellectually demanding and challenging. It was austerely metaphysical. Certainly, it was not for intellectual weaklings. It is important to be just to it.' As for those who studied this theology, 'we were far from being a body of cowed scholastics . . . My memory of my contemporaries is of a by and large cheerful body of men often given to laughter and quite content, happy, to live a hard life.' And overall: 'The pre-Vatican II time marked a low period in all church matters. Among the Irish Jesuits it marked a period of a certain unexamined confidence, of a simultaneous strange lack of confidence, of quite a remarkable degree of genuine zeal. . . . It was also marked by a paucity of imagination and by philistinism. (Imagination and non-philistinism are gifts not always granted in any age to most Jesuits.)'

Much of this is borne out by Professor John O'Meara, who was a novice and then a scholastic from 1933 until the mid-1940s. He writes of his noviceship with warm affection, recalling 'the special kind of happiness which one was fortunate to have had, even if some might judge it damaging

or just a waste of time'.[52] At Tullabeg he experienced 'a way
of life which I genuinely loved: that of study, good compan-
ionship and a common noble purpose'.[53] The books for the
philosophy course were out of date but the lecturers, one in
particular, strove to make up for the deficiency: he stressed
contemporary Jesuit writers 'as against the fashionable
Maritain and the less than tolerant Dominicans. . . . In the
main the approach was liberal . . . I enjoyed the course.'[54] But
the young man saw the other side of the times as well. It distressed him at Rathfarnham Castle, the house for scholastics
attending the university, to find extraordinary disciplinary
action taken against some of his colleagues who were
reported for making mild criticisms of the Rector and the
Provincial: 'A number of scholastics had ecclesiastical sanc-
tions read over them (a very grave and rare occurrence) as
they knelt before all in the refectory; a few were ordered to
repeat the thirty days' retreat of their noviceship; and two
quite innocent bystanders, so to speak, broke under the
tension of the affair as it climaxed, and had to repair to a
mental institution. The damage done interiorly to many
cannot be measured.'[55] The regime under which this happened was a brief aberration, Professor O'Meara leaves no
doubt, but it pointed to something wrong.

Whatever it was, it was not of long duration nor did it have
too wide-reaching an effect. The present writer can testify
that, as a schoolboy at Clongowes from 1945 to 1950, he was
aware of none of the disagreeable features of the system said
by some to have typified the immediately preceding years.
The priests, scholastics and brothers showed no sign of living
in a state of stress. Some stood out because they enthused
their classes better than others or had a better rapport with
their charges, or simply because they displayed amiable
personal eccentricities. Religion and general subjects alike
were taught on the whole with competent assurance; questioning or the presentation of alternative views was rarely
discouraged and often invited . . . although contumacious
ignorance received the short shrift it deserved. Discipline was
firm but invoked no more than necessary. Most of the time
and for most of the boys, it was a sane and happy place; its
modern historian, who was not himself at school there and

accordingly reports the findings of objective research, concludes that in these years the College 'achieved an era of benign quietude'.[56] That would scarcely have been possible if the Jesuit community lived under any strain of oppressive 'bossing'. There is little reason to believe that standards differed much in the other schools, or other houses, among which the Jesuits tended to circulate in the normal process of transfer from one posting to another. It is said, for example, that at Mungret the shortage of facilities for recreation (like a swimming pool) and for study (such as properly equipped science laboratories) was compensated for by the 'family atmosphere' and easy relations between staff and students.[57]

Beyond the absence of stress, an openness of mind could be met with among Jesuits of the 1940s which the modern age may consider unremarkable but which was quite other than the norm in the Ireland of the day. At Belvedere one winter morning early in 1941 a priest asked his class, 'Do any of you know the name of the famous writer who is being buried in Zurich today?. . . . His name was Joyce. . . . You will remember the name because you are going to hear it again. He was a student of Belvedere, some say the cleverest student this college ever produced. . . .'[58] To be a prefect in Clongowes it was necessary to be a member of the Sodality, and applicants for membership were elected or rejected by the existing members. In 1949, 'a small group of us resigned from the Sodality in protest at this discriminatory rule, to the bafflement of our gentle Spiritual Director, Father Gregory Ffrench'.[59] This revolt against what they understood to be the most revered institution of the Society of Jesus drew no thunderbolts on the heads of the boys involved. Father Ffrench interviewed each of them, discussed their motives and concluded sorrowfully, 'If you must, you must. God bless you.'[60] Such tolerance for the individual rights of conscience, without any patronising disparagement of the element of schoolboy bravado involved, not only enhanced the Spiritual Father's credibility but quite probably did more to strengthen the religious faith of the boys concerned than routine attendance at Sodality meetings would have done. Nothing so wins the respect of the adolescent than to be taken seriously when he is being serious; the adult who shows such sensitivity can reasonably hope that the respect he has been granted will extend to the values he represents. They were no blinkered clerics or fanatical Catholics, those Jesuits who could inculcate in the 1940s 'a questioning, not to say cynical, attitude to life; a love of reading, of argument; a perspective on religion which distinguishes the essentials from the optionals . . .'.[61] *O si sic omnes*

Jesuits discharge their vocation of service to God and the Church by seeking the needs to be met which they can best serve. This forms the basis of their involvement in education and in the evolution of public policy on social questions. It shows itself more immediately in the many-sided pastorate centred on their public churches and retreat houses, for spiritual needs have always been their first concern since Salmeron and Broet came to Ireland to discover the state of the Irish Church. The sending out of missionaries to town and countryside to revive a slackening faith was the main achievement of Father Holywood, and at the height of the penal days every effort was concentrated on making Mass and the sacraments available to the people. These activities never ceased. Each of the Jesuits' major public churches — Gardiner Street, The Crescent, St Ignatius' — had confraternities and local charities attached to them, and provided special spiritual exercises at appropriate times in the liturgical year: the preaching of the Seven Words on Good Friday was a particular feature of Jesuit churches; so also, as might be expected, were the sermons for the feasts of the Holy Name and the Sacred Heart.

These and myriad other devotions were probably never so popular as during the middle decades of the century. It is hard to imagine today the sheer fervour of Irish Catholics in those increasingly distant times. In 1926 at the 'Forty Hours Adoration' (exposition of the Blessed Sacrament) in the Jesuit church in Limerick 'an extraordinary scene of devotion began at midnight . . . the church was packed, chiefly by men . . . rosaries were recited and hymns sung . . . when 2 o'clock struck, the priest and his acolytes filed from the sacristy to the side altar for Mass . . . by this time not only was there not standing room but the worshippers flowed out into the street and thronged the corridors and other approaches to the church. . . .'.[62] The most phenomenal exercise of this kind under Jesuit auspices was the annual Novena of Grace in honour of Saint Francis Xavier. The principal centre for the nine days of prayer was Gardiner Street Church in Dublin, which is dedicated to the saint. An observer noted what it was like on one evening of the 1948 Novena: 'The church itself is filled to capacity by 6.30 p.m., although the devotions begin only at 7.45! And long before the beginning of the ceremony, the congregation has surged into the Ignatian chapel, has filled the corridors and Presbytery parlours, the laneway at Sherrard Street. Then the Concert Hall in Sherrard Street is filled with people, and there are still some 2,000 people outside the church in Gardiner Street, which is so densely packed that traffic cannot pass, and the Guards have to divert buses and cars around Mountjoy Square.'[63] A photograph of the crowd cramming the street bears out the estimate of numbers and, but for the reverent demeanour of the people and the absence of placards, could have been taken at a political rally of the period.

In retrospect, such demonstrations of piety suggest an imbalance in the popular religion of the time, an inverted pyramid of faith in which a minor observance attracted the enthusiasm that should have been reserved for the central truths of salvation, the preaching of the Gospel and the celebration of the Eucharist. On the other hand, the Jesuits used such devotions as the launching-pads, as it were, from which to convey the core messages of Christianity to receptive congregations. It was a technique grown from, and suited to, a type of religious mentality which no longer exists in the form in which it existed then. The old-style demonstrations of piety can be admired in their context but without regret for their decline, for they belonged to a religion riddled with maddening (i.e. mad-making) scrupulosity, intolerance and self-righteousness: faults which some devotions, especially that to the Sacred Heart, were preached to counteract. Despite its deficiencies, it was a religion also distinguished by mass loyalty and much holiness. If that be paradox, so be it.

A pastoral service to which the Jesuits have always brought a special competence has been the giving of retreats and missions: retreats, when the participants withdraw from the world for a few days to contemplate Jesus in the Gospel, to contemplate God; missions, when crash-programmes of sermons and devotions are presented to the people in their own surroundings, usually in a parish church but also involving visits to families in their homes, especially families in which sick or elderly people are being cared for. As we saw, the conduct of missions to reawaken dormant religious awareness in whole districts of Munster and Connacht was undertaken by the early Jesuits. Their successors in the nineteenth century were among many orders — the Redemptorists and Passionists in particular — who did much the same work in nineteenth-century Ireland when two hundred years of oppression, imperfect organisation and a chronic shortage of priests had brought about irregularities of religious observance (from dispensing with the formalities of marriage to low Mass attendance) and indulgence in what was deemed unseemly or immoral behaviour (on 'pattern days', when the feasts of local saints were celebrated, and at 'wakes', when neighbours came to commiserate on a death in the family — and to engage in traditional horseplay as well as copious drinking).[64] To this day, the 'mission crosses' put up to commemorate the descent of a spiritual task force a hundred years ago can be seen in many Irish parishes, as also in many French parishes where the idea of a permanent memorial to religious renewal originated.

The work of renewal being ongoing, the preaching of missions continued into the religiously more settled decades of the twentieth century. A permanent staff of Jesuit 'missioners' undertook parish missions: in the weeks after Easter in 1969, for example, they were found at work in Liverpool and the Irish-speaking Aranmore Island off the coast of Donegal, in Burtonport and Clara, in small parishes of Counties Kilkenny and Mayo and Waterford.[65] Fathers engaged in other work came to their aid to help meet the heavy demand in the summer. Sixty-six priests were listed for 106 retreats: these included two 30-day retreats (the full Exercises of Saint Ignatius); six diocesan retreats for clergy and two other clergy retreats; ninety-two convent and religious brothers' retreats.[66] It sounds like the early days of the Galway community writ large. In fact such activity was, and remains, an essential part of the Jesuit vocation. It has other aspects also. Ever since the days of Father Peter Kenney the Jesuits had been in demand as preachers on important occasions. In Holy Week, 1928, no fewer than six priests from Milltown Park 'preached in various places throughout Ireland'.[67] The Jesuits held their pulpit orators in high regard. It was considered worthy of note that in the same Holy Week of 1928 in Galway, 'Two Jubilarians preached "The Seven Words" on Good Friday. . . . Seldom has such a large audience remained for the whole three hours. The venerable preachers' eloquence was enhanced by the knowledge that Fr Byrne had preached from the same pulpit 40 years ago; and that Fr Murphy was preaching "The Seven Words" for the 14th time in 28 years.'[68] Another elderly Father Murphy preached on the same theme in Limerick two years later: '. . . in the pulpit Fr Tom seems to shed a quarter of a century. The closing passage, in which he brought the big congregation to their knees, was particularly fine. The laurels are still fresh on the brows of our older men . . .'.[69]

And there were residential retreats. In 1860 the famous and ubiquitous Father Edmund O'Reilly was given charge of the retreats to be held at the newly opened novitiate of Milltown Park in Dublin and on 18 March 1861 'the first Retreat for gentlemen' commenced.[70] In the mid-1870s the Sicilian refugee Father Sturzo, as 'Director of the Spiritual Exercises', built a large Retreat House at Milltown.[71] Further Retreat Houses were opened in Rathfarnham and, more recently, at Manresa House in Dollymount, both in the Dublin suburbs. These houses made it possible for the laity, either as individuals or in groups, to undergo the spiritual therapy of an enclosed retreat during which they resided in the house. It was an opportunity much availed of: in the first half of 1930, for example, twenty-four weekend retreats for men were provided at Rathfarnham and eight three-day retreats for boys; the number of men involved totalled 1,230 and the boys 329.[72] Retreats for women were arranged also and in later years forms of retreat were devised for engaged couples and married couples, for school-leavers (boys and girls attending together, to their mutual satisfaction) and other groups with a common interest or special needs. Residential retreats for past pupils or people associated with the college were held from time to time in Clongowes and Mungret. One more set of statistics, published in 1955,[73] helps illustrate the work of the Irish Jesuits for the care of souls in a single year:

438 enclosed retreats given to priests, brothers and nuns;
142 parish missions;
309 weekend retreats;
5,945 sermons preached.

Saint Ignatius laid down that in every church of the Society 'the word of God should be proposed to the people unremittingly by means of sermons, lectures and the teaching of Christian doctrine,' and that 'the same procedure . . . may also be followed outside the Society's church, in other churches, squares, or places of the region, when the one in charge judges it expedient for God's greater glory,' and further that Jesuits 'will endeavour to be profitable to individuals by spiritual conversations, by counselling and exhorting to good works, and by conducting Spiritual Exercises.'[74] The Irish Province has manifestly kept faith with these directives.

When the restored Irish Jesuits at last decided to provide themselves with a place in which a novitiate at home in Ireland could be conducted they bought a substantial country house in the south suburbs of Dublin called Milltown Park. To be exact, Mr Denis Redmond, whose son was a Jesuit and who lived nearby, bought the house: in 1858 there were still people about who would not sell their property to a religious order and least of all to the Jesuits.[75] It was thought safer to allow Mr Redmond to acquire it in his own name and have him make it over to the Society afterwards. This was duly done and the first eight novices arrived in 1860: two of them priests who had applied for entry to the Society, three new lay entrants and three Irish novices recalled from their training at Beaumont in England, where they had been sent for want of a novitiate at home. The house soon filled up as seven more Irish entrants arrived before the year was out, not to mention the contingent of Italians and Sicilians brought to Ireland by Father Sturzo. Perhaps the most unexpected novice in those early days was Father Patrick Corcoran, the

Administrator of Tuam Cathedral, who joined in 1862 'and lived to a great age'. With the retreats for the laity under way almost from the outset, Milltown must have been a busy place, and busier still after 1880 when the scholastics studying philosophy were sent there, followed a few years later by those from the short-lived College of Saint Ignatius in Temple Street (closed down, it will be recalled, when the Province took charge of University College). No doubt it was pressure of numbers, together with so many other activities that may in those days have been felt to be incompatible with the quiet and seclusion proper to novices, that inspired the purchase of the former palace of the Church of Ireland Bishop of Dromore in County Down.[76] The Jesuits renamed it Loyola House and brought the novices north from Milltown in 1884.

This was the first Jesuit residence to be securely established in Ulster, although Superiors of the old Mission and even Generals in Rome had more than once expressed the hope that the Society might acquire a permanent base in the Northern province. Dromore proved less than permanent. The buildings at Tullabeg became available following the amalgamation of the College with Clongowes. The novices shortly afterwards moved to Tullabeg and Dromore was disposed of: a very shortsighted step, because the strengthening of the Catholic Church in Ireland and the growth in numbers of the secular clergy had left bishops less inclined to invite or permit relatively independent religious orders to set up house in their dioceses. The irascibility of Bishop O'Dwyer in Limerick and Archbishop Walsh in Dublin towards the Jesuits whom they found *in situ* should have been fair warning! Ninety years would pass before the Jesuits were able again to open a house in Ulster. In a further rationalisation, the 'philosophers' were sent from Milltown to Mungret in 1888 and a year later it was decided that this part of the scholastics' training should be undertaken abroad. That facilitated revival of the project started in North Frederick Street, Dublin, in 1857 and almost immediately aborted: Milltown was made a theologate in 1889 — a house in which Jesuits would study theology during the years immediately prior to ordination. It enjoyed a high reputation from the outset, for 'an excellent staff of Professors was provided' and 'applications for places came in from many of the foreign Provinces'. It so continued for eighty years until it became the Milltown Institute in 1968, with students drawn more widely than from the Society alone.[77] It attained its ultimate status in 1974 as a papal *athenaeum* or university empowered to grant pontifical degrees up to, and including, doctorates in philosophy and theology. Known now as the Milltown Institute of Theology and Philosophy, it is governed by a Board of Trustees comprising the Irish provincial superiors of a number of religious orders; its Chancellor is *ex officio* the Jesuit General and its Vice-Chancellor the Irish Provincial of the Society. The Archbishop of Dublin is its Patron and at the time of writing its President is a Carmelite Father.[78]

In 1871 'a number of leading Catholics of Cork' petitioned their Bishop to allow the Jesuits to set up a College in the city[79] but nothing came of it. Following Dromore, no new Jesuit houses were opened in the country until 1909 when the Society left University College upon the establishment of the National University and acquired a residence for their academics nearby at 35 Lower Leeson Street — subsequently known as the House of Writers, to the chagrin of at least some Fathers living elsewhere who resented the implied elitism.[80] The Province also opened a hostel for lay university students at Winton Road, inconveniently situated beyond the Grand Canal. Through the munificence of 'a Mr Charles Kennedy, a man of considerable means and an old pupil of the Jesuits at Clongowes',[81] a handsome new hostel named University Hall was built in Hatch Street around the corner from the main university buildings in Earlsfort Terrace and connected by its garden with the House of Writers. From 1913 this provided lodgings in a collegiate atmosphere not only for students who had been pupils at Jesuit schools but for a number of others as well. For each it was a mind-broadening advantage, experienced by few of their contemporaries at the non-residential U.C.D., to rub shoulders daily with seventy other students from any and every faculty. In the early days extra-curricular occupations were not unknown: an eminent physician recalled how 'after the Easter Rebellion 1916. . . students would sometimes disappear for a while . . . they were engaged elsewhere in "political activities." '[82]

In the same year as they opened University Hall the Jesuits bought Rathfarnham Castle in the south-west suburbs of Dublin. Rathfarnham, like Dromore, had Church of Ireland episcopal associations: it was built by Adam Loftus, made Archbishop of Armagh by the first Elizabeth and then (as would happen to the Catholic Archbishop Cullen much later) translated to Dublin.[83] It passed through many hands and acquired some fine Georgian decoration by Angelica Kaufman and other artists before the Jesuits secured it as a residence for their 'juniors' who had completed their novice-ship and were studying for degrees at U.C.D. Some of the Fathers on the Mission Staff were incorporated in the community and it also became the home of the Tertian Fathers (Jesuits taking a renewal course through which they confirm their commitment to the spirit and the work of the Society following their ordination).[84] In 1922 a Retreat House was added to supplement the work being carried on in Milltown. For most people in Ireland, however, the Jesuits at Rathfarnham were above all the custodians of the seismograph, an instrument for recording the severity of earthquakes. Its readings were reported in the media whenever an earthquake occurred anywhere in the world. Father William O'Leary built his first seismograph at Mungret in 1911 when such instruments were very rare.[85] Inspired by Father Henry V. Gill, a Jesuit scientist, and encouraged by his Provincial, Father T. V. Nolan, he built another at Rathfarnham in 1916: for long it was the only seismograph of its kind in existence. In 1932 a type of instrument commonly in use by then was installed at Rathfarnham, not to replace the 'O'Leary Seismograph' but to give greater accuracy to the recordings. Rathfarnham took its place in the Jesuit Seismological Association which eventually had stations in Ireland, England, France, Spain, Italy, Australia and America. Father O'Leary became Director of a large observatory at Riverview College in Sydney. When fewer vocations to the priesthood, changes in Jesuit formation and the cost of maintaining large houses compelled the Jesuits to dispose of Rathfarnham in 1985 the seismograph was broken up and its parts given to various scientific museums.

The permanent location of the novitiate was by no means settled. From the mid-1920s to 1969 it was based at St Mary's, Emo, in County Laois. This house had formerly been Emo Park, the home of Lord Portarlington who, although a Protestant, had strongly supported the views on education held by his close friend, Father Delany, Rector of Tullabeg.[86] It would later feature in a novel, *There Was An Ancient House*, by Benedict Kiely who had for a short time been a Jesuit novice there. It was decided to close Emo in 1969 and the novitiate came to rest at Manresa, the seaside Retreat House at Dollymount on Dublin Bay. Tullabeg had meanwhile become home to the peripatetic 'philosophers' until they were sent abroad again briefly from 1962 until 1966, when they were re-assembled at Milltown.[87] Following the departure of the 'philosophers' Tullabeg became a retreat house.

A fair wind edged most of the Colleges gently down the decades towards the 1960s. Clongowes, Belvedere and the Crescent held to their civilised, predictable course, undergoing no major reforms and seeing little need for any. In Galway Saint Ignatius', Gaelicised as Coláiste Iognáid, had fully recovered from its closure between 1926 and 1929. A completely Irish-speaking staff had been quickly built up. Plays in Irish, expeditions to the Aran Islands, language refresher courses for teachers at Carraroe all made possible its acceptance by the Department of Education in 1934 as a 'Class A' school in which all subjects were taught through the medium of Irish.[88] The College remained a popular resort for Jesuits from other houses seeking 'villa' accommodation at holiday time and some guests arrived by the Atlantic liners which had begun again to drop anchor in Galway Bay.[89] Mungret remained in the doldrums until well into the 1950s but recovery began then under a succession of reforming rectors and prefects of studies who introduced improvements ranging from a better heating system to new classrooms and a wider curriculum. The pace of change accelerated rapidly after the arrival of Father John Kerr as Rector, following a Visitation of the Irish Province by an American Father McMahon who wondered why Father Kerr was teaching philosophy at Tullabeg when he should have been in a position of authority. New science laboratories, a new theatre, a swimming pool were matched by the imposition of high academic requirements for entrance — and a 50 per cent increase in the fees over a six-year period. But by the time Father Kerr left Mungret in 1968 'there were three applicants for every place in the lay school and many pupils were booked in for years ahead'.[90]

Meanwhile in 1950 the Jesuits had opened their first new school in Ireland in nearly 70 years. This was Gonzaga College, sited on land in the Dublin suburb of Ranelagh immediately adjoining Milltown Park. It represented a valiant effort to revive the *Ratio Studiorum*, the traditional Jesuit educational system, in the mid-twentieth century.

The other colleges, like virtually all Irish secondary schools, were caught in a web of constraints by having to prepare their pupils for the (new) Intermediate and Leaving Certificate exams set by the Department of Education. These were not unduly burdensome, unless candidates were seeking high marks to qualify for scholarships. Schools like Clongowes were able to ignore the Department's curriculum in such subjects as French and English until the year immediately preceding the Intermediate or the Leaving.[91] A solid grounding could thus be provided which gave pupils a richer and more appreciative acquaintance with the subject than if they had been confined to the curriculum alone. This grounding helped them, in a single year before an exam, to cope sufficiently with prescribed texts to secure tolerable, if not always spectacular, results. Nonetheless, although not to the same extent as the 'old Intermediate', during much of a young person's schooldays this system demanded concentration on passing the State exams rather than benefiting from the best education which a school, left to itself, might devise. In particular, it undermined the emphasis favoured under the *Ratio Studiorum* with its stress on speaking and writing, on clarity of thought achieved through a thorough knowledge of languages and especially of classical languages.

Gonzaga would endeavour to restore this noble ideal.[92] 'There would be a great emphasis on Languages and on Rhetoric. Greek and Latin would have an honoured place. But English and, hopefully, Irish would be equally important. The sciences would not feature on the curriculum. . . . The principle was that you first trained a man to think clearly and to express himself clearly before he tackled his professional subjects. Such at least was the hope, and such in broad outlines was the thinking behind the new school.'[93] To facilitate the drafting and teaching of Gonzaga's own curriculum it was decided not only to eschew the semi-specialty of science subjects but also to refrain from sending pupils forward for the State exams: they would sit only the matriculation exam for entry to the National University (which relied less on prescribed texts and more on individual ability than the Leaving Certificate). It was also decided that the 'matric' would be taken at the end of Fifth Year, leaving Sixth Year — the final year at school — free to prepare for entry into a world, academic or otherwise, in which a young man would have to know how to use his own resources without the feather-bedding of selection and pruning of texts undertaken by teachers, and without the benefit of the teachers' preparatory classwork. This transition year, devoted to reading widely and learning how to assemble knowledge effectively as well as how to present it, distinguished Gonzaga from most other schools until the late 1970s. Boys who underwent the experience spoke strongly in its favour once they discovered the advantages it gave them when they left school.

The decision to attempt a return to Jesuit basics was the brainchild of Father Thomas Byrne, Provincial in 1947 when the expansion of the south Dublin suburbs made it desirable to open a new secondary school. Implementation fell to the first Rector of Gonzaga, Father Charles O'Conor, under whom the plan worked well enough despite problems of cramped accommodation and ongoing building activities. After his time, in the 1960s and 1970s, it became inevitably less practicable. The exclusion of science began to look bizarre in a technological age and a place was tentatively found for it. New standards were being set for university entrance, as more applicants sought third level places than these institutions could accommodate: the 'points system', under which places were allocated by reference to the standard attained by applicants in the Leaving Certificate, meant that secondary students had to try to win the best results possible. This meant sitting the State exams and taking the range of subjects calculated to produce the highest score in 'points' for each student. The special curriculum devised for the school was accordingly undermined. Gonzaga had to offer the Department courses for the Leaving and, reluctantly, was forced to abandon the Sixth Year transitional approach. Parents, concerned for their sons' prospects in an Ireland where competition was increasingly becoming the norm in higher education, urged Gonzaga down this road. It thus, ineluctably and under the restrained guidance of a succession of dedicated Rectors and headmasters, became one more very good Jesuit school rather than a school radically different from the rest.

Another factor in the evolution of Gonzaga was the growing discomfiture of Jesuits — young Jesuits in particular — with providing quality education for the relatively better-off who could afford to pay for it.[94] This reflected the influence of the Second Vatican Council, which met from 1962 to 1965 and effected so powerful a change in the mind of the Catholic Church. One could say that its implications have still to be fully worked out in ecclesiastical thinking and practice as the century draws to its close. For Jesuits everywhere the final year of the Council had a further significance, for it brought the election of Father Pedro Arrupe as General of the Society, perhaps the most charismatic and prophetic holder of the office since Jan Philip Roothaan had consolidated its activities and firmly fixed its direction in the decades after the Restoration.

Father Arrupe, like his fellow-Basque Ignatius Loyola, was seized of the conviction the the Jesuits' duty lay in meeting the most urgent needs of the world in which they found themselves, and he had little doubt that the first of these needs in modern times was the pursuit of justice for the poor. This led to self-questioning in which he urged Jesuits everywhere to join with him. Thus, on Jesuit schools: 'We must honestly ask ourselves whether we are fostering, at least implicitly, elitism based on the ability to pay. If the answer is affirmative, we cannot avoid the next question: how can the situation be changed? If the situation cannot be changed, then the next question follows with ruthless logic: cannot our energies be used more effectively elsewhere?'[95]

Such considerations led the Jesuits in 1974 to propose that
Gonzaga become a Jesuit Comprehensive School, co-educational and non-feepaying, to be run by a board of management representing the Irish Province and the Minister for
Education.[96] A similar plan had already been given effect in
Limerick, where the Crescent had been converted successfully into a comprehensive of this kind on a new site at
Dooradoyle on the southern fringe of the city. In a clear
reflection of the emphases of Vatican II, the Gonzaga proposal
also indicated that the comprehensive 'would be a Jesuit
school, and therefore a Catholic one, but designed with the
specific aim of moving towards Christian unity, and exploring
the form of the Christian school as distinct from a Catholic
one. It would welcome children of other Christian faiths, and
ensure that their religious education was cared for as well as
that of Catholic pupils.' In this way, the Jesuits' service to the
Church and to their fellow-men would be discharged in a
non-elitist manner and their talents would be directed
towards meeting an urgent need in the Ireland of the day. As
it turned out, the State could not accept the proposal for
practical reasons (bearing on cost), other options were considered[97] and it was found in the end that the only feasible
course was to continue the school with little change.

To risk an over-simplification, the question posed by the
General was answered, in the case of Clongowes, Belvedere
and Gonzaga, by the consideration that the Jesuits were
justified in meeting the undoubted demand[98] for such schools
if they developed in their pupils a respect and commitment
to the 'option for the poor' that the pupils might be expected to advance in the professional and leadership roles which
many would afterwards find themselves exercising: in other
words, the colleges would be used consciously to promote
the Christian principle of justice. As Father Arrupe put it in
1973, the formation of 'men-for-others' was to be one of the
principal objectives of the Society's work in education.[99] In
Clongowes the promotion of social conscience long predated the Vatican Council. The work of its Social Study Club
featured among the school activities to which attention was
drawn during the centenary celebrations attended by John
Redmond in 1914. This group of boys had been inspired in

the previous year by Father Edward James Boyd-Barrett (who later left the Jesuits) to concern themselves with the relationship between poverty and industrialisation: the Dublin Lock-Out was a stimulus. Contact made with the St Vincent de Paul Society resulted in work by some of the older pupils of the school in the then appalling slums of Dublin, the founding of the Clongowes Boys Club for poor boys (a Belvedere Club was founded as well) and a Dublin housing scheme backed by the Clongowes Union. The organised group in the school did not last long and its approaches may sound patronising today but in their time they were well-intended, and not without consequences. The modern historian of Clongowes, who has compiled this information,[100] adds that the creation of the Catholic Workers' College referred to earlier can be traced to the influence of the Clongowes group on Father Edward Coyne, whom we have already met in connection with the Catholic social movement of the 1930s. In its modern form, the awareness of the boys is sharpened by a scheme of exchange visits in which boys from the Jesuit school stay for a time in the homes of under-privileged contemporaries, and vice versa.[101] How far the new thinking traceable to the Vatican Council and Father Arrupe has carried weight with ex-pupils of the Colleges awaits research. It may be found heartening, however, to note a story from the early post-concilar period:

> There were not a few quiet Jesuit cheers in October, 1971, when ten former students of Gonzaga mounted a protest picket at the gates of Castletown House where the past pupils' unions of Clongowes, Belvedere and Gonzaga were holding a £4-a-head dinner. The spending of about £3,000 on an evening's entertainment offended young radicals and many Jesuits alike.[102]

A point indeed, although, as can also be fairly said, 'radical protest . . . had charms which may not have been obvious to those who have given years of patient work to social action.[103]

A few years after the foundation of Gonzaga, Father Dermot Casey, S.J., opened St Declan's School and Child Guidance Centre in Dublin. It was not — and is not — a Jesuit institution; it is run by its own committee, but Father Casey set it up in 1958 and it therefore merits inclusion among the educational works of Irish Jesuits. It was established in the conviction that 'many nervous, highly-strung or otherwise emotionally disturbed children could be helped most effectively and more quickly in a special day school adapted to their special and individual needs.' When founded it was the only school of its kind in Ireland, and there were only three such schools in England. It continues today and many families have had the benefit of Father Casey's observation that 'a small amount of special psychological help given early on to a child and to its parents will prevent a great deal of trouble, distress and unhappiness later on'.[104]

The Provincial on whom the burden primarily fell of bringing the Irish Jesuits safely through the aftermath of Vatican II was Father Cecil McGarry, who came to office in 1968. To guide him he had the emphasis of the documents approved in 1965 and 1966 by the 31st General Congregation of the Society, which had elected Father Arrupe, as well as the exhortations which very quickly came from the new General himself. The Congregation chose two themes to stress, both of them conciliar. The first was an insistence on returning to the Society's origins, which meant developing a heightened awareness of its Founder's intentions. The second theme was the need to adapt the Society's organisation and activities to enable it better to cope with the intellectual, social and spiritual problems of the age. From the outset of his generalate Father Arrupe urged the Society to press on with this process of modernising itself in the spirit of Saint Ignatius (which involved *inter alia* Ignatian ideas of mobility and flexibility), in order that Jesuits might be able more easily to move into new areas of apostolic opportunity and need. And so 'Jesuits throughout the world began the task of integrating the decisions of the Congregation with their personal endeavours for renewal. As General, Father Arrupe indicated that he expected action. He said, "I do not want to defend any mistakes Jesuits might have made, but the greatest mistake would be to stand in such fear of making error that we would simply stop acting." '[105] Father McGarry acted promptly, to the great benefit of the Society in Ireland and to the admiration of Jesuits from other Provinces[106] which were slower to move.

It cannot have been easy. The Provincial discharged his unenviable task with courage, conviction and, it may reasonably be supposed, a degree of pain known to himself alone. While there were Jesuits in every age group who rejoiced to see the Congregation decisions implemented, what the Provincial had to do caused unhappiness to a number of older Fathers settled in their ways and harbouring no doubts concerning the work undertaken by the Irish Province in their lifetime. Also distressed were some younger men who had thrown themselves with enthusiasm into tasks given them in the recent past. If the Province was to adapt to new priorities some of the established activities would have to be curtailed, not least because of the fall in numbers which all orders began to suffer in the 1960s: eight Irish scholastics left the Jesuits in the year that Father McGarry took office,[107] which meant the intake of novices — averging seven a year[108] — did nothing to balance the natural losses through death and retirement. This imbalance was unlikely to improve. The Provincial did not act arbitrarily: he initiated internal discussions in each house to establish what the community was doing, and what it felt it should be doing. It would be no more than a small exaggeration to say that there were as many opinions as there were Jesuits.[109] But only the Provincial could make the ultimate decisions, and these involved abandoning some cherished commitments.

Perhaps his most distasteful duty was deciding where manpower could be saved. Suppression of a boarding-school was likely to bring maximum results, if only because it took so many men to provide supervision and administration as well as teaching. If a school had to go, Mungret was more vulnerable than Clongowes.[110] In the first place, there would still be a substantial Jesuit presence in Limerick between the community serving the public church and those attached to the Crescent (now the Crescent Comprehensive). Secondly, Mungret had already lost its apostolic school, which was half the reason for its existence. The Vatican Council had been the remote cause of this happening. The Council seemed to require philosophy and theology to be integrated in seminaries. Father Redmond Roche, Superior of the Apostolic School, could not see how this was to be guaranteed for the future, given the vocations crisis and an already evident shortage of competent lecturers. The vocations crisis also meant that institutions doing similar work, such as All Hallows in Dublin, were adequate to the need. The Apostolic School was accordingly suspended in 1967. The lay school, by contrast, was reaping the benefits of Father Kerr's rectorship. Demand for places constantly exceeded those available and the disappearance of the Apostolic School actually helped by removing an ambiguity from the overall purpose of Mungret. How far Clongowes was protected by its venerability as the first house of the restored Society in Ireland, or by its fame and continuing prestige, or (as was hinted *sotto voce*) by the fierce loyalty of its past pupils who would have made a far greater clamour if suppression were mooted than came from those of Mungret, must remain matter for speculation. One thing is certain. Father McGarry was not a man to flinch from any decision, however unpopular, if he believed it to be right. When he chose Mungret rather than Clongowes for suppression, it can be taken for granted that he did what he had prayerfully concluded to be his duty. Of course, there were many to say he was wrong: their arguments ranged from nostalgia to the new-found status of the lay school at Mungret and its long-established fecundity in vocations. But the critics who spoke thus were spared the responsibility of making the decision.

There were positive decisions also. In 1966 the State had proposed a scheme of 'free' — i.e. fully State-supported secondary education. Although it involved a reduction of 20 per cent in their income,[111] Coláiste Iognáid in Galway and the Crescent in Limerick entered the scheme. Now came the further proposal that the Crescent should become the keystone of a large comprehensive school of the kind outlined above in the account of developments at Gonzaga. At Dooradoyle in Limerick, under the inspired guidance of the Jesuit historian and Limerickman, Father Thomas J. Morrissey, this experiment in Irish education took off with dynamic vigour as a non-feepaying co-educational school to meet 'the diverse needs of the bright and the dull, the affluent and the

deprived'.[112] Personal initiatives received much encouragement, such as Father Michael Sweetman's protests against
inadequate housing for the poor of Dublin:[113] a stand which
inspired more than one young Jesuit to become involved in
activity for social reform and in time would result in the
services provided by Jesuits today to the socially deprived in
the suburban housing estates and the high-rise flats of the
modern capital. The teachings of the Vatican Council were
promoted by public lectures at Milltown Park which attracted
overflow audiences in the late 1960s and early 1970s.[114]

In the context of service to the Church, it may be that no
single development of recent years will turn out to have been
as significant as the generous support given by Father
McGarry to the Irish School of Ecumenics founded by Father
Michael Hurley of the Milltown community in 1970.[115] This
small but vitally important postgraduate institute offers
university degrees, nowadays from the University of Dublin
and formerly from the University of Hull, to students from
various Christian Churches and from Third World as well as
European countries who study theology together, gain first-
hand experience of one another's pastoral routine and
return to their duties in their own communions as informed
witnesses to the hope and possibility of Christian Unity. The
School functions under the patronage of senior representatives of the Roman Catholic, Church of Ireland, Presbyterian and Methodist Churches. The facilities of Milltown
Park have been made available to the School from the outset
and its international character was confirmed by the attendance of then General Secretary of the World Council of
Churches, Dr Eugene Carson Blake, at its formal inaugu-
ration in Milltown, where he delivered the opening address.
International Consultations on such topics as Mixed Marriages
and Human Rights have confirmed its repute. It has developed
a Centre for Peace Studies which underlines its significance
not only for the ecumenical movement in contemporary
Christendom but also for an Ireland still disrupted by violence
and tensions in the North which have deep roots in the
religious division of the past.

The emergence under Jesuit auspices of this independent
educational body, together with the attainment by the Milltown

Institute of pontifical university status, can stand for the quality of Cecil McGarry's leadership of the Irish Province. But it may well be that his ultimate memorial will be the option for the poor exercised today by Father Peter McVerry and other Jesuit champions of the homeless and deprived. Much of this began only after Father McGarry's term as Provincial ended in 1974 but it was his determination to give the Province a new direction, in obedience to the General Congregation and to Father Arrupe, that made possible an Irish Jesuit emphasis reminiscent of the old Mission dedicated to the poor of the Liberties and the dispossessed of the penal towns and countryside.

In 1974 the Society of Jesus was preparing for another General Congregation where momentous changes would be initiated which the next historian of the Irish Province will doubtless examine. For the present writer, this great event belongs so fully to the realm of current affairs that it cannot yet be brought within the bounds of history. What can be said is that the 350 Jesuits in Ireland that year lived in a Province of the Society which had been refurbished and prepared for whatever challenge might come. Wolfe and Nugent, Austin, Kenney and Delany could be assured that the ideal of Saint Ignatius was intact and that their spiritual heirs would see to it that God was made known through the activity proper to Jesuits of discerning and serving their neighbours' most pressing needs. Salmeron and Broet, no doubt, looked down in wonder and saintly puzzlement.

NOTES

Chapter 1, pp 11–46

1 Morrissey, 12.
2 Morrissey, 7.
3 Duanaire, 15. (This verse and those referred to in notes 4, 5, 7, 12, 13 and 33 are taken from poems in the first section of *An Duanaire*, described by the editor as 'echoes of the world before Kinsale, when love, learning, religion and human behaviour could be contemplated at leisure.')
4 Duanaire, 5.
5 Duanaire, 5.
6 Morrissey, 16.
7 Duanaire, 5.
8 Nicholls, Oxford II, 403; Quinn and Nicholls, Oxford III, 34–5.
9 Nicholls, Oxford II, 413; Quinn and Nicholls, Oxford III, 35.
10 Butlin, Oxford III, 152.
11 Toynbee, 154–6, 416.
12 Duanaire, 17.
13 Duanaire, 19.
14 Hayes-McCoy, Oxford III, 67.
15 Martin, Oxford II, 123.
16 Morrissey, 11.
17 Bangert, 58.
18 See Father Fergus O'Donoghue, S.J., on this point in *Studies*, Spring, 1991.
19 Bangert, 25.
20 Morrissey, 7.
21 Memorials, I, I, 6.
22 Morrissey, 21.
23 Morrissey, 32.
24 Morrissey, 30–32.
25 Bangert, 26–28.
26 Morrissey, 17.
27 Memorials, I, I, 7.
28 Morrissey, 56.
29 Morrissey, 39.
30 Hayes-McCoy, Oxford III, 138.
31 ibid.
32 Morrissey, 38.

33 Duanaire, 63.
34 Silke, Oxford III, 592.
35 Boylan, 76.
36 Hayes-McCoy, Oxford III, 90.
37 Hughes, III, 418–420 (text of Bull *Regnans in Excelsia*).
38 Morrissey, 47.
39 Morrissey, 91–6.
40 Bangert, 83 (quoting Brodrick, *The Progress of the Jesuits*, pp 234–5). If, however, Daniel was executed solely because he was an envoy of Fitzmaurice (see Morrissey, 97) it could be argued that he died as a rebel rather than 'for the faith'. In that case the distinction of being the Jesuit proto-martyr in Europe belongs to the English priest, Thomas Woodhouse, who was admitted to the Society while awaiting execution in the Tower of London. Basset (17) says Woodhouse was hanged in 1571, which would make him the proto-martyr in any event, but Bangert (83) gives the year as 1573.
41 Memorials, I, I, 9. A question arises whether O'Donnell (or as he is sometimes called, McDonnell) was not in fact the same man as Edmund Daniel, referred to in the previous note! Some accounts seem to assume this to be the case. The Memorials say nothing about Daniel's death and claim that O'Donnell was the first Jesuit martyr in Ireland. But this could be because of Daniel's political involvement (see previous note). The similarity of name and location, both of of ministry (Limerick) and execution (Cork), suggests a possible confusion. On the other hand, we are told a little more about the O'Donnell execution than the Daniel execution; the years of execution differ; so does the status accorded to the names (Daniel, a scholastic; O'Donnell, a priest). The list of 'Jesuits connected with the Irish Mission' (Memorials, I, II, eleven unnumbered pages following page 131) includes both Edmund Daniel and Edmund O'Donnell quite separately among those who entered the Society in 1561. The list also names 'Edmond of Ireland' as an entrant in 1555 and Father Bangert says (83), on the authority of Father Brodrick, that Daniel was known as 'Edmund the Irishman'. The present writer has opted for the likelihood of two men, who suffered death on different occasions, because this seems the most probable resolution of the bewildering nuggets of information and it avoids the danger of doing a historical injustice by omitting recognition of a Jesuit who died for his faith.
42 Memorials, I, I, 10.
43 ibid.
44 Morrissey, 72.
45 Morrissey, 42.
46 ibid.
47 Hayes-McCoy, Oxford III, 104.
48 Daniel-Rops, V, 334.
49 Bangert, 133.
50 Daniel-Rops, V, 334.
51 This neutral statement from Bangert, 82, is about as much as can usefully be said for want of any other evidence to explain what happened. It is important to stress that Father Wolfe seems to have remained on friendly terms with the General, Father Mercurian.
52 I am indebted to Father Morrissey's thesis for virtually all the factual information on this and the following pages concerning Archer's career, related events and quotations.
53 Hughes, III, 385.
54 Bangert, 121–3, 128–31.

55 Bangert, 104.
56 Silke, Oxford III, 614.
57 Morrissey, 294.
58 Morrissey, 357.
59 Memorials, I, I, 13–14. The attempt by Mountjoy (acting directly or through subordinates) to persuade Collins to become a Protestant and the words attributed to the Jesuit before his death are important to establish martyrdom since it could otherwise be argued that he was executed as a rebel taken *flagrante delicto* rather than because he stood by his religious beliefs.
60 Morrissey, 266.
61 Daniel-Rops, V, 183.
62 Clarke, Oxford III, 190–91.
63 Memorials, I, I, 20.
64 Memorials, I, I, 16.
65 Basset, 124.
66 These stories of the Holywood mission and the details provided in the succeeding paragraphs are taken from Memorials, I, I, 18–36, which in turn are based on contemporary records (mainly Holywood's reports to the Father General in Rome). Father Fergus O'Donoghue points out that, among the names arising in this connection, O'Kearney was Wall's nephew, although they were almost of the same age. They accompanied one another on their preaching trips.
67 Seathrún Céitinn (Geoffrey Keating), Duanaire, 85.
68 Silke, Oxford III, 624.
69 Silke, Oxford III, 619.
70 Memorials, I, I, 5.
71 Morrissey, 39.
72 Bangert, 14.
73 Silke, Oxford III, 614.
74 Clarke, Oxford III, 227.
75 Silke, Oxford III, 625.
76 Ó Cuív, Oxford III, 513.

Chapter 2, pp 47–84

1   Memorials, I, I, 15.
2   Bangert, 168, 258–9. The village settlements started in 1610 and Father Filde was working in Paraguay until 1626, when he died in Asunción (McErlean, Irish Jesuits, 58).
3   Bangert, 200–201.
4   Bangert, 219.
5   Daniel-Rops, VI, 141.
6   Basset, 176seq.
7   Bangert, 115–16.
8   Bangert, 155–7, 241–2.
9   Bangert, 242–5.
10 Bangert, 147.
11 O'Donoghue, 251.
12 Memorials (Short Memoirs), 25. The Barons Delvin were Nugents. The 12th Baron was created Earl of Westmeath in 1621 (Debrett, 1965, 1126).
13 O'Donoghue, 209.
14 O'Donoghue, 273, 277.
15 These developments are summarised in Oxford, VIII, 227–8.
16 O'Donoghue, 194.

17 O'Donoghue, 196–8.
18 O'Donoghue, 203. The foundation is sometimes referred to as a 'Jesuit university', but this is hyperbole.
19 Oxford VIII, 229. O'Donoghue, 246.
20 O'Donoghue, 201–3.
21 Factual details in this and the following paragraph are taken from O'Donoghue, 203–5.
22 O'Donoghue, 202.
23 Basset, 140.
24 O'Donoghue, 203.
25 Basset, 164.
26 See Basset, 140–42, for a contemporary account of these conditions.
27 Millet, Oxford III, 563.
28 Basset, 169–71.
29 Basset, 194.
30 Factual details in this paragraph are taken from O'Donoghue, 224–5, 242–4.
31 Clarke, Oxford III, 264.
32 O'Donoghue, 239.
33 O'Donoghue, 188.
34 Coonan, 49.
35 Coonan, 47–9.
36 Clarke, Oxford III, 264.
37 O'Donoghue, 189.
38 Memorials, I, VII, 326.
39 O'Donoghue, 272. The Nugent family had long-standing associations with the Irish language. 'One of the most important sixteenth-century manuscript collections of verse that has survived was handed down in the Nugent family of Delvin, and it contains a collection of poems for members of that family, one of whom was himself the author of poems in Irish.' (Ó Cuív, Oxford III, 522). When it was reported that Queen Elizabeth had expressed a wish to learn the language, the ninth Baron Delvin 'compiled a little primer of Irish' to help her! (Ó Cuív, op. cit., 511)
40 O'Donoghue, 345.
41 O'Donoghue, 302, 310.
42 O'Donoghue, 328 (footnote).
43 O'Donoghue, 345 (footnote).
44 O'Donoghue, 201.
45 O'Donoghue, 340.
46 O'Donoghue, 275.
47 O'Donoghue, 211–12.
48 O'Donoghue, 215.
49 Silke, Oxford III, 621.
50 Except as otherwise indicated, the account of the colleges which follows is based on Morrissey, Education, I, 7–74.
51 Bangert, 195.
52, 53 Silke, Oxford III, 620.
54 O'Donoghue, 212.
55 Silke, Oxford III, 621.
56 Silke, Oxford III, 628.
57 Memorials, I, V, 241–50.
58 Memorials, I, VI, 297–8.
59 Coonan, 139–41.
60 Coonan, 69.

61 Coonan, 122.
62 Coonan, 88–9. (The feast-day of Saint Ignatius is in fact 31 July).
63 Except as otherwise indicated, the account of the Jesuit Mission and the other religious orders during the Confederate and Cromwellian years (i.e. to the end of the present chapter) is based on the fully documented information in O'Donoghue, 258–364.
64 Coonan, 95.
65 Memorials (Short Memoirs), 15.
66 Bangert, 177.
67 Daniel-Rops, VI, 141.
68 The complex series of negotiations which culminated in this outcome, involving Rinuccini, the Supreme Council, Ormond and Inchiquin, are detailed in Corish, Oxford III, 327–35.
69 McErlean, Irish Jesuits, 63.
70 Memorials, I, VII, 317.
71 Basset, 148.
72 Ashley, 230–31.
73 Churchill, II, 230, 232.
74 Memorials, I, VII, 318.
75 Memorials, I, VII, 320. The diocesan priest was Thomas. The third brother, the Jesuit Father Robert Bathe, had either left Drogheda or escaped discovery. We know that Robert was not permanently resident in Drogheda because Verdier met him (see page 74) and Verdier did not visit Drogheda.
76 Memorials, I, VII, 323.
77 Memorials, I, VII, 322.
78 Memorials, I, VII, 321.
79 Memorials, I, VII, 328–9. Father Gellow's name is sometimes given as 'Gelouse'.
80 Bangert, 177.
81 Duanaire, 105.
82 Coonan, 308.
83 Memorials, I, VII, 324.
84 Duanaire, 103.
85 See Corish, Oxford III, 363 and 383–4, for a balanced account of the policy and practice regarding transportation to the West Indies.
86 McErlean, Irish Jesuits, 31.
87 Memorials, I, VII, 318.
88 McErlean, Irish Jesuits, 63. Silke, Oxford III, 631.
89, 90 Corish, Oxford III, 384. Bangert, 236 (re Ford).
91 Memorials, I, V, 243.
92 Memorials, I, VII, 319.
93 McErlean, Irish Jesuits, 36.
94 McErlean, Irish Jesuits, 40.
95 Memorials, I, VII, 329.
96 Memorials, I, V, 248–9.
97 McErlean, Irish Jesuits, 31.
98 Silke, Oxford III, 614.
99 McErlean, Irish Jesuits, 31–3.
100 McErlean, Irish Jesuits, 33.
101 McErlean, Irish Jesuits, 35.

Chapter 3, pp 85–130

1 Simms, Oxford III, 426.
2 Simms, Oxford III, 448–453.

3   Simms, Oxford III, 452.
4–5 Simms, Oxford III, 449.
6   Duanaire, 111.
7   Duanaire, 95.
8   Simms, 431.
9   The factual information, but not the comment, in this and the following two paragraphs is taken from McErlean, Irish Jesuits, 11–13, unless otherwise indicated.
10   Howard, *Studies*, Summer 1969, 197. No fewer than 56 clerical students were attending these schools in 1672. Of the 150 lay boys, 40 were Protestants: this led to the kind of pressure on the Dublin administration mentioned in the following paragraph and the schools were forced to close at the end of 1673. (Howard, op. cit., 197–8).
11   Simms, Oxford III, 430.
12   Memorials, I, VII, 330.
13   Howard, *Studies*, Summer 1969, 195, 197. Another victim of the Titus Oates affair was the Archbishop of Dublin, Peter Talbot, a former Jesuit who had resigned from the Society. He was charged with complicity in the 'Popish Plot' and imprisoned in Dublin Castle, where he died (Boylan, 378). His brother, John, was a Jesuit on the Irish Mission (Memorials, I, VII, 327) and another brother, Richard, became Earl of Tyrconnell and James II's Viceroy of Ireland.
14   Howard, *Studies*, Summer 1969, 198.
15   Howard, *Studies*, Summer 1969, 197–8, 202.
16   Millet, Oxford III, 562.
17   Howard, *Studies*, Summer 1969, 200. Simms, Oxford III, 447–8.
18   Memorials, I, VII, 330.
19   McErlean, Irish Jesuits, 33, 35–6.
20, 21, 22 Bangert, 200–204.
23   McErlean, Irish Jesuits, 36.
24   McErlean, Irish Jesuits, 12.
25   Silke, Oxford III, 632–3.
26   Simms, Oxford III, 433–4.
27   Simms, Oxford III, 435.
28   Memorials, I, II, eleven unnumbered pages inserted after page 131.
29   McErlean, Irish Jesuits, 35.
30   Memorials, I, VII, 328. Scope for an ecumenical evaluation of Andrew Sall was indicated by Rev. Terence MacCaughey of the Presbyterian Church and Trinity College, Dublin, in a lecture at Milltown Park on 14 November, 1990. Sall's conversion to the Church of Ireland would seem to have been actuated solely by conscience and, whatever about the 'polemical' nature of some of his public statements, he never criticised the Jesuits.
31   McErlean, Irish Jesuits, 38.
32   Silke, Oxford III, 621.
33   The factual information about Father Brown in this paragraph is taken from Memorials, I, VII, 327–8.
34   McErlean, Irish Jesuits, 40.
35   McErlean, Irish Jesuits, 42.
36   McErlean, Irish Jesuits, 43.
37   McErlean, Irish Jesuits, 38.
38   Basset, 259.
39   In this and the following paragraph, unless otherwise indicated, the factual details regarding the English Province during the reign of James II and the quotations from earlier writers are taken from Basset, 256–71.

40   Simms, Oxford III, 483.
41   In this and the following paragraphs, unless otherwise indicated, the factual details regarding King James's policy in Ireland and the Jacobite-Williamite war are taken from Simms, Oxford III, 478–508
42   Petrie, 460 .
43   Basset 268–69.
44   McErlean, Irish Jesuits, 42 .
45   McErlean, Irish Jesuits, 43–4.
46   Simms, Oxford III, 505 .
47   The details of the penal legislation which follow are taken from Oxford IV, 17–20 (Simms) and 37–8 (McCracken).
48   Basset, 269 .
49   The facts about Father Knoles in the following paragraphs and the extracts from his correspondence are taken from McErlean, Irish Jesuits, 44–5, and Memorials, I, VII, 331.
50   Ó Ríordáin, 58 .
51   Petrie, 157–8, 291–3.
52   Bangert, 196.
53   Father McErlean's phrasing .
54   McCracken, Oxford IV, 96 .
55   McCracken, Oxford IV, 92 .
56   McErlean, Irish Jesuits, 80.
57, 58 McErlean, Irish Jesuits, 46. Father Michael FitzGerald, a future Superior of the Mission, is the only name we have of a Jesuit residing in Galway at this time (McErlean, op. cit., 48).
59   McCracken, IV, 92, 94.
60   Ó Ríordáin, 53.
61   Duanaire, 151.
62, 63 Ó Ríordáin, 53 and 56, (translations of Gaelic prayers taken from *Our Mass our Life* by Diarmaid Ó Laoghaire, S.J.).
64   See Ó Ríordáin, 62, for a visitor's observations in Galway.
65   McErlean, Irish Jesuits, 45, 47.
66   Corish, 135.
67   Ó Ríordáin, 60.
68   Corish, 133.
69   The information which follows about devotion to the Sacred Heart is taken from Purcell, Message, 16–17.
70   Duanaire, 191.
71   Purcell, 16.
72, 73 McErlean, Irish Jesuits, 14. Father John St Leger, S.J., a native of Waterford, returned to his native city in 1742. It is recorded that 'with the aid of his friends in Spain he built the Church and Residence of St Patrick in Waterford, and for thirty-one years he had the charge of the parishes of St Patrick and St Olave in that city' (Memorials, I, VII, 334).
74   The biographical details in this and the following paragraph are taken from McErlean, Irish Jesuits, 47–8.
75   Unless otherwise stated, the factual information about the Dublin Jesuits in this and the following paragraphs is taken from McErlean, Irish Jesuits, 13–15 and (with Corcoran) 79–83.
76   Text in O'Riordan, Reportorium Novum, I, I, 140–53.
77, 78 McCracken, Oxford IV, 93.
79   The factual information about Dr Nary is taken from Meagher, Reportorium Novum, II, I, 129–38
80   Text in Brady, Reportorium Novum, II, I, 218–19.

81 McCracken, Oxford IV, 95.

82 McCracken, Oxford IV, 89.

83, 84 McCracken, Oxford IV, 95.

85 Estimate based on Cullen, Oxford IV, 161.

86 Ó Cuív, Oxford IV, 380.

87 Beckett, Oxford IV, li.

88 Corish, 138.

89 Foster, 208, quoting Corish, *The Catholic Community in the Seventeenth and Eighteenth Centuries* (Dublin 1981).

90 Bangert, 44.

91 The factual information about Fathers Austin, Bethagh and Mulcaile in this and the following paragraphs, together with quotations from their contemporaries, is taken from Memorials, I, VII, 333–337; Corcoran, Irish Jesuits, 83–5; and Burke Savage, Irish Jesuits, 103–5. The quotation from Charles Bowden is attributed to 'a work entitled "Tours through Ireland", published in 1791' (Memorials, I. VII, 334).

92 Ganss, par. 451. N.B. References to Ganss are to the numbered *paragraphs* of the Constitutions, not to pages.

93 Ganss, footnote to par. 451.

94, 95, 96 Ganss, pars. 447, 448, 451.

97, 98 Ganss, pars. 446, 447.

99, 100 Ganss, pars. 392, 395.

101, 102 Ganss, par. 623.

103 McCracken, Oxford IV, 39.

104 Simms, Oxford IV, 645.

105 '[Father Betagh] rewarded the most promising of them with a classical education. . . .' (Dr Blakes's sermon. Corcoran, Irish Jesuits, 85).

106 A Spanish diplomat's impression of their views at the time (Bangert, 364).

107 Daniel-Rops, VII, 219.

108 Bangert, 381.

109 Bangert, 372.

110 Bangert,387.

111 Daniel-Rops, VII, 70 .

112 Tocqueville, 129.

113 Tocqueville, 130.

114 Bangert, 372–9.

115 Bangert, 380. 'What is least forgivable in the Jansenists is that seeing the world as a *massa damnationis*, rushing to its own ruin, they could find no other remedy for its unhappiness but to make war on the Jesuits.' (Monsignor Ronald Knox, *Enthusiasm*, 203).

116 Bangert, 381.

117, 118 Daniel-Rops, VII, 219.

119 Bangert, 336, 410.

120 Daniel-Rops, VII, 220.

121 Daniel-Rops, VII, 219.

122 Bangert, 364.

123 Bangert, 381–2.

124 Daniel-Rops, VII, 220.

125 Daniel-Rops, VII, 218. It took a long time for the Papacy to concede that Pope Clement had submitted to improper pressure. But in the course of an address to Jesuit Provincials and the Assistants and Councillors of the General Curia on 27 February 1982, Pope John Paul II referred to 'the Society of Jesus which the enemies of Christ persecuted until they obtained its suppression'.

320   *To the Greater Glory*

(*Religious Life Review*, May-June 1982, 151). The then Irish Provincial, Father Joseph Dargan, was present and wrote afterwards of this papal address that 'There were many aspects of the Allocution which gave me a great sense of joy and hope. The most surprising part was when the Pope referred to the suppression of the Jesuits and said that this had been brought about by the enemies of Christ. This was the first time that any Pontiff had made such an admission' (op. cit., 145).

126 John, 18.38–19.12.
127 Bangert, 379.
128 References to the English Jesuits on the continent and in England from here to the end of the chapter are based, unless otherwise stated, on Basset, 319– 59.
129 The sources for the following account of the impact of the Suppression on the Irish Jesuits, unless otherwise stated, are Memorials, I, III, 133–150, and Burke-Savage, Irish Jesuits, 101–13.
130 Corish, Experience, 127.
131 Carpenter to Nuncio, 25 Sept 1773 (Curran, Reportorium Novum, I, I, 162).
132 Carpenter to Nuncio, 28 April 1774. (Curran, Reportorium Novum, I, I, 164).
133 Carpenter to Cardinal Marefoschi (Protector of Ireland), 11 Dec 1773; subsequent correspondence: Marefoschi to Carpenter, 26 Jan 1774; Carpenter to Marefoschi, 4 May 1774 (Curran, Reportorium Novum, I, I, 163).
134 Bangert, 402.
135 Carpenter to Sweetman, 23 Feb 1774 (Curran, Reportorium Novum, I, II, 400). In Waterford the Bishop gave dramatic demonstration of his faith in the Jesuits: 'at the time of the Suppression Dr William Egan, then Bishop of the diocese, declared St Patrick's a parish church, and appointed Father St Leger its first Parish Priest and Father Paul Power to be his assistant' (Memorials, I, VII, 334). For Father St Leger, see Note 72 above. Father Power was also a Jesuit (Burke Savage, Irish Jesuits, 113).
136 Wall, Reportorium Novum, I, I, 173–82.
137 Carpenter to Pastors and Superiors, 27 Oct 1780 (Curran, Reportorium Novum, II, I, 168).
138 Carpenter, pastoral letters, 1774–1775 (Curran, Reportorium Novum, II, I, 156–157).
139 Basset, 343–344 .
140 MacDonagh, I, 18. Father Harrington is buried in Templerobin Churchyard, Ballymore, Cobh. The tombstone erected by his pupils does not refer to his former membership of the Society (Yearbook, 1966, 96).
141 Taine, 342 .
142 Taine, 343 .

Chapter 4, pp 131–70

1 Daniel-Rops, VII, 242.
2 Estimate based on Daniel-Rops, VII, 244.
3 Bangert, 413.
4 Bangert, 405.
5 Bangert, 406.
6 Daniel-Rops, VII, 138.
7, 8, 9 Bangert, 416–18.
10 Unless otherwise stated, the account which follows of developments in England is based on Basset, 365–76.
11 The Archbishop's query arose from his concern regarding the Irish Jesuit Mission Funds, which he feared might be sent to the Jesuits in Russia. He knew of the compact between the ex-Jesuits and claimed that Archbishop

Carpenter had also known of it. When only two ex-Jesuits remained alive in Ireland (O'Callaghan and Betagh), Troy felt that the money should have been transferred to the Bishops but instead it had been willed to Stone by O'Callaghan. This, he argued, would have been justified only if the Jesuits had been restored. It was claimed that they had been restored in England and he sought clarification from Propaganda. This brought firm denials that there had been any restoration.

The Curia officials were more circumspect in conversation in Rome, where one of them told an agent of Troy's that he believed the Jesuits did not exist in the British Empire but that he could not swear to it! The agent wrote to Troy, 'I fear the ex-Jesuits have outwitted Propaganda and you all and that you will never touch a farthing of their money. The good but weak Mr Paul (Pius VII) is easily imposed upon . . . Such an artful and political body of men never existed. Tho' struggling now between life and death, they are daily publishing new works of lax doctrine. . . .'

Stone, in turn, waxed indignant with Troy for suggesting to Propaganda that the Jesuits might have been restored in England by a papal instruction given orally: the possibility had been raised by Stone in 1803 when he asked Troy to support a request to the Pope to do so but Troy should not have used Stone's phrase in writing to Rome. The English Provincial then expressed surprise that Troy would attempt to upset the disposition of property by a British subject by invoking 'the Spiritual Power' (It had been a serious offence since long before the Reformation to appeal to Rome against the provisions of English law).

The Archbishop was in fact boxed in. He could not himself put ecclesiastical pressure on Stone without risking prosecution under civil law. He could not initiate a civil action to dispute the will without producing the agreement between the ex-Jesuits and thereby risking seizure of the funds by the government on the ground that O'Callaghan's bequest had been for 'a superstitious use' or some other purpose still forbidden under the penal code. He could not even persuade Propaganda to bring pressure on Stone confidentially since Propaganda suspected, but could not aver, that the Pope had done something without the knowledge of the Congregation . . . as he had. The Pope had to be extremely cautious because of the French presence in Rome.

It should be stressed that Archbishop Troy, as he said himself, had 'no enmity against the Jesuits'. His anxiety was to preserve the funds for the purposes of the Irish Church. He was encouraged in this objective by his belief that some of the original funds might have been for the Irish colleges on the continent administered by the Jesuits before the Suppression, especially the Irish College in Rome.

(The information in this note regarding communications between Dublin, Rome and Stonyhurst has been kindly supplied by Father Henry Peel, O.P., from his researches into Archbishop Troy's 'Roman Correspondence' in the Dublin Diocesan Archives.)

12 Corcoran, Irish Jesuits, 86.
13 Unless otherwise stated, the account which follows of Irish developments up to the Restoration (including the early careers of future members of the Mission) is based on Memorials, I, I, 36–41 and I, IV, 187–204; and Burke Savage, Irish Jesuits, 86–91 and 109–12.
14 Possibly at the same time as Father O'Brien but the record is ambiguous.
15 Burke, 909; Costello 32. He resigned the Governorship 'as a protest against Lord John Russell's Papal Aggression Bill' (Memorials, I, VII, 343).
16 Text in Memorials I, II, 108–113.

17   McErlean, Irish Jesuits, 80–81.
18, 19 Pakenham, 110.
20   Pakenham, 124.
21   Unless otherwise stated, the account of the controversy which follows is based on Connolly, Oxford V, 36–55.
22   Corcoran, Irish Jesuits, 84.
23   Newman, 138.
24   Burke Savage, Irish Jesuits, 89.
25   Newman, 138; Burke Savage, Irish Jesuits, 90.
26   Text in Memorials, I, V, 265–9.
27   Memorials, I, IV, 204.
28   Memorials, I, VI, 306. The efforts made by Archbishop Troy of Dublin are outlined in Note 11 above.
29   Costello, 18.
30   Basset, 367.
31   Memorials, I, IV, 203.
32   Memorials, I, V, 270–71.
33, 34 Memorials, I, V, 268.
35, 36 Burke Savage, Irish Jesuits, 112.
37   Memorials, I, I, 41 and I, VI, 302.
38   Memorials, I, VI, 303; Burke Savage, Irish Jesuits, 97.
39   Ligthart, 102 .
40   Costello, 18.
41   Father John Grene in Memorials, I, VI, 305 .
42   Memorials, seriatim: e.g James McDonnell (entered 1822, sent to Rome and France); Michael Kelly (1822, to France); Robert More O'Ferrall (1823, to France); John Grehan (1843, to France); Edward Kernan (1839, to France and Belgium); Denis Murphy (1848, to France and Germany) .
43   Saxony was a Protestant country but the royal family was Catholic. Wogan Browne served 'as aide-de-camp to the king, by whom he was created a baron and made governor of Dresden and Commander of the Guards. . .he marched with Napoleon to the siege of Moscow' (Costello, 248). It would be interesting to learn whether he met any Jesuits on his progress across White Russia. Fourteen members of the Society in fact died while tending the sick and wounded stragglers of the Napoleonic army taken prisoner during its bitter retreat (Bangert 426).
44   In the middle ages, *Silva de Clongow*, from the Irish *Coill Cluana Gabhan* (the wood by the smith's meadow).
45   Costello, 24, where it is estimated that 'fifty guineas would be about £3, 500 in today's money'.
46   M. Sweetman, S.J., *The Clongownian*, 1964, 7.
47   MacDonagh, II, 127 .
48   MacDonagh, II, 192.
49   Bradley, 10.
50, 51, 52 Costello, 21–2. Among the points made by Father Kenney was his refusal to exclude Protestant pupils: his legal adviser, Denys Scully, had recommended him to take this line in dealings with the government to avoid the hazards raised by a recent court judgment against schools intended exclusively for Catholics (Costello, loc. cit.; Scully, 493).
53   Memorials, I, I, 49 and I, II, 102. Burke Savage, Irish Jesuits, 112.
54   Memorials, I, VI, 309–10; I, II, 122–3; I, III, 174–7.
55   Pakenham, Index.
56   Kee, 122.

57 Scully, 514 (footnote).
58 The account of the episode given here is based on letters of Father Kenney to
    Denys Scully from Clongowes, 29 May and 3 June 1814, from which this and
    the longer quotation (below) are also taken. Text in Scully, 512–16.
59 Costello, 22–3. Scully, 511. The significance of the Church of Ireland bishop's
    licence in such cases is obscure and merits more examination than can be
    undertaken here. I am indebted to Father Roland Burke Savage, S.J., for
    drawing my attention to the Catholic Relief Act of 1792 which removed the
    obligation on a Catholic to secure the licence 'to keep or teach school'. This,
    however, left open a range of questions touching the legality of the purpose
    for which property was bought, the endowment of schools for Catholics and
    the rights (if any) of religious orders. Denys Scully was the leading authority of
    the day on the penal laws and he guided the founder of Clongowes with great
    care through this quagmire in which the law was far from settled and quite
    recent judgments of the senior courts were ambiguous.
        Although he saw no positive value in the bishop's licence beyond the
    exemption it would provide from liability for window tax, Scully clearly
    considered that the safe course amid the legal uncertainties was to acquire
    such a licence. He gave Kenney detailed instructions on how to make his
    application and even stressed the importance of winning the appropriate
    Registrar's support by a promise that his fees would not be forgotten! Only
    when difficulties arose (of a bureaucratic rather than sectarian nature) did
    Kenney elect to proceed unlicensed.
        As it happened, from 1807 a licence giving exemption from window tax
    could have been had on application to the magistrates, a course apparently not
    considered in the case of Clongowes. It must therefore be assumed that
    Scully's and Kenney's interest in getting a *bishop's* licence had implications
    beyond mere tax avoidance. For what it may be worth, the present writer's
    belief is that a licence issued by a C. of I. bishop was seen as valuable evidence
    to produce if the Catholic purposes of the institution were invoked to negate
    a purchase or endowment. If a bishop of the Established Church had given
    permission for the enterprise, an illegal or 'superstitious' purpose could not
    easily be argued without impugning the bishop.
        Father Kenney's anxiety continued, despite the assurances he had received
    on the legality of opening the school. In February, 1815, he wrote to Scully
    from Clongowes: 'I am uneasy about this house & I beg that you will give a
    leisure moment to think, if there yet remain any legal move of putting it out of
    grasp.' More than a year later Sir Henry Parnell was saying that 'Mr Kenney's
    alarms have no foundation . . . he need not torment himself by giving way to
    them.' His fear, of course, was that the anti-Jesuit sentiments of a section of
    English opinion would provoke proceedings against the school. These
    proceedings would have had to be grounded in the provisions of the law and
    against these the Rector obviously felt insecure. The protection which he most
    obviously lacked was a bishop's licence.
        (The information and speculation in this note are based on Scully, 233–4
    [footnote], 493–5, 496–7, 510–11, 536, 584.)
60, 61 Basset, 370–372
62 Costello 22.
63 Memorials, I, I, 36.
64 Memorials, I, III, 157.
65 Memorials, I, II, 102.
66, 67 Costello, 26–27. Memorials, I, VI, 310.
68 Costello, 27–28.

69   Ganss, 83.
70   Memorials, I, II, 93.
71   Memorials, I, II, 116.
72   Memorials, I, II, 92.
73   Memorials, I, III, 169.
74   Bangert, 495.
75   Text of letters, from which this account of his adventures is taken: Memorials, I, II, 114–16.
76, 77 Memorials, I, VI, 310.
78   Memorials, I, VI, 311.
79   Andrews, Portraits, 139.
80   McErlean, Irish Jesuits, 81. Costello, 20.
81   Memorials, I, VI, 311 and Centenary (Restoration), 13.
82   Costello, 20.
83   Except as otherwise indicated, the factual information in this and the following paragraph on the St Leger brothers and Tullabeg is based on the obituaries by Father John Curtis, from which the quotations about Father John St Leger are also taken. The obituaries are published in Memorials, I, II, 104–6.
84   Basset, 370.
85   Costello, 31–2.
86   MacDonagh, I, 267.
87   Costello, 32. Kildare petition text, Memorials, I, I, 46.
88   Costello, 32. Basset, 391.
89   An unsuccessful application under the Act for a summons against the English Jesuits was made in London as late as 1902 (Basset, 391). In Ireland a member of the Educational Endowments Commission, Anthony Traill, FTCD, argued in the 1880s that the Jesuits were 'an Order not recognised by law', to which the Commission's chairman, Lord Justice Gerald Fitzgibbon, responded that their 'position in the history of learning and education is above the reach of Dr Traill's protest.' (Morrissey, Education, I, 211).
90   Burke Savage, Irish Jesuits, 92.
91   Memorials, I, VI, 310.
92   Memorials, I, III, 134.
93   Latitude of this kind seems in fact to have been exercised more widely. Before the Suppression about half of all pupils in Jesuit schools paid nothing while others paid something (information per Father Fergus O'Donoghue). No doubt these payments were in the nature of affordable voluntary contributions and, if they were not *demanded* by the Jesuits, the Ignatian principle need not have been offended: the Jesuits *did* accept alms — indeed, sometimes depended on them. Many of the schools on the continent enjoyed a 100 per cent endowment from wealthy patrons, which obviated the need for other support; part of the problem in English-speaking countries, as will be seen, was the paucity of endowment. But, at Clongowes, fee payments were demanded from the outset. Hence the question raised in the text.
94   Bangert, 435.
95   Details regarding this and other features of the evolution of Tullabeg will be found in Morrissey, Education, I, 267seq.
96, 97 Basset, 403.
98, 99, 100 Morrissey, Education, I, viii.
101   Except where otherwise indicated, the Clongowes charges are taken from Costello, 82.
102   Morrissey, Delany, 44 (Tullabeg Prospectus, 1877).
103   FitzGerald, *The Clongownian*, 1989, 56.

104 The author makes no apology for this deeply held, if undoubtedly subjective, conviction regarding the status of Clongowes!
105 Bradley, 81.
106 Andrews, Portraits, 137.
107 Morrissey, I, 192seq.
108 Morrissey, I, 178seq.
109 Unless otherwise stated, the information and quotations in this and the following paragraphs concerning the Maryland and Missouri Missions are taken from Bangert, 267–8, 479–85, 492–5.
110 Beards, 173.
111 Memorials, I, III, 153.
112, 113 Memorials, I, III, 154.
114 Memorials, I, IV, 211.
115 Burke Savage, Irish Jesuits, 98.
116 Memorials, I, IV, 213.
117 Memorials, I, II, 89.
118 Costello, 28.
119, 120, 121 Bishop Charles Sughrue of Kerry to Father Aylmer, 26 August 1819; Father Plowden to Father Kenney, 24 September 1819. Texts in Memorials, I, III, 152.
122 Basset, 377.
123 Memorials, I, VI, 312.
124 Memorials, I, I, 50 and I, VI, 309–10.
125, 126 Bangert, 433–5. Memorials, I, II, 123 (Clongowes community list, 1820–21) and I, VI, 312.
127 Memorials, Centenary (Milltown), 14.
128 Memorials, Centenary (Milltown), 15, 32, 33.
129 Memorials, I, III, 170.
130 Memorials, Centenary (Milltown), 15.
131 MacLoughlin, 46.
132 Memorials, Centenary (Restoration), 43.
133 Costello, 20.
134 Craig, 292. See also MacLoughlin, 56.
135 Memorials, I, III, 157.
136 Craig, note 2, 306.
137 Craig, 292.
138 Craig, Index, 357.
139, 140 Memorials, Centenary (Restoration), 43.
141 Shaw, under 'Mount-street, Lower' and in list of City occupiers, pages unnumbered.
142 Memorials, Centenary (Restoration), 44, 45.
143 McRedmond, 156–7.

Chapter 5, pp 171–225

1 e.g. by J. H. Newman. See Tristram 323.
2 Burke, 908–9.
3 Obituary by Father Curtis: Memorials, I, II, 102.
4 Andrews, Portaits, 131.
5 Memorials, I, II, 103–4.
6 Memorials, I, II, 107.
7, 8 Andrews, Portraits, 132.
9 Andrews, Portraits, 140.
10 MacLoughlin, 49.

326   *To the Greater Glory*

11 Andrews, Portraits, 141fn
12, 13 Craig, 230–31.
14 Unless otherwise indicated, the factual information (but not the comment) about Belvedere College which follows in this section is taken from Andrews, Portraits, 133–59.
15 MacDonagh, II, 202seq.
16 Shaw, under streets named (pages unnumbered).
17 Cruise, Portraits, 33.
18 Dudley Edwards, Portraits, 14.
19 Ligthart, 186–90.
20 Memorials, I, III, 171.
21 The factual information which follows about the Famine in Dublin is taken from Somerville-Large, 244–7.
22 Butler, 4.
23 Memorials, Centenary (Restoration), 18. The house was called 'Druid Lodge' and it was closed when the Jesuits were not allowed to build a church (by whom and why are not stated). The Jesuits about this time used to rent holiday accommodation in the same neighbourhood at Mount Salus, Dalkey, which Newman borrowed for use by English Oratorians in the early autumn of 1854 (McRedmond, 128). I an informed by Father Desmond Forristal, P.P., Dalkey, that according to local tradition the house in question was No. 2 Mount Salus.
24 McGrath, 251–2.
25 Memorials, Centenary (Restoration), 17.
26 Galvia Ignatiana, 1–3.
27 Memorials, Centenary (Restoration), 17. No such proposal is mentioned in Condon (the official history of All Hallows).
28, 29, 30 Memorials, Centenary (Restoration), 18–20. The request from Sydney was in fact to take charge of St John's Catholic College, which was affiliated to the University (Bygott, 29).
31 McRedmond, 7.
32 The factual information in this section about the Jesuits in Limerick is taken from Finegan, 7–39, unless otherwise indicated.
33 McRedmond, 103.
34 Memorials, I, II, 127.
35 Andrews, Portraits, 131.
36 Comerford, Oxford V, 377–8.
37 Author's personal knowledge.
38 Andrews, Portraits, 133.
39, 40, 41 Bangert, 431–3.
42 Ligthart, 201, 327.
43 McRedmond, *Studies*, Spring/Summer, 1978, 35–8.
44 Memorials, Centenary (Restoration),59.
45 Daniel-Rops, VIII, 300.
46 Quotations and factual information in this section about the Jesuits in Galway are taken from *Galvia Ignatiana*, unless otherwise indicated. NB: It is not always clear whether statements attributed to various persons in these manuscript papers are direct quotations or summaries of what was said. The expedient has been adopted, therefore, of using quotation marks where it seems certain *or likely* that the words recorded are a direct quotation.
47 Memorials, I, III, 105.
48, 49 Memorials, I, III, 163.
50 McRedmond, 6.
51 McRedmond, 84.

52, 53 Comerford, Oxford V, 378.
54   Morrissey, Education, I, 349.
55   Costello, 30–31.
56   Andrews, Portraits, 127.
57   Ligthart, 317.
58   Memorials, I, IV, 231–2.
59   Memorials, I, II, 101.
60   Memorials, I, II, 106.
61   Memorials, I, III, 159–60.
62   Memorials, I, IV, 230.
63   Memorials, Centenary (Restoration), 64–5.
64   Memorials, I, VIII, 395–6.
65   Memorials, Centenary (Milltown), 46.
66   Memorials, Centenary (Milltown), 44.
67   Unless otherwise indicated, quotations and information about Tullabeg in this section are taken from Morrissey, Education, I, 267–309.
68, 69 Andrews, Portraits, 145.
70   Ganss, par. 395 and passim.
71   Unless otherwise indicated, quotations and information about Clongowes in this section are taken from Costello, 78–82, 107–10, 131–4, 151–60.
72   It appears on very early prospectuses for Clongowes, Belvedere and the Crescent. Its arrival at Tullabeg was delayed, apparently until classes were instituted beyond the preparatory level. I have been unable to locate an early prospectus for Galway but the 1868 St Ignatius community list records Physics and Chemistry among the responsibilities of Father Thomas McEnroe.
73   Finegan, 10.
74   Memorials, I, III, 154, and Centenary (Restoration), 49.
75   Coldrey, 154.
76   Ganss, pars 378–83. This section of the Constitutions has to do with getting the student out of passively absorbing matter handed down by a lecturer, encouraging him instead to participate in acquiring and assimilating his own knowledge and his personal grasp of truth.
77   For a fascinating account of the promotion of drama by the Jesuits in Europe generally and at Clongowes in particular, see Costello, 151–60, from which this quotation is taken.
78   Andrews, Portraits, 136.
79   Finegan, 11.
80, 81 Galvia Ignatiana, 59–60.
82   Memorials, I, IV, 215.
83   Andrews, Portraits, 136fn.
84   Memorials, I, III, 158.
85   Costello, 24.
86   Facts and quotations concerning English public schools in this paragraph are taken from Woodward, 466–8.
87   Costello, 44.
88   Andrews, Portraits, 155.
89   Morrissey, Delany, 22.
90   Costello, 26.
91   Butler, 4. This sickly boy was to become a famous soldier, explorer, travel-writer and friend of the Canadian Indians. He lost his post as Commander of the British forces in South Africa on the eve of the Boer War because he opposed the jingoistic sabre-rattling of the clique dominated by Rhodes and Milner. He was a member of the first Senate of the National University of

Ireland, a Home Ruler and a supporter of the Gaelic League. These biographical details are given to illustrate, in view of what has to be said later about complaints of allegedly 'West British' attitudes in Jesuit schools, that it was entirely possible for an Irishman to make a career in the British establishment without abandoning his 'national spirit'.

92   Morrissey, Education, I, 280seq.
93   Andrews, Portraits, 155.
94   Morrissey, Delany, 22.
95   Costello, 44.
96   Costello, 87.
97   Morrissey, Delany, 21.
98   Morrissey, Delany, 22, 28–32; Morrissey, Education, I, 349.
99   Woodward, 469.
100 Morrissey, Education, I, 331seq.
101 Pollak, 21 December 1990.
102 See Coldrey, 69–76, from which facts and quotations concerning the complaints of anti-nationalism referred to in this paragraph are taken.
103 Gwynn, 7.
104 Costello, 78–80.
105 MacDonagh, II, 181. Clongowes reciprocated O'Connell's goodwill. A 'splendid reception' was organised there in November 1841 to celebrate his election as the first Catholic Lord Mayor of Dublin. 'The College was gaily ornamented. . . . Two addresses were offered to which O'Connell replied . . . Henry Meagher and Sir John Esmonde also spoke on the occasion amidst immense enthusiasm.' (Memorials, I, III, 156).
106 *Galvia Ignatiana*, 96. Hurling was being played in the same year at St Ignatius' but may have been introduced earlier.
107 Morrissey, Education, I, 277fn.
108 Finegan, 19, 22–3.
109 Finegan, 23.
110 Lyons, 91–2; Coldrey, 93–5; Morrissey, Delany, 33–6.
111 Morrissey, Delany, 32–6 (on which the references to Father Delany in this paragraph are also based).
112 *Galvia Ignatiana*, 112–21.
113 *Galvia Ignatiana*, 76.
114 Andrews, Portraits, 147fn; Costello, 61.
115 Morrissey, Education, I, 326.
116 Morrissey, Education, II, 495.
117 Costello, 45.
118 Morrissey, Delany, 62–3.
119, 120 Morrissey, Education, II, 498seq.
121 Finegan, 25.
122 Bradley, 74, quoting an article by Dominic Kelly in *The Rhetorician* (1889). A 'pandybat' was the leather strap, so known at Clongowes from the Latin *pando*, 'I hold out (my hand).'
123 Costello, 61.
124 Lyons, 92.
125 Andrews, Portraits, 147.
126 *Galvia Ignatiana*, 91.
127 Costello, 63.
128 Lee, 130.
129 The factual information in this section (but not the comments) regarding the origins of Mungret and its development is taken from the extended account in Morrissey, Education, I, 128seq., unless otherwise indicated.

130 Roantree, 43–54.
131 McRedmond, 70.
132 Roantree, 307.
133 Finegan, 13.
134 Quoted in Morrissey, Education, I, 128.
135 Newman, Letters and Diaries, XXIII, 343.
136 Roantree, 99–100.
137 Edward Byrne, Dermot Ryan, Desmond Connell.
138 John Charles McQuaid.
139 *Galvia Ignatiana*, 149–52.
140 Finegan, 29, 33–4.
141 I am grateful to Mr Padraig Folan for guidance on this important development for which documentation is surprisingly thin.
142 Quotations from Gogarty, 20–24.
143 Lysaght, 33–4, 39.
144, 145 Andrews, Portraits, 153.
146 Morrissey, Delany, 26–27.
147 Galway quotations from *Galvia Ignatiana*, 119.
148 Morrissey, Education, I, 247seq.
149 Costello, 199–202.
150 Morrissey, Education, I, 192.
151 Galway references in this and the following paragraph are taken from *Galvia Ignatiana*, 88–94 and 119–137.
152 Memorials, I, IV, 228.

Chapter 6, pp 226–70

1 to 5 Memorials, I, VII, 347–9. When the 'historical romance' appeared, an older Father is reported to have said that it was now time that Mr Finlay resumed 'the legitimate obscurity of a scholastic'.
6 McRedmond, vi.
7 Morrissey, Delany, 25.
8 Finegan, 18.
9, 10 Costello, 44–5.
11, 12, 13 Unless otherwise stated, factual references in this section to Father Delany, the Royal University and University College are based on Morrissey, Delany, passim; Curran, 69–81; Meenan, O'Brien, 22–35 and 141–6.
14 Lyons, 96.
15 Carefully compiled year-by-year tables, drawn up to show the superiority of University College to each of the Queen's Colleges, appear in Memorials, I, I, 62–4.
16 McRedmond, 183.
17, 18 Hopkins, 260.
19 Hopkins, 182 and 386.
20 Hopkins, 262.
21 Memorials, I, IV, 225.
22, 23 Curran, 76.
24, 25 *Studies*, March 1912, 3.
26 Meenan, O'Brien, 135fn.
27 *Studies*, Autumn 1968, 243seq.
28 Joyce, 168–9.
29, 30, 31 Curran, 80–81.
32 Felix Hackett in Meenan, L. and H., 64.
33 See comments in Bradley, 1–8; Costello, 167–71; Fallon, Portraits, 45–8.

34 Joyce, 8.
35 Joyce, 67.
36 Bradley, 4.
37 Costello, 168.
38 Bradley, 3 (quoting John C. Kelly, S.J.).
39, 40 Costello, 168–70.
41 For the amount of commentary on Joyce compared with that on Shakespeare: Professor Augustine Martin of U.C.D. in a television interview, *Booklines* programme, R.T.E., 31 January 1991.
42 The details of the 1866 voyage which follow are compiled from Father Dalton's recollections (Memorials, I, II, 81–7) and a letter sent home by Father Nolan shortly after the Jesuits' arrival in Melbourne (Soc. J. Australia, 28–33).
43 Memorials, I, V, 238.
44 Bygott, 21.
45 Morrissey, Delany, 18.
46 Soc. J. Australia, 25.
47 Unless otherwise stated, the factual information about the Church in Australia and the Jesuit Missions (Austrian and Irish) which follows in this section comes from Bygott, passim, and Memorials, I, V, 235–40. Page references are given for quotations.
48 Bygott, 27.
49 Memorials, I, VIII, 388–404. According to a story told in this biographical note on Father Duffy, he once attended a reception at Government House in Hobart. The Governor of Tasmania came up and embraced him, saying 'Though I know not your name, Reverend Father, I recognise you as the military chaplain who saved my life in the Crimean War. . . I was left for dead on the field. You placed me on your shoulders, and conveyed me to the ambulance, and tenderly cared me to recovery, and now I am proud to acknowledge the debt of gratitude I owe.'
50 Bygott, 81.
51 Bradley, 151. Father Kelly came from Tramore, Co. Waterford. Joyce mentions him as a schoolboy in Clongowes: 'at benediction . . . Dominic Kelly sang the first part by himself in the choir ' (Joyce, 43) .
52 Bygott, 179.
53 Year Book, 1932, 167.
54 Bangert, 157–60 .
55 Bangert, 172.
56 Bangert, 183–5, 279–83 .
57 Unless otherwise stated, most of the information about early Irish Jesuits referred to in this section is taken from McErlean, Irish Jesuits, 51–65.
58 O'Donoghue, 88 .
59 Soc. J. Australia, 49 .
60 Unless otherwise stated, factual information about the Hong Kong Mission is based on community lists, reports and articles in Year Books, 1928–1967. Specific references are given for quotations.
61 Year Book, 1935, 131–2, 179–80.
62 Year Book, 1935, 132 .
63 Bangert, 346 .
64 Bangert 280.
65 Year Book, 1941, 156.
66 Year Book, 1941, 151.
67 Ryan, 10–12. The factual details of the siege which follow are taken from Ryan, passim, and an account by the Superior of the Mission, Father Patrick Joy, in Year Book, 1947, 157–62.

68   See especially *Gaudium et Spes*, pars 53, 55, 56, 58 and 60.
69   Year Book, 1974, 39.
70   Unless otherwise stated, factual details about the Chikuni Mission in this section are taken from Year Books, 1951–1970. Specific references are given for quotations.
71   Year Book, 1951, 139.
72   Canisius, 2, 26–9.
73   Year Book, 1962, 64–5.
74   Year Book, 1960, 37–9.
75   Canisius, 35.
76   Rynne, I, 137; III, 21; IV, 69, 127, 140, 168.
77   Rynne, II, 254–60.
78   Memorials, I, II, 106.
79   Memorials, I, VII, 340–41.
80, 81 Memorials, I, VII, 343.
82   Costello, 95.
83   Bradley, 124, 128, quoting Lambert McKenna, S.J., and Rupert Coyle, S.J.
84   Costello, 95.
85   Bradley, 124, quoting an entry in Father Cullen's diary retrieved by Father McKenna.
86   Bradley, 128, quoting Father McKenna.
87   Bradley, 124, quoting Father McKenna.
88   *Milltown Studies*, Autumn 1989.
89   Bangert, 460.
90   *Milltown Studies*, Autumn 1989.
91   Dates and statistics from Bangert, 460, and Bygott, 313.
92   Viney, 22.
93   Kavanagh, 18–19.
94   Viney, 22.
95   Bygott, 209.
96   Bangert, 458.

Chapter 7, pp 271–311
1   Morrissey, Education, I, 214 seq.
2   Costello, 63–4.
3   Based on Lee, 23–4, and accompanying footnote.
4   Costello, 197. For details, see table, Costello, 198–9.
5   Finegan, 88.
6   Martin, Portraits, 51.
7   Bourke, 127.
8   Martin, Portraits, 57.
9   Ganss, 823.
10   Edwards, Portraits, 15.
11   O'Donovan, 42.
12   For a fascinating analysis of this attitude and subsequent changes of emphasis see Martin, Portraits, 49–62, from which references to *The Belvederian* in the following paragraph are taken.
13   Costello, 197.
14   Counihan references and quotations from O'Donovan, 158–60.
15   Morrissey, Education, 214 seq. Keogh, 30. Longford and O'Neill, 89.
16, 17 Meenan, *Studies*, Spring, 1962, 5.
18   Gaughan, I, 212–14.
19, 20 Meenan, *Studies*, Spring, 1962, 8.

21   Gaughan, I, 78; II, 102.
22   Meenan, O'Brien, 135.
23   Keogh, 168.
24   Whyte, 41.
25   Whyte, 73.
26   Neither Father Bangert, S.J., nor Henri Daniel-Rops identifies the Freemasons as a significant element in the story of the Suppression.
27   For a reasoned analysis of eighteenth-century Freemasonry by a preconciliar French Catholic historian in good standing, see Daniel-Rops, VII, 60–65. While recognising the anti-Christian element in Masonry, he concludes that 'History provides little or no evidence of a conspiracy; if such there was, it can have counted for very little in comparison with the demiurgic forces that came into play with the French Revolution. The "Masonic conspiracy" must be ranked with the "Jesuit conspiracy", whose spectre is raised from time to time.' And he cautions: 'Anyone who does believe in a Masonic conspiracy must refrain from associating the Jews with it.'
28   MacDonagh, II, 19–20.
29   See Daly, *Studies*, Spring/Summer 1978, 67.
30   Meenan, O'Brien, 133–4.
31   Morrissey, Education, I, 214–22.
32   Viney, 24–5.
33   Whyte, 64.
34   Whyte, 65.
35, 36 Whyte, 67.
37   Gaughan, II, 330.
38   Whyte, 70. Father Fergal McGrath, S.J., was a leading figure at the Clongowes Summer Schools (Costello, 188). 'These gatherings were at that time a major event in the intellectual life of the country. They were great fun, you met everybody, argued day and night and learnt a great deal' (Deeny, 58).
39, 40 Gaughan, II, 315.
41   Viney, 43–4. And see address by Father Edmond Kent, S.J., Year Book, 1955, 51–61.
42   Year Book, 112.
43   Unless otherwise indicated, the facts and quotations in the account which follows are taken from Keogh, *Studies*, Spring 1989, 82–95.
44   For a critical examination of the 'Catholic' elements in the constitution see Report of the Irish Theological Association working party, *The Tablet*, 10 June 1972, 557–9. See also McRedmond, *The Tablet*, 19 March 1977, 269–72, and McRedmond, *Law and Justice*, Trinity/Michaelmas 1981, 71–96.
45   Keogh, *Studies*, Spring 1989, 91–4.
46   Whyte, 73, 163–4.
47   e.g. Article 41, ss 1 and 2, Constitution of Ireland (The Family).
48   See Mr Justice Kenny's comments in the case of Ryan v. Attorney General (Kelly, 614–15).
49   Keogh, *Studies*, Spring 1989, 89, 95 (Note 8).
50   Viney, 27.
51   In a written communication to the present writer.
52   O'Meara, 54.
53   O'Meara, 78.
54   O'Meara. 76.
55   O'Meara, 67.
56   Costello, 213.
57   Viney, 42. Morrissey, Education, 236 seq.

58 O'Holohan, Portraits, 97.
59 FitzGerald, *The Clongownian* 1989, 58.
60 Personal recollection.
61 FitzGerald, *The Clongownian* 1989, 59.
62 Province News, September 1926, 8–9.
63 Year Book, 1949, 152.
64 Connolly, 89–90, 135–74, 200–213.
65, 66 Province News, July 1969, 311–12.
67 Province News, June 1928, 69.
68 Province News, June 1928, 70.
69 Province News, September 1930, 84.
70 Memorials, Centenary (Milltown), 13.
71 Memorials, Centenary (Milltown), 15–16.
72 Province News, September 1930, 82.
73 Year Book, 1955, 50.
74 Quotations from Ganss, pars. 645, 647, 648.
75 Details regarding the nineteenth-century development of Milltown Park and other Houses of Study in this and the following paragraph are taken from Memorials, Centenary (Milltown), 12–19 and 27–35.
76 A former resident was Bishop Thomas Percy, compiler of Percy's *Reliques of Ancient English Poetry* (1765), which influenced Wordsworth, Coleridge and the English Romantic movement. It is thought that Hopkins may have composed 'Tom's Garland' and 'Harry Ploughman' there, although he gave them their final form — got them 'ready for hanging on the line'—at Monasterevin (Hopkins, 271).
77 Viney, 43.
78 Prospectus, Milltown Institute, 1990–1991, 4–5.
79 Memorials, Centenary (Milltown), 31.
80 To the writer's personal knowledge. In fact 'house of writers' was a technical juridical term in the Society.
81 Details regarding University Hall from Finegan, Record, 9.
82 Quinlan, Record, 19.
83 Details regarding Rathfarnham Castle from Memorials, Centenary (Restoration), 27–39; Memorials, Centenary (Milltown), 44, and from *Rathfarnham*, 7–9.
84 The evolution of the tertianship from Saint Ignatius's original concept is outlined in Ganss, *pages* 234–5 (extended footnote).
85 Details regarding seismograph from Year Book, 1941, 139–47.
86 Morrissey, Delany, 31.
87 Viney, 43.
88 The successive developments leading to this recognition can be traced through the entries for Galway in the Year Books, 1929–1934, and the issues of *Irish Province News* during the same years.
89 Province News, October 1933, 12–13.
90 Morrissey, Education, I, 253–6.
91 Personal experience.
92 Unless otherwise indicated, the factual information regarding the foundation and development of Gonzaga is based on the detailed account by Father William Lee, S.J., in Gonzaga, 1985, 3–32, and 1986, 7–26.
93 Gonzaga, 1986, 5.
94 Gonzaga, 1986, 13. Viney, 41–2. Also the present writer's recollection of comments made to him at the time.
95 Quoted in Gonzaga, 1986, 13.
96 Text of proposal in Gonzaga, 1986, 13–16.

97   Outlined in Gonzaga, 1986, 12, 16–18.
98   Andrews, Portraits, 139, confirms the demand for Belvedere.
99   Bangert, 513.
100 Costello, 69–70.
101 Pollak, *Irish Times*, 21 December 1990.
102 Viney, 41.
103 Costello, 190.
104 Information about St Declan's and quotations from Yearbook, 1960, 55–6.
105 Bangert, 509–10.
106 Expressed to the present writer in 1971.
107 Viney, 27.
108 Viney, 35.
109 The writer was privileged to see a number of the reports from the houses at the time, having been requested as a sympathetic outsider to assist in preparing a summary for the Provincial.
110 The facts (but not the comments) regarding the suppression of Mungret are based on Morrissey, Education, 256–60.
111 Andrews, Portraits, 137.
112 Andrews, Portraits, 139.
113 Viney, 45–6.
114 Closed circuit television coverage had to be provided more than once in parlours adjacent to the large but crowded lecture hall. The series of Milltown Lectures, of which these were a continuation, had begun before the Vatican Council. The early lectures are said to have anticipated some of the Council's insights.
115 The information about the School of Ecumenics which follows is provided by the writer as a former Chairman of the School's Executive Board.

BIBLIOGRAPHY

Each bibliographical entry appears after the name of the author or abbreviated title by which it is mentioned in the Notes. Names of contributors to journals or other compilations who are referred to in the Notes also appear in this list, cross-referred to the entries with which they are associated.

Andrews, John Harwood — see Oxford.
Andrews, Paul, S.J. — see Portraits.
Ashley: *The Greatness of Oliver Cromwell*. Maurice Ashley. Hodder & Stoughton, London, 1957.
Bangert: *A History of the Society of Jesus*. Revised edition. William V. Bangert, S.J. Institute of Jesuit Sources, St Louis, 1971.
Basset: *The English Jesuits: from Campion to Martindale*. Bernard Basset, S.J. Burns & Oates, London, 1967.
Beards: *The Beards' New Basic History of the United States*. Charles A. Beard, Mary R. Beard, William Beard. Macmillan, London, 1960.
Bourke: *The O'Rahilly*. Marcus Bourke. Anvil Books, Tralee, 1967.
Boylan: *A Dictionary of Irish Biography*. Henry Boylan. Second edition. Gill & Macmillan, Dublin, 1988.
Bradley: *James Joyce's Schooldays*. Bruce Bradley, S.J. Gill & Macmillan, Dublin, 1982.
Brady, John — see Reportorium Novum.
Burke: *Burke's Irish Family Records*.
Burke Savage, Roland, S.J. — see Irish Jesuits.
Butler: *Sir William Butler: an Autobiography*. Constable, London, 1913.
Butlin, Robin Alan — see Oxford.
Bygott: *With Pen and Tongue: the Jesuits in Australia 1865–1939*. Ursula M. L. Bygott. Melbourne University Press, 1980.
Cahill: *Freemasonry and the Anti-Christian Movement*. Edward Cahill, S.J. Gill, Dublin, 1930 (first published 1929).
Canisius: *Thirty Years of Canisius 1949–1979*. (*The Canisian*, Vol 3, No 1). Canisius Secondary School, Chikuni, Zambia, 1979.
Churchill: *A History of the English-Speaking Peoples. Vol II, The New World*. Winston S. Churchill. Cassell, London, 1956.
Clarke, Aidan — see Oxford.
Clongownian: *The Clongownian*. Annually from 1895.
    Contributors quoted: M. Sweetman, S.J., G. FitzGerald.

336   *To the Greater Glory*

Coldrey: *Faith and Fatherland: The Irish Christian Brothers and the Development of Irish Nationalism.* Barry Coldry. Gill & Macmillan, Dublin, 1988.

Comerford, Richard Vincent — see Oxford.

Condon: *The Missionary College of All Hallows 1842–1891.* Kevin Condon, C.M. All Hallows College, Dublin, 1986.

Connolly: *Priests and People in Pre-Famine Ireland 1780–1845.* Sean J. Connolly. Gill & Macmillan, Dublin, 1982 (see also Oxford).

Coonan: *The Irish Catholic Confederacy and the Puritan Revolution.* Thomas L. Coonan. Clonmore & Reynolds, Dublin, 1954.

Corcoran, Timothy, S.J. — see Irish Jesuits.

Corish: *The Irish Catholic Experience.* Patrick J.Corish. Gill & Macmillan, Dublin, 1985. (See also Oxford.)

Costello: *Clongowes Wood: A History of Clongowes Wood College 1814–1989.* Peter Costello. Gill & Macmillan, Dublin, 1989.

Craig: *Dublin 1660–1860.* Maurice Craig. Alan Figgis, Dublin, 1980 (first published 1952).

Cruise, Francis R. — see Portraits.

Cullen, Louis Michael, — see Oxford.

Curran: *Under the Receding Wave.* C.P. Curran. Gill & Macmillan, Dublin, 1970.

Curran, Michael J. — see Reportorium Novum.

Daly, Rev Gabriel, O.S.A. — see Studies.

Daniel-Rops: *History of the Church of Christ.* Henri Daniel-Rops. In the English edition, ten volumes. Vols V (*The Catholic Reformation*), VII (*The Church in the Eighteenth Century*) and VIII (*The Church in an Age of Revolution*) translated by John Warrington; Vol VI (*The Church in the Seventeenth Century*) translated by J. J. Buckingham. Dent, London, 1962–1965.

Debrett: *Debrett's Peerage.* Kelly's Directories, Kingston-upon-Thames, 1965.

Deeny: *To Care and to Cure.* James Deeny. Glendale Press, Dun Laoghaire, 1989.

Duanaire: *An Duanaire 1600–1900: Poems of the Dispossessed.* Curtha in láthair ag Seán Ó Tuama, with translations into English verse by Thomas Kinsella. Dolmen Press (i gcomhar le Bórd na Gaeilge), Dublin, 1981.

Dudley Edwards, Owen — see Portraits.

Finegan: *Limerick Jesuit Centenary Record 1859–1959.* Francis Finegan, S.J. Sacred Heart College, Limerick. (See also Irish Jesuits and Record.)

FitzGerald, Gerald — see Clongownian.

Foster: *Modern Ireland 1600–1972.* R. F. Foster. Allen Lane, London, 1988.

Galvia Ignatiana: Jesuits in Galway: *Galvia Ignatiana.* Manuscript notes (109 pages), so headed, transcribed mainly by James Rabbitte, S.J., circa 1935, from various sources including Provincial Archives. Photocopies kindly provided by Mr Pádraig Folan, Coláiste Iognáid.

Ganss: *The Constitutions of the Society of Jesus.* Saint Ignatius of Loyola. Translated by George E. Ganss, S.J. Institute of Jesuit Sources, Saint Louis, 1970. (In quotations taken from Ganss, please note that the numbers refer to paragraphs of the Constitutions, not to pages, unless otherwise stated.)

Gaughan: *Alfred O'Rahilly.* J. Anthony Gaughan. Vol I, *Academic.* Vol II, *Public Figure.* Kingdom Books, Mount Merrion, Co. Dublin, 1986, 1989.

Gogarty: *It Isn't This Time Of Year At All!* Oliver St. John Gogarty. Sphere Books, London, 1983 (first published 1954).

Gonzaga: *The Gonzaga Record.* Published annually since 1985. Gonzaga College, Dublin. Contributor: W. Lee, S.J.

Gwynn: *Thomas Francis Meagher.* Denis Gwynn. O'Donnell Lecture. National University of Ireland. 1961.

Hackett, Felix — see Meenan, L. and H.

Hayes-McCoy, Gerard Anthony — see Oxford.

Hopkins: *Gerard Manley Hopkins*. Ed. Catherine Phillips. The Oxford Authors series, Oxford University Press, 1986.

Howard, Leonard — see Studies.

Hughes: *The Reformation in England*. Philip Hughes. Vol III, '*True Religion Now Established*'. Fifth, revised edition, three volumes in one. Burns & Oates, London, 1963.

Irish Jesuits: *The Irish Jesuits*. Bound typescript in Milltown Library of articles from various sources, mainly the Jesuit Year Book. Authors: John McErlean, S.J.; Timothy Corcoran, S.J.; Roland Burke Savage, S.J.; Francis Finegan, S.J. Identified in the Notes by author referred to, e.g. McErlean, Irish Jesuits, 62.

Joyce: *A Portrait of the Artist as a Young Man*. James Joyce. Grafton, London/Glasgow, 1977 (first published 1916).

Kavanagh: *Tarry Flynn*. Patrick Kavanagh. Penguin Books, London, 1978 (first published 1948).

Kee: *The Green Flag*. Robert Kee. Weidenfeld & Nicolson, London, 1972.

Kelly: *The Irish Constitution*. John M. Kelly. Second edition. Jurist Publishing Co. Ltd., University College, Dublin, 1984.

Keogh: *The Vatican, the Bishops and Irish Politics 1919–1939*. Dermot Keogh. Cambridge University Press, 1986. (See also Studies.)

Law & Justice: *Law & Justice: The Christian Law Review*. Biannual. The Edmund Plowden Trust, London.

Lee, William, S.J. — see Gonzaga.

Lee: *Ireland 1912–1985: Politics and Society*. J. J. Lee. Cambridge University Press, 1989.

Ligthart: *The Return of the Jesuits: the Life of Jan Philip Roothaan*. C. J. Ligthart, S.J. Translated by Jan J. Slijkerman, S.J. T. Shand, London, 1978.

Longford and O'Neill: *Eamon de Valera*. The Earl of Longford and Thomas P. O'Neill. Gill & Macmillan, Dublin, in association with Hutchinson, London, 1970.

Lyons: *Ireland Since the Famine*. F. S. L. Lyons. Collins/Fontana, London, 1973.

Lysaght: *Brendan Bracken*. Charles Edward Lysaght. Allen Lane, London, 1979.

McCracken, John Leslie — see Oxford.

MacDonagh: *Daniel O'Connell*. Oliver MacDonagh. Vol I, *The Hereditary Bondsman*. Vol II, *The Emancipist*. Weidenfeld & Nicolson, London, 1988, 1989. (See also Oxford.)

McErlean, John, S.J. — see Irish Jesuits.

McGrath: *Newman's University: Idea and Reality*. Fergal McGrath, S.J. Browne & Nolan, Dublin, 1951.

MacLoughlin: *Guide to Historic Dublin*. Adrian MacLoughlin. Gill & Macmillan, Dublin, 1979.

McRedmond: *Thrown Among Strangers: John Henry Newman in Ireland*. Louis McRedmond. Veritas, Dublin, 1990. (See also Studies; Law & Justice; The Tablet.)

Martin, Francis Xavier, O.S.A. — see Oxford; Portraits.

Meagher, John — see Reportorium Novum.

Meenan, O'Brien: *George O'Brien: a Biographical Memoir*. James Meenan. Gill & Macmillan, Dublin, 1980. (See also Studies.)

Meenan, L. and H.: *Centenary History of the Literary and Historical Society of University College Dublin 1855–1955*. Edited by James Meenan. Kerryman, Tralee, 1955. Contributors to Meenan, L. and H.: James Meenan, Felix Hackett et al.

Memorials: *Memorials of the Irish Province, S.J.* Sundry memoirs, letters, obituaries, historical essays etc., a number of them duplicated, bound under this general title. Various authors, mostly anonymous. Privately printed at various dates between 1899 and 1914. The volume includes the following sections —

'Short Memoirs of the Early Irish Jesuits Who Worked in Ireland Down to the Year 1840,' by Joseph McDonnell, S.J., printed by O'Brien & Ards, Printers, Dublin, 1903. Referred to in the Notes as: Memorials (Short Memoirs).

'A Short History of the Irish Province, S.J.' Part I. Referred to in the Notes as: Memorials, I, I, followed by page number.

'Memorials of the Irish Province, S.J.' Vol. I (misprinted as II), No. II. Clearly intended as a continuation of 'Part I', above, from which it is paged on. Referred to in the Notes as: Memorials, I, II, followed by page number.

'Memorials of the Irish Province, S.J.' Vol. I, Nos. III to VIII, continuing the series. Referred to in the Notes by volume, number and page, e.g. Memorials, I, IV, 223.

'Centenary Year. Short History of the Restoration of the Irish Province . . . etc. 1814–1914.' Printed by O'Brien & Ards, Dublin, 1914. Referred to in the Notes as: Memorials, Centenary (Restoration).

'Centenary Year. Short History of Milltown Park . . . etc. 1814–1914.' Printed by O'Brien & Ards, Dublin, 1914. Referred to in the Notes as Memorials, Centenary (Milltown).

Millet, Benignus, O.F.M. — see Oxford.
Milltown Studies: Published by the Milltown Institute, Dublin.
Morrissey: '"Archdevil" and Jesuit: the Background, Life and Times of James Archer from 1550 to 1604.' Thomas J. Morrissey, S.J. Unpublished M.A. thesis, N.U.I. 1968.
Morrissey, Delany: *Towards a National University: William Delany, S.J. (1835–1924).* Thomas J. Morrissey, S.J. Wolfhound Press, Dublin, 1983.
Morrissey, Education: 'Some Jesuit Contributions to Irish Education'. Thomas J. Morrissey, S.J. Unpublished PhD thesis, N.U.I. 1975.
Newman: *Maynooth and Georgian Ireland.* Jeremiah Newman. Kenny, Galway, 1979.
Newman, Letters and Diaries: *The Letters and Diaries of John Henry Newman.* Edited by Charles Stephen Dessain et al. Nelson, London, sequentially from 1961.
Nicholls, Kenneth William — see Oxford.
Ó Cuív, Brian — see Oxford.
O'Donoghue: 'The Jesuit Mission in Ireland, 1598–1651'. Fergus O'Donoghue, S.J. Unpublished PhD thesis, Catholic University of America, Washington D.C., 1981.
O'Donovan: *Kevin Barry And His Time.* Donal O'Donovan. Glendale Press, Sandycove, Co. Dublin, 1989.
O'Holohan, Frank — see Portraits.
O'Meara: *The Singing-Masters.* John O'Meara. Lilliput Press, Dublin, 1990.
Ó Ríordáin: *Irish Catholics: Tradition and Transition.* John J. Ó Ríordáin. Veritas, Dublin, 1980.
O'Riordan, William M. — see Reportorium Novum.
Oxford: *A New History of Ireland.* Ed. Art Cosgrove, T. W. Moody, F. X. Martin, F. J. Byrne, W. E. Vaughan. Vol II, *Medieval Ireland 1169–1534.* Vol III, *Early Modern Ireland 1534–1691.* Vol IV, *Eighteenth Century Ireland 1691– 1800.* Vol V, *Ireland Under the Union I 1801–1870.* Vol VIII (Chronology). Vol IX (Genealogies, Lists). Oxford, at the Clarendon Press, 1976–1989. Referred to in the Notes by contributor, volume and page, e.g. Nicholls, Oxford II, 413.

Contributors to Oxford *New History of Ireland* quoted: J. H. Andrews; R. A. Butlin; A. Clarke; R. V. Comerford; S.J. Connolly; P. J. Corish; L. M. Cullen; G.A. Hayes-McCoy; J. L. McCracken; 0. MacDonagh; B. Millet, O.F.M.; K. W. Nicholls; B. Ó Cuív; D. B. Quinn; J. J. Silke; J. G. Simms.
Pakenham: *The Year of Liberty.* Thomas Pakenham. Hodder & Stoughton, London, 1969.

Portraits: *Portraits: Belvedere College 1832–1982*. Ed. John Bowman and Ronan O'Donoghue. Gill & Macmillan, Dublin, 1982. Referred to in the Notes by contributor and page number, e.g. Andrews, Portraits, 124.
    Contributors to *Portraits* quoted: O. Dudley Edwards; F. X. Martin, O.S.A.; P. Andrews, S.J.; F. O'Holohan; F. R. Cruise.
Petrie: *The Jacobite Movement*. Sir Charles Petrie. Eyre & Spottiswoode, London, 1959.
Pollak: *The Jesuits*. Andy Pollak. *Irish Times*, 20 and 21 December 1990.
Province News: *Irish Province News*. Newsletter for private circulation (within Irish Province).
Purcell: *The First Jesuit*. Mary Purcell. Gill, Dublin, 1956.
Purcell, Message: *Message and Messenger*. Mary Purcell. Irish Messenger, Dublin, 1987.
Quinlan, Harold — see Record.
Quinn, David Beers — see Oxford.
Rathfarnham: *Rathfarnham, Gateway to the Hills*. Local History Group, Rathfarnham Guild, Irish Countrywomen's Association, 1990 .
Record: *University Hall Dublin: Record 1913–1973*. Edited by J.B. Stephenson, S.J. Irish Messenger, Dublin, 1973.
    Contributors quoted: Francis Finegan, S.J., Harold Quinlan.
Religious Life Review. Bimonthly. Dominican Publications, Dublin.
Reportorium Novum: *Reportorium Novum: Dublin Diocesan Record*. Vols I, 1955, and II, 1956. Thereafter biennially to 1963–1964. C. J. Fallon, Dublin, to 1956. Thereafter Browne & Nolan, Dublin.
    Contributors to *Reportorium Novum* quoted: J. Brady; M. J. Curran; J. Meagher; W. M. O'Riordan; M. Wall.
Roantree: 'William Monsell, M.P., and the Catholic Question in Victorian Britain and Ireland'. Dermot S. Roantree. Unpublished doctoral thesis, N.U.I. 1990.
Ryan: *Jesuits Under Fire in the Siege of Hong Kong, 1941*. Thomas F. Ryan, S.J. Burns Oates & Washbourne, London and Dublin, 1944.
Rynne: A contemporary account.of the debates and decrees of the Second Vatican Council in four volumes. Xavier Rynne. Vol I, *Letters from Vatican City*. Vol II, *The Second Session*. Vol III, *The Third Session*. Vol IV, *The Fourth Session*. Faber & Faber, London, 1963–1966.
Scully: *The Catholic Question in Ireland and England, 1798–1822: The Papers of Denys Scully*. Ed. Brian MacDermot. Irish Academic Press, Blackrock, Co. Dublin, 1988.
Shaw: *The Dublin Pictorial Guide and Directory of 1850*. Henry Shaw. Reprint, with an introduction by Kevin B. Nowlan. Friar's Bush Press, Belfast, 1988.
Silke, John Joseph — see Oxford.
Simms, John Gerald — see Oxford.
Soc. J. Australia: *The Society of Jesus in Australia*. Bound volume in Milltown Library with manuscript note: 'This contains two or three long articles on the Society in Australia, written in the "Woodstock Letters" by Fr Watson, S.J.'.
Somerville-Large: *Dublin: the First Thousand Years*. Peter Somerville-Large. Appletree Press, Belfast, 1988.
Studies: an Irish Quarterly Review. Published for, and later by, the Irish Jesuits, Dublin, March 1912 to date. Referred to in the Notes by contributor, issue and page number, e.g. Howard, *Studies*, Summer 1969, 192.
    Contributors to *Studies* quoted: G. Daly; L. Howard; D. Keogh; J. Meenan; L. McRedmond.
Sweetman, Michael, S.J. — see Clongownian.
Tablet: *The Tablet*. Weekly, since 1840. The Tablet Publishing Company, London.
Taine: *Les Origines de la France Contemporaine: l'Ancien Régime*. H. Taine. Seizième édition. Hachette, Paris, 1891.

Tocqueville: *France Before the Revolution.* Alexis de Tocqueville. Translated by Henry Reeve. Third edition. John Murray, London, 1888.

Toynbee: *A Study of History.* Arnold Toynbee. Abridgement of Volumes I-VI by D. C. Somervell. Oxford University Press, 1946.

Tristram: *John Henry Newman: Autobiographical Writings.* Edited by Henry Tristram. Sheed & Ward, London, 1956.

Viney: *The Jesuits in Ireland 1542–1974.* Michael Viney. Articles from the *Irish Times,* 1–5 November 1971. Revised and updated to 1974 with the author's approval by Hugh Duffy, S.J., and reprinted as a booklet with the editor's permission. Page references in the Notes are to this booklet.

Wall, Maureen — see Reportorium Novum.

White and Wynne: *Irish Stained Glass.* James White and Michael Wynne. The Furrow Trust/Gill & Son, Dublin, 1963.

Whyte: *Church and State in Modern Ireland 1923–1970.* J. H. Whyte. Gill & Macmillan, Dublin, 1971.

Woodward: *The Age of Reform 1815–1870.* E. L. Woodward. Oxford University Press, 1949 (first published 1938).

Year Book: *The Jesuit Year Book,* incorporating the Irish Jesuit Directory. Published annually by the Irish Province from 1928.

INDEX

attitudes to, 48-50
Superiors' length of office, 69, 75, 98
and papal authority, 90-1
international influence of, 99-100, 131-3
Suppression of, 114-21, 124, 127
Restoration, 133, 141-2, 143, 152
Brothers, 154-5
and liberal Catholicism, 184-6
Restoration Centenary, 196
Tertian Fathers, 300
option for the poor, 304-6
modernisation, 307-8
Jews, 278-9
John, Don, of Austria, 2
John Baptist, Brother, 252
John XXIII, Pope, 266
Joy, Fr Patrick, 253, 258, 260
Joyce, James, 163, 168, 213, 222, 281, 292
training of, 238-40

Kane, Fr, 224
Kane, Fr Robert, 191, 283
Kaufman, Angelica, 300
Kaunda, Kenneth, 265
Kavanagh, Patrick, 269
Keane, John B. (architect), 170
Keating, Fr Edward, 122, 186
Kelly, Fr, 242, 244, 250
Kelly, Fr Clement, 122
Kelly, Fr Dominic, 249
Kelly, Fr Edward, 180
Kelly, Fr Ignatius, 101, 102, 104
Kelly, Fr John C., 238
Kelly, Fr Thomas, 180
Kelly, Fr William, 241
Kennedy, Charles, 299
Kennedy, Hugh, 235
Kennedy, Fr Richard, 260
Kenney, Fr Peter, 158, 159, 172, 227, 267, 296, 311
early career, 135-8
Vice-President, Maynooth, 141
and Mission funds, 142-51
American Visitations, 144-5, 156, 164-6, 168, 172

Rector, Clongowes, 152-5, 162, 200, 221, 243
buys Tullabeg, 156-7
and fee-paying schools, 161
recommended for bishopric, 167
Kenny, Fr Peter, 191, 194, 224
Kerr, Fr John, 301-2, 309
Kerry, Bishop of, 179
Kerry, Co., 38, 89
Kettle, Tom, 234, 236, 273-4
Kieffer, Fr, 232
Kiely, Fr Bartholomew, 238
Kiely, Benedict, 301
Kildare, Dowager Countess of, 50, 51, 59, 76
Kildare, Earl and Countess of, 24
Kilkea Castle, 50, 68, 70, 76
Kilkenny, 65, 98
Jesuit activities in, 28, 52, 75, 87, 88
Confederation of, 58, 64-74
novitiate, 66, 74, 82-3, 111
bubonic plague, 78
Killiney residence, 178, 179
Kinsale, Battle of, 31-2
Knoles, Fr Anthony, 98-9, 101, 102, 104-6
Kohlmann, Fr Anthony, 165

labour movement, 272, 279, 306
Labour Party, Australia, 246, 247
Lambert, Matthew, 24
Lane, Fr, 37
Latin, Fr James, 68
Latin America, 47, 119
Laynez, Fr Diego, 16
Le Brocquy, Louis, 238
Lea, Fr Charles, 24
Leaving Certificate, 302, 303-4
Ledochowski, Fr Wladimir, 250
Legion of Mary, 264
Leibniz, G. W., 129
Leinster, 37, 42, 53, 60
Leinster, Duke of, 122, 158
Leitrim, Co., 39
Lemaire, Fr, 224
Lenan, Fr Patrick, 44

Tuite, Fr James, 192
Tullabeg, 169, 173, 176, 178, 192,
    196, 211, 224, 242, 272, 301
    established, 155, 156-8
    novitiate, 159, 160
    fees, 160, 162
    corporal punishment, 201
    descriptions of, 201-2, 291
    English influence, 202-4
        amalgamated with Clongowes,
        212-13, 298
    lay staff, 223
    matriculation, 229
    stained glass, 238
typhus, 153-4, 172, 178

Ulster, 39, 60, 64, 66, 67
Union, Act of, 139-40
United Irishmen, 139
United States of America, 117, 128,
    185, 226, 251
    Visitations to, 144-5, 156, 164-6,
    172
    Civil War, 195
    Fr Ronan visits, 221
    Pearl Harbour, 258
    Visitation from, 301
University Church, Stephen's Green,
    170, 231-2, 236
University College, Dublin, 213,
    230-6, 245, 275, 278, 298, 299,
    300
    Jesuits on staff, 237-8
University Hall, Hatch St, 299
University of Paris, 91
Urban VIII, Pope, 67, 68
Ussher, Dr James, Archbishop of
    Armagh, 46, 49, 70, 83

Valtorta, Dr Henry, Vicar Apostolic,
    Hong Kong, 253, 254
Vatican, 18-19, 26, 100
    political involvement, 28, 33
    and Jesuits, 48, 119
    and Irish mission, 55-6
    and Rinuccini's excommunica-
    tions, 72
    authority of, 90

temporal power eliminated,
    184-5
Vatican II, 162, 185, 261, 266, 271,
    304-10
Vaughan, Dr, Archbishop of
    Sydney, 245, 249
Verdier, Fr Mercure, 72-6, 82, 142,
    145
Verry, Fr Peter, 311
vespers, 108
Veto controversy, 140, 167
Victor Emmanuel, King of Sardinia,
    186
Vincentians, 206, 229
Viney, Michael, 289, 290
Vitelleschi, Fr Muzio, 51-2, 53, 55-6,
    57, 59-60, 68-9
    and 1641 rebellion, 66, 67
vocationalism, 284-6
vocations, 20
Voltaire, Francois, 115, 117, 118,
    119, 120, 129, 131

Wadding, Fr Ambrose, 63
Wadding, Fr Luke, OFM, 63, 71
Wadding, Fr Luke, SJ, 63, 83-4
Wadding, Fr Michael, 252
Wadding family, 57
Wah Yan College, Hong Kong, 255,
    257, 258, 260, 261-2
wakes, 295
Wall, Fr Walter, 43-4
Walsh, Dr William, Archbishop of
    Dublin, 235-6, 298
Walsh, Fr Peter, OFM, 90-1, 92
Walshe, Fr James, 78
Ward, Fr John, 126, 127
Waterford, 65, 74, 78, 79, 84, 86,
    93, 98, 105, 121, 122
    Jesuit activities in, 52, 53, 82, 87
    Jesuit administrative centre, 99,
    103-4
    St Patrick's chapel, 103-4
Welensky, Sir Roy, 265
Wellington, Duke of, 200
Wentworth, Viscount, 56-8, 63, 86
Werribee Seminary, Australia, 248
West Indies, 82, 252